## TENTH EDITION

# Elite Deviance

**David R. Simon**
*University of North Florida*

**PEARSON**

Boston  Columbus  Indianapolis  New York  San Francisco  Upper Saddle River
Amsterdam  Cape Town  Dubai  London  Madrid  Milan  Munich  Paris  Montréal  Toron
Delhi  Mexico City  São Paulo  Sydney  Hong Kong  Seoul  Singapore  Taipei  Tokyo

**Publisher:** Karen Hanson
**Editorial Assistant:** Joseph Jantas
**Executive Marketing Manager:**
  Kelly May
**Marketing Assistant:** Janeli Bitor
**Media Editor:** Tom Scalzo
**Production Manager:** Meghan DeMaio
**Creative Director:** Jayne Conte

**Cover Designer:** Suzanne Duda
**Cover Image:** © Vege / Fotolia
**Full-Service Project Management/**
  **Composition:** Papitha Ramesh,
  Element LLC
**Printer/Binder/Cover Printer:**
  R. R. Donnelley & Sons

**Library of Congress Cataloging-in-Publication Data**

Simon, David R., 1944-
  Elite deviance / David R. Simon. — 10th ed.
    p. cm.
  Includes bibliographical references and index.
  ISBN-13: 978-0-205-21628-4
  ISBN-10: 0-205-21628-5
  1. White collar crimes—United States.   2. Deviant behavior—United States.
3. Elite (Social sciences)—United States.   4. Corporations—Corrupt
practices—United States.   5. United States—Moral conditions.   I. Title.
  HV6769.S56 2012
  364.16′80973—dc23

                                                              2011029583

10 9 8 7 6 5 4 3 2 1

ISBN-10: 0-205-21628-5
ISBN-13: 978-0-205-21628-4

*For all my children, especially little David, and grandchildren, and for Jeannie—for all the reasons. May you all experience a more democratic and equal world.*

# CONTENTS

# PREFACE

This is the tenth edition of this book. Throughout its 30 year history, this text has stressed several themes. These include the following:

1. The notion that elite deviance in and of itself is a great social problem in American life. Elite deviance consists of criminal and deviant acts by the largest corporations and the most powerful political organizations.
2. Elite deviance stems from a system of political economy in which power and wealth are increasingly concentrated in the hands of a power elite.
3. Within this power elite there has emerged a series of criminal and deviant acts that has been termed "the higher immorality."
4. Elite deviance is intimately interrelated to each and every type of non-elite deviance.
5. The solution to the problems posed by elite deviance involves a serious restructuring of the major institutions of postmodern society: the polity, economy, and mass media.

As this edition of *Elite Deviance* goes to press, there are numerous scandals that remained unresolved and are under investigation. Some of these include the following:

- The conduct of the wars in Iraq, Afghanistan, and a secret war in Pakistan is riddled with corruption on all sides.
- At home, the nation and much of the world remains mired in the worst economic slump since the Great Depression of the 1930s. One in four American homeowners is behind on their mortgage payments and home foreclosure remains at the highest rate since the 1930s. The middle class has experienced no growth in real income since the 1980s, and America's distribution of wealth is more unequal now than at any time in its history.
- A scandal over the salary and compensation of America's CEOs, especially those firms that were recipients of federal bailout funds.

Not since the Reagan era of the 1980s have there been so many scandals in both corporations and government. Since its initial publication, the book has never wavered in its approach to its subject, namely, that the intense maldistribution of power and wealth among the nation's power elite has given rise to a set of criminal and deviant practices that C. Wright Mills termed the higher immorality. As the new millennium dawned, it became crystal clear that these practices, described in depth in this ninth edition, are now global in scope.

xii   PREFACE

These global deviant practices have come to include such crimes as international money laundering; global environmental pollution; illegal wars, which include alliances with known arms smugglers, drug traffickers, and global crime syndicates; export of toxic waste and products that have been banned for sale in the United States because they endanger the public health and safety, and the like.

Likewise, the new millennium has brought absolutely no improvement in the political system in the United States. Hundreds of millions of dollars were spent in the 2000 and 2004 elections by political action committees and super-rich candidates, excluding meaningful third-party candidates from offering alternative policies to the nation's pressing problems. The chaos in Florida demonstrated that the right to vote might be abridged at any time in the United States and in any number of ways. As discussed throughout the text, corruption is a way of life in American politics and has been since the nation was founded. Knowledge of improprieties is but one reason why the voter turnout in America is the lowest of any modern democratic nation.

## Elite Deviance and the New Millennium

This tenth edition of *Elite Deviance* appears at the dawn of a new millennium, an era characterized by new global realities. The global nature of elite deviance and its consequences are noted throughout this edition.

Since George W. Bush took office, an epidemic of scandal and corruption has taken place. The scale of wrongdoing in this administration exceeds that of both Richard Nixon's Watergate era and Ronald Reagan's Iran-Contra scandal.[1]

These scandalous episodes have raised serious issues that are discussed throughout this book:

- Numerous crimes of election fraud and electioneering occurred in both 2000 and 2004. Can Americans still trust that voting is a basic and meaningful part of American democracy? Discussed in Chapters 1 and 7.
- Under Bush, the inequality of wealth and income and the growth of poverty have all increased. What consequences are caused by political equality and economic inequality? These issues are discussed in Chapters 1, 2, and 9.
- The epidemic of corruption in the White House and in Congress was the leading issue in the 2006 election. What are the consequences of this political alienation for the future of American politics and society? These issues are discussed in Chapters 1, 7, 8, and 9.
- The corporate crime wave during the first Bush administration (2001–2004) has resulted in a huge number of verdicts, as well as a new round of corporate scandals. What are the penalties for corporate crime, and what new sorts of business scandals are now emerging? This topic is discussed in Chapters 1–4.

- Within the Defense Department there has been a new round of immense waste, fraud, and abuse. This corruption, which has taken place because of the Afghanistan and Iraq wars, involves the president and vice president, as well as numerous defense contractors. For the first time since the American Revolution, the U.S. military has hired hundreds of private citizens and corporations to "outsource" everything from torturing prisoners to doing laundry and cooking food for the troops. Many of these firms have overcharged the government, engaged in fraud, sold defective weapons, and violated basic security procedures and human rights. These and other military-related scandals are discussed in Chapters 5, 7, 8, and 9.
- Likewise, the war on terrorism, and the actions taken in Afghanistan and Iraq have raised numerous issues about the United States as a trustworthy actor on the world stage, its quest for oil and empire, and its warlike nature.[2] These issues profoundly affect the public's confidence in the government, our economic and political futures, and numerous other social problems plaguing America and the world. These issues are discussed in Chapters 1, 7, and the epilogue.
- At home there have been terrible acts of fraud and deception related to victims of Hurricane Katrina, as well as other domestic social needs.[3] These issues are discussed in Chapter 1 and the epilogue.
- The Bush administration is criticized by many observers as one of the most secretive, mendacious, and manipulative in American history.[4] Bush's own family has been accused of numerous crimes and illegal secret dealings with Nazis, terrorists, and the Saudis.[5] The important issues raised by the rule of a corrupt dynasty are discussed in Chapters 1, 8, and 9.

Elite deviance is a massive global and social problem, with numerous aspects. This book examines a large number of white-collar deviance topics:

- Chapter 1 introduces readers to both the concept of elite deviance and a description of the environment in which these acts of great harm take place. Within the United States as well as globally, the distribution of power and wealth is becoming ever more concentrated, making it more and more difficult to exercise any control over what elites do.
- Chapter 2 presents the higher immorality—an institutionalized set of deviant practices that are now global in scope. This is especially true of elite cooperation with global crime syndicates involved in the $850 billion global narcotics trade and the vast amount of money laundered by legitimate financial institutions, lawyers, and other elite professionals.
- Chapters 3 and 4 discuss the contemporary nature of corporate deviance. The multibillion price tag and hundreds of thousands of lives taken by global corporate crime make this form of deviance one of the world's most serious social problems. Add to these figures the pollution

and resource depletion that are a result of global mass consumption and the gravity of these practices becomes truly immense.

- Chapter 5 is devoted to various types of global elite deviance. International arms smuggling, the dumping of toxic wastes, and the sale of products banned for sale in the United States because of their toxic nature constitute yet another scandal. The chapter also contains an examination of human rights violations by regimes receiving U.S. foreign and military aid. As examined, the Obama sent another 30,000 troops to Afghanistan, some to uncover corruption, only to experience an increase in corruption among US troops and private contractors.
- Chapters 6, 7, and 9 detail the nature of modern graft and corruption. Scandal in our era has become an institutionalized feature of America's power elite, one, as noted, with global ramifications.
- Chapter 8 contains an analysis of the causes of elite deviance and argues that a genuine sociological theory of such deviance must account for causal factors on the macro, immediate milieu, and individual levels of analysis. The chapter discusses how these various causes interrelate, as well as how elite deviance is interrelated with other types of wrongdoing.
- Finally, the epilogue examines the types of policy changes viewed as necessary for the reduction of elite deviance. This section also contains solid suggestions for becoming more informed about and involved in the struggle against the social injustices embodied in elite deviance.

## Supplementary Materials for the Instructor

*Instructor's Manual and Test Bank* (ISBN 0205216323): The Instructor's Manual and Test Bank has been prepared to assist teachers in their efforts to prepare lectures and evaluate student learning. For each chapter of the text, the Instructor's Manual offers different types of resources, including detailed chapter summaries and outlines, learning objectives, discussion questions, classroom activities and much more.

Also included in this manual is a test bank offering multiple-choice, true/false, fill-in-the-blank, and/or essay questions for each chapter. The Instructor's Manual and Test Bank is available to adopters at www.pearsonhighered.com.

*MyTest* (ISBN 0205216307): The Test Bank is also available online through Pearson's computerized testing system, MyTest. MyTest allows instructors to create their own personalized exams, to edit any of the existing test questions, and to add new questions. Other special features of this program include random generation of test questions, creation of alternative versions of the same test, scrambling question sequence, and test preview before printing. Search and sort features allow you to locate questions quickly and to arrange them in whatever order you prefer. The test bank can be accessed from anywhere with a free MyTest user account. There is no need to download a program or file to your computer.

*PowerPoint Presentations* (ISBN 0205020658): Lecture PowerPoints are available for this text. The Lecture PowerPoint slides outline each chapter to help you convey sociological principles in a visual and exciting way. They are available to adopters at HYPERLINK "http://www.pearsonhighered. com" www.pearsonhighered.com.

## Supplementary Materials for the Student

*MySearchLab*

MySearchLab contains writing, grammar, and research tools and access to a variety of academic journals, census data, Associated Press news feeds, and discipline-specific readings to help you hone your writing and research skills. In addition, a complete eText is included. MySearchLab can be purchased with the text (ISBN 020586371X) or separately (ISBN 0205239927).

## Acknowledgments

Many family members and colleagues have my sincere thanks for the roles they have played in this new edition. Likewise, my new colleagues at the University of North Florida deserve my heartfelt appreciation for their encouragement in completing this new edition, especially Dr. Henry Thomas of the Political Science Department. My thanks also go to Martin Schwartz and Joque Soskis for their stimulating ideas and loan of valuable research materials. My thanks go also to Martin Schwartz and Joque Soskis for their stimulating ideas and loan of valuable research materials.

## ENDNOTES

1. See, for example, Dean, J. (2004). *Worse than Watergate*. New York: Warner Books; Rich, F. (2006). *The greatest story ever sold: The decline and fall of the truth*. New York: Penguin; Phillips, K. (2004). *American dynasty*. New York: Penguin; Huffington, A. (2004). *Fanatics and fools*. New York: Hyperion; Scheer, C., et al. (2003). *The five biggest lies Bush told us about Iraq*. New York: Seven Stories; Laurent, E. (2004). *Bush's secret world*. Malden, MA: Polity Press; Lindorff, D. (2004). *This can't be happening: Resisting the disintegration of American democracy*. Monroe, ME: Common Courage Press; and Willis, C. (ed.). (2004). *The I hate George W. Bush reader*. New York: Thunders Mouth Press; and Miller, M. C. (2004). *Cruel and unusual: Bush/Cheney's new world order*. New York: Norton.

2. Ritter, S. (2006). *Target Iran: The truth about the White House's plans for regime change*. New York: Nations Books; Burbach, R., & Terbell, J. (2004). *Imperial overstretch*. New York: Zed Books; Blum, W. (2005). *Freeing the world to death: Essays on the American empire*. Monroe, ME: Common Courage Press; Judis, J. (2004). *The folly of empire: What George W. Bush could learn from Theodore Roosevelt and Woodrow Wilson*. New York: Scribner; and Scheuer, M. (2005). *Imperial hubris: Why the West is losing the war on terror*. Washington, DC: Potomac Books.

3.    See, for example, Piven, F. F. (2004). *The war at home*. New York: New Press; and Phillips, K. (2006). *American theocracy*. New York: Viking. These scandals and unmet needs are examined in Chapters 1, 2, 6, and 8.

4.    See Chomsky, N. (2005). *Imperial ambitions*. New York: Metropolitan Books; Moore, M. (ed.). (2004). *The Official Fahrenheit 9/11 Reader*. New York: Simon and Schuster; Rich, F. *The greatest story ever sold* (pp. 95–227); Boehlert, E. (2006). *Lapdog: How the press rolled over for Bush*. New York: Free Press; Fritz, B., et al. (2004). *All the President's spin: George W. Bush, the media, and the truth*. New York: Touchstone; and Rampton, S., & Stauber, J. (2006). *The best war ever: Lies, damned lies, and the mess in Iraq*. New York: Jeremy P. Tarcher/Penguin.

5.    Unger, C. (2004). *House of Bush, house of Saud*. New York: Scribner; and Landau, S. (2003). *The Pre-emptive empire: A guide to the Bush kingdom*. London: Pluto Press.

# 1

# The Nature of Elite Deviance

## Scandal-Plagued America

The nation is experiencing the most devastating economic crisis since the Great Depression of the 1930s, as well as some of the lowest levels of public confidence in government and corporations that have ever been witnessed by pollsters. This confluence is a product of the corrupt influence of corporate lobbying on government, corporate fraud, and the emergence of a political economy wherein those running for office are completely dependent on corporate money for election financing.

The seeds of this crisis were planted during the Reagan era's ideology of deregulation of business. In 1999, the financial services industry spent a record $417 million to have the Glass-Stegall Act of 1933 overturned. The act prohibited bank-holding companies from owning other financial companies, such as investment banks.

The result was a significant deregulation of the entire financial services industry, including the ability of banks and insurance firms to engage in risky ventures, and a virtual deregulation of the real estate mortgage industry. This deregulation, along with the easing of credit rules resulted in a whole new series of financial service industry rackets. Stated another way, the financial industry was given a license to steal, and the regulatory agencies were told to look the other way if any irregularities surfaced. The result was an obsession with greed not seen since the 1980s.

Following the September 11, 2001 terrorist attack on the United States, the Bush administration decided that America should become "the ownership society," and that the American dream of home ownership should become a reality for as many people as possible. The result was a significant lowering of credit rates by Alan Greenspan's Federal Reserve and a massive $1.3 trillion subprime (not well qualified) mortgage market in which so-called "predatory lending practices" resulted in mortgage loans to consumers who were unable to repay them.

It was not unusual for people making $20,000 a year to be lent $500,000 with no down payment required on their homes. Home buyers of modest means were talked into signing mortgage applications by a group of greedy real estate brokers and lenders. In some cases, lending practices were so

1

fraudulent that even dead people were given loans. In 500,000 subprime loan cases, credit scores, employment, and income information were fraudulently altered by real estate brokers in order to gain bank approval, so-called NINJA-No Income, No Job, No Application loans. Mid-level real estate brokers, agents, appraisers, and fraudulent lenders were indifferent to inflated housing prices, or the perils of talking consumers into borrowing beyond their means because mortgages were quickly packaged into new security products and sold to various new investors. Homeowners were quickly overwhelmed by unmanageable debt and had their houses taken from them during the foreclosure crisis that now encompasses one in every 10 U.S. homes.

These mid-level nonelite deviants also hid high fees and interest rates in mortgage contract details without explaining them to homeowners. Often, lenders were indifferent as to whether a home went into foreclosure or not. The loans had already been purchased as CDOs (see below), and fees pocketed, or phony default provisions were used to foreclose on homes that were worth far more than their owner's loan balances.

Next, the deregulating of financial services made possible the invention of new investment securities, including $4 trillion in "collateralized debt obligations" (CDOs). CDOs are pooled groups of individual subprime loans, originally rated AAA, and then found to be in serious risk of default. These instruments were sold to cities, school districts, foreign governments and banks, and pension funds.

There was also an additional $1.5 trillion in "liars' loans" (called ALTE and Option Arm Mortgages) that were made at variable rates, were due to reset at much higher payments in 2009–2010 that will cause a second mortgage crisis.[1] These loans were guaranteed by monoline insurance firms, but the insurance on them is worth about as much as the paper their policies are printed on. The small insurance companies that wrote the policies on these loans were highly leveraged (lacked the assets to guarantee the worth of the loans they insured).

An additional Wall Street racket was added with the invention of the credit default swap (CDS). "Credit default swaps are insurance-like contracts that promise to cover losses on certain securities in the event of a default. They typically apply to municipal bonds, corporate debt and mortgage securities and are sold by banks, hedge funds and others. The buyer of the credit default insurance pays premiums over a period of time in return for peace of mind, knowing that losses will be covered if a default happens. It's supposed to work similarly to someone taking out home insurance to protect against losses from fire and theft. Except that it doesn't. Banks and insurance companies are regulated; the credit swaps' market is not. As a result, contracts can be traded—or swapped—from investor to investor without anyone overseeing the trades to ensure the buyer has the resources to cover the losses if the security defaults. The instruments can be bought and sold from both ends—the insured and the insurer."[2]

# The Bailout Rackets

The U.S. economy is now faced with a crisis of unknown proportions. (1) The amount of leveraging to back CDSs is unknown. What is known is that the amount of American CDSs is well over $45 trillion, and could easily produce an even more serious financial meltdown. (2) What is also clear is that "after receiving billions in aid from U.S. taxpayers, the nation's largest banks say they can't track exactly how they're spending it. Some twenty-one banks wouldn't even talk about what they've done with their federal bailout funds under The Federal Asset Relief Program (TARP) when asked by the Associated Press in December 2008."[3] The Treasury Department never asked the banks how the money would be spent. The head of the congressionally appointed oversight relief panel, Elizabeth Warren, says her new office didn't even contain a phone with which to call recipients of TARP funds and ask the most basic questions.

(3) The FBI is struggling to find enough agents and resources to investigate all of the financial fraud cases stemming from the failures of the subprime mortgage market, American International Group insurance, Washington Mutual, Country Wide Mortgage, Bear Sterns, Lehman Brothers, Fannie Mae, and Freddie Mac. Indictments and case dispositions may be several years in the making, if they are made at all. *This* is the largest series of fraud cases in American history.

(4) Currently, 1 in 10 U.S. homes is worth less than its owners' mortgage. Some experts predict that by 2010's end, the number will be one in five. The resulting defaults have touched off the worst financial calamity since the Great Depression. Two million people lost their jobs in 2008, and many economists fear the current 9.7% unemployment rate could reach as high as 10% by 2012. The real unemployment rate is much closer to 17%. The recession has resulted in a global financial meltdown with unknowable international consequences. What is known is that on October 6 and 7, 2008, global stock-market losses totaled $6.5 trillion, and that global losses on worthless securities are estimated at $1.4 trillion.[4]

In the current economic insanity bank costs are kept secret by their allies at the Federal Reserve. The Fed has never been audited and guards its independence like a dog with a new bone. What we do know is that the companies first "affected were those directly involved in home construction and mortgage lending such as Northern Rock and Countrywide Financial, as they could no longer obtain financing through the credit markets. Over 100 mortgage lenders went bankrupt during 2007 and 2008. Concerns that investment bank Bear Stearns would collapse in March 2008 resulted in its fire-sale to JP Morgan Chase. The crisis hit its peak in September and October 2008. Several major institutions failed, were acquired under duress, or were subject to government takeover. These included Lehman Brothers, Merrill Lynch, Fannie Mae, Freddie Mac, Washington Mutual, Wachovia, and American International Group. ... Between June 2007 and November 2008,

Americans lost an estimated average of more than a quarter of their collective net worth. By early November 2008, a broad U.S. stock index the S&P 500, was down 45 percent from its 2007 high. Housing prices had dropped 20 percent from their 2006 peak, with futures markets signaling a 30–35 percent potential drop. Total home equity in the United States, which was valued at $13 trillion at its peak in 2006, had dropped to $8.8 trillion by mid-2008… Total retirement assets, Americans' second-largest household asset, dropped by 22 percent, from $10.3 trillion in 2006 to $8 trillion in mid-2008. During the same period, savings and investment assets (apart from retirement savings) lost $1.2 trillion and pension assets lost $1.3 trillion. Taken together, these losses total a staggering $8.3 trillion. Since peaking in the second quarter of 2007, household wealth is down $14 trillion."[5]

By 2010, the public had become outraged that the financial debacle had triggered the worst unemployment crisis since the Great Depression. Total unemployment and underemployment reached 20% of the American workforce by early 2010, before it began a slight decline. A number of the firms involved in the 2008–2009 multibillion dollar bailouts by the federal government (e.g., Goldman Sachs, J.P. Morgan Chase) initially granted six-figure bonuses that outraged a recession-weary public. Even now, "three out of the four largest banks in America (J.P. Morgan Chase, Bank of America, and Wells Fargo) are now larger than before the bailout. The four largest banks in America have assets equal to more than 50 percent of the entire annual U.S. gross domestic product. These four big banks now issue two-thirds of all credit cards, half of the mortgages and control nearly 40 percent of all bank deposits. Just five American banks (J.P. Morgan Chase, Bank of America, Citigroup, Goldman Sachs, and Morgan Stanley) own a staggering 95 percent of the $290 trillion in risky derivatives held at commercial banks."[6]

At last the myth of the lack of seriousness involved in white-collar crime has been painfully pierced. Sadly, the FBI complains of a shortage of agents to prosecute all the potential fraud cases in the financial crises.

"The civil suit filed by the Securities and Exchange Commission (in April, 2010) accused Goldman of 'defrauding investors by misstating and omitting key facts' about a financial product based on subprime mortgage-backed securities, and creating and selling a mortgage investment that was secretly devised to fail." The move marked the first time that regulators have taken action against a Wall Street deal that helped investors capitalize on the collapse of the housing market. Goldman itself profited by betting against the very mortgage investments that it sold to its customers. On July 15, 2010, "Goldman agreed to pay $550 million to settle federal claims that it misled investors in a subprime mortgage product as the housing market began to collapse in 2007."[7]

The securities were a key contributor to the financial crisis that peaked in 2008 because many contained risky mortgages. The charges are believed to be the first brought against a Wall Street firm for speculating on the collapse of the housing market"[8] in which 1 million foreclosures were predicted for

2010. Meanwhile, in March 2010, the Office of Inspector General of the Securities and Exchange Commission revealed that, during the last 5 years, over 30 regular and contract employees were accused of various ethical violations for watching pornography on the Internet for thousands of hours (while neglecting to regulate the very financial industry that brought about this crisis).[9] Obsessive greed has come very close to resulting in economic suicide.

Sadly, there are no signs that the global financial crisis will ease anytime soon.[10]

- The central banks of Ireland and Greece are being bailed out of bankruptcy by the International Monetary Fund.[11]
- One out of every 34 Americans who earned wages in 2008 had no income—none at all—in 2009, according to dramatic findings uncovered by David Cay Johnston. Wages fell in 2009 for average Americans, median income Americans, and all Americans except those at the very top, who saw a fivefold leap in their incomes, according to the Social Security data. Johnston blamed the recession, but also pointed to the so-called "free trade," calling it "nothing more than tax-subsidized mechanisms that encourage American manufacturers to close factories, fire workers, and use cheap labor in China for products they send right back to the United States."[12]
- Dubbed "Operation Broken Trust," U.S. Attorney General Eric Holder and his Justice Department team have arrested so far (December 7, 2010) 343 defendants allegedly responsible for scamming 120,000 victims out of $8.3 billion. Most of the schemes so far uncovered by Holder have targeted the usual collection of vulnerable investors: small communities, churchgoers, the elderly, bereaved families, and disabled individuals.[13] Thus far, not one major Wall Street firm's executives have been sent to prison for defrauding its investors.[14]
- Mortgage Electronic Registration Systems Inc. (MERS) was created by Countrywide and Fannie Mae. Its members created a "paperless" system so that they could line their pockets by originating and flipping phony mortgage loans into the so-called mortgage backed security trusts and then selling trillions of dollars of bonds to investors around the world. By reporting false profits from these sales Fannie Mae's and Countrywide's executives were able to make hundreds of millions of dollars in "bonuses."[15]

"A 2009 ruling by the Kansas Supreme Court held that MERS, a private company that registers mortgages electronically and tracks changes in ownership, has no standing in real estate foreclosure proceedings. One-half of all new mortgages in the U.S. are registered with MERS and recorded in its name. MERS facilitated the process where banks would purchase pools of mortgages and then securitize them—basically chopping them into pieces and selling them off to investors. MERS reduced the transparency of the mortgage market to such an extent that the homeowner no longer knew who held the mortgage note. It may have been held by one bank in Frankfurt, or pieces of it held by hedge funds and insurance companies. This ruling has since spread to other states; hence, Bank of America responded by halting foreclosures as it regroups and reassesses its foreclosure procedures."[16]

And as more news comes out "you can be sure that MERS will find itself and its top executives in a tricky dance...because either they knowingly created a process that broke the law in at least 23 states...or they lack a thorough understanding of their core business requirements (and corporate responsibility)...or the banks asked them to break the law." Ed Harrison points out that "The crisis in foreclosure documentation is much deeper than the specific issue of robo-signers, which has precipitated the halt in foreclosures by major banks. The fact is the mortgage process in the United States is broken because securitization has created a Byzantine mess that is wholly unsuited for the large number of foreclosures now ongoing."[17]

During the previous administration, the Center for American Progress released a one-page document detailing "Intimigate." The document showed that the White House developed a pattern of firing, intimidating, and defaming anyone who had the courage to tell the truth about Iraq. In fact, the Iraq policy makers whose influence grew in the White House are largely those who parsed and distorted intelligence and misled the American people.[18]

One of the most senior officials in the White House during that time, Vice President Cheney's chief of staff Lewis Libby, was convicted of lying to the FBI. Libby's sentence was recently (2007) commuted by President Bush.[19] Libby lied about leaking the name of CIA agent Valerie Plame, which may have been part of an administration effort to destroy the credibility of Plame's husband, Ambassador Joseph Wilson, who wrote an article critical of the claim that Iraq had obtained nuclear fuel rods from an African country.[20] The army's top civilian official resigned in March 2007 due to a scandal over care and conditions for wounded Iraq War veterans at Walter Reed Army Medical Center in Washington, DC, and in other veterans' hospitals. Army secretary Francis Harvey resigned one day after firing the general in charge of Walter Reed. Harvey's resignation was requested by defense secretary Robert Gates.[21]

These incidents and numerous others documented throughout this book are symbolic of the major scandals that have made elite wrongdoing of major concern in America. The public believes that money has a pervasive influence in political campaigns, wherein candidates often spend millions of dollars to secure $100,000-a-year positions. The crisis of confidence continues to this day. Moreover, large corporations have proved every bit as deviant as political organizations.

## Scandals Within the Economic Sphere

The public's sagging confidence in major U.S. institutions extends beyond Wall Street. Increasingly, big business has come to be viewed with distrust and cynicism.

In 1978, the Senate revealed that, between 1945 and 1976, approximately 350 U.S. corporations admitted to making bribes of some $750 million to officials of foreign governments. Many of these companies made such payments without informing their stockholders.[22] Moreover, the Watergate investigation revealed that more than 300 corporations illegally contributed to President Nixon's 1972 reelection campaign.[23] No corporate executives were sent to prison for their involvement in concealing or making such payments. Advertising is full of examples of fraudulent claims for products. And the stock market has been manipulated to defraud clients, as was revealed in 1975, when officials of the Equity Life Insurance Company were indicted for manipulating the price of shares by inventing thousands of nonexistent insurance policies. Between $2 and $3 billion was lost by thousands of investors, making this the largest investment fraud to date. Equity's chairman, along with several other company officials, were convicted of the crime but received suspended sentences or prison terms that varied from only 2 to 8 years.[24] By 1982, it was estimated that price-fixing among corporations cost the consumer $60 billion per year. In addition, between 1970 and 1980, 117 of 1,043 major corporations (11%) had committed at least one serious criminal offense, including 28 cases of bribery, kickback, or illegal rebates; 21 cases of illegal campaign contributions; 11 cases of fraud; and five cases of tax evasion. In all, 50 executives were sent to jail, and 13 fines were levied in excess of $550,000 (ranging to a high of $4 million).[25]

Perhaps the largest energizer of negative feelings toward big business has been the realization that corporations are guilty of what we might call "chemical crimes." Through dumping of waste products into the air, water, and landfills and the production of products that pollute unnecessarily, businesses have assaulted the public with pollutants, with dangerous implications for the health of present and future generations.

Of the many examples of this chemical assault, we will describe one in some detail, Love Canal.

From 1942 to 1953, the Hooker Chemical Company dumped more than 20,000 tons of toxic chemical waste into the Love Canal near Niagara Falls, New York. After Hooker sold the dump site to the local board of education in 1953 for one dollar, an elementary school and playground were built on the site, followed by a housing development. For at least 20 years prior to 1977, toxic chemicals had been seeping through to the land surface. However, in 1977, highly toxic black sludge began seeping into the cellars of the school and nearby residences. Tests showed the presence of 82 chemicals in the air, water, and soil of Love Canal; among them were 12 known carcinogens, including dioxin, one of the deadliest substances ever synthesized. There is evidence that Hooker Chemical knew of the problem as far back as 1958 but chose not to warn local health officials of any potential problems because cleanup costs would have increased from $4 million to $50 million.

In April 2010, a Horizon Deep Water oil well, leased by British Petroleum, exploded in the Gulf of Mexico, killing 11 oil workers and spilling over 315 million gallons of crude oil into the Gulf. Fears arose that some of the oil may make its way into the Gulf Stream, up the East Coast of the United States and even to the North Atlantic Coastal regions of United Kingdom.

Knowledge of the existence of toxic chemicals in the area caused a financial hardship for the residents. Once word of the contamination got out, their homes became worthless. But much more important, tests revealed that the inhabitants of this area had disproportionately high rates of birth defects, miscarriages, chromosomal abnormalities, liver disorders, respiratory and urinary disease, epilepsy, and suicide. In one neighborhood a few blocks from Love Canal, a survey by the homeowners' association revealed that only one of the 15 pregnancies begun in 1979 ended in the birth of a healthy baby; four ended in miscarriages, two babies were stillborn, and eight others were born deformed.[26]

In 2002 and 2003 came a flood of corporate scandals involving large corporations such as Enron, Tyco, Halliburton, WorldCom, Adelphia Communications, K-Mart, Global Crossing, Merck, Qwest, Reliant Energy, ImClone, and Xerox Corporation. Most of them involved corporations, with the aid of their accountants, inflating the worth of their assets, massive fraud, and lying to the workers, stockholders, and the public. Collectively, these scandals cost the American economy over $200 billion and the loss of 1 million jobs. They also negatively affected an already severely depressed stock market and prolonged a serious recession in which the real unemployment rate has reached around 10%.[27]

Today, it is now clear: Love Canal is merely the tip of the U.S. waste iceberg.

- In the summer of 2006, a Public Interest Research Group (PIRG) report revealed that more than 2,300 daily temperature records were set in July alone. This record warmth is the result of global warming. The PIRG report analyzed 2000–2006 temperature data from 255 major weather stations and found that temperatures were above normal almost everywhere during the period. Global warming, which is the result of carbon dioxide emissions in the atmosphere, is caused largely by corporate pollution and auto emissions.[28] The amount of global warming from fossil fuel and other emissions, deforestation of rain forests, and other causes has doubled since 1960.[29] Former vice president Al Gore won an Oscar in 2007 for his documentary *An Inconvenient Truth*, which alarmingly details the potential destructive effects of global warming if current trends are not reversed.[30]

Similarly, scores of opinion polls registering mounting public distrust, cynicism, and alienation regarding the most powerful U.S. economic and political institutions and the individuals who head them could be discussed. What is most important for our purposes, however, is that the characteristics that these incidents share are what we call *elite deviance*. These characteristics include the following:

1. The acts are committed by persons from the highest strata of society: members of the upper and upper-middle classes. Some of the deeds

mentioned earlier were committed by the heads of corporate and governmental organizations; others were committed by their employees on
behalf of the employers.

2. Some of the acts are crimes in that they violate criminal statutes and
carry penalties such as fines and imprisonment.[31] Other acts violate
administrative or civil laws, which may also involve punishment.
Included are acts of both commission and omission.[32] Other acts, such
as U.S. presidents lying to the public about the Vietnam War, although
not illegal, are regarded by most Americans as unethical or immoral
(i.e., deviant). Thus, elite deviance may be either criminal or noncriminal in nature.

3. Some of the actions described previously were committed by elites
for personal gain (e.g., members of Congress who accepted bribes), or
they were committed by the elites or their employees for purposes of
enhancing the power, profitability, or influence of the organizations
involved (e.g., when corporations made bribes overseas for the purpose of securing business deals).

4. The acts were committed with relatively little risk. When and if the
elites were apprehended, the punishments inflicted were in general
very lenient compared with those given common criminals.[33]

5. Some of the incidents posed great danger to the public's safety, health,
and financial well-being.

6. In many cases, the elites in charge of the organizations mentioned were
able to conceal their illegal or unethical actions for years before they became public knowledge (e.g., Hooker Chemical's dumping of poisonous chemicals and the presidential misuses of the FBI and CIA). Yet the
actions mentioned were seemingly compatible with the goals of such
organizations (i.e., the maintenance or enhancement of the organization's power and/or profitability).[34]

## A Theory of Elite Deviance

Elite deviance, in all its forms, now constitutes a major social problem for
American society and, as will be explored, much of the world as well. This
does not mean, however, that there is a consensus concerning what constitutes deviance. Notions of elite wrongdoing, white-collar crime, and
related concepts are now the focus of intense debate in the social sciences.
In this regard, the conflict perspective and the evidence amassed in support of it offer the best starting point concerning a causal theory of elite
deviance.

Criminologists and students of criminal justice tend to focus on the
study of individual criminals in their research. The criminal justice system
itself was originally established to protect the rights of accused persons, not

to discover the causes of or ways to prevent criminal activity. As a result of this bias in American society, the social sciences focus heavily on individual crimes, individual rights, and individual cases. This is especially the case with street crimes (e.g., homicide, robbery, burglary, and rape), which receive the lion's share of attention and resources in law enforcement, the courts, and correctional institutions. Street crimes are also the primary preoccupation of both the criminology and criminal justice fields.

This is not to say that the street crime problem is unimportant. Indeed, as we will examine later in this book, street crime, organized crime, and elite deviance are interrelated in numerous ways (see Chapter 8). In fact, the crime problem in the United States is actually rooted in a system in which lower-class criminals, organized crime, a corrupt public sector, and deviant corporations cooperate for purposes of profit and power.

Thus, our examination begins with the proposition that crime and deviance are societally patterned. This means that certain sociological factors cause crimes to be committed by both individuals and organizations. Among the most important of these factors in American society is the U.S. power structure itself.

## The U.S. Social Structure: The Power Elite

The view of the U.S. social structure that we support is the one advocated by the late C. Wright Mills.[35] Mills proposed that the dominant institutional structures of American life constitute a power elite of the largest corporations, the federal government, and the military. These dominant institutions are headed by elites, people whose positions within organizations have provided them the greatest amounts of wealth, power, and often prestige of any such positions in the nation. Immediately below this power elite is a subgroup of corporations that constitute the mass media. The source of their power is communications, which clearly differentiates elites from nonelites in American society. A sizable Washington press core waits for the daily pronouncements of political elites. Moreover, 90% of the commercials on prime-time television (TV) are sponsored by the nation's 500 largest corporations.[36]

The corporate, political, and military worlds are interrelated in numerous ways. Most members of the president's cabinet come from the ranks of big business and return there when their government service ends; numerous Pentagon employees, civilian and military, are employed by weapons industry firms upon retirement.

These interrelationships mean that the deviance within this elite often involves two or more organizations: one or more corporations and one or more government agencies. Power and private wealth are concentrated in the hands of the elite. Together, these institutions determine primary societal objectives, priorities, and policies, and thus greatly influence the so-called lesser institutions (i.e., the family, religion, and education). The elite dominate these lesser socializing institutions and thus shape the American social character.

***The Evidence for a Power Elite.***   In the United States, elites own both great riches and the ability to make decisions that affect the conduct of nonelites (political power), but studies reveal that they also exert a great deal of control over such resources as education, prestige, status, skills of leadership, information, knowledge of political processes, ability to communicate, and organization. "Moreover, elites [in America] are drawn disproportionately from ... society's upper classes, which are made up of those persons ... who own or control a disproportionate share of the societal institutions industry, commerce, finance, education, the military, communications, civic affairs, and law."[37]

One recent study concludes that there are 5,416 positions within the nation's most powerful economic, governmental, military, media, legal, civic, and educational institutions. These positions constitute a few 10-thousandths of 1% of the population. Yet the amount of resources that they control is immense. Among families, personal wealth (net worth) is highly concentrated: As of 2005, "the richest 10 percent of the adult population possesses 69.8 percent of the country's household wealth, the second-highest share of any democratic developed nation. The top 1 percent possesses 33.4 percent of net wealth, including more than half of the total value in publicly traded stocks. Though the American Dream, or the perception that Americans enjoy high social mobility, played a key role in attracting immigrants to the United States, particularly in the late 1800s, some analysts find that the United States has relatively low social mobility compared to Western Europe and Canada."[38]

- In industry, 100 out of 200,000 corporations control 55% of all industrial assets. The largest 500 industrial corporations control three-quarters of manufacturing assets. The largest 800 corporations employ one of every five workers in the civilian labor force.[39]
- In transportation and utilities, 50 out of 67,000 companies control two-thirds of the assets in the airline, railroad, communications, electricity, and gas industries.[40]
- In banking, 25 out of over 12,000 banks control over 50% of all banking assets. Three of these banks, Bank America, Citicorp, and Chase Manhattan, control almost 20% of such assets.
- In insurance, 10 out of 2,048 firms control over half of all insurance assets. Two insurance companies, Prudential and Metropolitan Life, control nearly one-quarter of such assets.[41]

In 1983, 50 corporations controlled the vast majority of all news media in the United States. At the time, Ben Bagdikian was called "alarmist" for pointing this out in his book, *The Media Monopoly*. In the fourth edition of the book, published in 1992, he wrote, "In the U.S., fewer than two dozen of these extraordinary creatures own and operate 90% of the mass media"— controlling almost all of America's newspapers, magazines, TV and radio stations, books, records, movies, videos, wire services, and photo agencies. He predicted then that eventually this number would fall to about half a dozen companies, a number that was greeted with skepticism. When the sixth edition of *The Media Monopoly* was published in 2000, the number had fallen to six. Since then, there have been more mergers, and the scope has expanded to include new media like the Internet market. More than *one in four* Internet users in the United States now log in with AOL Time-Warner, the world's largest media corporation.

In 2004, Bagdikian's revised and expanded book, *The New Media Monopoly*, shows that only five huge corporations—Time Warner, Disney, Rupert Murdoch's news corporation, Bertelsmann of Germany, and Viacom (formerly CBS)—now control most of the media industry in the United States. General Electric's NBC is a close sixth.[42]

Media corporations are often perceived as somehow different from other corporations because they produce news and entertainment. The truth is that large media firms "share members of the board of directors with a variety of other large corporations, including banks, investment companies, oil companies, health care and pharmaceutical companies, and technology companies."[43] The following list shows board interlocks for five global media conglomerates, ABC/Disney, NBC/GE, CBS/Viacom, CNN/Time Warner, and Fox/News Corp.:

### *ABC/Disney*

Boeing
Casella Waste Systems
CB Richard Ellis Services
City National Bank
Columbia/HCA Healthcare
Doubleclick
Edison International
FedEx
Jenny Craig
LM Institutional Fund Advisors I
Lozano Communications
Northwest Airlines

On Command Corp.
Pacific American Income Shares
Shamrock Holdings
Sotheby's N. America
Staples
Starwood Hotels & Resorts
Sun Microsystems
SunAmerica
Trefoil Investors
UNUM Provident
Verdon-Cedric Productions
Xerox

### *NBC/GE*

Alcatel
Anheuser-Busch
Ann Taylor
Avon

Banco Nacional de Mexico
Cambridge Technology
    Partners
Catalyst

Champion International
Chase Manhattan
Choice-Point
Chubb Corporation
Coca-Cola
Community Health Systems
Dell Computer
Delphi Automotive
Fiat
Home Depot
Honeywell
Illinois Tool Works
International Speedy
Internet Security Systems
Invemed
Morgan Chase & Co.
Kellogg
Kimberly-Clark

Knight-Ridder
Microtune
Morgan Guaranty Trust
National Service Industries
New York Stock Exchange
Oglivy & Mather
Penske
Planet Hollywood
Scientific Atlanta
State Street Bank and Trust
Sun Microsystems
Texaco
TIAA-CREF
Total Systems Services
TRICON Global Restaurants
Unifi
Unilever
WinStar

### CBS/Viacom

Akamai Technologies
Amazon.com
American Express
American Home Products
 Corporation
Atlas Air
Avnet
Bank One
Bear Sterns Companies
Boston Properties
Cardinal Health
Care Capital
Chase Manhattan
CineBridge Ventures
Credit Suisse First Boston
 Corporation
CVS
Daimler Chrysler
Dell
DND Capital Partners
Downeast Food
 Distributors

Electronic Data Systems
Ezgov.com
Genuity
Honeywell
Morgan Chase & Co.
Lafarge Corporation
Louisiana Marine Transport
Maersk Group
MBIA
MovieTickets.com
New York Stock Exchange
Orion Safety Products
PartnerRe
Pfizer
Polaris Venture Capital
Prudential Insurance
Rockwell International
 Corporation
Sonesta
Ventro
Verizon
Visteon

### CNN/Time Warner

Allstate Insurance
American Express
American International
AMR
Barksdale Group
Catellus Development
Chevron
Citigroup
Colgate-Palmolive
Community Health Systems
Dell Computers
Eagle River
Exult
Fannie Mae
FedEx
Forstmann Little & Co.
Hills & Co.
Hilton Hotels
Interpublic Group

Kleiner Perkins Caufield
  & Byers
Lucent
Morgan Stanley Dean Witter
New York Stock Exchange
Nextel Communications
Oakwood Homes Corporation
Park Place Entertainment
Pearson plc
PepsiCo
Pfizer
Pharmacyclics
Sears
Sun Microsystems
TCW
Webvan
Westfield America Corporation
XO Communications
ZG Ventures

### Fox/News Corp.

Allen & Company
Bayou Steel Corporation
Beijing PDN Xiren Info. Tech. Co.
British Airways
Championship Auto Racing
  Teams
Commonwealth Bank of Australia
Compaq
Gateway
John Swire and Son Pty.
Kleiner Perkins Caufield & Byers

New York Stock Exchange
One.Tel
Phillip Morris
PMP Communications
RM William Holdings
Rothschild Investment
Sanoma of Finnland
Six Flags
Valence Technology
Western Multiplex Corporation
Worldcom

Another myth about the mass media is its "left-wing" orientation. The truth is that the mass media are owned by very conservative executives. Edward Herman and Noam Chomsky believe that a series of five "filters" explain why the mainstream media function as propagandists for the interests of the power elite. They explain, "Only stories with a strong orientation to elite interests can pass through the five filters unobstructed and receive ample media attention. The theory also explains how the media can conscientiously function when even a superficial analysis of the evidence would indicate the preposterous nature of many of the stories that receive ample publicity in the press and on the network news broadcasts."[44]

The first filter that influences media content is that ownership of the media is highly concentrated among a mere five for-profit global corporations. Many of these firms own stock and other firms in other industries and nations. Their needs for profit profoundly influence both news content and the overall nature of media products.

A second filter is advertising, which is the primary source of the media's income. The media are not in the business of criticizing the nature of consumer capitalism, the sexist, racist, and alienating nature of advertising content (see Chapters 3 and 4), or the overall structure of the global capitalist system.

A third filter is termed *sourcing*, where "the mass media are drawn into an interdependent relationship with powerful sources of information, especially corporate and governmental elites and their employees. The media rely heavily upon news provided them by corporate and government sources, which have their own political and economic interests to promote. These sources have their own public relations personnel who "feed" their own views to the media, in effect creating a subsidy (i.e., free or inexpensive information) for news outlets. Thus, the media are careful not to offend important suppliers of news."[45] Furthermore, these corporate and government sources are instantly credible by accepted journalistic practices. Antielite sources, on the contrary, are regarded with utmost suspicion and have tremendous difficulty passing successfully through this filter.

Herman and Chomsky's fourth filter is the development of right-wing corporate "flak" producers such as Accuracy in Media to harass the mass media and put pressure on them to follow the corporate agenda. This filter was developed extensively in the 1970s, when major corporations and wealthy right wingers became increasingly dissatisfied with political developments in the West and with media coverage of these developments. These flak producers have actively promoted the (absurd) notion that the media are bastions of liberalism and fundamentally hostile to capitalism and the "defense" of "freedom" around the world. Although ostensibly antagonistic to the media, these flak machines provide the media with legitimacy and are treated quite well by the media. News outlets treat Accuracy in Media as an unbiased source and regularly report their opinions.

The final filter is the ideology of the evil threat, which provides the ideological basis for the propaganda model. From the late 1940s to the early 1990s, anticommunism ("the evil empire") was integrated into American journalism. Today Islamic terrorism (Islamo-fascism) is a central aspect of the "axis of evil" faced by America and its allies. When threats of evil fervor are aroused, the demand for serious evidence to support claims of danger to the nation is suspended by the media, and propagandists can serve as objective experts.

Likewise, if journalists or editors question the enemy threat, they must do so in a way that passes through the other four filters, and in ways that do not threaten the media's interests.

One additional basis of this great concentration of power and resources is the income and wealth possessed by the elite, that is, its economic power. Such wealth is owned by relatively few individuals in families and corporations.

International data now indicate that wealth is more unequally distributed in the United States than in other modern democracies.

One study of the 250 largest U.S. corporations found that all but a handful (17) had at least one of their chief executives sitting on the board of at least 1 additional corporation in the top 250. Some of them even held seats on competing companies, a practice that has been illegal since 1914 with the passage of the Clayton Antitrust Act. Moreover, even people who serve on the board of directors of one company may serve as an executive of another company. This situation has been found to exist for more than 250 directors of the top 500 corporations.[46]

- More important than such interlocks is the shared ownership that characterizes U.S. corporate capitalism, concentrated among large banks and wealthy families. Many of these banks administer the trust funds of wealthy individuals or other sources of capital with which they purchase stock. Collectively, the number of boards interlocked by members of these corporations includes 700 companies. Most important, these networks of interlocking directorates tend to remain stable over time.[47]

What do all these facts mean? The largest 500 or so manufacturing firms and some 50 financial institutions, controlling two-thirds of all business income and half the nation's bank deposits, are interlocked by directorships and controlled by less than 0.5% of the population. Put simply, U.S. corporate assets reside in a few hands. More specifically, half of all assets in industry, banking, insurance, utilities, transportation, telecommunications, and the mass media are controlled by a mere 4,500 individual presidents and directors.[48] This concentration allows a very small corporate community to exercise power over one-third of the nation's gross national product and considerable indirect influence over the remainder of the nation's goods and services.[49] This is true because corporate leaders can invest money where and when they choose; expand, close, or move their factories and offices at a moment's notice; and hire, promote, and fire employees as they see fit. These powers give them direct influence over the great majority of Americans who depend on wages and salaries for their incomes. They also give the corporate rich indirect influence over elected and appointed officials because the growth and stability of a city, state, or the country as a whole can be jeopardized by a lack of business confidence in government.[50]

*The Political Elite.* Aside from the economic elite, the nation also possesses a political elite. The political elite, to a significant extent, overlaps with, yet is independent from, the economic elite. The corporate managers, owners (super-rich individuals and families), and directors are, for the most part, members of the American upper class. Membership in the upper class is typically measured by such indicators as (1) one's name in the *Social Register*, an exclusive list of influential persons published in major U.S. cities and containing the names of about 138,000 persons; (2) attendance at elite private secondary schools and universities; (3) membership in exclusive social clubs and annual attendance at upper-class vacation retreats (e.g., Bohemian Grove, Pacific Union Club, Knickerbocker Club); and, of course, (4) seats on boards of the largest interlocked corporations.[51]

The political elite differs from the corporate or economic elite in that it includes persons occupying "key federal government positions in the executive (presidential), judicial (the Supreme Court and lesser federal courts), and legislative (congressional) branches [and] . . . the top command positions in the Army, Navy, Air Force, and Marines."[52] Numerous studies reveal that the political elite is composed of persons from both the upper-middle class (lawyers, small businesspeople, doctors, farmers, educators, and other professionals) and the upper class. The upper class tends to dominate the federal branch of the government, whereas upper-middle-class professionals make up the preponderance of the legislative branch. A study of presidential cabinets, from McKinley to Nixon, examining the degree to which cabinet heads were recruited from the ranks of big business, indicated that, from 1897 to 1973, big business supplied from 60% (under McKinley) to 95.7% (under Nixon) of presidential cabinet members.[53]

Another study found that 63% of the secretaries of state, 62% of the secretaries of defense, and 63% of the treasury secretaries have been members of the national upper class.[54] A few examples of the members of the power elite include the following:

- John Foster Dulles was secretary of state from 1953 to 1960. Before his appointment he was senior partner in a prestigious law firm, Sullivan and Cromwell, and sat on the boards of numerous corporations: Bank of New York, American Bank Note Company, United Railroad, International Nickel of Canada, American Cotton Corporation, and European Textile Corporation. Dulles was also a trustee of leading civic organizations: the New York Public Library, the Rockefeller Foundation, and the Carnegie Endowment for International Peace. His brother, Allen, was director of the CIA (1953–1961) and a member of the Warren Commission, the panel set up by President Johnson to investigate the assassination of President Kennedy.

- Alexander Haig, secretary of state in 1981–1982, is currently president of United Technologies Corporation, a major defense contractor. Haig is a former four-star U.S. Army general; former Supreme Commander of NATO forces in Europe; former assistant to President Nixon; former deputy commander of the U.S. Military Academy in West Point, New York; and former deputy secretary of defense. He is the man most responsible for the terms set down in the pardon of President Nixon following the Watergate scandal.

Corporate position has rarely been better represented in government than it is by the position of secretary of the treasury.

- George Bush's treasury secretary, Nicholas Brady, was a former chairman of Dillion Read & Company, a major Wall Street investment firm, and member of the board of directors of Purolator, National Cash Register, Georgia International, and Media General.
- Jimmy Carter's treasury head, Michael Blumenthal, is president of the Bendix Corporation, former vice president of Crown Cork Company, and trustee of the Council on Foreign Relations.

Thus, it makes little difference whether the White House is run by Republicans or Democrats; those who run the government largely tend to come from corporate backgrounds and share remarkably similar educational and cultural experiences and affiliations.

As of 2003, at least 40 of the 100 U.S. senators are millionaires, including 22 Republicans and 18 Democrats. These figures indicate an increasing gulf between average Americans and their so-called representatives. Even Congress members with "modest" net worth make salaries of $154,700, with leadership positions paying $171,900 annually.

- First is Massachusetts senator John Kerry, whose estimated net worth is between $164 million and $211 million. His wife is part owner of the Heinz Corporation and has a net worth of close to $1 billion.
- Second is Senator Herb Kohl of Wisconsin, whose net worth is $111 million. Kohl owned a chain of stores before going into politics; currently he owns the Milwaukee Bucks basketball team.
- Senator John J. Rockefeller of West Virginia has a net worth of $81.6 million; Senator Jon Corzine of New Jersey, a former Wall Street executive, is worth $71 million, and Senator Dianne Feinstein, of California, married to businessman Richard Blum, is worth $26.3 million.
- Two Republicans worth millions are banking heir Peter Fitzgerald of Illinois, worth $26.1 million, and former Senate majority leader Bill Frist of Tennessee, worth $15.1 million. Frist's family founded HCA, the nation's largest for-profit hospital chain. Frist placed his money in blind trusts valued at between $6.5 million and $31 million.

The vague methods of the congressional reportage requirements conceal many millions of dollars of assets and income. Some items are grouped into broad categories (e.g., $1 million to $5 million), and the assessed value of a permanent home—exceeding $1 million in some cases—does not require reporting at all.

A disclosure would probably demonstrate the percentage of senators who are millionaires is well over 50%. The U.S. House of Representatives also contains a number of millionaires among its 435 members, including former House Speaker Nancy Pelosi ($92 million held jointly with her businessman husband, Paul).[55]

Although it is true that economic power and state or government power are interlinked, they are not related in a conspiratorial fashion. This is an important point because a number of people who have written on the subjects of elite power and political corruption do believe in conspiracies.[56] A second distorted view of the elite has been put forth by certain muckraking journalists, who hold that while the state and the upper class are relatively independent, certain "moral and legal lapses in this independence" occur.[57] This view purports that the business class gets what it desires from government by engaging in all manner of corruption, lobbying, and other forms of illegal or unethical behavior.

The view expressed in this book is that the conspiratorial view of elite behavior is simplistic. Even though conspiracies do occur from time to time and always will, such explanations do a disservice to the complex nature of elite power and elite deviance.

The conspiratorial view of the elite is unrealistic for a number of reasons. First, not only are the elite somewhat diverse as to class background, but they are ideologically diverse, as well. That is, political opinions among elites range from conservative to social democrat. Although it is true that the elites agree on the basic rules of politics (i.e., free elections, the court system, and the rule of law) and believe in the capitalist economic system, they disagree considerably about such issues as the power of business, civil rights, welfare, and foreign policy.[58]

Second, elites do not control the federal government because they do not possess a monopoly of political power. The structure of capitalist society is such that elite rule is faced with economic and other crises (e.g., inflation, unemployment, war, racism) that lead nonelite interests to demand changes consistent with their interests (e.g., unemployment benefits in periods of high unemployment). As William Chambliss has concluded, "The persistence of and importance of the conflicts resolved through law necessarily create occasions where well-organized groups representing [nonelite] class interests manage to effect important legislation."[59]

Third, the conspiratorial view relating to elites dominating the state through corruption masks some of the most important unethical patterns that characterize much of elite deviance. For example, during the hearings regarding his appointment as vice president in the mid-1970s, Nelson

Rockefeller was questioned about his gift-giving habits but was not held "accountable for the shootings at Attica (prison) or ... for the involvement of Chase Manhattan [Bank] in the repressive system of South African racism."[60]

Likewise, the right wing's conspiratorial view of a capitalist elite plotting to lead the nation into communism hides much of the unethical behavior of corporations that results as a consequence of the structure of corporate capitalism itself. As mentioned, about one-third of the economy is dominated by corporate giants. Such giantism means that, in many manufacturing (e.g., cereals, soups, autos, and tires) and financial industries, a handful of firms (often four or fewer) accounts for more than half the market in a particular industry or service. Such situations are often characterized by artificially high prices due not to secret price-fixing conspiracies but to a practice known as price leadership. This results when one firm decides to raise prices on a given product and is then copied by the other major firms in the same field. The costs of these monopolistic price distortions are discussed in depth in Chapter 3. This and other unethical practices considered in detail in this volume are not accounted for by conspiratorial views of the economy and government and the linkages between them.

Our position is that it is more fruitful to consider deviance within the context of the relationships between business and governmental organizations, the functions performed by government, and the internal organizational structure of both the corporate and political organizations that constitute the elite sectors of society. In sum, we concur with Michael Parenti's view that "elite power is principally systemic and legitimating rather than conspiratorial and secretive."[61]

## Economy-State Linkages and the Functions of Government

To understand the interrelationships between the economy and the state is to comprehend how elites attempt to formulate and implement public policy. These interrelationships are based on connections among corporations, large law firms that represent large corporations, elite colleges and universities, the mass media, private philanthropic foundations, major research organizations (think tanks), political parties, and the executive and legislative branches of the federal government. Key examples of these interlocks of moneys, personnel, and policies are pictured in Figure 1.1.

Aside from the major corporations and the federal government, the rest of the organizations are included for several reasons:

1.  Twenty-five universities and colleges listed in Figure 1.1 control 50% of all educational endowment funds and include some 656 corporate and other elites as their presidents and trustees. Moreover, only 50 foundations out of 12,000 control 40% of all foundation assets.[62] The officers of such foundations often have experience in elite corporations, educational institutions, and/or government.

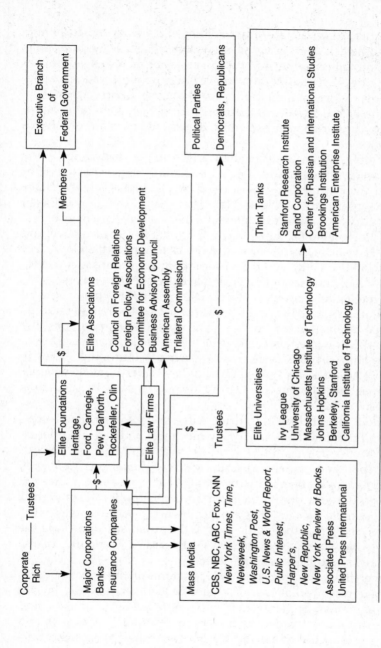

**FIGURE 1.1** *The Capitalist Elite: Links among the Ruling Elite*

*Source:* Adapted from Domhoff, G. W. (Spring 1974). State and ruling class in corporate America. *The Insurgent Sociologist, 4, 9.* By permission of G. William Domhoff and *The Insurgent Sociologist.*

2. The elite civic associations bring together elites from the corporate, educational, legal, and governmental worlds. Such organizations have been described as "central coordinating mechanisms in national policy making."[63] These organizations issue public position papers and investigative reports on matters of domestic and foreign policy. Membership in one or more of these organizations is sometimes a prerequisite to a high-ranking post within the executive branch of the federal government.

   For example, the majority of the Carter cabinet (including Jimmy Carter himself) served on the Trilateral Commission prior to assuming office. The commission was formed by David Rockefeller, chairman of the board of the Chase Manhattan Bank; heir to the Exxon fortune; graduate of Harvard; member of the boards of directors of B.F. Goodrich, Rockefeller Brothers, Inc., and Equitable Life Insurance; and trustee of Harvard. Rockefeller is also the chairman of the Council of Foreign Relations (CFR). Almost all recent secretaries of state, including Cyrus Vance and Henry Kissinger, have been CFR members.[64]

3. The mass media are concentrated in that there are three major TV and radio networks, NBC, ABC, and CBS. These networks are also multinational corporations that own or are owned by other corporations. For example, NBC is owned by General Electric, a major manufacturer of appliances and weapons systems components. Controlling shares in the three TV networks are owned by five New York commercial banks: Chase Manhattan, Morgan Guaranty, Citibank, Bankers Trust, and the Bank of New York.[65]

   The media also include the major wire services, Associated Press and United Press International, from which most national and international news make its way into U.S. radio, TV, and newspapers. Regarding newspapers and newsweeklies, the *New York Times*, the *Washington Post*, *Time*, *Newsweek* (owned by the *Washington Post*), and *U.S. News & World Report* are regarded as the most influential publications in their field.[66] Most cable TV networks are also owned by media conglomerates. One exception is the holdings of Ted Turner, which include the Cable News Network (CNN), stations WTBS and TNT, and the Atlanta Braves, Hawks, and Falcons sports teams.

   Moreover, the major sponsors of TV programs on the three networks are other large corporations. The media tend to portray deviant behavior as violent behavior that is perpetrated by poor nonelites. As one recent study concludes, the crime reported in TV news and newsmagazines includes kidnappings and particularly gruesome murders. "Ordinary people who carry out nonviolent crimes or violate the mores rarely appear in national news."[67] However, "the economically powerful, such as officers of large corporations and holders of great wealth, are filmed or written about rarely, and then usually for reasons having little to do with their economic power, [except] when they are involved in some conflict with the federal government or are having legal difficulties."[68]

Overall, the media function to portray crime and deviance as a problem created by nonelites and to describe corporate capitalism as a system characterized by competition, freedom, and, while flawed, the best of all existing worlds. As a *Time* magazine profile put it: "Plainly capitalism is not working well enough. But there is no evidence to show the fault is in the system—or that there is a better alternative. ... For all its blemishes capitalism still holds out the most creative and dynamic force that any civilization has ever discovered: the power of the free ambitious individual."[69]

Such propagandistic exercises are also characteristic of numerous TV commercials and public service announcements (often prepared by the elite National Advertising Council) that insist that the oil companies are "working to keep your trust" or that our "economics quotients" (knowledge about the U.S. economic system) could stand improvement. Thus, one overall function of the mass media is to ensure the continuation and growth of the system of corporate capitalism.

4. Twenty-eight superfirms do much of the legal work for the corporations, mass media, and educational and civic foundations. In addition, senior lawyers in such firms often fill posts on various foundations and civic and educational institutions and from time to time assume various posts within the executive branch of the federal government. A good example of one such superlawyer is Paul Warnke, President Carter's chief negotiator in the Strategic Arms Limitation Talks. Warnke is also a member of the Trilateral Commission, a director of the CFR, a former assistant secretary of defense, and partner in a Washington law firm that included former defense secretary Clark Clifford.[70]

5. Finally, there are numerous elite-related think tanks, primarily research institutes. In general, these operations receive moneys from both public and private sources, depending on the type of research that they do. For example, about 5% of the Department of Defense's research and development budget in the 1960s and early 1970s went to such research organizations.[71]

Think tanks perform a very wide variety of research tasks and are closely allied with the business arm of the American power elite. For instance, the American Enterprise Institute (AEI) is allied with the conservative wing of the Republican Party and southern Democrats. Its activities primarily involve studies, the end products of which are policy proposals aimed at enhancing the profitability and power of its corporate clients.[72]

• In the 1970s new "think tanks," especially the AEI and the Heritage Foundation, were established and richly endowed by corporate money. The right-wing Heritage Foundation was started with a $250,000 donation from Colorado beer tycoon Joseph Coors. AEI's patrons included AT&T ($125,000), Chase Manhattan Bank ($125,000), Exxon ($130,000), General Electric ($65,000), General Motors ($100,000), and Procter & Gamble ($165,000). AEI quickly became a "primary source of Washington opinion" shaping the policy positions of Washington politicians and the mass media.[73]

The AEI and other think tanks also prepare studies for influential big-business lobby groups, such as the National Association of Manufacturers and the United States Chamber of Commerce. In short, think tanks provide valuable research aid in achieving the policy aims of elites, both inside and outside of government. Figure 1.1 depicts the structures that supply personnel, money, and policy to the federal government but does not describe the processes used by or the benefits from the state sought by elites. Such means and benefits are important in that when they are abused, they constitute forms of elite deviance. These benefits will be discussed in following sections.

*Lobbying.*    The principle of majority rule is sometimes violated by special interests, which, by deals, propaganda, and the financial support of political candidates, attempt to deflect the political process for their own benefit. Individuals, families, corporations, and various organizations use a variety of means to obtain numerous benefits from congressional committees, regulatory agencies, and executive bureaucracies. To accomplish their goals, lobbyists for the special interests "along with the slick brochures, expert testimonies, and technical reports, ... still have the slush fund, the kickback, the stock award, the high paying job offer from industry, the lavish parties and prostitutes, the meals, transportation, housing and vacation accommodations, and the many other hustling enticements of money."[74]

The existence of lobbyists does not ensure that the national interests will be served or that the concerns of all groups will be heard. Who, for example, speaks for the interests of schoolchildren, minority groups, the poor, people who are mentally retarded, renters, migrant workers, in short for the relatively powerless? And if there is a voice for these people, does it match the clout of lobbyists backed by the fantastic financial resources of the elite?

In fairness, it must be stressed that the success of such lobbies is not ensured.

Big economic interests don't always win. The cargo preference bill was defeated. So was the 1979 sugar quota. The Consumer Cooperative Bank bill passed the House by one vote and became law. Sometimes scandal or the weight of evidence can push Congress in the right direction. And it must be noted that when a congressman from Michigan votes to bail out Chrysler, or a congressman from Wisconsin votes for dairy price supports, he is also voting to benefit his own constituents. This may not favor the public interest, but it is predictable politics, not personal corruption... . To receive money from an interest doesn't mean a member of Congress is controlled, per se. There are indentured politicians and there are principled conservatives; the former virtually auction their souls to the highest bidder while the latter may truly believe that the government shouldn't be forcing pharmaceutical firms to pre-market test their drugs.[75]

Nevertheless, corporate lobbies usually do exert a significant influence.

*Financing Political Campaigns.*    Perhaps one of the most elite-dominated and undemocratic features (at least in its consequences) of the U.S. political system is a result of the manner in which campaigns are financed. Political campaigns are expensive, with statewide campaigns sometimes costing hundreds of thousands of dollars and national campaigns running into the millions. This money is raised from contributions, and campaign contributions now represent a major scandal for both political parties. In the 1996 presidential elections the Democratic Party attempted to raise $200 million for the Clinton–Gore re-election campaign. Some of the tactics used involved clear violations of federal law.

Between 1983 and 1988, 163 savings and loan (S&L) political action committees (PACs) gave $11 million to congressional candidates, with donations increasing 42% just before the S&L bailout was authorized by Congress.[76] The campaign donations from the S&L industry resulted in the most massive financial scandal in U.S. history. Members of various S&Ls allowed Democratic Congress members to use S&L-owned yachts for fundraising purposes and even paid for one influential congressman's dinners, which amounted to $20,000 for a single year. S&L lobbyists also contributed to the establishment of a business school for Utah senator Jake Garn, who coauthored a bill allowing S&Ls to engage in all manner of questionable financial practices. The final cost to the public may be over $1 trillion. (See Chapter 2 for details.)

Thus, the passage of favorable laws or the defeat of unfavorable ones may directly result from the finances of special interests. So, too, may the special interests receive beneficial governmental rulings and the maintenance of tax loopholes. As these investments pay off, it is only rational for the special interests to donate to the candidates of both parties to ensure that their interests are served. The result is that the wealthy have power, while the less well-to-do and certainly the poor have little influence on officeholders.[77]

By law, corporations cannot directly contribute any of their funds to political parties or candidates. However, because corporations apparently find that political contributions help them, many have contributed to political campaigns illegally. This can be done either by giving money to employees, who in turn make individual contributions, or by forcing employees to contribute to a party or candidate as a condition of employment. Watergate showed that many companies engaged in fraudulent bookkeeping practices to cover up their political expenditures.

To counter the potential and real abuses of large contributors, the 1976 presidential campaign was partially financed from public funds; about $20 million was allocated to each of the two major candidates. Congress, however, refused to provide a similar law for its members or potential members. As a result, the moneys contributed to congressional candidates rose sharply. In 1978, the total gifts from all reporting interest groups to candidates for Congress was $35 million, compared with $22.6 million in 1976 and only $12.5 million in 1974. The most discussed phenomenon in campaign financing today is undoubtedly the PAC.

> PACs are "nonparty," "multicandidate" political committees that maintain a separate, segregated fund for political contributions: "nonparty" because they are set up by interest groups, "multicandidate" because they distribute their largesse to at least five candidates ("political contributions" only; no charity to be mixed in here).[78]

Although some PACs are established by the numerous single-issue groups, such as the National Rifle Association and environmental or anti-abortion causes, the vast majority of PAC money stems from corporate interests. Thus, in the 1981–1982 congressional campaign, corporate PACs spent $50 million of the $83 million given to candidates, a tenfold increase over the amount given to candidates in 1972. Seven million dollars of that money (more than 7%) came from oil and gas interests. The chairs of the House and Senate energy committees received funds from 34 and 37 energy PACs, respectively.[79]

PAC money is now far and away the largest source of congressional campaign funds, with business PAC contributions favoring Republicans over Democrats by a ratio of two to one. Indeed, in the 1970s there were about 600 PACs in Washington. By the 1992 election, there were 4,585, and all but about 365 of these were corporate in nature. "Candidates have become so dependent on PAC money that they actually visit PAC offices and all but demand contributions."[80] The beer distributors' PAC is called six-PAC. There is also a Beef-PAC, and an Ice Cream-PAC. These PACs may donate up to $5,000 to each congressional candidate in both primary and general election campaigns. During the 1991–1992 political campaign, all Democratic congressional candidates raised $360 million, whereas Republican candidates raised $293 million. The GOP National Committee raised an additional $85.4 million, whereas the Democratic National Committee raised $65.7 million. The vast majority of these funds (about 80%) came from PACs.

What do PACs expect from the Congress members receiving their funds? Votes on important pieces of legislation. For example, in 1992, Senator David Prior, an Arkansas Democrat, sponsored a bill that would link a huge tax break for establishing factories in Puerto Rico with stable prices for prescription drugs. Nine of the top 10 recipients of drug PAC money from 1981 to 1991 voted for tabling (thus killing) this unfavorable legislation.[81]

By the late 1980s, politicians from all sides had become alarmed about the dangers of PACs to democracy. Senator Charles Mathias remarked that the current system of financing congressional elections threatened to "erode public confidence in the electoral process and in government itself."[82] Conservative Barry Goldwater stated that unlimited spending in political campaigns "cuts at the very heart of the democratic process."[83] Despite such pronouncements, in 1988 the ill effects and influence of PACs continued unabated.

- Fifty-one U.S. senators and 146 members of the House of Representatives are either founders or officers of Washington, DC, tax-exempt organizations that produce either research statistics or corporate propaganda for lobbying purposes.[84]
- In 1960, fewer than 400 lobbyists were registered with the U.S. Congress. By 1992, 40,000 were registered.[85] These 40,000 people represent mostly American and foreign corporations. Much of this growth came in the 1970s and 1980s when the capitalist class decided it was underrepresented in the nation's capital. Eighty percent of the Fortune 500 corporations established "public-affairs offices" (lobby groups) in Washington.[86]
- In 2000, the Republican Party insisted that its financial base was primarily small contributors, but research by the *New York Times* revealed that the GOP had received $90 million from a small pool of wealthy individuals, some of whom kept their contributions secret. An elite group of 739 contributors provided two-thirds of the Republicans' $137 million "soft money," the unrestricted donations. Some contributors were directed by GOP officials to make their donations in secret ways. Those people and corporations that gave at least $250,000 between 1999 and 2000 were labeled Platinum Level members. The Federal Election Commission showed only 54 such corporations and individuals because donors were asked to split their funds into smaller checks, thus making their origin harder to trace.[87]

These examples not only illustrate the dangers of PAC influence in Congress but also indicate why many of the laws designed to control corporate crime were so weakened during the Reagan years. (See Chapter 2 for further discussion of these issues.)

Meanwhile, in Congress, one effect of PAC money has been to alter the very structure of power within the institution. Representative Jim Wright of Texas was elected Speaker of the House after giving $312,000 of his own campaign funds to 141 members. Moreover, consider that senators now spend 60% to 70% of their time raising the money needed to be re-elected; during an entire 6-year term, as much as $10,000 per week must be raised.[88] Finally, political parties have found loopholes in election laws, laundering moneys through state party committees, which allows them to spend beyond the $54 million limit in presidential campaigns. Such moneys have included massive contributions from individuals (e.g., $1 million from Joan Kroc of McDonald's and $503,263 from a former U.S. ambassador) that federal financing of election laws was designed to stop.[89]

*Candidate Selection.*   Closely related to our discussion of PACs is the process by which political candidates are nominated. Being wealthy or having access to wealth is essential for victory because of the enormous cost of running a successful campaign. It cost up to $5.5 million to elect a senator and/or representative in 1992.[90] This means, then, that the candidates tend to represent a limited constituency, the wealthy. "Recruitment of elective elites remains closely associated, especially for the most important offices in the larger states, with the candidates' wealth or access to large campaign contributions."[91]

The two-party system also works to limit candidates to a rather narrow range. Each party is financed by special interests, especially business.

> When all of these direct and indirect gifts (donations provided directly to candidates or through numerous political action committees of specific corporations and general business organizations) are combined, the power elite can be seen to provide the great bulk of the financial support to both parties at the national level, far outspending the unions and middle-status liberals within the Democrats, and the melange of physicians, dentists, engineers, real-estate operators, and other white-collar conservatives within the right wing of the Republican party.[92]

As affluent individuals and large corporations dominate each party, they influence the candidate selection process by giving financial aid to those sympathetic with their views and by withholding their support from those who differ. The parties, then, are constrained to choose candidates with views congruent with the elite moneyed interests.

## Benefits That Elites Seek From the State

A number of factors about the current historical era bear on the nature of elite deviance. Over the past 20 years, the United States has experienced the most dramatic economic and political change of the post–World War II era. Unfortunately, this unprecedented change has contributed to a wave of elite deviance that is virtually out of control.

Economically, the United States is no longer the dominant power it once was. Its share of the world's income is now half of what it was two decades ago. The U.S. manufacturing base has severely declined, and millions of manufacturing jobs located in the nation's Northeast and Midwest have been relocated overseas, where labor is cheaper, taxes are lower, and raw materials are more accessible (see Chapter 5). Two-thirds of the workforce now engages in service-sector positions, and one-quarter of all jobs are now government related.

As a result of these changes, corporations grow not by expanding plants and equipment, and thus creating new jobs but by buying other corporations. Another related effect of these economic changes is insider trading scandals on Wall Street.

In addition, the United States experienced an era of inflation accompanied by unemployment from the 1970s to the early 1990s. Although the rate of inflation has slowed in recent years, in real terms, American workers are no better off economically than they were 20 years ago. One result has been an outbreak of criminal and unethical behavior at all levels of society. The unemployment rate has settled at about 7%, a level that would have been viewed with some alarm 25 years ago. Today, it is viewed as an improvement, which is an indication of just how much economic decline Americans have become accustomed to.

Central to our understanding of elite deviance is the relationship between the corporate and political institutions. Many contemporary conflict theorists believe that the central contradiction of the capitalist order is now focused on the state. The political institution is being asked to perform two contradictory functions. On the one hand, politically influential corporations demand state assistance in capital accumulation (profit expansion) through tax relief, lucrative government contracts, subsidies, loans, and loan guarantees. Corporations also receive military protection of their overseas markets and investments. But, on the other hand, for its legitimacy to be maintained, the state must meet the demands placed on it for public assistance: social programs designed to aid those suffering from poverty, unemployment, homelessness, mental illness and retardation, drug addiction, and other problems arising in modern capitalist societies.

The result is that the state is caught in the middle. The demand for state services and expenditures consistently exceeds state revenues. One consequence of this situation is a massive deficit, which can be reduced in only three ways.

1. Reduce support for corporate programs (e.g., defense contracts, subsidies, loans, corporate taxes). This is unlikely, due to corporate influence in the policy-making process.
2. Cut social programs for the unemployed, poor, elderly, and other needy groups. If too much is cut, it will appear that the government is serving the wealthy and powerful at the expense of those in need, which would prompt a massive withdrawal of legitimacy by ordinary people. This in turn might result in mass resistance to fighting additional wars to preserve corporate holdings, a tax revolt that might increase debt, or a new political movement designed to redistribute wealth, income, and political power in a more democratic fashion.

3. Raise taxes for citizens. This is unpopular among those who vote and is thus something that no serious candidate wishing to be elected would propose.[93]

The situation is made worse by the competitive sector of the economy, the 12 million small and medium-sized businesses that suffer the crises of farm foreclosures, bank failures, and bankruptcy. In recent decades, these businesses have struggled against high interest rates and suffered declining demand for their goods and services because corporate America has transferred millions of jobs to places with lower wage scales, both in the United States and overseas.

Corporate deviance also plays a role in these processes. Indeed, Harold Barnet has argued that marketing unsafe products, polluting the environment, and violating health, safety, and labor laws all help to increase corporate profits by transferring various costs to consumers, workers, and the public in general.[94] Moreover, the appalling lack of enforcement of corporate crime laws and the lenient sentences handed down in the few cases that get convictions serve further to indicate that the state functions largely to encourage capital accumulation, not to repress elite wrongdoing.

## The Higher Immorality and Links Between Various Kinds of Crime

Many have characterized the 1980s and 1990s as a period in which the individual focus was on self-concern, personal survival, and greed.[95] This personal focus was aided and abetted by a conservative, probusiness administration that somehow made greed seem moral and corruption an everyday fact of political life (see Chapter 2). The result was a wave of scandal in the corporate, political, and military worlds. It was spawned by the centralization of power within large organizations composing the elite and covered up by the mass media, which continually provided diversion, distraction, and socialization to the very norms of the elite.

Mills argued that the power elite had managed to institutionalize deviant behavior within its ranks. This is significant, in part, because sociologists usually consider deviant behavior as constituting abnormal episodes and characterizing a minority of people. Various chapters ahead contain evidence demonstrating that deviance and crime among many segments of the nation's economic, political, and military elite are frequent. Moreover, the deviance within the elite differs markedly from that of other social classes because it involves so much more money, power, and resources than are available to people in other strata.

The higher immorality consists of a group of acts and behaviors intended to increase profit and power (see Chapter 2). However, the nature of the higher immorality has changed within recent years. Corporate crime and political scandal are now interrelated not only to each other but also to other types of crime and deviance.

The American drug problem is a central example. More than $200 billion of the world's $600 billion in illegal drugs is consumed in the United States. Drugs can be smuggled into the United States with the cooperation of banks (which launder drug money) and political elites (who accept payoffs), both here and in countries of origin. General Manuel Noriega, onetime leader of Panama, was convicted in 1992 for accepting bribes from the Latin American cocaine cartel. At the same time, Noriega was a longtime employee of the CIA, which for years had known of his involvement in the drug trade. The CIA has also been involved in various aspects of drug trafficking for more than 40 years in Europe, Southeast Asia, and most recently Latin America (see Chapter 2).

After being smuggled in, the drugs are often distributed to street gangs and peddlers by organized criminal syndicates, one of whom is the Italian American Mafia. At its lowest level, the American drug problem is directly related to the vast majority of property crimes committed by street criminals who seek money in support of drug habits. Hundreds of murders each year are committed by gangs seeking to control territory in the drug trade. Thus, crime at all levels of American life is now interrelated, as organized crime and supposedly legitimate elites cooperate for a variety of reasons in international drug traffic.[96]

From what we have said about lobbying, election financing, and candidate selection, it is obvious that much of the higher immorality involves political activities and for good reasons. The state not only regulates the capitalist economy, but also federal, state, and local governments now account for 32.2% of the gross national product. Two-thirds of these goods and services stem from spending by the federal government alone.[97] Thus, elites seek favorable legislation (or prevention of unfavorable legislation), as well as tax breaks, subsidies, and lucrative government contracts. Such contracts include everything from multibillion-dollar weapons systems to office furniture and paint. These contracts not only are influenced by the decisions of congressional members but are also often the charge of various bureaucrats within the federal government.

For example, the Government Services Administration is in charge of securing virtually all office supplies for the entire federal government. Thus, favors from lobbyists are also from time to time dispensed to bureaucrats, as well as elected members of Congress. These favors are illegal when they include kickbacks (payments by contractors that usually involve a certain percentage of the contract in which a firm is interested). But other favors may simply include the promise of a job with the company upon completion of government services. Although not illegal, these types of deals are unethical.

In addition, many independent regulatory agencies (e.g., the Federal Communications Commission, Interstate Commerce Commission, Federal Trade Commission) have some impact on virtually every large and small business in the United States. The personnel in these agencies are not infrequently the target of various lobbying and other efforts (e.g., the promise of a job in the industry that they regulate). Often, certain staff members of these agencies come from the industries that they oversee, and in some cases, the industries involved requested the initial regulation.

Finally, it is important to realize the influence that elites possess over the enactment or lack of enactment of legislation that defines what is and is not against the law in the first place. Examples of such influence are legion.

- The automobile industry got the Justice Department to sign a consent decree that blocked any attempt by public or private means to sue car manufacturers for damages occurring from air pollution.
- Many of the nation's antitrust laws appear, on the surface, to be actions that regulate business. However, many of these laws were actually requested by big business. Such laws, as we will see in Chapter 2, exclude new competitors from the marketplace and have been used to reduce the influence of labor unions. These laws have also functioned to increase public confidence in the quality of food and drugs by having such products certified safe by government inspection. For example, the 1906 Meat Inspection Act received a lot of support because of the muckraking activities of Upton Sinclair, who exposed the bad conditions in the meat processing industry. However, this act also delighted the large meat packers; it helped them to export successfully by meeting the high safety standards required by European countries. Nonetheless, the action crippled smaller companies. Americans were left with poor-quality meat and low wages.[98]

Such laws often help to create uncompetitive (monopolistic) situations and are usually welcome (even favored) by big business. Moreover, such laws are rarely enforced, and the penalties for breaking them tend to be minuscule. Numerous additional examples could be cited showing how, time and again, corporate officials and politicians have, without penalty, violated laws or prevented acts from being made public that involved the theft of great amounts of money or the taking of many lives.

Another of the great problems in dealing with elite deviance is that all laws are not administered equally. The laws that are administered most strictly tend to be those related to the deviance of the powerless nonelites. This process works in very subtle ways but nevertheless ensures a bias in favor of the more affluent.

One way in which this bias operates is illustrated by examining the priority given the investigation and prosecution of corporate crimes within the federal government. Despite some of the advances noted in recent years, corporate crime remains a low priority.[99] As of 1992, the federal government still possessed no centralized statistical capability to index the extent of elite and other white-collar crimes. Yet for years the FBI, through its Uniform

Crime Reports, has monitored street crimes involving both violence and crimes against property (e.g., burglary).

Clearly, white-collar crime does not draw the attention of government and law enforcement officials. And for this reason it does not draw the resources. In fact, the Reagan administration cut back funding designated for white-collar prosecutions by the Justice Department. By 1990, the FBI had only 650 agents to investigate 7,000 fraud claims in connection with the massive S&L scandal. The FBI has estimated that it needed a minimum of 1,000 agents to do an adequate job.[100]

The Criminal Justice section of the American Bar Association issued this conclusion: "For the most part within the Federal agencies with direct responsibility in the economic crime offenses area, available resources are unequal to the task of combating economic crime. ... In cases where seemingly adequate resources exist, these resources are poorly deployed, underutilized, or frustrated by jurisdictional considerations."[101]

Thus, the bias of the federal law enforcement effort, as well as state and local efforts (see Chapter 2), remains slanted toward the crimes of nonelites.

## The Classification of Elite Deviance

The bias of the law enforcement effort in areas other than elite deviance has had dramatic consequences for the scholarly study of such acts. Federal granting agencies and elite foundations have historically provided little funding for the study of elites. The first empirical study of elite deviance was not published until 1940 (Sutherland's *White Collar Crime*), and there has been what Clinard and Yeager describe as "little follow-up research, with only minimal study being carried out on illegal corporate behavior."[102]

With such minimal study devoted to the subject, such terms as *white-collar crime* have become ambiguous. A former head of the FBI defined white-collar crime as "crimes that are committed by nonphysical means to avoid payment or loss of money or to obtain business or personal advantage where success depends upon guile or concealment."[103] Moreover, he applied the term to crimes committed by persons from every level of society, including both elites and nonelites.

The Justice Department's current definition of white-collar crime is so ambiguous that it is difficult for criminological researchers to determine the targets of FBI investigations in this area. This definition of white-collar criminality includes just about everything that is both illegal and nonviolent, involving "traditional notions of deceit, deception, concealment, manipulation, breach of trust, subterfuge, or illegal circumvention."[104]

> This definition is so nonspecific that it could include everything from welfare cheating by the poor to antitrust violations by upper class business. ... What is clear is that the Justice Department has drastically altered and expanded the usual definition of white-collar crime as it has previously been understood by both academic social science and law enforcement.[105]

The view of elite deviance discussed here differs considerably from these definitions. First, our concern is only with persons of the highest socioeconomic status. That is, we have defined the elites of U.S. society as comprising corporate and government officials. We have done this because of the enormous wealth and power that reside in the nation's political economy and the relationship between the economic and political institutions. We have, therefore, not included in our discussion labor unions or organized criminal syndicates, except insofar as there are deviant relationships between these organizations and corporate and governmental entities (e.g., the CIA hired Mafia members to assassinate Castro).

Second, unethical and immoral acts are an important category of elite deviance, a view that is not shared by all students of the subject. One criminologist described a similar classification as "definitional quicksand."[106] In a way, this is true. What is criminal is often easily understood by studying only those acts that are codified in criminal statutes. This would make our task relatively easy. But such an approach overlooks many complexities. For example, in most instances, "only a short step separates unethical tactics from violations of law. Many practices that were formerly considered unethical have now been made illegal and [are] punished by government."[107] Such acts include air and water pollution, bribes made overseas by multinational corporations, the disregard of safety and health standards, and false advertising. Thus, what is considered unethical at one time often becomes illegal later.

Let us concede that the definition of what is unethical is, like deviance itself, often in the eye of the beholder and thus subject to intense debate. Nevertheless, as one observer states: "It is all too human to bracket law breaking with immorality, to assume that a person who offends against the law is ipso facto less moral than one whose activities remain within the legally permitted. Yet a few moments' honest reflection will convince us that the mere fact of transgressing the legal code or not tells us very little about our spiritual condition."[108]

The position taken herein is that it is unavoidable and indeed desirable that students of deviance concern themselves with our spiritual condition. As Galliher and McCartney, two criminologists, have pointed out:

> [If] sociology makes no moral judgment independent of criminal statutes, it becomes sterile and inhuman, the work of moral eunuchs or legal technicians. ... If moral judgments above and beyond criminal law were not made, the laws of Nazi Germany would be indistinguishable from the laws of many other nations. Yet the Nuremberg trials after World War II advanced the position that numerous officials of the Nazi government, although admittedly acting in accordance with German laws, were behaving in such a grossly immoral fashion as to be criminally responsible. ... In the Nuremberg trials, representatives of the Allied governments, France, England, the Soviet Union, and the United States, explicitly and publicly supported the idea of a moral order and moral judgments independent of written law. ...

However, defining elite deviance need not be so controversial or so subjective. There is an objective definition of such deviance that can be scientific, if by scientific one means concepts that can be measured. One such concept is harm. In this book, elite deviance refers to acts by elites and or the organizations that they head that result in any of the following types of harms[109]:

1. *Physical harms* include death and/or physical injury or illness.
2. *Financial harms* include robbery, fraud, and various scams not legally defined as fraud but which, nevertheless, result in consumers and investors being deprived of their funds without receiving goods or services for which they contracted.
3. *Moral harms* are the deviant behavior of elites (people who head governmental or corporate institutions) that forms a negative role model that encourages deviance, distrust, cynicism, and/or alienation among nonelites (members of the middle and lower classes).

For example, President Nixon resigned from office in 1974 because of the Watergate scandal. Following this, confidence in government fell dramatically and has never recovered.

Not all harmful conditions are social problems. Harms become social problems only if they are socially patterned. Socially patterned harms are traits, characteristics, or behaviors exhibited by groups of people or institutions. Thus, the inclusion of unethical acts in the study of elite deviance represents not merely a residual category but also the cutting edge of a neglected and important field of inquiry.

Third, our view of white-collar crime differentiates acts of personal enrichment from acts that are committed on behalf of one's employer.[110] This often becomes a difficult distinction to maintain when studying the deviance of elites because some elites own the organizations in which (and on behalf of which) they commit such acts. This distinction is probably easier to maintain when discussing political corruption than it is when discussing economic deviance. However, many politicians receive illegal payments or campaign contributions for the purpose of winning elections, not necessarily for the purpose of hiding such moneys in secret bank accounts or making other personally enriching expenditures.

Also, some acts of employees committed on behalf of employers are indirectly personally enriching and committed for the purpose of ensuring job security or obtaining a promotion within the organization. This is not to say that employees never embezzle funds for personal use or that politicians do not take graft for the purpose of adding to their personal bank accounts. The point is simply that the distinction between acts that are personally enriching and acts committed on behalf of maintaining and/or increasing the profitability or power of an organization in which one is an owner or employer is difficult to maintain.

Therefore, our view of elite deviance includes three types of acts: (1) economic domination, (2) government and governmental control, and (3) denial of basic human rights.[111]

## Acts of Economic Domination

Acts of economic domination include crimes and unethical deeds that are usually committed by single corporations or by corporations in league with other organizations (e.g., the CIA). Typically, such crimes include violations of antitrust laws, which prohibit the formation of monopolies, price-fixing, and false advertising. These crimes also involve defrauding consumers, polluting the environment, and bribing politicians, both at home and overseas. Acts of economic domination also include crimes committed by business such as not correcting unsafe working conditions and deliberately manufacturing unsafe goods and hazardous medicines and foods. And, in some instances, corporations illegally enter into business ventures with organized criminal syndicates.

However, some acts of economic deviance that are illegal in the United States are legal abroad. For example, an organic mercury fungicide, banned by law for sale in the United States, was used in Iraq to coat by-products of 8,000 tons of wheat and barley. This resulted in 400 deaths and 5,000 hospitalizations among Iraqi customers.[112]

Dumping of unsafe products is a $1.2 billion per year business. It is perceived as being unethical by journalists, government officials, and certain businesspeople. Nonetheless, it is not illegal.

## Crimes of Government and Governmental Control

This category includes tax loopholes and other forms of "corporate welfare," including subsidies and certain special favors granted in doing business with the government and numerous acts involving the usurpation of power. Involved here are the Watergate crimes, crimes of electioneering, and other acts involving violations of civil liberties, and designed to perpetuate a given administration and to enrich its members. Also included are crimes committed by the government against persons and groups that are supposed threats to national security, such as crimes of warfare and political assassination.[113]

Related to offenses viewed as threats to national security are violations of individual civil rights, including illegal surveillance by law enforcement agencies, infiltration of law-abiding political groups by government agents, and denials of due process of law.

Many unethical acts are also committed by governmental organizations and officials. Some examples include classifying certain types of information as secret simply to cover up embarrassing incidents, making campaign promises that candidates know that they cannot or will not keep, defining a situation as a genuine crisis when no real crisis exists, letting out government contracts without competitive bidding, and allowing cost overruns on such contracts.

## Elite Deviance as a Denial of Basic Human Rights

Related to both deviance by corporations and deviance by governments are actions that contribute to various types of social injuries. Included here are threats to the dignity and quality of life for specific groups and humanity as a whole. Such practices as racism and sexism, especially sexual harassment, either political or economic, fall into this category. In addition is the threat to the human race posed by nuclear arms. Although such notions of humanity are not always part of a nation's laws, they should enter into any value judgments made concerning the worth and dignity of individuals.

A body of international agreement and law contains basic notions concerning human rights. Most nations of the world, including undemocratic nations, now agree that such rights should include the provision of basic material needs and freedom from torture, arbitrary arrest and detention, assassination, and kidnapping.

Thus, the criminal and unethical acts of corporations and government and the violations of basic human rights that are part of certain bodies of international agreements subscribed to by the United States constitute the subject matter of elite deviance.

## Conditions Leading to Elite Deviance

In the remainder of our inquiry into the various types of elite deviance, several assumptions will be made regarding the causes, costs, and consequences of such actions. First, organizations are often characterized by what has been termed "the shield of elitist invisibility."[114] This refers to their actions as well as the heads of political organizations and governmental agencies frequently being shrouded in secrecy. Corporate management and government officials are often shielded from the press, government investigators, and boards of directors (in the case of corporations) by virtue of the power that they possess over information. For example, the illegal payments made by the Gulf Oil Company during the 1970s were kept secret from the board of directors by Gulf's chief executive officer for more than 18 months after the scandal made headlines.

Such deceptions are possible in huge organizations. Corporations are often international organizations, characterized by "complex and varied sets of structural relationships between the boards of directors, executives, managers, and other employees on the one hand, and between parent corporations, corporate divisions, and subsidiaries on the other."[115] These complex relationships often make it impossible for outsiders and many insiders to determine who is responsible for what. Such structural complexities make it relatively easy to perform numerous acts that corporate managers wish to be kept secret. Next, the benefits involved in such deviance far outweigh the risks of apprehension and penalty. Although estimates of the cost of corporate crime are made infrequently and most date back to the 1970s and early 1980s, two congressional studies have put the figure between $174 and $200 billion annually.[116] This is more than the cost of all other types of crime plus the cost of running the entire criminal justice system combined. No source can give exact estimates concerning the costs of political corruption and various kickbacks, but the *New York Times* estimated that business bribery and kickbacks, at least a portion of which goes to politicians, may run as high as $15 billion per year.[117] Thus, the monetary rewards of corporate and political crime are without parallel.

Coupled with these rewards are minimal risks. From 1890 to 1970, only three businesspeople were sent to jail for violations of the Sherman Antitrust Act (see Chapter 2 for details), and from 1946 to 1953, the average fine levied in such cases was $2,600 (with $5,000 being the maximum possible).[118] Thus, there is very little incentive not to violate some laws. And as criminologist Donald Cressey has stated, "Some businessmen have so little respect for the law that they would prefer an antitrust indictment to being caught wearing argyle socks. ... They do so because they do not believe in these laws. This is another way of saying that they consider such laws ... illegitimate."[119]

The prime goal of business is to make a profit, and, according to the business ideology, government regulation is often viewed as meddling (see Chapter 2). In summary, organizational structure, complexity, and primary goals (autonomy and profit) all help to shield top-level officials from the scrutiny of the press and the law. In addition, the lenient penalties established for much elite deviance are ineffectual deterrents.

## Consequences of Elite Deviance

The consequences of elite deviance to U.S. society are thought to be monumental by most experts. Consider the following:

1. It is estimated that five times as many persons die each year from illnesses and injuries contracted on the job (100,000–200,000 persons) than are murdered by all street criminals.[120] (See Chapters 3 and 4 for details.)

2. We have observed that public confidence in U.S. economic and political elites has drastically declined with revelations of elite deviance. In addition, many criminologists believe that deviance by elites provides either motivation or rationalization for nonelites to commit profit-oriented crimes.[121]

3. The power of elites to help shape criminal law and its enforcement raises serious questions regarding the racial and class biases of the

criminal justice system's traditional equating of the crime problem in the United States with street crime.

4. The monetary costs of elite deviance are thought to contribute substantially to inflation. Estimates range from $17.7 to $231 billion a year in the prices added to goods and services. (See also Chapter 8.)

5. It will be demonstrated that elite deviance has been an important cause of the persistence and growth of organized crime in the United States. This assistance has been provided by both economic and political elites (see Chapter 2).

One sociologist has argued that there exists a symbiotic (mutually interdependent) relationship between deviance by elites and deviance by nonelites because elite deviance greatly affects the distribution of power in society. Much elite deviance is aimed at maintaining or increasing the proportion of wealth and power that rests in elite hands. Given the inequitable distribution of such resources, the most powerless and economically deprived members of society suffer from social conditions "that tend to provoke powerless individuals into criminality."[122] Likewise, it is possible that elites, who view themselves as respectable members of society, view the deviance of the powerless as the genuinely dangerous type of crime faced by society. Such attitudes result in elites viewing themselves as morally superior to nonelites and the crimes that elites commit as not really criminal. Thus, elites may be even more likely to violate legal and ethical standards because of the deviance of nonelites, which is in part caused by the inequitable distribution of resources, the existence of which is in turn related to elite power.

Finally, the consequences listed previously regarding elite deviance constitute a mere beginning. The relationship between the acts of the powerful and those of the powerless, especially deviant acts, has not been well investigated by scholars. Moreover, the behavior of elites, insofar as it effects an alienation and loss of confidence among nonelites, undoubtedly has additional negative consequences about which we have much to learn. What is clear is that elite deviance possesses numerous important social, economic, and political consequences for all society. Only a few of the most dramatic of these consequences will be examined in this volume.

## Conclusion

This chapter has introduced the topic of elite deviance. Because of the Vietnam conflict, Watergate, the Iran-Contra scandal, the S&L bailout, and numerous recent incidents involving corporate and governmental wrongdoings, elite deviance has become a major public concern. Closer examination reveals that the deviant acts of economic and political elites are not random events. They are related to the structure of wealth and power in the United States and to the processes that maintain such structures.

Moreover, aside from being illegal or unethical (at least according to the norms maintained by persons outside the organization committing the deviant act), elite deviance has several basic characteristics:

1. It occurs because it furthers the goals of economic and political organizations, that is, the maintenance or increase of profit and/or power.
2. It is committed with the support of the elites who head such organizations. Such support may be open and active or covert and implied.
3. It may be committed by elites and/or employees acting on their behalf.[123]

Such deviance is important because it holds many negative consequences for society, including high prices, dangerous products, and the increased motivation to commit deviance on the part of nonelites.

Despite all the public attention recently devoted to elite deviance, it remains a poorly understood and hence unresolved social problem in U.S. society. As corporations and government now touch nearly every aspect of our daily lives, it behooves us all to learn as much as possible about the dimensions of and possible solutions to this type of deviant behavior.

## CRITICAL THINKING EXERCISE 1.1
### Researching the Power Elite

Obtain a list of the members of the Clinton cabinet from *The World Almanac* or *The World Almanac of U.S. Politics*. Then look up and tabulate the backgrounds of the cabinet members in *Who's Who?* or other references using the criteria for upper-class membership given in this chapter. These criteria include

1. Having one's name in the *Social Register*
2. Attendance at private elite preparatory schools and universities (the elite universities are listed in Figure 1.1)
3. Membership in exclusive social clubs and annual attendance at upper-class vacation retreats (e.g., Bohemian Grove)
4. Membership on board of directors of the nation's largest corporations
5. Upper-class income—typically in the millions of dollars per year—and upper-class wealth—typically in the tens of millions of dollars

Show your results in a table that distinguishes between upper-class and non-upper-class cabinet members. You may also wish to examine some of the backgrounds of undersecretaries in various cabinet posts.

## ENDNOTES

1. Talbott, J. R. (2008).*Obamanomics* (p. 70). New York: Seven Stories.
2. Morrissey, J. (March 17, 2008). Credit default swaps: The next crisis. *Time.Com*, 1.
3. Apuzzo, M. (December 23, 2008). Bankers are bailing out on questions. *Associated Press.Com*, A-1.

4. Gumbel, P. (October 20, 2008). The meltdown goes global. *Time*, 32–36.

5. Ibid.

6. http://sanders.senate.gov/newsroom/news/?id=875c3ef4-5598-4bb3-9515-5692d0cc2a24 (10/22/2010)

7. http://topics.nytimes.com/top/news/business/companies/goldman_sachs_group_inc/index.html

8. http://news.yahoo.com/s/afp/20100417/bs_afp/usbankingpropertygoldmancompany-fraud

9. http://www.docstoc.com/docs/documentpreview.aspx?doc_id=36077124

10. *60 Minutes*. (December 2008). The Federal Reserve was recently audited, thanks to a clause in the recently passed Dodd-Frank Bill. It was discovered that Fed has made some $16 trillion in loans to banks and mortgage firms, but has done very little to create jobs for middle class Americans.

11. See Foster, J. B., & Magdoff, F. (2009). *The great financial crisis* (p. 26ff). New York: Monthly Review Press.

12. http://www.minyanville.com/businessmarkets/articles/bailout-eurozone-bankruptcy-portugal-spain-ireland/11/29/2010/id/31390

13. http://www.huffingtonpost.com/phil-trupp/operation-broken-trust-th_b_793292.html

14. See the documentary *Inside job*. Warner Brothers, 2010.

15. http://livinglies.wordpress.com/2008/12/09/mers-scandal-exposed-and-explained/

16. http://www.thebremnergroup.com/news/mers-scandal-or-smokescreen/(10/15/2010)

17. http://www.knowyourmortgagebanker.com/blog/mers-scandal-part1(10/18/2010)

18. http://www.commondreams.org/news2003/0930-12.htm

19. http://www.nytimes.com/2007/03/07/opinion/07weds1.html

20. http://www.capitolhillblue.com/artman/publish/article_7564.shtml

21. http://www.npr.org/templates/story/story.php?storyId=7700555&ft=1&f=7

22. Roebuck, J., & Weeber, S. C. (1978). *Political crime in the United States: Analyzing crime by and against government* (p. 86). New York: Praeger.

23. Clinard, M., & Yeager, R. (August 1978). Corporate crime: Issues in research. *Criminology*, 2, 260.

24. See Conyers, Jr., J. (March 1980). Corporate and white-collar crime: A view by the chairman of the house subcommittee on crime. *American Criminal Law Review*, 17, 290; and Blundell, W. E. (1978). Equity funding: I did it for the jollies. In J. Johnson & J. Douglas (eds.). *Crime at the top: Deviance in business and the professions* (pp. 153–185). Philadelphia: J. B. Lippincott.

25. Ross, I. (1983). How lawless are big companies? In L. A. Wollan (ed.). *Florida 2000: Creative crime control* (pp. 39–46). Tampa: Florida Endowment for the Humanities (originally appeared in *Fortune*, December 1, 1980).

26. Nader, N., & Brownstein, R. (May 1980). Beyond the love canal. *Progressive*, 44, 28, 30.

27. See, for example, Lyman, M. D., & Potter, G. W. (2004). *Organized crime* (3rd ed., pp. 444–446). Upper Saddle River, NJ: Prentice-Hall.

28. Hilts, R. (December 13, 1993). 50,000 deaths a year blamed on soot in air. *San Francisco Chronicle*, A-8.

29. "The Dirty Seas," *Time*, August 1, 1988: 48.

30. http://thinkprogress.org/2006/06/20/global-warming-emissions-double/; Gore, A. (2006). *An inconvenient truth* (pp. 76–77). New York: Melcher Media.

31. Geis, G. (1974). Upper world crime. In A. Blumberg (ed.). *Current perspectives on criminal behavior: Original essays in criminology* (pp. 114–137). New York: Knopf.

32. See Kramer, R. (1984). Corporate criminality: The development of an idea. In E. Hochstedler (ed.). *Corporations as criminals* (pp. 1–38). Beverly Hills: Sage; and Little, C. (1983). *Understanding deviance and control* (p. 214). Itasca, IL: Peacock.

33. See Thio, A. (1978). *Deviant behavior* (p. 353). Boston: Houghton Mifflin.

34. See Mintz, M., & Cohen, J. (1976). *Power, Inc.* New York: Viking, xix.

35. See especially the following by Wright Mills, C. (1959). *The sociological imagination*. New York: Oxford University Press; *The power elite*. New York: Oxford University Press, 1956; and *Character and social structure*. New York: Harcourt, Brace, and World, 1953 (with

Hans Gerth). Other useful works include Simecca, J. (1978). *The sociological theory of C. Wright Mills.* Port Washington, NY: Kennikat; *Society and freedom: An introduction to humanist sociology.* New York: St. Martin's Press, 1981; and J. Eldridge, C. *Wright Mills.* New York: Tavistock, 1983.

36. See Parenti, M. (1991). *Make believe media: The politics of entertainment.* New York: St. Martin's Press; and Barnouw, E. (1978). *The sponsor.* New York: Oxford University Press.

37. Dye, T., & Zeigler, H. (2002). *The irony of democracy* (10th ed., p. 4). Belmont, CA: Wadsworth. For an excellent summary of the evidence supporting the existence of an elite, see Kerbo, H., & Della Fave, R. (Winter 1979). The empirical side of the power elite debate. *Sociological Quarterly, 20,* 5–22.

38. Ibid., 14, 19, 235; http://en.wikipedia.org/wiki/United_States

39. See Dowd, D. (1993). *U.S. capitalist development since 1776: Of, by, and for which people?* (pp. 113–115). New York: M. E. Sharpe.

40. Dye, T. (1983). *Who's running America?* (3rd ed., p. 38). Englewood Cliffs, NJ: Prentice Hall.

41. Dye, T. (1986). *Who's running America?* (4th ed., pp. 16–19). Englewood Cliffs, NJ: Prentice Hall.

42. Media Reform Information Center. (January 31, 2007). http://www.corporations.org/media/

43. Ibid.

44. The political economy of the mass media: Edward S. Herman interviewed by Robert W. McChesney (August 2007). *Monthly Review,* January 1989; http://www.chomsky.info/onchomsky/198901.htm

45. See, for example, Kappeler, V., & Potter, G. (2005). *The mythology of crime and criminal justice* (4th ed., pp. 5–18). Long Grove, IL: Waveland Press; Germond, J. (2004). *Fatman fedup* (pp. 43–50). New York: Random House.

46. These figures are taken from Evans, P., & Schneider, S. (1980). The political economy of the corporation. In S. McNall (ed.). *Critical issues in sociology* (p. 221). Chicago: Scott, Foresman.

47. Ibid. (p. 222).

48. Dye (4th ed., p. 176).

49. Garson, G. D. (1973). *Power and politics in the United States* (pp. 181, 182, 185). Lexington, MA: D. C. Heath.

50. Domhoff, G. W. (1983). *Who rules America now?* (p. 77). Englewood Cliffs, NJ: Prentice Hall. Such power also stems from the fact that the U.S. upper class contributes heavily to political parties, campaigns, and PACs (see discussion that follows). Moreover, its media ownership aids it in gaining an "impact on the consciousness of all (social) classes in the nation." From Gilbert, D., & Kahl, J. (1982). *The American class structure* (pp. 348–349). Homewood, IL: Dorsey Press.

51. See Domhoff, G. W. (1967). *Who rules America?* (pp. 87–96). Englewood Cliffs, NJ: Prentice Hall; *The power elite and the state: How policy is made in America.* Hawthorne, NY: Aldine de Gruyter, 1990; and The American power structure. In M. Olsen & M. Marger (eds.). *Power in modern societies* (pp. 170–195). Boulder: Westview, 1993, for evidence concerning the national upper class and their policy-making role.

52. Dye, T. R., & Pickering, J. W. (November 1974). Governmental and corporate elites: Convergence and differentiation. *Journal of Politics, 36,* 905.

53. Freitag, P. (December 1975). The cabinets and big business: A study of interlocks. *Social Problems, 23,* 137–152.

54. Kerbo, H. In Olsen & Marger (eds.). *Upper class power* (pp. 223–237).

55. Johnson, J. (July 7, 2003). 40 millionaires in US senate. http://www.wsws.org/articles/2003/jul2003/sen-j07_prn.shtml

56. This point and the discussion that follows are based on Garner, R. A. (1977). *Social change* (pp. 252–254). Chicago: Rand McNally. For a right-wing conspiratorial view, see Allen, G. (1971). *None dare call it conspiracy.* Rossmor, CA: Concord Press; and Robertson, P. (1991). *The new world order.* Dallas: Word.

57. Garner (p. 253).

58. For a summary of such differences, see Dye (2nd ed., pp. 190–195).

59. See Chambliss, W. (ed.). (1975). *Criminal law in action* (p. 230). Santa Barbara, CA: Hamilton.

60. Garner (p. 253).

61. Parenti, M. *Power and the powerless.* (p. 22). New York: St. Martin's Press.

62. Dye (4th ed., p. 153).

63. Dye (2nd ed., p. 126).

64. Ibid. (p. 29).

65. See White, T. H. (1973). *The making of the president 1972.* New York: Atheneum. Chapter 8; Domhoff, G. W. *Who rules America?* (pp. 79–83).

66. Parenti, M. *Democracy for the few* (p. 168). See also Parenti, M. (1993). *Inventing reality: The politics of the news media* (2nd ed., p. 29). New York: St. Martin's Press.

67. Gans, H. J. (1979). *Deciding what's news* (p. 12). New York: Pantheon.

68. Ibid. (p. 14).

69. Tabor, G. M. (April 21, 1980). Capitalism: Is it working? *Time*, 55.

70. Dye (2nd ed., pp. 115–116).

71. Klare, M. T. (1972). *War without end* (p. 77). New York: Knopf.

72. Domhoff, G. W. (1978). *The powers that be: Processes of ruling class domination in America* (p. 118). New York: Vintage.

73. Greider, W. (1992). *Who will tell the people?: The betrayal of American democracy* (p. 51ff). New York: Simon & Schuster. This is one of the best books on the ills of the American political system.

74. Parenti, M. *Democracy for the few* (p. 226).

75. Green, M., & Newfield, J. (April 21, 1980). Who owns congress?" *Village Voice*, 16.

76. Waldman, M. (1990). *Who robbed America? A citizen's guide to the savings and loan scandal* (p. 65). New York: Random House.

77. See Weaver, Jr., W. (March 13, 1977). What is a campaign contributor buying?" *New York Times*, E-2.

78. Etzioni, A. (1984). *Capital corruption* (p. 3). New York: Harcourt, Brace, and Jovanovich.

79. Cooper, W. C. (May 7, 1983). Take back your dirty PAC money. *Nation*, 565; Green, *Who runs congress?* 30–31.

80. Wagman, R. (ed.). (1993). *The world almanac of U.S. politics* (p. 19). Mahwah, NJ: Funk & Wagnalls.

81. Drake, D., & Uhlman, M. (1993). *Making drugs, making money* (p. 41). Kansas City, MO: Andrews & McMeel.

82. Mathias, C. (July 1986). Should there be financing of congressional campaigns? *Annals of the American Academy of Political and Social Science, 486*, 65.

83. Ibid. (p. 66). See also Bolling, R. (July 1986). Money in politics. *Annals of the American Academy of Political and Social Science, 486*, 76–80, for additional comments by a leading federal politician.

84. See Greider (p. 51).

85. Perot, R. (1992). *Not for sale at any price* (p. 140) New York: Hyperion.

86. Greider (p. 52 ff).

87. Van Natta, Jr., D., & Broder, J. M. (August 1, 2000). The few, the rich, and the rewarded donate the bulk of G.O.P. gifts. *New York Times*, A-1.

88. Sherrill, R. (August 27, September 3, 1988). Deep pockets. *Nation, 247*, 170.

89. Galtney, L. (November 7, 1988). A case of legal corruption. *U.S. News & World Report, 20*, 21–23.

90. R. Wagman, 17. See also Garvey, E. (September 1993). Campaign reform? Get real. *Progressive*, 18–20. Garvey notes that the average cost of a Senate seat in 1992 was $3.5 million, and the average House seat cost $555,000.

91. Burnham, W. D. (1975). Party system and the political process. In W. N. Chambers & W. D. Burnham (eds.). *The American party system* (2nd ed., p. 277). New York: Oxford University Press.

92. Domhoff, *The powers that be* (p. 148).

93. This perspective is discussed in O'Conner, J. (1973). *The fiscal crisis of the state.* New York: St. Martin's Press; Barnet, H. (January 27, 1981). Corporate capitalism, corporate crime. *Crime and Delinquency,* 4–23; and Cullen, F. T., et al. (1987). *Corporate crime under attack: The Ford Pinto case and beyond.* Cincinnati: Anderson, Chapter 2.

94. Barnet (pp. 4–6).

95. Two of the most interesting works on this topic are Derber, C. (2004). *The wilding of America* (3rd ed.). New York: Worth; and Messner, S., & Rosenfeld, R. (2001). *Crime and the American dream* (3rd ed.). Belmont, CA: Wadsworth.

96. Mills, J. (1986). *The underground empire.* New York: Dell.

97. Paulson, M. (October 5, 1974). What is business afraid of? *National Observer,* 14.

98. See Hills, S. (ed.). (1988). *Corporate violence: injury and death for profit.* Totowa, NJ: Roman & Littlefield; and Simon, D. R. (March 1988). Book review essay: White-collar crime and its future. *Justice Quarterly, 5,* 157, 159.

99. See Conyers (pp. 291, 299), and Chapter 2 of this volume.

100. Hedges, S., & Witkins, G. (July 23, 1990). The bulletproof villains. *U.S. News & World Report,* 18.

101. ABA Section on Criminal Justice, Committee on Economic Offenses, March 1977, 6–7, cited in Conyers (p. 290).

102. Clinard & Yeager (p. 256).

103. Webster, W. In Conyers (ed.). *Examination of FBI theory and methodology* (p. 276).

104. Attorney General of the United States, *National priorities for the investigation and prosecution of white-collar crime.* Washington, DC: Government Printing Office, 1980, ii.

105. William Domhoff D.G. (1978). The Powers That Be: Processes of Ruling Class Domination in America. New York: Vintage, (p. 148).

106. See Geis (p. 117).

107. Clinard & Yeager (pp. 107, 204).

108. Mays, J. B. (1967). *Crime and the social structure* (p. 39). London: Faber & Faber.

109. The following discussion is based on Schrager, L., & Short, J. F. (February 1978). Toward a sociology of organizational crime. *Social Problems, 25,* 407–419; and Simon, D. R. (1995). *Social problems and the sociological imagination* (pp. 13–18). New York: McGraw-Hill.

110. See Edelhertz, H., et al. (1977). *The investigation of white-collar crime* (p. 7). Washington, DC: Government Printing Office.

111. For an extended discussion of this typology, see Quinney, R. (1977). *Class, state and crime* (pp. 50–52). New York: McKay/Longman.

112. See Dowie, M. (November 1979). The corporate crime of the century. *Mother Jones, 9,* 24.

113. Quinney (p. 51).

114. Scott, W. C., & Hart, D. K. (1979). *Organizational America* (p. 40). Boston: Houghton Mifflin.

115. Clinard & Yeager (p. 265).

116. Demaris, O. (1974). *Dirty business* (p. 12). New York: Harper's Magazine Press. See also Coleman, J. W. (1992). *The criminal elite* (3rd ed., 6–8). New York: St. Martin's Press.

117. See "Companies' Payoffs in U.S. come under new scrutiny." *New York Times,* March 16, 1976, A-1.

118. See Nader, R., & Green, M. (April, 29, 1972). Crime in the suites. *New Republic,* 19. The maximum fine was raised to $55,000 in 1955; however, this is still a pittance compared with the multimillion-dollar profits of most large corporations.

119. Cressey, D. (November/December 1978). White collar subversives. *Center Magazine, 6,* 44.

120. See "Job Hazards." *Dollars and Sense, 56,* April 1980, 9.

121. Thio (pp. 85, 89).

122. Conyers (p. 293).

123. For further discussion of these issues, see Ermann, M. D., & Lundman, R. J. (eds.). (1993). *Organizational deviance* (4th ed., pp. 7–9). New York: Oxford University Press.

# CHAPTER

## 2

# Elite Deviance and the Higher Immorality

## The Nature of the Higher Immorality

Sociologist C. Wright Mills once remarked that "as news of higher immoralities breaks [people] often say, 'Well another one got caught today,' thereby implying that the cases disclosed are symptoms of a much more widespread condition."[1] Mills used the term *higher immorality* to describe a *moral insensitivity*[2] among the most wealthy and powerful members of the U.S. corporate, political, and military elite (which he termed the *power elite*). For Mills, the higher immorality translated into a variety of unethical, corrupt, and sometimes illegal practices, which were viewed as a systematic, institutionalized feature of contemporary U.S. society.

In business and in government, Mills felt, many transactions are accomplished by interpersonal manipulation. One type of such manipulation by the successful is using a *false front:* pretending to be interested in what others have to say, attempting to make others feel important, and radiating charm and self-confidence (despite one's own insecurities). Obviously, if social relations are based on insincere feelings, these activities would be characterized by a good deal of alienation on the part of the participants.

In addition, Mills believed that some business and political arrangements include the favors of prostitutes. The sexual favors of these high-priced call girls are often paid for with executive expense account allotments[3] (which will be discussed later). Aside from interpersonal manipulation and the peddling of high-priced vice, the higher immorality also includes the following:

1. Unethical practices relating to executive salaries and expense accounts
2. Unfair executive and corporate tax advantages
3. The deliberate creation of political and/or economic crises by the power elite
4. The manipulation of public opinion
5. The violation of antitrust and other laws relating to political corruption

Since Mills described these various types of deviance in the 1950s, the nation has witnessed scandal after scandal involving these forms of the higher immorality. Thus, an up-to-date analysis of the nature and significance of the higher immorality is in order.

This chapter is concerned with executive salaries and expense accounts, laws relating to the incomes of corporate executives and corporations, the creation of phony crises by the power elite, and violations of antitrust laws. We also consider one form of the higher immorality only hinted at in Mills's provocative analysis: the relationships between the wealthy and powerful and members of organized crime. We begin with a microcosm of the higher immorality, the massive inequality of wealth, income and power.

## Case Study: Inequality of Wealth, Income, and Power in America[4]

"Some of the information may come as a surprise to many people. In fact, I *know* it will be a surprise and then some, because of a study published in 2010 showing that most Americans have *no* idea just how concentrated the wealth distribution actually is. Then there's the added shock that they think the "ideal" wealth distribution is far more equal than what they wrongly assumed to be the current wealth distribution.

First, though, some definitions. Generally speaking, *wealth* is the value of everything a person or family owns, minus any debts. However, for purposes of studying the wealth distribution, economists define wealth in terms of *marketable assets*, such as real estate, stocks, and bonds, leaving aside consumer durables like cars and household items because they are not as readily converted into cash and are more valuable to their owners for use purposes than they are for resale. Once the value of all marketable assets is determined, then all debts, such as home mortgages and credit card debts, are subtracted, which yields a person's *net worth*. In addition, economists use the concept of *financial wealth*—also referred to in this document as "nonhome wealth"—which is defined as net worth minus net equity in owner-occupied housing. It thus reflects the resources that may be immediately available for consumption or various forms of investments.

"We also need to distinguish wealth from *income*.[5] Income is what people earn from work, but also from dividends, interest, and any rents or royalties that are paid to them on properties they own. In theory, those who own a great deal of wealth may or may not have high incomes, depending on the returns they receive from their wealth, but in reality those at the very top of the wealth distribution usually have the most income. (But it's important to note that for the rich, most of that income does not come from "working": in 2008, only 19% of the income reported by the 13,480 individuals or families making over $10 million came from wages and salaries.)"

"As you read through these numbers, please keep in mind that they are usually 2 or 3 years out of date because it takes time for one set of experts to collect the basic information and make sure it is accurate, and then still more time for another set of experts to analyze it and write their reports.

It's also the case that the infamous housing bubble of the first 8 years of the 21st century inflated some of the wealth numbers.[6]

So far there are only tentative projections—based on the price of housing and stock in July 2009—on the effects of the Great Recession on the wealth distribution. They suggest that average Americans have been hit much harder than wealthy Americans. Edward Wolff, the economist we draw upon the most in this document, concludes that there has been an "astounding" 36.1% drop in the wealth (marketable assets) of the median household since the peak of the housing bubble in 2007. By contrast, the wealth of the top 1% of households dropped by far less: just 11.1%. So as of April 2010, it looks like the wealth distribution is even more unequal than it was in 2007."

"One final general point before turning to the specifics: people who have looked at this document in the past often asked whether progressive taxation reduces some of the income inequality that exists before taxes are paid. The answer: not by much, if we count *all* of the taxes that people pay, from sales taxes to property taxes to payroll taxes (in other words, not just income taxes). And the top 1% of income earners, who average over $1 million a year, actually pay a *smaller* percentage of their incomes to taxes than the 9% just below them."[6]

## The Wealth Distribution

"In the United States, wealth is highly concentrated in a relatively few hands. As of 2007, the top 1% of households (the upper class) owned 34.6% of all privately held wealth, and the next 19% (the managerial, professional, and small business stratum) had 50.5%, which means that just 20% of the people owned a remarkable 85%, leaving only 15% of the wealth for the bottom 80% (wage and salary workers). In terms of financial wealth (total net worth minus the value of one's home), the top 1% of households had an even greater share: 42.7%. Total assets are defined as the sum of (1) the gross value of owner-occupied housing; (2) other real estate owned by the household; (3) cash and demand deposits; (4) time and savings deposits, certificates of deposit, and money market accounts; (5) government bonds, corporate bonds, foreign bonds, and other financial securities; (6) the cash surrender value of life insurance plans; (7) the cash surrender value of pension plans, including IRAs, Keogh, and 401(k) plans; (8) corporate stock and mutual funds; (9) net equity in unincorporated businesses; and (10) equity in trust funds. Total liabilities are the sum of (1) mortgage debt; (2) consumer debt, including auto loans; and (3) other debt."

"In terms of types of financial wealth, the top 1% of households has 38.3% of all privately held stock, 60.6% of financial securities, and 62.4% of business equity. The top 10% have 80% to 90% of stocks, bonds, trust funds, and business equity, and over 75% of nonhome real estate. As financial wealth is what counts as far as the control of income-producing assets, we can say that just 10% of the people own the United States of America."[7]

"In 2007, the average White household had 15 times as much total wealth as the average African American or Latino household. If we exclude home equity from the calculations and consider only financial wealth, the ratios are in the neighborhood of 100:1. Extrapolating from these figures, we see that 70% of White families' wealth is in the form of their principal residence; for blacks and Hispanics, the figures are 95% and 96%, respectively."

"And for all Americans, things are getting worse: as the projections to July 2009 make clear, the last few years have seen a huge loss in housing wealth for most families, making the gap between the rich and the rest of America even greater, and increasing the number of households with *no* marketable assets from 18.6% to 24.1%.

Here are some dramatic facts that sum up how the wealth distribution became even more concentrated between 1983 and 2004, in good part due to the tax cuts for the wealthy and the defeat of labor unions: Of all the new financial wealth created by the American economy in that 21-year period, fully 42% of it went to the top 1%. A whopping 94% went to the top 20%, which of course means that the bottom 80% received only 6% of all the new financial wealth generated in the United States during the 1980s, 1990s, and early 2000s."

## The Relationship Between Wealth and Power

"Power ... is the ability (or call it capacity) to realize wishes, or reach goals, which amounts to the same thing, even in the face of opposition. Leaving those discussions for the philosophers, at least for now, how do the concepts of wealth and power relate?"

"First, wealth can be seen as a "resource" that is very useful in exercising power. That's obvious when we think of donations to political parties, payments to lobbyists, and grants to experts who are employed to think of new policies beneficial to the wealthy. Wealth also can be useful in shaping the general social environment to the benefit of the wealthy, whether through hiring public relations firms or donating money for universities, museums, music halls, and art galleries."

"Second, certain kinds of wealth, such as stock ownership, can be used to control corporations, which of course have a major impact on how the society functions.

Third, just as wealth can lead to power, so too can power lead to wealth. Those who control a government can use their position to feather their own nests, whether that means a favorable land deal for relatives at the local level or a huge federal government contract for a new corporation run by friends who will, in turn, hire this government leader after leaving office. If we take a larger historical sweep and look cross-nationally, we are well aware that the leaders of conquering armies often grab enormous wealth, and that some religious leaders use their positions to acquire wealth."

"There's a fourth way that wealth and power relate. For research purposes, the wealth distribution can be seen as the main "value distribution" within the general power indicator I call "who benefits." What follows in the next three paragraphs is a little long-winded, I realize, but it needs to be said because some social scientists—primarily pluralists—argue that who wins and who loses in a variety of policy conflicts is the only valid power indicator, whereas philosophical discussions don't even mention wealth or other power indicators."

"Here's the argument: if we assume that most people would like to have as great a share as possible of the things that are valued in the society, then we can infer that those who have the most goodies are the most powerful. Although some value distributions may be unintended outcomes that do not really reflect power, as pluralists are quick to tell us, the general distribution of valued experiences and objects within a society still can be viewed as the most publicly visible and stable outcome of the operation of power."

"In American society, for example, wealth and well-being are highly valued. People seek to own property, to have high incomes, to have interesting and safe jobs, to enjoy the finest in travel and leisure, and to live long and healthy lives. All of these "values" are unequally distributed, and all may be utilized as power indicators. However, the primary focus with this type of power indicator is on the wealth distribution sketched out in the previous section."

"The argument for using the wealth distribution as a power indicator is strengthened by studies showing that such distributions vary historically and from country to country, depending upon the relative strength of rival political parties and trade unions, with the United States having the most highly concentrated wealth distribution of any Western democracy except Switzerland. For example, in a study based on 18 Western democracies, strong trade unions and successful social democratic parties correlated with greater equality in the income distribution and a higher level of welfare spending."

"If the top 1% of households have 30%–35% of the wealth, that is, 30 to 35 times what we would expect by chance, we infer they must be powerful. And then we set out to see if the same set of households scores high on other power indicators (it does). Furthermore, if the top 20% have 84% of the wealth (and recall that 10% have 85% to 90% of the stocks, bonds, trust funds, and business equity), that means that the United States is a power pyramid. It is tough for the bottom 80%—maybe even the bottom 90%—to get organized and exercise much power."

## Income and Power

"The income distribution also can be used as a power indicator. It is not as concentrated as the wealth distribution, but the top 1% of income earners did receive 17% of all income in the year 2003, 21.3% in 2006, and 23% in 2009.

That's up from 12.8% for the top 1% in 1982, which is quite a jump, and it parallels what is happening with the wealth distribution.[8] This is further support for the inference that the power of the corporate community and the upper class have been increasing in recent decades."

"The rising concentration of income can be seen in a special *New York Times* analysis of an Internal Revenue Service report on income in 2004. Although overall income had grown by 27% since 1979, 33% of the gains went to the top 1%. Meanwhile, the bottom 60% were making less: about 95 cents for each dollar they made in 1979. The next 20%—those between the 60th and 80th rungs of the income ladder—made $1.02 for each dollar they earned in 1979. Furthermore, the *Times* author concludes that only the top 5% made significant gains ($1.53 for each 1979 dollar). Most amazing of all, the top 0.1%—that's one-tenth of 1%—had more combined pretax income than the poorest 120 million people.[9]"

"But the increase in what is going to the few at the top did not level off, even with all that. As of 2007, income inequality in the United States was at an all-time high for the past 95 years, with the top 0.01%—that's one-hundredth of 1%—receiving 6% of all U.S. wages, which is double of what it was for that tiny slice in 2000; the top 10% received 49.7%, the highest since 1917. However, in an analysis of 2008 tax returns for the top 0.2%—that is, those whose income tax returns reported $1 million or more in income (mostly from individuals, but nearly a third from couples)—it was found that they received 13% of all income, down slightly from 16.1% in 2007 due to the decline in payoffs from financial assets."

"And the rate of increase is even higher for the very richest of the rich: the top 400 income earners in the United States. According to an analysis by David Cay Johnston—recently retired from reporting on tax issues at the *New York Times*—the average income of the top 400 tripled during the Clinton Administration and doubled during the first 7 years of the Bush Administration. So by 2007, the top 400 averaged $344.8 million per person, up 31% from an average of $263.3 million just 1 year earlier."

"How are these huge gains possible for the top 400? It is due to cuts in the tax rates on capital gains and dividends, which were down to a mere 15% in 2007, thanks to the tax cuts proposed by the Bush Administration and passed by Congress in 2003. As almost 75% of the income for the top 400 comes from capital gains and dividends, it is not hard to see why tax cuts on income sources available to only a tiny percent of Americans mattered greatly for the high-earning few. Overall, the *effective* tax rate on high incomes fell by 7% during the Clinton presidency and 6% in the Bush era, so the top 400 had a tax rate of 20% or less in 2007, far lower than the marginal tax rate of 35% that the highest income earners (over $372,650) supposedly pay. It's also worth noting that only the first $105,000 of a person's income is taxed for Social Security purposes, so it would clearly be a boon to the Social Security Fund if everyone—not just those making less than $105,000—paid the Social Security tax on their full incomes."

"A key factor behind the high concentration of income, and another likely reason that the concentration has been increasing, can be seen by examining the distribution of all "capital income": income from capital gains, dividends, interest, and rents. In 2003, just 1% of all households—those with after-tax incomes averaging $701,500—received 57.5% of all capital income, up from 40% in the early 1990s. On the contrary, the bottom 80% received only 12.6% of capital income, down by nearly half since 1983, when the bottom 80% received 23.5%."

"Another way that income can be used as a power indicator is by comparing average CEO annual pay to average factory worker pay, something that has been done for many years by *Business Week* and, later, the Associated Press. The ratio of CEO pay to factory worker pay rose from 42:1 in 1960 to as high as 531:1 in 2000, at the height of the stock market bubble, when CEOs were cashing in big stock options. It was at 411:1 in 2005 and 344:1 in 2007, according to research by United for a Fair Economy. By way of comparison, the same ratio is about 25:1 in Europe."[10]

"It is even more revealing to compare the actual rates of increase of the salaries of CEOs and ordinary workers; from 1990 to 2005, CEOs' pay increased almost 300% (adjusted for inflation), whereas production workers gained a scant 4.3%. The purchasing power of the federal minimum wage actually *declined* by 9.3%, when inflation is taken into account."

"Although some of the information I have relied upon to create this section on executives' versus workers' pay is a few years old now, the AFL/CIO provides up-to-date information on CEO salaries at their Web site. There, one can learn that the median compensation for CEOs in *all* industries as of early 2010 is $3.9 million; it is $10.6 million for the companies listed in Standard and Poor's 500, and $19.8 million for the companies listed in the Dow-Jones Industrial Average. As the median worker's pay is about $36,000, then you can quickly calculate that CEOs in general make 100 times as much as the workers, that CEOs of S&P 500 firms make almost 300 times as much, and that CEOs at the Dow-Jones companies make 550 times as much."

"But how such a large gap could develop? The proximate, or most immediate, factor involves the way in which CEOs are now able to rig things so that the board of directors, which they help select—and which includes some fellow CEOs on whose boards they sit—gives them the pay they want. The trick is in hiring outside experts, called "compensation consultants," who give the process a thin veneer of economic respectability."[11]

"The process has been explained in detail by a retired CEO of DuPont, Edgar S. Woolard, Jr., who is now chair of the New York Stock Exchange's (NYSE) executive compensation committee. His experience suggests that he knows whereof he speaks, and he speaks because he is concerned that corporate leaders are losing respect in the public mind. He says that the business page chatter about CEO salaries being set by the competition for their services in the executive labor market is "bull." As to the claim that CEOs deserve ever-higher salaries because they "create wealth," he describes that rationale as a "joke," says the *New York Times*."

"Here is how it works, according to Woolard:

The compensation committee [of the board of directors] talks to an outside consultant who has surveys you could drive a truck through and pay anything you want to pay, to be perfectly honest. The outside consultant talks to the human resources vice president, who talks to the CEO. The CEO says what he'd like to receive. It gets to the human resources person who tells the outside consultant. And it pretty well works out that the CEO gets what he's implied he thinks he deserves, so he will be respected by his peers."

"The board of directors buys into what the CEO asks for because the outside consultant is an "expert" on such matters. Furthermore, handing out only modest salary increases might give the wrong impression about how highly the board values the CEO. And if someone on the board should object, there are the three or four CEOs from other companies who will make sure it happens. It is a process with a built-in escalator."

"As for why the consultants go along with this scam, they know which side their bread is buttered on. They realize the CEO has a big say-so on whether or not they are hired again. So they suggest a package of salaries, stock options and other goodies that they think will please the CEO, and they, too, get rich in the process. And certainly the top executives just below the CEO don't mind hearing about the boss's raise. They know it will mean pay increases for them, too.[12] There is a much deeper power story that underlies the self-dealing and mutual back-scratching by CEOs now carried out through interlocking directorates and seemingly independent outside consultants. It probably involves several factors. At the least, on the worker side, it reflects an increasing lack of power following the all-out attack on unions in the 1960s and 1970s, which is explained in detail by the best expert on recent American labor history. That decline in union power made possible and was increased by both outsourcing at home and the movement of production to developing countries, which were facilitated by the breakup of the New Deal coalition and the rise of the New Right. It signals the shift of the United States from a high-wage to a low-wage economy, with professionals protected by the fact that foreign-trained doctors and lawyers are not allowed to compete with their American counterparts in the direct way that low-wage foreign-born workers are."

"On the other side of the class divide, the rise in CEO pay may reflect the increasing power of chief executives as compared to major owners and stockholders in general, not just their increasing power over workers. CEOs may now be the center of gravity in the corporate community and the power elite, displacing the leaders in wealthy owning families (e.g., the second and third generations of the Walton family, the owners of Wal-Mart). True enough, the CEOs are sometimes ousted by their generally go-along boards of directors, but they are able to make hay and throw their weight around during the time they are king of the mountain. (It's really not much different than that old children's game, except it is played out in profit-oriented bureaucratic hierarchies, like no other sector of society, like government, willing or able to restrain the winners.)"

"The claims made in the previous paragraph need much further investigation. But they demonstrate the ideas and research directions that are suggested by looking at the wealth and income distributions as indicators of power."

# The Higher Immorality and the Political Economy

Mills's notion of the higher immorality has rarely been viewed as a theory of elite crime. However, closer examination will reveal that it is indeed a set of theoretical propositions concerning an institutionalized set of behaviors among the U.S. power elite. In this section, we explore the general parameters of the higher immorality within the political economy.[13]

## Corporate Compensation: Salaries, Taxes, and Perks

As the higher immorality involves the pursuit of money, the mechanisms by which money is obtained and retained are very important. As Mills put it, "Higher income taxes have resulted in a whole series of collusions between the big firm and higher employee. There are many ingenious ways to cheat the spirit of the tax laws, and the standards of consumption of many high-priced men are determined more by complicated expense accounts than by simple take-home pay."[14]

The accuracy of Mills's description can be gauged by a study of all the various rewards granted top corporate executives. Perhaps the most innovative scheme used by corporate executives to raise their own salaries concerns the management of General Dynamics (GD), a major defense contractor with a long history of defense fraud convictions (see Chapter 5). In 1991, although GD was busy laying off 30% of its workers, its chairman, William Anders, asked stockholders to approve $7.6 million worth of bonuses for GD's top 25 executives. The bonuses, tied to the performance of GD stock, were approved by 77% of the company's stockholders. In light of the layoffs, the bonuses were the subject of angry worker demonstrations.[15]

The situation at GD is symbolic of a national debate over executive pay. Three-fourths of the American people now believe that corporate executive salaries are too high, and the Securities and Exchange Commission has ruled that executive pay can come before corporate stockholders for a vote. Excessive corporate compensation is a fundamental reason for the great inequality of wealth and income in America (see Chapter 1).[16]

In 2005, the average CEO of a Standard & Poor's 500 company received $13.51 million in total compensation, a 16.14% increase in CEO pay over

2004. Since 1985 there has been "an unprecedented growth in compensation only for top executives and a dramatic increase in the ratio between the compensation of executives and their employees."[17]

Boards of directors too often have awarded compensation packages that go well beyond what is required to attract and retain executives and have rewarded even poorly performing CEOs. These executive pay excesses have served to increase the inequality of both wealth and income by taking money from shareholders—including the retirement savings of America's working families.

Recent scholarly studies have linked CEO stock options to accounting fraud and unethical schemes. Stock options guarantee the benefits of share price increases with none of the risk of share price declines. For this reason, stock options can serve as a powerful incentive for executives to "cook the books."

According to new research, certain CEOs may be backdating their own stock-option grants to maximize their value. According to the *Wall Street Journal*, "Year after year, some companies' top executives received options on unusually propitious dates."[18]

Excessive CEO pay occurs because CEOs have too much power to exact what economists' call *economic rents* from shareholders—the equivalent of monopoly profits. These rents, known as *agency costs,* arise from the separation of ownership and control. At approximately two-thirds of the largest companies, the CEO is the board's chair, making it impossible to objectively monitor and evaluate CEO "performance."[19]

CEOs also dominate the election of directors. The vast majority of directors are handpicked by incumbent management. Because of the proxy rules, it is cost prohibitive for shareholders to run their own director candidates. Moreover, even if a majority of shareholders withhold support from directors, they are still elected to the board at most companies.

Ultimately, shareholders have to be able to trust their boards of directors to set responsible CEO pay packages. For this reason, CEO pay will be reformed only when corporate boards are made more accountable. Until then, CEOs will continue to influence the size and form of their own compensation, and CEO pay will continue to rise. In 2010, the average corporate executive made 530 times as much as the average assembly line worker in the United States. This is up from a ratio of 301:1 in 2000, and 901:1 in 1990.[20]

*Why Is Executive Pay So High?*    Such increases are rarely tied to company performance. For example, in February 2005, the NYSE ruled that its former chair, Richard Grasso, had too much power in setting his $187.5 million compensation and took unfair advantage of his personal relationships with NYSE board members to have his compensation approved. Executive compensation is highly correlated with the salaries of committee members in charge of approving executive salaries.[21] Thus, corporate executives possess the power to reward themselves by placing people on corporate boards who are predisposed to vote executive pay increases. CEOs are also likely to get raises if other CEOs are getting them, thus effectively reversing the law of supply and demand.

One of the most widely used and effective devices for amassing corporate wealth is the corporate stock option. A *stock option* is "a right given a corporate executive to buy his company's stock at some time in the future, at a specified price the date the option is granted."[22] For example, suppose that an executive is given an option to buy 100,000 shares of his or her company's stock on January 15, 1991, and on that day the price of such stock is $75 per share. If the executive contracted to buy the stock at $50 per share back in 1989, he or she may still buy at that price. The profit on the stock amounts to $25 per share on 100,000 shares, or $250,000. The executive does not pay income tax on this windfall but does pay capital gains tax. Such taxes, however, are only 40%, considerably less than the income tax one would pay on such an amount.

Another stock-option plan permits executives to purchase stock at its book-value price. Rather than buy stock at market prices, executives buy it at a price per share equal to the company's assets minus its liabilities. This price rarely declines and usually increases greatly, regardless of stock market swings. Later, executives are permitted to sell the stock to the company at its new book value. The perks (perquisites) of corporate life are not limited to salaries, bonuses, and stock options. Indeed, the corporate compensation landscape now represents a form of corporate socialism for top executives.

Today, 75% of executive compensation consists of nonsalary bonuses, stock options, and related perks.

All in all, the success of American corporate executives has undermined the public's faith in the U.S. economic system, caused a brain drain of bright people from teaching and public service, and helped to create a "greed is good" attitude among middle- and lower-level managers. The result is an unprecedented cynicism of employees toward companies and bosses.[23]

Other advantages secured by the elite, especially those relating to tax laws and private foundations, are also important because they have, in some instances, facilitated both political and economic crimes.[24] Such advantages deserve a closer look.

## Welfare for the Well-Off: Tax Breaks

The U.S. system of government has produced what is known as a dual-welfare system. Programs for the poor are termed *relief, welfare, assistance*, or *charity*.[25] Programs for the rich, however, are called *tax expenditures, subsidies, price supports, parity*, and the like.

The dual-welfare system is an integral part of the higher immorality, allowing the rich to become richer at the expense of the middle class and the poor. Mark Zepezauer and Arthur Naiman have recently put the costs of corporate welfare at $448 billion, "about 3.5 times as much as the $130 billion we spend yearly for the poor."[26] Such "wealthfare" includes subsidies, tax deductions, tax exemptions, tax-free investments, excessive government pensions, and $172 billion worth of fraud and waste in the Defense Department (see Chapter 5 for details).[27]

The expected deficit for fiscal 2006 was $400 billion. In 2005, about $27 billion in earmarks (pet projects in various congressional districts) made it into appropriations bills, excluding an additional $25 billion earmarked for the highway transportation bill. Many corporate subsidies are disguised as earmarks. For example, defense contractor Northrop Grumman Corporation lacked enough insurance to cover losses from Hurricane Katrina at its Mississippi shipyards. The U.S. Senate approved $140 million for rebuilding the shipyards, and Northrop made record profits of $2.4 billion in 2005, even with the Katrina loss. This means large corporations may have no future motivation to acquire insurance at all, making them more dependent on tax subsidies.

Wal-Mart, the world's largest corporation, receives an astounding amount of corporate welfare. Wal-Mart employees are eligible for federal assistance due to low pay and the company's unaffordable health insurance plan; $2.5 billion in federal welfare went to Wal-Mart employees in 2004. Wal-Mart personnel managers actually encourage their employees to apply for welfare. Moreover, Wal-Mart received government subsidies for store and distribution center construction: $150 million worth through 2003 from local, state, and federal governments to open 47 distribution centers in 32 states.

Likewise, although victims of Katrina are lucky if they receive aid from volunteers in fixing or rebuilding their homes, the home of Confederacy president Jefferson Davis received $38 million for restoration. Congress also allocated $700 million to relocate train tracks that it just voted $250 million to repair after Katrina. Money to fight the Colorado bark beetle's pine tree destruction was also included in the Katrina relief law, as was $15 million for New England shell fisherman to reduce the 2005 impact of red tide.[28]

One mechanism by which rich individuals and corporations are allowed to retain their wealth is the tax loophole (now called *tax expenditures* by government). In fact, 90,000 corporations paid no federal income taxes whatsoever 1 year. Since 1981, the maximum corporate tax rates allowed by law have been cut from 46% to 34%.[29]

In the 1940s, corporate income taxes accounted for 33% of federal income tax receipts. The figure now stands at 15% and has remained constant since the late 1980s. All of corporate America now pays less in taxes than those paid by families in just three states, New York, California, and Ohio.[30]

Many special deductions keep the tax bills of corporations and the rich below those of average Americans (on a percentage basis). Some of these are discussed next.

## The Asset-Depletion Range

Over half the benefits from asset depletion go to the largest 103 U.S. manufacturing corporations.[31] This tax law makes an allowance for wear and tear on equipment by allowing a depreciation deduction. In reality, there is no way of knowing how long a piece of equipment will last; it merely depends on how quickly a given company decides to replace it. Before the asset-depletion allowance, most equipment had to be depreciated over a 10-year period for tax purposes. Now, however, a company is allowed to depreciate equipment over an 8-year period, 20% faster than before. Of course, such equipment lasts 8 years, 10 years, or even longer. The odd thing about the asset-depletion range is that it comes at a time when 25% of the nation's plant capacity is already underused. Hence, the need for new equipment is suspect.

In 1993, the federal Omnibus Budget Reconciliation Act became law. The law gives corporations some of the most confounding deductions in American history.

- A "potato chip" deduction clause allows merging corporations to depreciate their product names and intangible assets. Thus, over a 15-year period, companies are allowed to deduct for all manner of secret ingredients in product formulas (e.g., floor waxes and deodorants), as well as for brand names: Doritos, Quaker, and Kellogg's. Moreover, the law states that past attempts to write off such intangibles are now legal, even if they were previously denied by the Internal Revenue Service (IRS) or courts. Thus, corporations can now file for refunds from previous years.
- The act also contains a variety of special laws. Banks that made bad loans can deduct these as bad debts. Foreign-owned companies are taxed at rates lower than American companies. Poorly run corporations that are losing money can now get refunds from previous years.
- Corporations can now deduct executive salaries and interest payments on borrowed money, much of which has gone for mergers in recent years (as discussed in Chapter 3). The deductions on interest alone total $200 billion. Thus, in 1991–1992, Stone Container paid no federal corporate income taxes on its $493 million earnings due to its deduction for interest on its debt. Moreover, the owners of this debt (bondholders) escaped taxes on the part of their individual incomes that Stone paid in interest to them.

- Currently, there is an ongoing debate concerning whether or not to abolish the federal estate tax (always called the death tax by those advocating its abolition). Only 1.6% of the population inherit $100,000 or more, while over 90% get nothing. "The rich already have a new way to avoid inheritance taxes forever—for generations and generations—thanks to bankers. After Congress passed a reform in 1986 making it impossible for a "trust" to skip a generation before paying inheritance taxes, bankers convinced legislatures in many states to eliminate their "rules against perpetuities," which means that trust funds set up in those states can exist in perpetuity, thereby allowing the trust funds to own new businesses, houses, and much else for descendants of rich people, and even to allow the beneficiaries to avoid payments to creditors when in personal debt or sued for causing accidents and injuries. About $100 billion in trust funds has flowed into those states so far. You can read the details on these "dynasty trusts" (which could be the basis for an even more solidified "American aristocracy.")

The results of these deductions constitute nothing less than a scandal. Money is used for mergers, which, in turn, result in plant closings and the loss of over 2.5 million middle-class jobs in recent years. Corporate taxes decrease, executive salaries increase, unemployment reaches depression levels, and what's left of the American middle class is saddled with an increased tax bill."[32]

## Taxes and Multinational Corporations

Many multinational corporations take advantage of foreign tax credits, which allow a company to pay taxes on profits made overseas, where taxes are usually less, and to pay no taxes on such profits in the United States. This has made some nations, including Liechtenstein, Panama, and Liberia, tax havens for large corporations. The practice of setting up dummy corporations overseas to which items are sold only on paper (for purposes of tax avoidance) is also common.

## Misappropriated Charity: Foundations

Despite the tax advantages granted to corporations, individuals who own controlling interests in corporations also tend to do all they can to ensure that their fortunes are passed on to their kin. To escape inheritance and other taxes, a boon to such individuals has been the tax-exempt foundation.

The purpose of a foundation is supposedly to facilitate charitable contributions. As of 2003, a mere 2.8% of all foundations controlled $100 million or more in assets, accounting for 5.9% of total foundation assets and 45% of all foundation donations.[33] Setting up a tax-exempt foundation exempts all assets therein from income and capital gains taxes, as well as most inheritance taxes. On the surface, this seems morally upright because such funds are, after all, given to worthy causes. Underneath, however, the reality is somewhat different.

Foundations excel at investing money and escaping taxation. A government study of 1,300 foundations found that 180 owned 10% or more of a corporation's stock (often enough to gain a controlling interest in a company).[34] Far from being strictly charitable, foundations play a major role in the corporate decisions that affect the private sector of the economy, as well as politics.

Moreover, there have been incidents of government interference by awarding private foundation grants. This has especially been the case with the CIA. In 1966, the CIA disbursed $400,000 through the J. M. Kaplan Fund to a research institute. The institute in turn financed research centers in Latin American countries, which also drew support from the Agency for International Development (a U.S. foreign-aid agency), Brandeis and Harvard universities, and the Ford Foundation. The CIA also sponsored the travel of various social scientists to communist countries. The Kaplan Fund had also been financed by foundations, although it was not even listed with the IRS. This suggests that the foundation was fraudulently created by the CIA. Seven other foundations were discovered to have been CIA-created conduits, but the purposes or amounts of money given have never been made public. Why the CIA went into the charity business, which is a clear violation of its charter, has also gone unexplained.[35]

Foundation money has been used for a number of causes that have nothing whatever to do with charity, which represents one more form of the higher immorality. The Ford Foundation, for example, has lent large sums of money to private corporations, in effect competing with private banks. Howard Hughes created the Hughes Medical Institute to insure the liabilities of a number of Hughes's own companies.

Other foundations have made loans to businesspeople for the purpose of closing business deals. Foundation grants have also been used for the following:

1. Bankrolling political candidates
2. Financing experiments with school decentralization in slums in which African Americans live
3. Supporting militant political organizations, on both the left and right
4. Financing the foreign travels of the staff of U.S. senators
5. Financing activities of moderate (middle-class) civil rights organizations, which have largely failed to understand or alleviate the problems of poor ghetto blacks (who rarely receive such money without strings)[36]

In short, foundations have been used for deviant purposes that have nothing whatever to do with charity.

To say the least, "subsidies go to a bewildering array of industries, seemingly without rhyme or reason."[37]

- The United States owns power plants in Nevada that produce electricity for about one penny per kilowatt. As a result, the citizens of Las Vegas (with its huge neon signs) pay 5.6 cents per kilowatt for electricity, while residents in the Northeast pay 12 cents per kilowatt for their unsubsidized electricity.

## The Creation of Crisis

One aspect of the higher immorality identified by Mills concerns the concept of *crisis*.

> Crisis is a bankrupted term because so many men in high places have evoked it to cover up their extraordinary policies and deeds. As a matter of fact, it is precisely the absence of genuine crisis that has beset our morality. For such crises involve situations in which men at large are presented with genuine alternatives, the moral meanings of which are clearly open to public debate. Our higher immorality and general weakening of older values have not involved such crises.[38]

Perhaps nothing in our recent experience so confirms Mills's words as the current war in Iraq.

In his introduction to a collection of classic readings in sociological theory, Mills argues that one result of reading sociology ought to be learning how to make sense of the news, how to relate events to each other and to the more general concepts of the cultures they represent, and the trends of which they are a part.[39] Although much news "coverage has to do with 'white-collar crime,' with crime syndicates operated on business lines . . . and many other forms of fraud and deceit," it is not enough to view each item as it occurs; one must come to see the items as part of a whole. If you remember how often elite corruption is reported (as well as learn how much of it goes unreported),[40] you will observe that a pattern of themes begins to emerge. Among these themes are the following:

1. The extent of manipulation (propaganda and lying) as a form of exercising power. In our era this has come to mean the creation of a crisis (which the public is manipulated into believing is true) where no real crisis exists. The crisis is then used as an excuse to make money for corporate interests and to illegally further the power of government agencies.

   In recent years the United States and much of the world has experienced these fabricated crises on a regular basis:

   - The ongoing decade old war in Iraq had nothing to do with the 9/11/2001 terrorist attack on the World Trade Center, nor did Iraq possess weapons of mass destruction.[41]

- In 2011, the politicians in Minnesota completely shut down the state government by refusing to pass a state budget. The "crisis" was resolved when it was learned that no more revenues from the state lottery, admissions to state parks, or beer licenses would be issued.[42]
- Likewise, in summer 2011, members of congress turned what should have been a routine vote to raise the national debt ceiling $2.5 trillion turned into a near government shutdown that would have resulted in lowering the U.S. government's credit rating, increased interest rates for individuals and businesses in the midst of the worst economic crisis since the 1930s, and stopped the government from meeting many of its important financial obligations.[43]

2. The extent of semiorganized irresponsibility, meaning that no specific person in an organization is typically blamed for a scandal. Instead, organizations operate according to the principle of "plausible deniablity" wherein blame is shifted to lower-level employees and elites are held blameless.

- In July 2011, media mogul Rupurt Murdoch was struggling to save his huge media empire on both sides of the Atlantic. He was forced to shut down his London tabloid <u>News of the World</u> because the paper's reporters had systematically bribed British police officers to gain access to the cell phone numbers of British politicians and members of the Royal Family, actor Hugh Grant, families of murder victims, and families of soldiers killed in Iraq and Afghanistan.[44]

  While Murdoch has apologized for the hacking scandal, "in full-page adverts, Murdoch pledged "concrete steps" to resolve the issue in a bid to regain the initiative after losing Les Hinton, head of Dow Jones, publisher of the Wall Street Journal, and Rebekah Brooks, head of News Corp's British newspaper arm, on" July 15, 2011.[45]

  Meanwhile, while Murdoch himself has denied any knowledge of the hacking–scandal, the FBI has begun an investigation to see if Murdoch ordered any of his American reporters to hack into the phones of the victims' families of the 9/11/2001 World Trade Center bombing, or violated America's Foreign Corrupt Practices Act by bribing officials in Britain.[46]

3. The extent to which propaganda techniques and plausible deniability find so many employees willing to engage in them, and who, in turn, are corrupted by the work they do. Why is this so? "Does it not reveal ... the supremacy of cash and kudos (recognition and praise from on high) as the all-American values?"[47]
4. Finally, and most crucial "is not one revealing image of contemporary American society a network of rackets" (i.e., coordinated scandals, scams, frauds and deceits)? [42]

## Antitrust Laws

Mills believed that much corporate crime results because it is often good business to break the law. As he said, businesses "obey these laws, when they do, not because they feel that it is morally right, but because they are afraid of being caught." Therefore, such laws "exist without the support of firm moral conviction. It is merely illegal to cheat them, but it is often considered smart to get away with it."[48]

There are several reasons why businesses sometimes consider it smart to break the laws that regulate their activity. First, many laws are ambiguous and contain exemptions and exclusions, leaving a great deal of room for interpretation by the courts. Second, many laws regulating business activity are hardly strict in their penalties. Indeed, many items of business laws are settled in civil rather than criminal courts. Imprisonment under such laws is rare, and the fines imposed for breaking them many times amount to no more than a slap on the wrist. Finally, the enforcement of such laws is often lax because government devotes comparatively few resources to catching corporate offenders. This lack of enforcement can be explained by examining the Sherman Act (1890), the Federal Trade Commission Act (1914), and the Robinson-Patman Act (1936).

The Sherman Act prohibits "unreasonable restraints upon and monopolization of trade."[49] The act also outlaws arrangements that result in price-fixing or limiting access to trade or commerce (e.g., dividing markets). However, the act is loaded with exclusions and ambiguities. Thus, the Sherman Act only applies to monopolies in trade (commerce), not to monopolies in manufacturing. Moreover, under a series of cases in 1911 involving American Tobacco and Standard Oil, it was ruled that the act applied only to *unreasonable* trade combinations and did not exclude consolidation per se. The definition of a *reasonable* combination, of course, is a matter of judicial opinion. Under the Sherman Act's price-fixing definitions, businesses that are already regulated by the federal government (such as the Civil Aeronautics Board's regulation of the nation's airlines) are excluded from the law. This exclusion also applies to interstate water carriers, railroads, and trucks. Other loopholes are present in the act, as well. Although the act specifies that it is illegal to fix the price of a product by agreement, this practice is legal in states that authorize it under so-called fair laws.[50]

In 1914, the Federal Trade Commission Act was passed, making it unlawful to restrict competition and to engage in unfair and deceptive trade practices. However, the power of the FTC is limited to issuing cease-and-desist orders, which it can do only upon securing the permission of a federal court. The FTC can recommend prosecution of criminal cases, but the Justice Department is specifically charged with this task.

In 1936, the Robinson–Patman Act made it illegal to discriminate between various buyers of products by charging different prices to different buyers. But the act has several limitations. First, it applies only to products, not to services, which are supposedly covered by other laws. In addition, the law specifically exempts U.S. companies that have joined together for purposes of export. The antitrust laws also exempt such items as bank mergers, agricultural cooperatives, and insurance companies, which are unregulated by state laws.[51]

During the Reagan–Bush years, the enforcement of antitrust and other laws designed to control corporate crime became a very low priority. So lax was the enforcement that, by 1982, 60% of corporations had failed to pay their fines following conviction or court settlement. As a result, $38 billion in fines were outstanding.[52] Moreover, the Reagan administration made clear its dislike of the very structure of antitrust laws. In 1986, it sent to Congress a package designed, in effect, to repeal some key provisions of the Clayton Act, especially those prohibiting mergers that reduce competition and hence create monopoly. It was proposed that the government prove the *significant probability*, not just the *possibility*, of monopoly before antitrust sanctions could be applied. Federal courts would have had to evaluate proposed mergers, considering their effects not simply on U.S. markets but on world markets as well. Most important, the Reagan proposal allowed a 5-year exemption from antitrust laws for corporations found to be seriously injured by imports, especially shoes, steel, and textiles.[53]

The Clinton administration showed the same reluctance to enforce the antitrust laws in a meaningful way. Its one great exception concerns its suit against Microsoft, the computer software giant. Microsoft agreed to stop a number of licensing practices, which will give computer manufacturers more freedom in installing programs from other companies. Microsoft used to receive a royalty for each computer sold, even if its operating systems were made by other manufacturers that had a contract with Microsoft for Microsoft's Windows or DOS operating systems. This discouraged the selling of other operating systems, such as Novell's Dr. DOS or IBM's OS-2. The agreement could give Microsoft more competition for dominance over the personal computer (PC) market.[54]

## The Higher Immorality and Corporate Crime

If Mills's view of corporate crime is correct, one would expect two effects: (1) widespread violations of antitrust laws and (2) the presence of attitudes condoning such violations. Ample evidence exists to support both propositions. First, two studies have documented the fact that corporate illegalities are widespread.

- Edwin Sutherland, who coined the term *white-collar crime*, studied the illegalities of 70 large corporations from 1890 to 1945. He found that there had been 980 decisions against these corporations. Every corporation had at least 1 decision against it, and the average number of decisions was 14.[55] Criminal courts made 159 of the 980 decisions, 45 were made by courts that were under either civil or equity jurisdiction, and 361 were settled by government commission. Of the 70 corporations studied by Sutherland, 30 either were illegitimate in origin or became involved in illegal activities. Eight others, he found, were probably illegal in origin or in beginning policies. The finding of original illegitimacy was made with respect to 21 corporations in formal court decisions from other historical evidence in other cases. What Sutherland's study implies is that 60% of the corporations, or 42 in number, with an average of four convictions each, are habitual criminals.[56]

- A study of the largest 582 publicly owned corporations indicated that more than 60% of such firms had at least one legal action initiated against them during 1975 and 1976. The 300 parent manufacturing firms in the study had an average of 4.8 actions initiated against them by federal agencies. Yet fewer than 10% of the violations resulted in any criminal penalties. Moreover, in less than 1% of the federal enforcement actions was a corporate officer sent to jail for failing to carry out corporate legal responsibilities.[57] When a jail term was imposed, "sentences almost never exceeded six months."[58]

Corporate executives seem well aware that many businesspeople engage in either criminal or unethical action. A 1961 survey in the *Harvard Business Review* of some 1,700 businesspersons revealed that four out of seven believed that individuals "would violate a code of ethics when asked and 70 percent of 500 believed that price fixing is a common occurrence in their industries."[59]

Corporate executives and small businesspersons engage in unethical or illegal behaviors for several other reasons, too. One important factor is the capitalist economic system and its dependence on continued profits and economic growth. When antitrust and other business laws are enforced with such laxness and the penalties involved are so minimal, violations of such laws become rational from a profit standpoint. Quite simply, it is much more profitable to violate such laws than to obey them.

Second, most corporate executives who are caught breaking the law often believe that what they have done does not violate the law in any serious sense. Typically, even though found guilty, they believe that they have not harmed anyone.[60]

Third, corporate criminal behavior, like any other type of behavior, is learned. In the case of corporate executives, it is the corporate environment, not the street gang or the college education, that teaches and sometimes demands the learning of such behavior. A 1973 study by the American Management Association concluded that corporate executives and businesspeople must often sacrifice personal morals and ethics in order to remain in business. "About 70 percent . . . admit they have been expected, frequently or on occasion, to compromise personal principles in order to conform either to organizational standards or to standards established by their corporate superiors."[61]

In one famous case, the convicted executives made it clear that their motives in fixing prices were to increase the profits for the company and further their own careers.

As Robert Sherrill recently asked,

> When is a crime not officially a crime? Simple: When the laws against that activity are not enforced. Antitrust laws—those almost mythical beings so revered by populists—have been on the books for several generations and are supposed to be used to prevent the kind of concentration of market power that leads to price-fixing and the death of competition. . . . That's why the Federal Trade Commission used the antitrust laws to block Rite Aid's proposed $1.8 billion purchase of Revco, a combination that would have created the nation's largest drugstore chain. Antitrust laws were used … to pry fines from *Reader's Digest* ($40 million) and U.S. Healthcare ($1.2 million). Nowhere was this clearer than in the aerospace and military industry, where, in one of the largest mergers in U.S. history, Boeing bought McDonnell Douglas to become the only—yes, only—manufacturer of commercial jets in the United States, catapulting it ahead of Lockheed Martin, the number-one military contractor, as the world's largest aerospace company. This pairing-off received the same enthusiastic government support that a series of multibillion-dollar military industry mergers have received from the Clinton Administration over the past four years.
>
> Other industries have been promised the same support. Last June the FTC proposed that antitrust enforcers let cost savings justify mergers that would otherwise be considered illegal because they were anticompetitive.
>
> What's more, the commission adopted new rules that would speed mergers and acquisitions by radically shortening the time the FTC takes to consider cases alleging anticompetitive conduct or consumer fraud.[62]

## Penalties: The Double Standard

Corporate officials convicted of price-fixing and other corporate crimes invariably receive light sentences (see Chapter 3). McCormick's data (see endnote 59) demonstrate that the heaviest jail sentence imposed in a price-fixing case from 1890 (the year the Sherman Antitrust Act was passed) until 1969 was 60 days. Actually, it was not until the 1961 electrical conspiracy case (discussed at length in Chapter 3) that any businesspersons "were actually imprisoned purely for price-fixing and monopolization. No individuals were sent to jail until twenty years after the passage of the act."[63] In fact, in almost three-fourths of the cases (73.1%), convictions were gained not by the government proving any wrongdoing but by pleas of *nolo contendere*, under which defendants merely refuse to acknowledge guilt, instead of admitting guilt, and accept whatever sentence is imposed, thereby avoiding being labeled criminal by the court. Finally, only 45% of the cases under the Sherman Act have been criminal in nature; the majority were tried as civil matters, which involved no jail terms. Of those cases in which jail terms were imposed and actually served, only 2% were tried under the Sherman Act, and almost all these came under the act's statutes concerning labor unions. (Unions assisting nonunion labor to gain control over a labor market is a violation of section 6 of the Sherman Act.)[64]

The laxness with which antitrust laws are enforced is in part attributable to the meager resources devoted to such enforcement. Within the Justice Department, outside Washington, local federal prosecutors (U.S. attorneys) are charged with enforcement of federal laws. In its 94 local offices, there are fewer than 2,000 attorneys for the entire nation, only 200 of whom prosecute fraud cases. At the state level, only 30 of 50 state prosecutors had consumer fraud units. Although some white-collar prosecutions can cost more than a million dollars, only 40 state prosecutors had budgets that exceeded a million dollars, whereas three had budgets in excess of $500,000. All state prosecutors combined employ fewer than 7,000 attorneys. (The federal government alone employs more than 10,000 lawyers.)[65]

## Public Awareness

Corporate crime, as well as other types of white-collar illegalities, is made worse by the ignorance and unwitting cooperation of the public. This is not to suggest that the public is necessarily stupid or gullible. Rather, it is to confirm the fact that, until very recently, consumer education and violations of law by corporations were not part of the public's general knowledge or specific education in the United States. The nature of profitable crime is such that it is invisible. As Thio has stated, "It may be difficult for the victims to know that they are victimized, even if they want to find out the true nature of their victimization. Grocery shoppers, for example, are hard put to detect unlawful substances [such] as residues of hormones, antibiotics, pesticides, and nitrates in the meat they buy."[66]

Even when corporate criminals are caught and convicted, the news media, which are made up of corporations, have not faithfully reported such incidents. Although many criminologists believe that public shame is a key aspect of criminal penalties,[67] the media have failed to do their part. "Even when prosecutions have resulted in conviction, most of the news media—including *Time* and *Newsweek*, the networks, and the *New York Times*—have failed repeatedly to recognize the importance of adequate reporting and have ignored the cases or have treated them trivially."[68]

The mass media, until recently, have very much underreported corporate criminality. Such reporting may be partially responsible for convincing corporate criminals that the illegal acts that they commit are not real crimes.

Coupled with the large majority of antitrust violations that are tried as civil matters, this means that little stigma and little public shame are associated with such crimes. Whether this will change in the face of growing public resentment of big business is yet an open question. At the moment, it is safe to conclude that antitrust and other corporate violations are the most profitable form of crime and carry little risk of detection and genuine punishment.

## Organized Crime and the Business Elite

As a formal matter, *organized crime* is defined as "business enterprises organized for the purpose of making economic gain through illegal activities."[69] We are reminded that organized crime, to be defined as such, must display certain features:

> We have defined organized crime as an integral part of the American social system that brings together (1) a public that demands certain goods and services that are defined as illegal, (2) an organization of individuals who produce or supply those goods and services, and (3) corrupt public officials who protect such individuals for their own profit or gain.[70]

However, for most people, organized crime has taken its meaning over the past 20 years from the television series, books, movies, magazine articles, and congressional hearings (televised no less) on the Mafia, or Cosa Nostra.

The image of organized crime, as presented in the mass media, is that of a secret international organization of Italian and Sicilian gangsters who, through corruption and violence, are successful in exerting their will in every task that they undertake. But the media image of organized crime is misleading, especially when the relationships among legitimate businesspeople, politicians, and syndicate criminals are examined.

That is, an element of the higher immorality in the activities of organized crimes is largely unexplored. The higher immorality applies to organized crime insofar as legitimate corporate and political elites utilize the services of the Mafia (or Cosa Nostra) for unethical or illegal purposes. This takes place when organized crime (1) assists economic and political elites in repressing threats to the established order; (2) assists businesses in profit-making ventures; and/or (3) assists federal officials in carrying out U.S. foreign policy objectives.

### Organized Crime and Repression

Modern organized crime in the United States began in 1929 when the treasurer of Atlantic City, New Jersey, Enoch Lewis "Nucky" Thompson proudly hosted the first convention of nation-wide organized crime members called the "Seven Group." The Group's members included organizer Charles "Lucky" Luciano, as well as Benjamin "Bugsy" Siegel, Mayer Lansky,

Frank Costello, Louis "Lepke" Buchalter, and Dutch Schultz, née Arthur Flegenheimer, from New York, Joe Adonis from Brooklyn; as well as members from Northern New Jersey, Boston, Philadelphia, and Alphonse "Al" Capone from Chicago. By 1929, the Seven syndicate had made alliances with 22 mobs from Maine to Florida, and west to the Mississippi River. Organized crime has long assisted certain business and political elites in preventing and/or suppressing the powerless in society. Throughout the 1920s, businesspeople entered into union contract negotiations with gangster-dominated unions in order to insure themselves against upsets of any kind (e.g., union unrest). Often businesspeople would join with each other by creating trade associations, and the newly formed associations would negotiate with the gangster-dominated unions. Such organizations kept competition from other businesses not belonging to such associations at a minimum. The costs of such protection were usually passed on to consumers. These activities stabilized markets in small, competitive industries, such as trucking, garments, baking, and cleaning and dyeing. When Prohibition ended, gangsters moved into the movie industry using these same tactics.[71]

Mafia figures have been recruited by businesses and politicians to quell labor unrest in a variety of settings.

- In the 1940s, Detroit automobile companies used gangsters to suppress efforts to unionize the auto industry. Gangsters such as D'Anna and Adonnis were given a monopoly over the haul-away business at the Ford Motor Company in return for gaining control of the autoworker unions in the city. And even after the American Federation of Labor (AFL) succeeded in unionizing the auto industry, Ford still hired mobsters to act as strikebreakers. In 1945 and 1946, there were 41,750 strikes in the United States, more than in the previous 10 years combined, so the need for strikebreakers was clear. Use of gangsters for this purpose was curtailed in the 1950s as unions supported governmental policies related to the cold war, and militant unionism, often associated with communism, declined.[72]
- During the late 1930s and early 1940s, the International Longshoreman's Association (ILA) was infiltrated by organized criminals in New York Harbor. The docks of New York Harbor are made up of very narrow piers and gridiron street layouts, and congestion is a continual problem. Such congested conditions make it easy to disrupt traffic on the docks. These peculiar physical conditions were part of the reason why gangsters were hired to infiltrate the local ILA. Because of the congestion, drivers did not bring their own loaders to the docks. Rather, loaders were hired at the pier. Loaders could be hired only through loading bosses, who were ILA union members. Bosses charged high prices for using the labor that they controlled, and a syndicate organization, Varick Enterprises, Inc., dominated this trade by charging all truckers a per-ton tax, whether they used the loaders or not. While

standardized rates were eventually worked out, the Varick organization, along with the ILA and the local Tammany Hall political machine, kept control of the loading and other rackets along the docks.

- In the late 1930s, the West Coast ILA was a so-called clean union headed by a labor radical named Harry Bridges. Bridges had taken his union out of the ranks of the AFL to the Congress of Industrial Organizations (CIO), an act of militant independence. Fearing such independence, as well as the strong socialist sentiment among some New York dockworkers, mobster Albert Anastasia murdered Peter Panto, a radical longshoreman leader, who worked on the Brooklyn docks. Militant left-wing union activity continued throughout the 1940s until 1951, when more than a million trade unionists from 12 unions (one-fifth of the CIO membership) were expelled from the CIO in response to the Report of the Investigation of Communism in New York City Distributive Trades.

Other brutal attacks on union dissidents by mobsters occurred throughout the 1940s. This fear concerning socialism within the U.S. labor movement is responsible for the persistence of organized crime's involvement in labor racketeering and violence, at the behest of certain corporate elites. Of course, "both employers and unions have hired gangsters to help them in industrial disputes. It has been employers who have benefited the most. One of the underlying factors was a desire to keep real wages down, and the constant use of terror to destroy rank and file organizations was condoned because of the general American fear of radicalism in the docks, so crucial to the working of the system."[73]

Labor unions are not the only entities that have been repressed by syndicate criminals. Some sociologists feel that organized crime has significantly contributed to the control of U.S. ghettos. Michael Tabor has argued that a conspiracy exists in the U.S. ghetto between organized crime and the police, who are corrupted by organized criminals. Tabor's analysis centers on the role of organized crime in the distribution of heroin in ghetto areas. His contention is that the selling of heroin and the creation of a small army of heroin addicts within the ghetto keep persons who might otherwise challenge the existing social order strung out on dope and in a state of perpetual escapism from inhumane ghetto conditions.[74]

Moreover, Stephen Spitzer has argued that organized crime helps to control problem populations in a number of ways. First, organized crime creates a parallel opportunity structure, a means of employment in illegal activities for persons who might otherwise be unemployed and possibly politically discontent. The goods and services provided by organized crime to the underclasses in society do deflect their energies from the sources of their oppression.[75] In this view, organized crime, insofar as it gains a monopoly over illegal goods and services, actually aids and maintains the public order because monopoly brings with it security that one will make profits and as a result lessens the need for violence.

There is some evidence that the theses of both Tabor and Spitzer are correct. We know that heroin addiction is highly concentrated in the ghetto areas of the United States and that certain illegitimate gambling activities (such as numbers running) not only give poor people a source of hope that they will become wealthy but also provide a source of employment. The *New York Times* has estimated, for example, that the numbers racket employs thousands of people in Harlem alone.[76]

## Organized Crime and Profits

Aside from aiding with the control of so-called problem populations, organized crime has increased the profits for certain legitimate businesses. The most obvious source of profit provided by organized crime is as an important customer of corporations. For example, it was estimated that, by 1940, bookies were the fifth-largest customer of AT&T.[77] Moreover, the members of organized crime are themselves consumers of many goods and services. Given the $50 to $80 billion estimates of organized criminal enterprise, the amount of money spent by syndicate members as both capitalists and consumers serves as a rather significant market. As Quinney has stated,

> Organized crime and legitimate businesses may mutually assist one another, as in regulating prices or commodities or enforcing labor contracts. Interdependence between the underworld of crime and the upper world of business ensures that both systems will be maintained. Mutual assistance accompanied by the profit motive provides assured immunity.
>
> Organized crime has grown into a huge business in the United States and is an integral part of the political economy. Enormous amounts of illegitimate money are passed annually into socially acceptable endeavors. An elaborate corporate and financial structure is now tied to organized crime.[78]

The reach of underworld business is extensive, in terms of both economic and social impact. Organized crime remains a billion-dollar-a-year untaxed business in the United States. It includes the traditional Italian–Sicilian Cosa Nostra, as well as numerous motorcycle gangs and drug-profiteering organizations of other origin. Despite 1,200 Mafia convictions made during the 1980s, organized crime remains a powerful force in American life.

The most powerful crime family is the Genovese family of Manhattan. Their profits come through infiltration of labor unions (e.g., the Teamsters), waterfront ports, and fish markets (New York's Fulton) through domination of the ILA casinos in Atlantic City and Las Vegas; bid rigging on local construction projects; and selling stolen jewelry (swag) to Manhattan jewelry exchanges (after which it is resold to the public).[79]

There is also evidence that a number of large corporations (e.g., in the 1960s, Pan American Airways and the Howard Hughes Corporation) have entered into partnership with organized crime in a number of gambling casinos and resort ventures in both Las Vegas and the Caribbean.[80] Apparently, certain members of the corporate elite are not above obtaining capital from organized crime for purposes of expanding markets. It is not known how much capital has come from criminal syndicates for ventures of this type, but, as mentioned in Chapter 1, obtaining such capital is now against the law under the Racketeer Influenced and Corrupt Organizations (RICO) Act.

Unquestionably the most important contemporary organized crime phenomenon is global organized crime.[81] The end of the cold war created new opportunities for transnational organized crime. "Transparent national borders, fewer trade restrictions, and truly global financial and telecommunications systems provide significant opportunities for criminal organizations to expand operations beyond national boundaries."[82] Russian organized crime has formed an unholy alliance with Sicilian, Asian, Mexican, and Colombian syndicates, and the results are devastating.[83]

- In Russia, thousands of poorly guarded nuclear warheads and hundreds of unsafe reactors (20,000 safety violations during 1993 inspections and 78 shutdowns for safety reasons) are rusting away on the Soviet fleet, many with nuclear fuel aboard. The Russian Academy of Sciences estimated in 1995 that the Russian Mafiya now owns 50%–80% of all voting stock in Russia's legitimate corporations.[84]
- Drug cartels from Colombia, Russia, Italy, Japan, and China instantly transfer huge sums around the world with "wire" (actually satellite) transfers, using offshore banks. The cartels manipulate accounts drawn in the names of "shell" corporations. The economies of a number of tiny sovereign nations, like the Cayman Islands, are completely dependent on laundering transactions.

Organized crime groups from the former Soviet Union, Asia, and Italy are forming partnerships among themselves as well as with the drug barons of Latin America. All syndicates are engaging in corruption on a grand scale.

- In 1995, more than 6,000 Italian bureaucrats, corporate executives, and politicians (among them a staggering 438 deputies and senators) were under investigation or had been indicted on various corruption charges. One estimate is that the Mafia has paid $140 billion in bribes to executives and officials over the past decade.[85]
- The Colombian cartels now trade cocaine to the Italian Mafia in exchange for heroin. The Colombian Cali cartel now earns $4 billion annually from cocaine and has invested hundreds of millions in banks in Russia, Europe, and the United States.
- In Mexico,[86] the former Mexican federal deputy attorney general Eduardo Valle Espinosa resigned his official post in frustration in May 1996 and estimated that at least half of Mexico's federal police chiefs and attorney generals receive illegal payoffs from drug dealers. Some police chief candidates now pay $1 to $2 million just to get hired; from 1988 to 1994, the brother of the former president of Mexico transferred

more than $80 million from a Citibank (a U.S. bank) branch in Mexico through Citibank's New York headquarters to a secret Swiss bank account. Mexico's chief drug czar had to resign in 1997 when it was learned that he had ties to Mexico's drug cartel.

- Of the approximately 1.5 million U.S. vehicles stolen each year, several hundred thousand are illegally exported out of the country to Central America and Eastern Europe. One Colombian criminal, Gabriel Taboada, testified at a U.S. Senate committee hearing that he bribed diplomats, who are exempt from paying duty on imported cars, "to import cars in their name."[87] The diplomats were paid $25,000 to $50,000 per car.

Approximately $2.8 trillion in currency is laundered annually utilizing various global financial institutions, making money laundering the third-largest industry in the world. Federal law requires that banks report all cash deposits of $10,000 or more to the IRS. In 1975, only 3,000 such activities were reported. By 1988, 5.5 million were reported annually. It is now estimated that the total amount of drug money laundered each year is an immense $300 billion, about half of all funds connected to the worldwide drug trade. Of this amount, $100 billion is laundered in the United States. Nine-tenths of this amount ends up overseas, often in secret Swiss accounts, from which it can then be freely moved. This outflow of money contributes substantially to the nation's foreign trade deficit.[88]

One of the largest money-laundering operation ever uncovered took place in 1989. U.S. banks were used to ship $1 billion a year to cocaine traffickers. The drug profits were disguised as stemming from phony front businesses (wholesale gold and jewelry) run largely out of Los Angeles. Another money-laundering investigation in 1990, Operation Polar Cap, resulted in the freezing of hundreds of bank accounts in 173 American banks, more than half of which were in New York and Florida. The accounts contained some $400 million in Colombian drug profits. Other sources of laundered money are storefront check-cashing and money-transmitting services, most of which are unlicensed and run by newly arrived or illegal immigrants. Most of these are in states with only a few regulators, who are thus unable to keep up with the growth of such businesses. This is especially true of Florida, Texas, New York, and California. Each year such operations take billions in cash from drug dealers and send it overseas. These storefront operations also defraud honest customers by failing to send their money to requested addressees. Many customers cannot complain because they are either newly arrived immigrants ignorant of the law or illegals.[89]

A number of major U.S. banks have been more than willing to overlook the IRS reporting requirement, sometimes receiving a 1.5% to 2% commission from drug-trafficking depositors for doing so. Other sources of money laundering are investment firms, such as Shearson/American Express and Merrill Lynch, and jewelry wholesalers.

- In the 1980s, the famous Pizza Connection case resulted in the conviction of more than 400 Mafia members in Sicily and the United States on numerous charges, including heroin trafficking. The Pizza Connection cons laundered tens of millions of dollars in cash through a number of New York City banks. The banks then electronically wired the millions of dollars into secret accounts in Swiss banks so that they could not be traced. The Pizza Connection traffickers also deposited $5 million in cash with the Merrill Lynch brokerage firm in $5, $10, and $20 bills over a 6-week period. Merrill Lynch not only accepted these dubious deposits, but it also provided the couriers transporting the money with extra security. The same couriers also laundered $13.5 million through accounts at the E. F. Hutton & Co. investment firm, which also provided security for them.
- The CIA and the Mafia played an important role in establishing the World Finance Corporation. This Florida company laundered drug money and supported terrorist activities in the early 1970s.
- In 2000, it was reported that the major multinational tobacco corporations hired global organized crime syndicates in North and South America, Asia, and elsewhere to sell cigarettes on the black market in the 1990s. Today it is estimated that one in every three cigarettes is sold on the black market in order to avoid taxation. Further, in exchange for their cooperation in this scheme, the tobacco firms agreed to launder money for the Latin American cocaine cartels.[90]

Organized crime in the 1990s became an active force on Wall Street, forming partnerships with investment houses and other financial institutions for illegal purposes. The American Mafia has established a network of stock promoters, securities dealers, and the all-important "boiler rooms" that sell stocks nationwide through hard-sell cold calling.

- Four Mafia families, as well as elements of the Russian Mafiya, directly own or control perhaps two dozen brokerage firms that make markets in hundreds of stocks. Other securities dealers and traders are believed to pay extortion money or "tribute" to the Mob as just another cost of doing business on Wall Street.
- Using offshore accounts in the Bahamas and elsewhere, the Mob has engineered lucrative schemes involving low-priced stock under Regulation S of the securities laws. Organized-crime members profit from the run-up in such stocks and also from short-selling the stocks on the way down. They also take advantage of the very wide spreads between the bid and ask prices of the stock issues controlled by their confederates.
- The Mob's activities seem confined almost exclusively to stocks traded in the over-the-counter "bulletin board" and NASDAQ small-cap markets. By contrast, NYSE and American Stock Exchange issues and firms apparently have been free of Mob exploitation.

Wall Street has become so lucrative for the Mob that it is allegedly a major source of income for high-level members of organized crime, few of whom have ever been publicly identified as having ties to Wall Street. Don Abramo, who may well be the most active reputed mobster on Wall Street, has remained completely out of the public eye, even staying active on Wall Street after his recent conviction for tax evasion.

All these endeavors require the cooperation and corruption of corporations, government regulators, and banks. These entities are not pawns in the hands of organized criminal syndicates, but part of its fabric.[91] The illegal drug business, both domestically and internationally, cannot exist without the willing participation of money-laundering banks and corrupt public officials, and these legitimate outlets are a major part of America's crime and drug problems.

## Organized Crime and the Political Elite

In 1975, revelations by the Senate Intelligence Committee disclosed the hiring of organized crime members by the CIA in the 1960s for the express purpose of assassinating Premier Fidel Castro of Cuba.[92] Thus, organized crime (at certain times, at least) has functioned as an instrument of U.S. foreign policy.

Such activities allegedly began during World War II when the underworld figures in control of the New York docks were contacted by navy intelligence officials in order to ensure that German submarines or foreign agents did not infiltrate the area. It was thought that waterfront pimps and prostitutes could act as a sort of counterintelligence corps. The man whose aid was sought for this purpose was Lucky Luciano; he was reportedly very successful in preventing sabotage or any other outbreaks of trouble on the New York docks during the war. Following his arrest and conviction for compulsory prostitution in 1936, Luciano was granted parole and given exile for life in 1954 in exchange for the aid he provided during the war.

Mafiosi assistance was also enlisted in other war-related efforts. Some locals were used by the Allies during the invasion of Sicily in 1943. Vito Genovese, a New York gangster, who had earlier escaped to Italy to avoid a murder charge, became an "unofficial advisor to the American military government."[93] After the war, local mafiosi were installed as mayors in many locations in Sicily because they were antisocialist. And in France in 1950, the CIA recruited a Corsican gangster, Ferri-Pisani, to form an elite terror squad for use on the Marseilles docks. Socialist dockworkers had refused to move shipments of U.S. arms bound for use in Vietnam in support of the French military effort there. Corsican gangsters were also used to assault the picket lines of communist unions in France and to harass union officials. The concession granted these international criminals in exchange for such aid was the privilege of using Marseilles as the center for Corsican heroin traffic. In Pearce's words, "The CIA had helped build the French Connection."[94]

In Cuba, it is known that the dictator Fulgencio Batista allowed Mafia financier Meyer Lansky to set up gambling casinos in Havana in 1933. Following Castro's closing of the casinos in the early 1960s, organized crime figures were recruited by the CIA to aid in assassinating Castro. In Vietnam in the 1960s and early 1970s, organized crime figures cooperated with the CIA in setting up Asia's Golden Triangle, Southeast Asia's center for heroin distribution. This triangle stretches for some 150,000 square miles across northeast Burma, northern Thailand, and northern Laos. The CIA's involvement included transporting opium using its own airline, Air America.[95]

Organized crime has long served as a source of campaign funds for political elites on virtually every level of U.S. politics—local, state, and national.[96]

One of the most famous of these incidents involves John F. Kennedy and the presidential election of 1960. During the primaries a deal was struck between Kennedy's father and New Jersey mobster "Skinny" D'Mato. Votes were purchased by gangsters in West Virginia, who then paid off local sheriffs responsible for the vote counting. Kennedy's opponent, Hubert Humphrey, also tried to bribe local sheriffs to fix the election, but did not have as much money as the Kennedy campaign. During the national election, John Kennedy also funneled moneys to Chicago Mafia boss Sam Giancana via a mistress shared by the two men, Judith Campbell.[97]

Likewise, Lyndon Johnson greatly disliked the Kennedy brothers. In private conversations, he referred to J.F. Kennedy as "Sonny Boy," and described him once as a "little scrawny fellow with rickets." The Kennedys seemed to have little respect for him either, referring to him as "Uncle Cornpone." John Kennedy told Arthur Schlesinger that Johnson was a man who lied all the time and was incapable of truth telling.

By November 1963, Johnson was a man in potential trouble: corrupted by both his ties to organized crime, and his alliances with cronies whose corruption threatened his entire career. His pal Billy Sol Estes had been involved in scandals since 1961 by the swindling of millions of taxpayers' dollars in bogus cotton allotment schemes and subsidies for fictitious machinery grants. Johnson was allegedly implicated with Estes in these swindles. Then there was Johnson's relationship with his personal secretary for 8 years, Bobby Baker. Baker was being investigated for and accused of influence peddling, financial manipulations, and directing a prostitution ring serving the politically powerful in Washington. Baker also had Mafia ties to gangsters in Las Vegas, Chicago, Louisiana, and the Caribbean.

Robert Caro, in a 1981 article, claimed that men had come into LBJ's office for years, handing him envelopes full of cash, even as vice president. One oil company lobbyist testified that he paid Johnson $50,000 in the 3 years that he was Kennedy's vice president. Johnson also allegedly funneled at least $50,000 a year of Carlos Marcello's gambling profits. In return, Johnson helped stop in committee all antiracket legislation that could have harmed Marcello's interests.

At the time of John F. Kennedy's assassination, Attorney General Robert Kennedy reportedly had assembled an inch-thick file on the Marcello–Johnson connection, which he was seriously considering pursuing. If he had charged Johnson, LBJ faced both political ruin and a possible prison term for involvement in the Estes or Baker affair. One European investigative journalist claimed that the Baker scams were the hidden key to the J.F. Kennedy assassination, which had already been planned by others.

Madeleine Brown, Johnson's mistress, recalled a party hosted by Clint Murchison, oil millionaire founder of the Dallas Cowboys, on Thursday evening, November 21, 1963. In attendance were Richard Nixon, J. Edgar Hoover, and Lyndon Johnson. LBJ allegedly told Ms. Brown, "that after tomorrow, the Kennedys would never embarrass him again."

Hours after the Kennedy assassination, all the available evidence, including the weapon, clothing, and the Zapruder film, was either on its way to Washington or under the control of the FBI or the Secret Service. Within 3 days of the murder, the presidential limousine was removed to a Cincinnati workshop where its rebuilding destroyed important evidence, including two unexplained marks, a dent in the chrome windshield, and a bullet mark on the windscreen. The person who had the power to issue such orders was the new president, Lyndon Johnson.[98]

The Reagan administration also had important relationships with organized crime figures. These include

- The endorsement of the Teamsters Union in the 1980 election.
- The friendship of Reagan's close friend and campaign manager Senator Paul Laxalt with Allen Dorfman, the man responsible for the supervision of the Teamster's Central States Pension Fund, which the American Mafia used as their personal loan source. Laxalt was also close to Moe Dalitz, a leading Las Vegas mobster, who contributed $50,000 to Laxalt's first senatorial campaign.
- Teamster Union president Jackie Presser was appointed as a senior economic adviser of his presidential transition team. His appointment was arranged by Senator Laxalt. Reagan also met with another Teamster president, Roy Williams, in 1980, the day after Williams had taken the Fifth Amendment in front of a Senate committee concerning his ties to organized crime.
- Another union with longtime organized crime connections is the International Longshoreman's Association. Reagan was the first president ever to deliver a speech to the association, despite the fact that over 30 of its officials had been convicted of criminal charges.
- Reagan appointed as secretary of labor Raymond Donovan, despite the fact that an FBI investigation of Donovan's background revealed both business and social ties with Mafia figures and Donovan's participation in fraud schemes with a leading New Jersey organized crime figure.

- Other Reagan administration officials with known associations included national security adviser Richard V. Allen, CIA director William Casey, deputy CIA director Max Hugel, as well as Reagan's personal friends Walter Annenberg and Frank Sinatra.

As a result of all these ties, the Mafia became very influential in the Reagan administration:

- Investigations of Mob activities in Las Vegas were curtailed and a political corruption hotline closed down thanks to Senator Laxalt.
- During Donovan's tenure as labor secretary, union official prosecutions declined by 30%.
- A 33% cutback in FBI investigation into traditional Mafia rackets was imposed.
- Two federal taxes on gambling were repealed.
- Reagan commuted the sentences of 10 white-collar criminals, all with Mafia ties.[99]

At the national level, opposing organized crime factions appear to be linked to opposing political parties. For example, following the presidential election in 1968, the Nixon administration undertook a campaign against organized crime. This campaign was, in fact, directed at those elements of organized crime most closely allied with Nixon's Democratic opponents, especially Meyer Lansky. Under pressure from investigations by the FBI and IRS, Lansky sold his Las Vegas casino interests to Howard Hughes and his Miami-based bank interest to Nixon confidant Bebe Rebozo. In the meantime, Teamsters Union leaders made an arrangement with the Nixon White House that resulted in clemency for jailed Teamsters chief Jimmy Hoffa in return for a campaign contribution. Also, Nixon was promised the availability of Teamsters pension funds should hush money be needed to silence the Watergate burglars.

The final attack on the Lansky faction of organized crime was a result of the Nixon administration's war on drugs. The Republicans tried to close off Lansky's heroin sources by pressuring the Turkish government to enforce laws against growing opium. Between 1969 and 1973, the amount of opium brought from Turkey into the United States fell by 50%. Efforts against Lansky's Latin American opium suppliers were also instituted.

By the early 1970s, Southeast Asia's Golden Triangle had become a major new heroin source for the U.S. organized crime syndicate of Santos Trafficante Jr., a Lansky rival in the heroin trade. Trafficante had ties to both the Nixon White House and the Laotian Chiu Chow syndicate, a major opium source in Southeast Asia and the owner of the Laotian Pepsi Cola Company, whose U.S. counterpart had longtime ties to the Nixon organization.[100]

There is ample evidence now of links between traditional Italian–Sicilian organized crime and international drug smugglers from Colombia and Mexico, who import cocaine and heroin. Nontraditional organized crime groups in the United States, including the Japanese Yakuza, the Hell's Angels motorcycle gang, Jamaican and Chinese American vice groups, and many street gangs made up of numerous minority groups, also have ties to the Mafia through illegal drug trade, prostitution, and gambling.[101] (These links, including alliances with terrorists, are further explored in Chapter 9.)

These illustrations have led some criminologists to conclude that organized crime has served and continues to serve the domestic and foreign political goals of the U.S. political and economic elites. Finally, it is important to understand that, despite recent convictions of aging godfathers in New York and Sicily, organized crime is in key respects stronger than ever. Virtually all the illegal gambling, arms, and drug trade remain intact.[102]

Certainly, illegal drug trafficking has proved much more intractable than nearly anyone had believed. A chief reason for the tenacity of the drug trade is the corruption of and cooperation with legitimate political and at times economic elites by organized criminal syndicates, which are now an integral portion of the higher immorality.

## The Vatican Bank Scandal

The man known as "God's banker," and his links to a secret organization, which included former Nazi war criminals, P-2, and the Masons, continues to haunt the Vatican and its various allies since it was revealed in 1975. The scandal is immensely complex and was even tangential to the plot of *The Godfather Part III*. The details constitute the essence of scandals of the postmodern era: assassinations, money laundering, narcotics trafficking, secret Swiss bank accounts, and a complex web of corruption involving the Catholic Church, American and European intelligence agencies, business executives, politicians, and mafiosi. The scandal almost defies brief summation. Below is one such attempt:[103]

1. Pope John Paul I died only 33 days following his election as pope (August 26, 1978–September 28, 1978), one of the shortest reigns in papal history. The official cause of death was a heart attack, but there was much confusion regarding the details of this sudden death, and many believe the pope was murdered by his enemies. The leading theory was that John Paul I died from an overdose of digitalis, a drug that members of the secret P-2 organization carry with them as a matter of course.

2. John Paul I strongly favored ecumenism and a reduction of church wealth. He was determined to reverse the church's position on contraception, clean up the Vatican bank, and dismiss many cardinals who were Masons and members of the secret P-2 Lodge. He was about to make a series of dismissals and new appointments and remove those accused of financial and other misdeeds. All this has been construed as a motive for his murder.

3. The P-2 Lodge was founded in 1877 and was known as Propaganda Due (P-2). It became a secret lodge in 1970 to recruit right-wing members to curb the rise of communism in Italy. When P-2 became embroiled in a financial scandal, its offices were inspected by Italy's police and its membership lists were found. It was discovered that the organization had links to the Italian intelligence ministries, senior military staff, and even top figures in the nation's media. Forty-eight members of the Italian parliament were secret members, along with four cabinet ministers. The organization was soon officially disbanded, but it continued to operate secretly. P-2 continues operating within Vatican circles today. P-2 members also include intelligence agents, including representatives of the CIA.

4. The Vatican Bank (or Istituto per le Opere di Religione, IOR), was established in the 19th century and was personally owned and operated by the reigning pope. IOR made loans for religious projects all over the world. The bank's history involved exploiting its status, engaging in risky speculation, and scandals that included money laundering. Money was invested with Roberto Calvi, head of the elite Banco Ambrosiano, at the time the largest privately owned financial institution in Italy (also controlled by the Vatican). Calvi was eventually convicted for currency fraud in 1981 (more than $1.3 billion was missing from bank funds). Later, the money was traced to accounts owned by the Vatican. Using a false passport, Calvi fled to England, where he was found dead, hanging from a bridge in London in June 1982. His corpse was found dangling from a rope, with 14 pounds of brick and stone in his pockets, and his hands tied behind his back, a fact that was ignored by the coroner who pronounced the affair a simple suicide. Calvi's family insisted on a second inquest. The second inquest, begun in 1998, but not concluded until 2002, found that Calvi had been murdered.[104] In October 2005, five alleged members of the Italian Mafia went on trial in Italy for the murder of Roberto Calvi. One of them, Pippo Calo, a man known as "the Mafia's cashier," is already serving a life term in jail for unrelated Mafia crimes.[105]

5. Another participant in the scandal was Michele Sindona, P-2 member, CIA operative, and adviser to Pope Paul VI. Sindona was poisoned in 1986 in his prison cell. The massive fraud was also linked to the Masons, the Mafia, arms dealers, and moneys funneled through the CIA to support Solidarity in Poland. Sindona was a prominent insider in the hierarchy of the Illinois Republican Party. He also worked with the Inzerillo crime family (relatives of New York's Gambino family) and invested Mafia funds in various banks and holding companies, including the Liechtenstein-based Fasco, linked to the Banca Privata Finanziaria, an entity founded in 1930 by a fascist ideologue.

6. In September 1998, Italian and French police swept into Cannes and arrested Licio Gelli, a fugitive since May, and called "the Puppet Master"

for his role in numerous bizarre scandals and postwar covert operations. Gelli was involved in secret dealings dating from World War II; many of these events involved the Vatican. Some involved the role played by the Holy See in operating the "ratline," an expatriation movement for Nazis and other war criminals. Others included a financial deal linking the papacy with illegal Mafia drug money and Nazi confiscated funds flowing through the IOR. Gelli was also a high-ranking Italian intelligence agent, and a founder of P-2. What Gelli brought with him to P-2 were more than 150 secret dossiers on high-ranking politicians, business executives, and other powerful Italians. Calvi and his bank were also involved with Gelli's P-2. Gelli had been in the fascist Black Shirts Battalion in the Spanish civil war wherein the church-backed General Franco. During World War II he served as a key liaison officer to the elite German SS Division headed by Nazi henchman Hermann Göring. In the cold war era, Gelli spied for Italy, Britain, and by some accounts the Soviet KGB.

7. After World War II, the Vatican used its resources in supplying passports, money, and other support for church-run "ratlines." Many Nazis and their supporters were transported out of Europe to safer havens in the Middle East, Britain, Canada, Australia, New Zealand, the United States, and South America. Nazi organizations like ODESSA (Organization of Former Officers of the SS) and "The Spider" took advantage of this service, and by some accounts the Vatican ratline provided support to as many as 30,000 Nazis. Among those receiving Vatican help were former Gestapo operatives Klaus Barbie, Adolph Eichman, Dr. Joseph Mengele (the "White Angel" or "Angel of Death" of the Auschwitz death camp), Gustav Wagner, commandant of Soirbibor concentration camp, and Franz Stangl of the Treblinka camp. Members of the Waffen SS "Galician Division" were resettled as well. Through its IOR, the Vatican reportedly laundered $100 million in Nazi-imposed church taxes, as well as money for the escaped Nazis confiscated from Jews and other victims of Nazi madness in wartime Yugoslavia. Meanwhile, the IOR became a postwar haven for "offshore" funds deposited by corporations, organized crime, intelligence services, and other groups.

8. Both Calvi's Banco Ambrosiano and the Vatican's Istituto per le Opere di Religione (IOR) engaged in money laundering. An American bishop, Paul Marcinkus, head of the IOR, laundered money for a CIA covert operation, "Stay Behind," which gave money to Italian prime minister Silvio Berlusconi, who himself laundered money for organized crime figures.

9. Calvi began skimming from the funds flowing through his bank to prop up bad loans, and began laundering drug money for the Mafia. He may also have sought financial help from a secret Catholic group, Opus Dei ("God's Work"), and traveled to London to meet with the group's treasurer. But Calvi had made too many enemies, and his

skimming operation threatened to become a major scandal. In 1992, a Mafia defector claimed that Calvi had been murdered on orders from a British drug dealer, Franceso DiCarlo. The Reagan administration paid $300 million in secret CIA discretionary funds to cover the Vatican bank's debts.

10. In 1998, court documents were made public that traced the money trail from the Corleone Mafia family to investments in the Vatican bank. There was also a report that a Vatican finance representative attended the meeting where the conspiracy to murder Calvi was discussed.

11. In November 1999, Ukrainian Holocaust survivors, later joined by Serb and Jewish plaintiffs, filed a class action lawsuit against the Vatican's IOR, alleging Vatican complicity in laundering of Nazi deposits including the proceeds from several Croatian concentration camps where 500,000 Serbs were murdered between 1941 and 1945. The suit was overturned in 2002 but was successfully appealed and reopened in March 2004. In October, 2010, attorney Jonathan Levy asked the European Commission to investigate the Vatican's complicity in the depositing of Jewish assets in the IOR, the acronym for the Italian Istituto per le Opere di Religione, known as the Vatican Bank, during World War II's Serbian Holocaust.

Jonathan Levy, one of the plaintiffs' counsels, suggests the Vatican is particularly vulnerable to legal process since it has only enjoyed U.S. recognition since 1983 as a sovereign entity. Levy said, "Many of the Vatican's activities fall outside the traditional actions of a state, particularly when it comes to financing the Church." There has also been a massive pedophilia scandal cover-up stemming from 1962 Vatican instructions involving protecting guilty priests, a violation of international law as well as the United Nations Convention on the Rights of the Child, to which the Vatican is a signatory.

# Conclusion

This chapter has discussed a series of acts that involve the exercise of elite power. C. Wright Mills coined the term *higher immorality* to denote what he felt was systematic corruption among the U.S. economic and political elite. The features of the higher immorality discussed are unique in that most of the acts are not against the law. Indeed, certain types of executive compensation, including expense accounts and stock options, corporate income taxes, and government subsidies to businesses and wealthy individuals, represent special favors that elites have secured for themselves by the passage of special legislation and are therefore perfectly legal. But what is legal is not necessarily moral or just.

The consequences of corporate tax loopholes are serious. First, such privilege creates cynicism among the majority of taxpayers, who are very much aware that the nation's tax laws favor the rich and powerful. Second, special loopholes for the wealthy create larger government deficits and increase inflation by billions of dollars per year. Third, government subsidies, which go largely to big businesses, violate the basic principles of free enterprise. Why, for example, should Lockheed and Chrysler be allowed loan guarantees to ensure that they will remain in business while only about 1 in 10 of the new businesses begun in this country survives more than 5 years on average?[106]

We also discussed how political and economic elites attempted to convince the public of the reality of the energy crisis of the 1970s. Yet, when one looks at the facts, as well as at who profited from this so-called crisis, such reality becomes suspect. The energy crisis clearly resulted in huge increases in oil company profits, elimination of competition from independent oil dealers, and fuel bill increases for the billions for consumers serviced by multinational oil companies. Even the government's own studies indicated that the energy crisis of 1973–1974 was due to the oil companies' anticompetitive practices, not to a genuine shortage of crude oil. Such manipulation by elites, involving the creation of favorable media images of their activities and the suppression of important facts, is not illegal unless lied about under oath. Yet how many people consider such activities moral, ethical, or just?

Finally, we described the long history of goods and services provided to political and economic elites by members of organized criminal syndicates. Members of Mafia families have suppressed labor unions, lower-class ghetto dwellers, and anticapitalist political movements; provided capital for certain business ventures; and, on numerous occasions, aided political elites in the execution of U.S. foreign and military policy. In return for such services and capital, certain elites have allowed the activities of organized criminal syndicates to grow and prosper. This, in turn, has contributed to the flourishing of the drug trade in many cities, as well as the corruption of politicians on all levels by organized U.S. crime members (see Chapter 6). The use of capital from illegal businesses is now against the law. And the CIA suffered no little embarrassment when it was revealed that Mafia members had been recruited to assassinate Fidel Castro. Thus, the use of organized criminal syndicates to further the goals of economic and political elites contributes to criminal activity at all levels of U.S. society and occasionally results in scandal for elites. This contributes further to the decline of public confidence in elite rule.

While many of the activities that constitute the higher immorality are not illegal, they are widely regarded as unethical and often possess serious consequences for nonelites. Our discussion tends to confirm Mills's thesis that the higher immorality is an institutionalized feature of the elite power in the United States. Certainly, our discussion of the S&L scandal demonstrated that all the behaviors described in this chapter are still central to the deviance of the power elite.

# CRITICAL THINKING EXERCISE 2.1
## The Higher Immorality

Look up the categories having to do with corporate crime in the latest complete *New York Times Index* or the *Wall Street Journal Index*.
These categories include the following:

1. Antitrust violations
2. Pollution law violations
3. False advertising
4. Fraud
5. Sexual harassment

Do you notice any patterns with respect to which industries have the most violations? Many violations take place in the petroleum, automobile, and drug industries. Do these firms serve as models of corporate behavior for others? Were any specific corporations involved in more than one violation?

# ENDNOTES

1. Wright Mills, C. (1963). A diagnosis of our moral uneasiness. In I. H. Horowitz (ed.). *Power, politics, and people* (p. 331). New York: Ballantine.
2. Kreisberg, B. (1975). *Crime and privilege* (p. 4). Englewood Cliffs, NJ: Prentice Hall. For a brief historical view of the higher immorality and corporate crime, see also Balkan, S., et al. (1980). *Crime and deviance in America* (pp. 182–184). Belmont, CA: Wadsworth.
3. Wright Mills, C. (1963). Plain talk on fancy sex. In I. H. Horowitz (ed.). *Power, politics, and people* (pp. 324–329). New York: Ballantine. For remarks by some expense account girls themselves, see Ray, E. I. (1976). *The Washington fringe benefit*. New York: Dell. The service Ray performed while on the payroll of Congressman Wayne Hayes touched off a scandal in Washington that resulted in Hayes leaving Congress. Ray's story closely parallels Mills's description of the goals and means of the expense account girl. An anonymous article, Landis, J. (1980). The corporation prostitute. In, *Sociology: Concepts and characteristics* (4th ed., pp. 354–359). Belmont, CA: Wadsworth, claims that some corporations hire prostitutes on a permanent basis for help in closing a variety of deals, including bidding on factory sites, mergers with other companies, political lobbying, undercutting competitors, gathering stockholder proxy votes, and securing oil leases (ibid., 355).
4. The following is excerpted from G. William Domhoff. "Who Rules America?," http://sociology.ucsc.edu/whorulesamerica/April, 2010, with permission of the author.
5. http.Senate.Sanders.Gov. (28 November 2010).
6. See also Wright, E. O. & Rogers, J. (2011). *American society: How it really works*. New York: W.W. Norton; Chapter 12.
7. Huffington, A. (2010). *Third world nation*. New York: Crown, 2010; Introduction.
8. See also Gross, M. (2009). *National suicide* (pp. 278–286). New York: Berkley.
9. See also http://en.wikipedia.org/wiki/Distribution_of_wealth (November, 2010).
10. See Moore, M. (2010). *Capitalism: A love story*. Warner Brothers, and Michael Moore.com.
11. For other corporate tricks see Markopolos, H. (2010). *No one would listen* (pp. 287–328). Hoboken, NJ: Wiley.
12. See also http://www.aflcio.org/corporatewatch/paywatch/(2010).

13. See Hagan, F., & Simon, D. R. *Crimes of the Bush era*, presented at the 1993 meeting of the American Society of Crim inology, Phoenix, Arizona.

14. Mills. *A diagnosis of our moral uneasiness* (p. 334).

15. Lynne Walker, S. (1991). Pickets protest GenDyn bonuses. *San Diego Union*, May 30.

16. Phillips, P., & Project Censored. (2000). *Censored 2000: The year's top 25 stories* (p. 115). New York: Seven Stories.

17. *2005 trends in CEO pay.* http://www.aflcio.org/corporatewatch/paywatch/pay/index.cfm

18. *The perfect payday. Wall Street Journal*, March 18, 2006.

19. http://www.aflcio.org/corporatewatch/paywatch/pay/index.cfm.

20. http://thinkprogress.org/2005/08/30/average-ceo-makes-430-times/.

21. Bok, D. (1993). *The cost of talent: How executives and professionals are paid and how it affects America* ( New York: Free Press).

22. Blumberg, P. (Spring 1978). Another day, another $3,000: Executive rip-off in corporate America. *Dissent*, 2, 159.

23. See, for example, Derber, C. (1992). *Money, murder, and the American dream: Winding from Wall Street to Main Street* (pp. 97–99). Boston: Faber & Faber; Stein, C. (December 14, 1993). What Bok really thinks. *Boston Globe*, 78; and Kanter, D., & Mirvis, P. (1989). *The cynical Americans* (pp. 27–40). San Francisco: Jossey-Bass.

24. See, for example, Lundberg, F. (1968). *The rich and the super-rich* (pp. 433–435). New York: Bantam.

25. Tussing, D. (January/February 1974). The dual welfare system. *Society*, 2, 50–58.

26. Zepezauer, M., & Naiman, A. (1996). *Take the rich off welfare* (p. 6). Tucson, AZ: Odionian.

27. Ibid., 4–5.

28. Captain Ed. (May 24, 2006). *Trackback pings*. http://www.captainsquartersblog.com/mt/mt-cqtb.cgi/7050; http://portland.indymedia.org/en/2005/07/320707 .shtml, *Portland Independent* (July 2, 2005); http://www.nationalreview.com/kudlow/200601131453.asp (January 13, 2006).

29. *USA Today*, July 2, 1985, 5-B. See also Rodgers, H. (Spring 1978). Welfare policies for the rich. *Dissent*, 2, 141; Hart, G. The economy is decaying: The free lunch is over. *New York Times*, April 21, 1975; and Jackson, J. (1987). Courage of conviction: The call of conscience. In R. Bellah et al. (ed.). *Individualism and commitment in American life* (p. 363). New York: Harper & Row.

30. See Bartlett, D., & Steele, J. *America: Who really pays the taxes* (p. 24). New York: Touchstone/Simon & Schuster, 1994.

31. For valuable discussions on these issues, see Stern, P. (1973). *The rape of the taxpayer* (pp. 214, 232). New York: Random House; and Ackerman, F. (1982). *Reaganomics: Rhetoric vs. reality* (pp. 50–54). Boston: South End Press.

32. Bartlett and Steele, 140–49. See Domhoff, G. W. (April, 2010). *Who RULES America?*. http://sociology.ucsc.edu/whorulesamerica/.

33. *The foundation directory* (11th ed.). New York: The Foundation Center, 1987, xiv.

34. Lundberg, 292.

35. Examples cited in Demaris, O. (1974). New York: Harper's Magazine Press, pp. 303–304.

36. Examples cited in ibid. (pp. 317–318).

37. Katznelson, I., & Kesselman, M. (1975). *The politics of power* (p. 142). New York: Harcourt, Brace, Jovanovich.

38. Wright Mills, C. (1963) "A Diagnosis of Our Moral Uneasiness," in Power, Politics, and People, I. H. Horowitz (ed.) (p. 338). New York: Ballantine, 1963.

39. Wright Mills, C. (ed.), (1960). *Images of man* (pp. 16–17). New York: Braziller.

40. For a good overview of important unreported stories, see Project Censored's annual list of important underreported and unreported stories at http://www.projectcensored.org/publications/index.htm; http://www.alternet.org/story/16274/.

41.  Scheer, Christopher (2003) "Ten Appalling Lies We Told about Iraq," *AlterNet* http://www.alternet.org/story/16247/.
42.  "The Rachel Maddow Show," MSNBC (14 July 2011).
43.  The Associated Press, (7/15/2011).
44.  Bernstein, Carl, "Is Phone-Hacking Scandal Murdoch's Watergate?," *Newsweek* (11 July 2011).
45.  Abbas, M., "Murdoch Apologizes for Hacking Scandal," *Reuters* (16 July 2011).
46.  Ibid
47.  Mills, C. W. (Ed.) (1960) *Images of Man* (New York: Braziller):16.
48.  Mills. *A diagnosis of our moral uneasiness* (pp. 335–336).
49.  Vancise, J. G. (1979). *The Federal antitrust laws* (3rd rev. ed., p. 7). Washington, DC: American Enterprise Institute.
50.  Bequai, A. (1978). *White collar crime: A 20th century crisis* (p. 96). Lexington, MA: D. C. Heath.
51.  Ibid., 100–101.
52.  Sherrill, R. (November 28, 1988). White-collar thuggery. *Nation*, 573.
53.  *Newsweek*, January 27, 1986, 46.
54.  See *San Francisco Chronicle*, July 17, 1994, C-1, C-4.
55.  Quoted in Lundberg (p. 137).
56.  Sutherland, E. Crime of corporations. In G. Geis & R. F. Meier (eds.). *White-collar crime* (rev. ed., p. 73) New York: Free Press, 1977.
57.  Clinard, M. B. (1979). *Illegal corporate behavior* (p. 108). Washington, DC: Law Enforcement Assistance Administration.
58.  McCormick, A. E. (October 1977). Rule enforcement and moral indignation: Some observations on antitrust convictions upon the societal reaction process. *Social Problems*, 25, 34.
59.  Bequai (pp. 148–150).
60.  National Council on Crime and Delinquency (March 26, 1979). *Criminal Justice News Letter*, 7, 2.
61.  Cited in Rogow, A. (1975). *The dying of the light* (p. 89). New York: Putnam.
62.  Sherrill. *White-collar thuggery* The Nation (28 November 1988): (p. 573).
63.  Clinard, M., & Quinney, R. (1973). *Criminal behavior systems: A typology* (2nd ed.). New York: Holt, Rinehart and Winston.
64.  Cited in Rogow. (p. 89).
65.  Smith, R. (1970). The incredible electrical conspiracy. In M. Wolfgang et al. (eds.). *The sociology of crime and delinquency* (p. 363). New York: Wiley.
66.  Thio, A. (1988). *Deviant behavior* (p. 352). Boston: Houghton Mifflin.
67.  Geis, G. (1974). Upper world crime. In A. S. Blumberg (ed.). *Current perspectives on criminal behavior* (pp. 132–133). New York: Knopf.
68.  Ibid. (p. 116).
69.  Ianni, F. A. J., & Ianni, F. (Eds.), (1976). *The crime society: Organized crime and corruption in America*. New York: New American Library, xvi.
70.  Clinard & Quinney (p. 225).
71.  See McIntosh, M. (1973). The growth of racketeering. *Economy and Society*, 2, 63, 64; Johnson, N. (2010). *Boardwalk empire* (pp. 99–100). Melford, NJ: Plexus.
72.  The items in this section are from Pearce, F. (1976). *Crimes of the powerful* (p. 140). London: Pluto Press.
73.  McIntosh. (p. 64).
74.  See Tabor, M. (1971). The plague: Capitalism and dope genocide. In R. Perrucci & M. Pilisuk (eds.). *The triple revolution emerging* (pp. 241–249). Boston: Little, Brown.
75.  Spitzer, S. (February 1975). Toward a Marxian theory of deviance. *Social Problems*, 22, 649.
76.  For details, see *New York Times*, January 30, 1975, 1; March 21, 1975, 41; August 7, 1975, 38; and November 4, 1975, 38.

77. King, R. (1975). Gambling and crime. In L. J. Kaplan & D. Kessler (eds.). *An economic analysis of crime* (p. 40). Springfield, IL: Charles C. Thomas.

78. Quinney, R. (1975). *Criminology: Analysis and critique of crime in America.* (p. 145) Boston: Little, Brown.

79. Behar, R. (September 3, 1990). The underworld is their oyster. *Time,* 54–57.

80. See Reid, E. (1969). *The grim reapers* (pp. 138–39). New York: Bantam; and Kohn, H. (May 20, 1976). The Nixon–Hughes–Lansky connection. *Rolling Stone,* 41–50, 77–78.

81. See Brandt, D. (January–March 1995). As criminal capitalism replaces communism: Organized crime threatens the new world order. *NameBase NewsLine,* 8.

82. Office of International Criminal Justice. (Winter 1996). *Bulletin,* 1.

83. Viviano, F. (June–July 1995). The empire of crime. *Mother Jones,* 17ff.

84. Senator Kerry, J. (1997). *The new war* (p. 161). New York: Simon & Schuster.

85. Viviano. (p. 17ff).

86. Kerry. (p. 160).

87. Ibid. (p. 73).

88. Harris, L. (1991). *The heroin epidemic* (pp. 52–53). New York: Macmillan.

89. Ibid. (pp. 61–62).

90. *The Toronto Globe and Mail,* February 10, 2000.

91. Kappeler et al., (1993). *The mythology of crime & criminal justice* (2nd ed., p. 85). Prospect Heights, IL: Waveland.

92. See Dolbeare, K., & Edelman, M. (1977). *American politics* (3rd ed., pp. 85–89) Lexington, MA: D. C. Health, for Senate Intelligence Committee Report excerpts on this and other CIA assassination plots.

93. Pearce (p. 149).

94. Ibid. (p. 150).

95. Ibid. (p. 151).

96. For a detailed account of organized crime as a source of political campaign contributions, see Chambliss, W. (1978). *On the take: From petty crooks to presidents* (pp. 150–168). Bloomington: Indiana University Press.

97. Simon, D. (2004). *Tony Soprano's America: The criminal side of the American Dream* (pp. 38–39). New York: Westview; *The Rat Pack* (pt. 4). New York: Arts and Entertainment Network, 1999.

98. Court TV Crime Library, http://www.crimelibrary.com/terrorists_spies/assassins/.

99. See Lyman, M. D., & Potter, G. W. (2004). *Organized crime* (3rd ed., pp. 450–464). Upper Saddle River, NJ: Prentice-Hall; Moldea, D. (1986). *Dark victory: Ronald Reagan, MCA and the mob* (pp. 260; 346–47). New York: Viking.

100. For details, see Chambliss; and Block, A., & Chambliss, W. (1981). *Organizing crime* (pp. 34–37). New York: Elsevier.

101. See the *President's Commission on Organized Crime Task Force Report.* Washington, DC: Government Printing Office, 1987, for a discussion of the new Mafia–drug connection.

102. For confirmation of continuing Mafia strength, see *New York Times,* October 9, 1988, 1; and Simon, *Tony Sopraro's America* (pp. 67–76).

103. The following discussion is based on Yallop, D. (1984). *In God's name: An investigation into the murder of Pope John Paul I* (pp. 4, 106–56). New York: Bantam, and http://www.bloomberg.com/news/2010-10-26/holocaust-survivors-ask-eu-commission-to-probe-vatican-bank-over-nazi-loot.html

104. http://www.atheists.org/catalogue/special.html.

105. *BBC World News.* (October 6, 2005). http://news.bbc.co.uk/1/hi/world/europe/4313960.stm

106. See Maccoby, M., & Terzi, K. A. (1974). Character and work in America. In P. Brenner et al. (ed.). *Exploring contradictions: Political economy in the corporate state* (p. 128). New York: McKay/Longman.

# 3   Corporate Deviance: Monopoly, Manipulation, and Fraud

## Costs of Corporate Crime

Sociologist Stanton Wheeler, in his presidential address to the 1975 annual meeting of the Society for the Study of Social Problems, chided his colleagues for their neglect of one particular area of criminality: "the patterns of illegal activity that lie at the core of large-scale corporate, industrial society."[1] The magnitude of this omission was revealed in 1978 by the first comprehensive investigation of corporate crime. Sociologist Marshall Clinard and his associates gathered data on the illegal actions of the 582 largest publicly owned corporations in the United States. Among their findings were that, during a 24-month period, (1) 60% of these corporations had a legal action instituted against them by a federal agency for criminal activity; (2) of those corporations having had at least one violation, the average number of violations was 4.2, with one corporation being formally accused by the government on 62 occasions; and (3) almost one-half of the violations occurred in the oil refining, automobile, and drug industries (a rate 300% greater than their size in the sample indicated).[2]

According to a 2003 estimate, corporate crime, which includes antitrust, advertising law, and pollution law violations, costs American consumers an estimated *$3 trillion. The amount taken in all bank robberies that year was 6,000 times less.* This figure is 40 times more than estimated losses from street crime.[3] Studies of punishment in corporate crime cases reveal that only about 2% of corporate crime cases result in imprisonment.

## Penalties for Corporate Crime

Just as the Bank of New York and other multinational banks have been able to escape penalties for money laundering (see Chapter 2), so it is that many large corporations escape punishment for corporate crime on a regular basis.

- Antitrust cases are a great rarity in the United States.[4] However, a 1998 Benchmark survey of 1,694 large- and medium-sized American firms found that 27% of the respondents indicated that their organization knowingly broke the law "at least sometimes." In addition, a 1997 survey by the Human Resource Management/Ethics Resource Center found that 61% of 747 human resource professionals felt that their firms did not provide ethics training, and 47% felt that there was at least some pressure to compromise the organization's ethics code to achieve business goals.[5]

- Small, privately held businesses account for more than 95% of all of the corporate convictions each year.[6]
- In recent years there has emerged a strange pattern concerning corporate punishment. Corporations now take out numerous insurance policies that cover everything from fraud by rogue traders to the costs of violating environmental laws. The risk of loss due to violating the law has now effectively been shifted to an insurance company, assuming that no prison sentence is handed down when a corporation is caught. Prison sentences are extremely rare in corporate crime cases, and the average prison sentence from 1996 through 1998 has been between 2.4 and 6 months.[7] There are more prosecutions of corporate fraud cases now due to the corporate scandals of 2002–2003.

A U.S. Department of Justice study found that 80% of the penalties levied against corporate criminals were $5,000 or less.[8]

- "95 percent of Americans believe that U.S. corporations should have more than one purpose (making money). They also owe something to their workers and the communities in which they operate, and they should sometimes sacrifice some profit for the sake of making things better for their workers and communities.
- More than 70 percent of both political parties' contributions now come from corporations.
- 71 percent of Americans believe that business has gained too much power over too many aspects of American life.
- 72 percent of Americans believe business has benefited more than consumers from deregulation."[9]

In 1890, when the Sherman Act was passed, the violation was a misdemeanor subject to up to 1 year in prison and a $5,000 fine (raised to $50,000 in 1955). In 1974, violation of the Sherman Act became a felony, subject to 1 to 3 years imprisonment and a maximum fine of $100,000 for individuals and $1 million for corporations. The sentencing guidelines set sentences at 18 months in 1977, and the individual fine was increased to $250,000 in 1984. In 1990, the maximum fine became $350,000 for individuals and $10 million for corporations.

In 1999, the Antitrust Division of the U.S. Justice Department proposed that the maximum Sherman Act fine be raised to $350,000 for individuals (or twice the gain from the crime or twice the victim loss), up to

3 years' imprisonment, and a maximum corporate fine of $100 million. Most global antitrust conspiracies greatly exceed the 1997 $10 million fine amount.[10]

- A 1990 study by Amitai Etzioni found that between 1975 and 1984, 62% of the Fortune 500 companies were involved in one or more incidents of corrupt behavior (bribery, price-fixing, tax fraud, or violations of environmental regulations).[11]
- A *Multinational Monitor* study in 1992 of the 25 largest Fortune 500 corporations' activities between 1977 and 1990 found that all the corporations were either found guilty of criminal behavior or fined and required to make payment for civil violations.[12]

The fact that so few studies have been done on corporate crime rates speaks volumes concerning the way powerful corporate interests have been able to define the American crime problems as a "street" (i.e., lower-class) problem. The neglected subject of corporate deviance is the focus of this chapter, as well as the next. Specifically, this chapter is devoted to five areas of corporate deviance: the problems generated by (1) monopoly, (2) price-fixing, (3) price gouging, (4) deceptive advertising, and (5) fraud.

## Monopolies

As noted in Chapter 1, the United States has moved from competitive capitalism to a stage of monopoly capitalism. Karl Marx, well over 100 years ago, correctly predicted this current stage.[13] Free enterprise, he argued, would result in some firms becoming bigger and bigger as they eliminated their opposition or absorbed smaller competing firms. The ultimate result of this process would be the existence of a monopoly in each of the various sectors of the economy. Monopolies, of course, are antithetical to the free-enterprise system because they determine the price and the quality of products, thus interfering with the balance of supply and demand. This, as we will see, increases the benefits for the few at the expense of the many.

According to a 1982 report, the following industries were dominated by shared monopolies: razors and razor blades (the four largest firms control 99% of the market); light bulbs (91%); cigarettes (90%); electronic calculators (90%); linoleum (90%); clocks and watches (84%); refrigerators (82%); cereals (80%); sugar (67%); and roasted coffee (66%). Four packers sell more than 70% of all beef imported into the United States; only two firms manufacture commercial jets; three wholesalers distribute more than 90% of prescription drugs; and three firms control nearly 80% of the confectionary market.[14]

Shared monopolies raise the costs of products to consumers. For example, in 1980, the Federal Trade Commission (FTC) released the results of an 8-year study that showed that consumers paid more than $1.2 billion in higher prices for ready-to-eat cereals over a 15-year period. The commission alleged that these overcharges of 15% were the direct result of the monopoly in the cereal industry held by three companies: Kellogg, General Mills, and General Foods. In just 1 year, consumers paid $100 million more for cereals than they would have had there been a more competitive market.[15]

The existence of shared monopolies indicates the extent of concentration of U.S. business. The evidence is clear that the assets of U.S. businesses are highly concentrated in the hands of a few giants. The 200 largest, for instance, have increased their share of U.S. industry from 45% in 1945 to 61% in 2001.[16] Two processes account for the superconcentration of assets among a few corporations: (1) growth through competition, where the fittest survive, and (2) growth through mergers. Of the two, the latter is the more significant.

Since the globalization of markets in the early 1990s, the tendency in manufactured goods industries and other commodities and services has been toward more oligopolization. In raw materials three firms control almost 75% of the global market in iron ore. In manufacturing, Owens Illinois controls roughly half the global capacity to supply glass containers. In heavy equipment, General Electric supplies 60% of large gas turbines and 60% of large wind turbines. In processed materials, Corning produces 60% of the glass for flat-screen televisions (TVs). In sneakers, Nike and Adidas control a 60% share of the global market. Oligopoly characterizes global banking, meatpacking, oil refining, and grains.

By 2005:

- The world's top 10 seed companies had increased their control from one-third to one-half of the global seed trade.
- The top 10 biotech firms had increased their share from just over half to nearly three-quarters of world biotech sales.
- The market share of the top 10 pesticide manufacturers rose from 80% to 84%.
- The top 10 pharmaceutical companies control almost 59% of the legal drug market.

In 2004, the global value of corporate mergers was $1.95 trillion—a 40% increase over the $1.38 trillion in 2003.[17]

## The Corporate Frankenstein

Corporate mergers have become identified with a new type of Wall Street crime: insider trading. In a recent study Data Resources examined some

130 stocks, 70% of which ran up sharply in value just before corporate take-overs, "suggesting that insider trading is rampant" among investors.[18] More-over, "mergers, acquisitions and spinoffs totaled $659 billion in 1996, up 27 percent from $519 billion in 1995."[19]

Corporate mergers in the 1990s were devastating to American workers. According to the *New York Times*, more than 43 million jobs have been erased in the United States since 1979. Increasingly the jobs that are disappearing are those of higher-paid, white-collar workers, many at large corporations, women as well as men, many at the peak of their careers.

Nearly three-quarters of all households have had a close encounter with layoffs since 1980 according to a new poll by the *New York Times*. In one-third of all households, a family member has lost a job, and nearly 40% more know a relative, friend, or neighbor who was laid off.

"One in ten adults or about 19 million people, a number matching the adult population of New York and New Jersey combined, acknowledged that a lost job in their household had precipitated a major crisis in their lives, according to the *New York Times* poll."[20]

In 2004–2005, Sony bought MGM for $3 billion, K-Mart purchased Sears for $11 billion, Sprint purchased Nextel for $35 billion, Johnson and Johnson bought Guidant for $25.4 billion, Procter and Gamble acquired Gillette for $55 billion, SBC purchased AT&T for $16 billion, and Verizon acquired MCI for $6.6 billion.[21]

Why do these biggest of businesses feel the urge to merge? The goal of bigness appears to be control. Eugene Rostow has summarized this phenomenon: "The history of corporations is the best evidence of the motivation for their growth. In instance after instance [it] appears to have been the quest for monopoly power, not the technological advances of scale."[22]

The ever-greater concentration of power and resources in a few cor-porations has important negative consequences for U.S. society, exacer-bating many social problems.[23] Foremost is the overpricing that occurs when four or fewer firms control a particular market. A study by the FTC estimated that if the control of the four largest firms in an industry were reduced from 50% to 40% of sales, prices would fall by at least 25%. When industries are so concentrated that four or fewer firms account for 70% of sales, they are found to have profits 50% higher than the less concentrated industries.[24]

The existence of monopolies is costly to consumers in other ways because consumers ultimately bear the costs of advertising and product changes. The irony is that consumers, even though squeezed by monopolies, are forced to finance the continuation of monopolies.

Overpricing leads to lost output because of fewer sales and excess capacity. Lost output is detrimental for three reasons. First, it reduces potential economic activity. Second, lower output substantially reduces tax revenues that, if not reduced because of lower output, could either reduce the tax burden for all or be spent to alleviate social problems. Third, another negative consequence of overcharging by monopolies is inequitable transfer cost. Excessive prices bring excessive profits. These profits then redistribute income from purchasers to the stockholders of the corporations, and 47% of stocks are owned by the wealthiest 0.5% of the population.[25] As a result, a relative handful of stockholders (the already wealthy) reap the dividends. Thus, overcharging redistributes wealth, but in the direction of greater inequalities. As Newfield and Greenfield concluded:

> It is this tiny minority of shareholding Americans that gather in the super-profits generated by the power of big business to stifle competition and manipulate prices without fear of challenge. When we recognize that officers of these superbusinesses often collect more money from their stock-holdings and stock-option privileges than from their salaries, we can see where much of our money goes: not to the community at large, not to wage earners, not into more efficient products, but into the bank accounts, trust funds, and holdings of the richest 1.6 percent of Americans.[26]

Put in a stronger and even more compelling way, two Stanford economists have argued that if there were no monopolies, (1) 2.4% of U.S. families would control not 40% of the total wealth but only 16.6% to 27.5%, and (2) 93.3% of U.S. families would be better off. Only the wealthiest 6.7% would be worse off. According to these estimates, without monopoly, the current maldistribution of wealth in the United States would be as much as 50% less.[27]

Heavily concentrated industries are also sources of inflation. When consumer demand falls, for example, the prices of products in concentrated industries tend to rise. This occurs in such different industries as automobile manufacturing and professional sports. As evidence, economist John Blair studied 16 pairs of products, one group from a concentrated industry (i.e., where a shared monopoly existed), the other group from a more competitive industry (e.g., steel building materials vs. lumber; pig iron vs. steel scraps). During the two recessions of the 1950s, the price of every unconcentrated product fell, whereas the price of 13 of the 16 concentrated products actually rose.[28]

In other words, when a few corporations are large enough to control an industry, they are immune from the rules of a competitive economy. The immediate consequences for consumers are that they will pay artificially high prices. Shared monopolies also cause inflation because they can automatically pass on increased labor costs or increased taxes to the consumer. In competitive industries, however, a corporation may be forced to reduce its profit if it wants to continue to get a share of the market. Moreover, the tendency toward parallel pricing in concentrated industries means that prices only rise. When an industry leader such as General Motors or U.S. Steel announces a price increase of 7%, within a few days, similar increases are announced by their so-called competitors. As Ralph Nader and his associates have noted, "Each firm gladly increases its profit margin by getting the same share of a larger pie. There is no incentive to keep prices down, for then all the other firms will have to come down to that price which means the same share of a smaller pie."[29]

It is impossible to know exactly how much monopolies contribute to inflation. Certainly, the profits generated by lack of competition, rather than efficiency or product superiority, are hidden contributors. The existence of monopolies also has important political consequences. The concentration of economic power undermines the democratic process in two fundamental ways. The first is overt, as the powerful marshal their vast resources to achieve favorable laws, court decisions, and rulings by regulatory agencies. They have the lobbyists, lawyers, and politicians (as noted in Chapter 1) to work for their interests. Second, more subtly (but real, nonetheless), the powerful get their way because of the bias of the politicoeconomic system. Such time-honored notions as "our economic interests abroad must be protected" and "tax incentives to business will benefit everyone" and "bigness is goodness" go unchallenged because we have been socialized to accept the current system as proper. Thus, decisions continue to be based on precedent, and the idea that "what is good for General Motors is good for the country" prevails. As long as such notions guide decision making, the interests of the wealthy will be served at the expense of the nonwealthy.[30]

For defenders of a competitive free-enterprise system, the existence of monopolies and shared monopolies should be attacked as un-American because the economy has become neither free nor competitive. Green made the following observation:

> Huey Long once prophesied that fascism would come to the United States first in the form of anti-fascism. So too with corporate socialism. Under the banner of free enterprise, up to two-thirds of American manufacturing has been metamorphosed into a "closed enterprise system." Although businessmen spoke the language of competitive capitalism, each sought refuge for themselves: price-fixing, parallel pricing, mergers, excessive advertising, quotas, subsidies, and tax favoritism. While defenders of the American dream guarded against socialism from the left, it arrived unannounced from the right.[31]

In summary, the negative consequences of shared monopolies are important to our understanding of elite deviance in two ways. First, monopolies are themselves deviant because they disproportionately redistribute wealth and advantage toward the already advantaged. And, second, the existence of monopolies aids in creating an environment in which deviant acts are encouraged. An examination of the automobile industry will illustrate these interrelated phenomena.

## Price-Fixing

The sine qua non of capitalism is competition. We have seen, though, that the tendency toward concentration makes a mockery of the claim that the U.S. version of capitalism is competitive. The existence of shared monopolies allows the few corporations that control an industry to eliminate price wars by parallel pricing and product homogeneity. The parallel-pricing, tacit collusion by supposed competitors achieves a common price, and product homogeneity means that prices will be roughly equal because the competitors produce goods with similar specifications. Both practices are common and have the consequence of equal prices, regardless of whether the leading companies in an industry conspire to do so.

The typical practice among the large corporations that dominate an industry is *parallel pricing*. Currie and Skolnick describe how this works:

> Administering prices doesn't involve actual agreements among the large corporations not to undercut one another's prices; such direct "price fixing" is illegal. Instead, the usual pattern is one of "price leadership," in which there is a tacit understanding that if one company raises its prices, the others will follow. This ensures that competition through prices is diminished in the concentrated industries. The effect on the consumer is that prices in such industries … rarely go down and almost always go up, short of a really dramatic slowdown in the economy. This is one key reason why prices have often continued to rise even during recessions.[32]

Prices are also manipulated to maximize profits through collusive activities of the companies supposedly in competition with each other. This practice is called *price-fixing*. It refers to the explicit agreement among competitors to keep prices artificially high to maximize profits. Price-fixing is illegal, and complaints are monitored and brought to court by the Antitrust Division of the Justice Department. The illegality of price-fixing, however, has not deterred competing companies from conspiring to make abnormal profits through this practice, which costs consumers about $60 billion a year.[33] One review of cases from 1963 to 1972 in which price-fixing was proved revealed that the practice occurred among companies producing and marketing the following: steel wheels, pipe, bedsprings, metal shelving, steel castings, self-locking nuts, liquefied petroleum gas delivery, refuse collection, linoleum installation, swimsuits, structural steel, carbon steel, baking flour, fertilizer, railroads, welding electrodes, acoustical ceiling materials, hydraulic hose, beer, gasoline, asphalt, book matches, concrete pipe, drill bushings, linen, school construction, plumbing fixtures, dairy products, fuel oil, auto repair, brass fittings, plumbing contracting, bread, athletic equipment, maple floors, vending machines, ready-mix concrete, industrial chemicals, rendering, shoes, garage doors, automobile glass, and wholesale meat. In addition, review these current examples:

- Just 1 week before its shareholders' meeting, Archer Daniels Midland (ADM) pled guilty to price-fixing of several commodities commonly used in processed foods (e.g., corn syrup, citric acid, and lysine) and paid a $100 million criminal fine—the largest criminal antitrust fine ever—for its role in conspiracies to fix prices to eliminate competition. The two-count felony charges filed against ADM alleged that the company conspired with other producers (including previously charged Ajinomoto Co., Inc.; Kyowa Hakko Kogyo Co. Ltd.; and Sewon America, Inc.) in the lysine and citric acid markets to set prices and allocate sales from 1992 to 1995.

Under the plea agreement, all executives and employees of ADM, except for two, were protected from prosecution if they cooperated with the government. Moreover, ADM's stock went up after the announcement of the plea.

"There are a whole number of ADM executives who committed these crimes," said the cofounder of the ADM Shareholders Watch Committee of Hallandale, Florida, who argued that the executives responsible for the crimes should have been indicted first. ADM's political campaign contributions to both political parties insulated ADM and its executives from a just result.

Moreover, there is no disclosure in the plea agreement about the specifics of this crime. The government provided little information on who was involved. One estimate is that the citric acid price-fixing cost clients $400 million, whereas the lysine price-fixing cost $100 million. Under federal sentencing law, the $500 million total loss could be doubled, thus putting ADM's potential criminal exposure at $1 billion. But the Department of Justice defended the $100 million fine, saying no one at ADM got off the hook.

Federal officials noted that because of ADM's crimes seed companies, large poultry and swine producers, and ultimately farmers paid millions more to buy lysine, an amino acid used by farmers as a feed additive to ensure the proper growth of livestock. Lysine is a $600 million a year industry worldwide. In addition, manufacturers of soft drinks, processed foods, detergents, and other products paid millions more to buy the citric acid additive, which ultimately caused consumers to pay more for these products. Citric acid is a flavor additive and preservative and is used in soft drinks, processed food, detergents, pharmaceuticals, and cosmetic products. Citric acid is a $1.2 billion a year industry worldwide.[34]

Examining a number of price-fixing cases, several researchers have tried to determine whether a pattern can be found. They concluded that "conspiracy among competitors may arise in any number of situations but it is most likely to occur and endure when numbers are small [few companies involved], concentration is high (when four or fewer firms control fifty percent or more of the market), and the product is homogeneous."[35] Of the top 100 corporate crime cases of the 1990s, 20 of them involved antitrust matters like price-fixing and another 20 involved fraud.

- The single largest corporate crime of the last decade was a worldwide scheme to fix the price of certain vitamins and ended when Hoffman–La Roche was assessed a $500 million fine, the largest criminal fine ever levied.
- Likewise, between 1997 and 2000, five of America's largest music firms and three of the largest music retailers overcharged consumers by $480 million. The settlement of the case lowered CD prices by about $5 each.[36]

We should not forget, however, that collusive arrangements to keep prices or fees artificially high are not limited to industrial sales. Price-fixing, in one form or another, often occurs in real estate fees, doctors' fees, lawyers' fees, and tax accountants' fees, to name a few. Although the government continues to prosecute price-fixing cases, the problem continues. Apparently, the potential for increased profits is too tempting. Moreover, when individuals have been found guilty, the punishment has been more symbolic than real. Thus, the incentives remain. Once again, profit is the primary source of motivation and the customer be damned.

The extra profits garnered through price-fixing arrangements have an obvious impact on customers, who pay higher prices for goods and services. But they also have negative indirect effects. Two of these subtle consequences are especially noteworthy. First, larger than necessary expenditures fuel inflation. And, second, extra profits exacerbate the gap between the haves and the have-nots.

So serious had price-fixing become that on June 22, 2004, the Antitrust Criminal Penalty Enhancement and Reform Act became law. The changes made through this law dramatically increased maximum penalties and jail terms for individuals and corporations involved in price-fixing, bid-rigging, and other Sherman Antitrust Act offenses:

- The maximum prison sentence is increased from 3 to 10 years;
- The maximum individual fine is increased from $350,000 to $1 million;
- The maximum corporate fine is increased from $10 million to $100 million.

These changes brought the consequences for price-fixing, bid-rigging, and other Sherman Act violations into line with the accounting-fraud crimes established under the Sarbanes-Oxley Act of 2002. A second extremely costly corporate crime is fraud.

For an illustration of price-fixing, let's examine the most blatant incident in modern U.S. history.

## Case Study: The Electrical Conspiracy

From the mid-1940s through the 1950s, virtually all electrical manufacturing firms were actively involved in collusive activities to keep prices high.[37] Twenty-nine companies, but principally General Electric (GE) and Westinghouse, eventually were found guilty of conspiring to fix prices, rig bids, and divide markets on electrical equipment valued at $1.75 billion annually. The amount of profit generated from price-fixing in the electrical industry was considerable. "The result of these machinations was grossly inflated prices. Generator prices rose 50 percent from 1951 to 1959, while wholesale prices on all commodities rose only 5 percent. The Senate Small Business Committee later asserted that Westinghouse had bilked the Navy by a 500 percent overcharge on certain gear assemblies, and GE had charged 446 percent too much on another contract."[38]

An example of how the prices were fixed occurred in so-called competitive bidding for new business. Public agencies (e.g., utilities, school districts, and the government) required companies to make sealed bids for the cost of their products. The conspiring companies used this seemingly competitive practice to ensure high prices by rotating business on a fixed-percentage basis. That is, each company was allowed the proportion of the sales equal to the proportion of the market that they had controlled prior to the conspiracy. For sealed bids on circuit breakers, for example, the four participating companies divided the sales so that GE received 45%, Westinghouse 35%, Allis-Chalmers 10%, and Federal Pacific 10%.

Every 10 days to 2 weeks, working-level meetings were called in order to decide whose turn was next. Turns were determined by the ledger list, a table of who had received what in recent weeks. After that, the only thing left to decide was the price that the company picked to win would submit as the lowest bid.[39]

Four grand juries investigated price-fixing allegations in the electrical industry and handed down 20 indictments involving 45 individuals and 29 corporations. At the sentencing hearing in 1961, Judge Ganey levied fines totaling $1,787,000 on the corporations and $137,000 on different individuals. The highest corporate fines were against GE ($437,500) and Westinghouse ($372,500). Seven individuals were given jail sentences of 30 days (later reduced to 25 for good behavior), and 20 others received suspended sentences. In addition, the individuals were assessed fines ranging from $1,000 to $12,500. The corporations also faced settlements to injured parties. By 1964, for example, some 90% of the 1,800 claims against GE had been settled for a total of $160 million.

Several significant conclusions can be drawn from this electrical conspiracy case. First and most obvious, this antitrust conspiracy illustrates the willful and blatant violation of the law by some of the leading corporations in the United States. Second, the highest officials in the guilty corporations escaped without fines and jail sentences. Those found guilty were vice presidents, division managers, and sales managers, not presidents and chief executive officers. Moreover, the sentences were mild, considering the huge amounts of money involved. The government even ruled that the companies' payments of fines and settlements could be considered a business expense and therefore tax-deductible.[40]

This type of crime is underplayed by the media. For example, on the day that the defendants pleaded guilty or nolo contendere (no contest), only four of the largest 22 newspapers made the story front-page news, and four well-known papers, the *Boston Globe*, *New York Daily News*, *Christian Science Monitor*, and *Kansas City Times*, completely omitted the story. Five days later, when the sentencing occurred, 45% of the 20 newspapers with one-fifth of all the newspaper circulation in the United States did not consider the story front-page news.[41]

The parties convicted did not consider their acts immoral. Two quotes illustrate this point. First, the president of Allen-Bradley, Fred L. Loock, said "It is the only way a business can be run. It is free enterprise." Second, a GE official said, "Sure, collusion was illegal, but it wasn't unethical."[42]

The punishment for those judged guilty was incredibly light, given the magnitude of the case—a maximum of $12,500 and 30 days in jail. But more important is the discrepancy found when the sentences for these types of crimes are compared to those given to individuals guilty of street crimes. Some extreme examples are provided by Nader and Green:

> A year after seven electrical manufacturers were sent to jail for 30 days apiece, a man in Asbury Park, New Jersey, stole a $2.98 pair of sunglasses and a $1 box of soap and was sent to jail for four months. A George Jackson was sent to prison for ten years to life for stealing $70 from a gas station, his third minor offense; and in Dallas one Joseph Sills received a 1,000-year sentence for stealing $73.10. Many states send young students who are marijuana first offenders to jail for five to ten years' sentences. But the total amount of time spent in jail by all businessmen who have ever violated antitrust laws is a little under two years.[43]

In all probability, antitrust cases like the electrical conspiracy represent only a small portion of the actual amount of price-fixing in U.S. industry.[44] The potential profits are too tempting for many business executives, and the chances of getting caught are slim. The likelihood of escaping conviction, if caught, is great because of two factors: (1) the deals are made in secret and masked by apparently legal activity (e.g., sealed bids), and (2) the government's antitrust budget is very small.

# Price Gouging

Because many private corporations are entirely profit oriented, they take whatever advantage they can to sell their products or services at the highest possible prices. Shared monopolies, as we have seen, use their control of the market to increase prices an average of 25%. Price-fixing, of course, is another tactic to maximize profits. In this section, we discuss yet another manifestation of profit-maximizing behavior: price gouging, or taking extraordinary advantage of consumers because of the bias of the law, monopoly of the market, manipulation of the market, or contrived or real shortages.

Whatever the means used, price gouging is a form of deviancy. Let's examine the procedures used in three areas: (1) selling to the disadvantaged, (2) taking advantage of events, and (3) making extraordinary profits through convenient laws and manipulation.

## Taking Advantage of the Disadvantaged

Low-income consumers are the victims of price gouging from a variety of merchants, banks and finance companies, landlords, and the like. The poor pay more due to several factors, including higher rates of street crimes in their neighborhoods, which raise the cost of doing business, and the economic marginality of the poor, making their credit especially risky. But even when these rationales are accounted for, the poor are the victims of unusually high prices, which of course tends to perpetuate their poverty. Many food chains find that it costs 2% or 3% more to operate in poor neighborhoods, yet low-income consumers pay between 5% and 10% more for their groceries than those living in middle-income areas. Perhaps the best example of price gouging by ghetto stores is that they tend to raise prices on the first and the 15th of each month because these are the days when welfare checks are received. Similarly, there is evidence that grocers in the Mississippi Delta raised prices when food stamps were introduced.[45]

Banks and other financial organizations also take advantage of the poor. Because they are not affluent and therefore have inadequate collateral or credit standing, the poor must pay higher interest rates or may be forced to deal with loan sharks because they are denied resources through legitimate financial outlets.

The greater risk of lending to the poor is used to justify extremely high prices in poor neighborhoods. In the jewelry business, for example, the normal markup is 100%, but for jewelry sold in poor neighborhoods, the markup often is 300% or higher. A ring selling wholesale for $50 will sell for up to $300 in the poverty market. To protect themselves from default, credit jewelers in such a situation will try to get the maximum down payment, say, $60.

If so, the dealer has already made a $10 profit, and the future payments mean even more profit.[46]

The merchants in poor areas engage in such price gouging for several reasons: (1) the stores are essentially monopolies (no competition present); (2) the stores can argue legitimately that their costs are higher than in middle-class areas (although their prices, as we have seen, tend to exceed their increased risks by a wide margin); (3) the poor are unorganized and have no access to the powerful in society; (4) the poor are often unaware of the available avenues through which to complain of abusive practices; and (5) the poor tend to be apathetic because of the hopelessness of trying to change the practices of powerful banks, supermarket chains, finance companies, and other seemingly monolithic organizations.

Cross has summarized the economic plight of the poor: "Caught in a vicious cycle of poverty, the poor and the stores which serve them are trapped by the worst aspects of the free enterprise system. And it is likely that the poor are also at the receiving end of a greater amount of deliberate fraud and price discrimination than the suburban middle class."[47]

## Taking Advantage of Unusual Events

The sharp entrepreneur is always looking for special events that might lead to spectacular profits. For example, in the summer of 2004, parts of the American Southeast were hit by four hurricanes. Florida's consumer services commissioner's office received more than 3,000 consumer price-gouging complaints by gas stations, motels, and other retail outlets.

In the mid-1970s, a worldwide shortage caused the price of sugar to increase rapidly for U.S. consumers, bringing a concomitant rise in a number of products containing sugar. The cost of candy bars increased while their size dwindled (the price tripled while the bar shrank to one-third its former size). The cost of soda also increased markedly during this period. Canned soda from vending machines went from 15 to 25 cents a can. Interestingly (and revealing of the tendency of corporations to gouge whenever possible), the cost of diet soda (which, of course, contains no sugar) went up in price to 25 cents as well. When the sugar shortage subsided, the cost of soda stayed at the shortage-created level and continued to increase. Also, all major soda companies had the same pricing strategy, a form of parallel pricing or price-fixing. Oil companies used Hurricane Katrina (2006) as a reason to boost gas prices from $2.66 to $2.99 per gallon, claiming that reduced output from oil refineries was causing a lack of gasoline supplies.[48]

## Making Extraordinary Profits Through Deception

Although there are many examples of price gouging because of deception, we will focus on this phenomenon in one industry: the pharmaceutical industry. The sale of prescription and nonprescription drugs is a large industry, representing 10% of all medical costs in the United States.

- Mary Nathan suffers from a rare condition called Gaucher's disease, which is potentially fatal. The drugs she takes for it cost $270,000 per year. She worries about what will happen when she reaches the maximum amount that her insurance will pay. Her experience with drug costs is representative of the problems that stem from this $77 billion per year industry.
- When drug prices in the United States increased 81% between 1980 and 1985, the Drug Manufacturers Association told Congress that the increases were merely temporary, but during the following 6 years (1986–1992) drug prices increased another 66%. In 1993, the average prescription drug cost $22.50 (vs. $6.62 in 1980). In the 1990s, prescription prices increased almost 9% per year, far exceeding inflation in other costs.[49]

Why are Americans charged so much for prescriptions? The drug companies claim that it costs $231 million on average to bring a new drug to market, and they are merely recuperating their investment costs. Yet, consider the case of premarin, a hormone found in horses' urine. The drug has been used for more than 50 years, and all research and development costs on the drug were recovered long ago. Since 1985, however, the cost of the drug has increased 75% (from 20 to 35 cents for a daily dose). The real reason for this great price increase is profit margins.

Sidney Wolfe of the Public Interest Research Group claims that 104 of the 287 most frequently prescribed drugs are too dangerous to use. Their side effects can cause death in some cases.

The pharmaceutical firms spend thousands of dollars for each of the nation's doctors in order to convince them to prescribe their drugs. Also, a great deal of misleading and fraudulent advertising is associated with the drug industry. In 1992, 150 health professionals examined 109 full-page ads for drugs in medical journals. The group found that more than 90% of the ads violated the FDA's standards in some way.[50]

In 1988, 16 drug companies sponsored some 34,000 symposia for doctors at a cost of $89.5 million. These events are held in expensive locations and are little more than long commercials designed to get doctors to prescribe various drugs. The meetings often contain misleading claims about various drugs and are not subject to oversight by the FDA due to their private nature.[51]

The American pharmaceutical industry made $20 billion in profits on $200 billion in sales in 2004, a 12% profit margin. This is the highest profit margin of any industry in the country. The top executives of large drug firms earn from $1.9 million to $13 million per year, and the nation is poorer and less healthy for the actions of this industry. About half of all prescription drugs come in two forms: under a brand name or under the generic name. Although the drugs are identical chemically, the brand-name form is much more expensive and therefore profitable.

The situation in drug sales is very different from that of the typical purchaser–seller relationship. The choice of prescription drugs is made not by the consumer but by the physician, whose decision is based not on price but on knowledge. Doctors prescribe drugs they know about, and most of their information is supplied by large pharmaceutical firms, which spend from $3,000 to $5,000 per doctor per year promoting their own brand-name drugs.

Drug manufacturers also benefit by the proliferation of drugs, which leaves physicians inundated with a virtual sea of drugs and drug names. For example, 61 firms offered their own version of one chemical compound, Pentaerythritol tetranitrate (PETN). Busy physicians will opt, in most cases, for the drugs with which they are most familiar, and drug firms do all they can to familiarize doctors with their branded (and expensive) products. But drug companies have done more than just advertise their products to physicians. According to Ben Gordon, a drug consultant to the U.S. Senate for 20 years, "The larger drug manufacturers have been misleading and lying to the American public, to the medical profession, and to the Congress about the quality of their drugs, as against that of the generic drugs."[52] They have used several scare tactics, such as films in which generic drugs were compared to defective cars and warnings to pharmacists that the increased use of generic drugs would cause the druggists' insurance rates to increase.[53]

Another tactic used by drug firms has been to lobby for laws prohibiting generics to be substituted for the branded drugs prescribed by physicians. At one time, all 50 states had such laws, but in recent years, many have been changed. In late 1978, 40 states and the District of Columbia allowed pharmacists to substitute generic drugs for brand-name prescription drugs. Also, in 1984, Congress finally passed a law that eliminated the costly and time-consuming delays facing companies seeking government approval to market generic drugs.

Many of them simply can't do it. They trade-off drugs against home heating or food. Some people try to string out their drugs by taking them less often than prescribed, or sharing them with a spouse. Others, too embarrassed to admit that they can't afford to pay for drugs, leave their doctors' offices with prescriptions in hand but don't have them filled. Not only do these patients go without needed treatment but their doctors sometimes wrongly conclude that the drugs they prescribed haven't worked and prescribe yet others—thus compounding the problem.

The people hurting most are the elderly. ... At the end of 2003, Congress passed a Medicare reform bill that included a prescription drug benefit (that began) in 2006, but its benefits are inadequate to begin with and will quickly be overtaken by rising prices and administrative costs. ...

In 2001, nearly one in four seniors reported that they skipped doses or did not fill prescriptions because of the cost. (That fraction is almost certainly higher now.) Sadly, the frailest are the least likely to have supplementary insurance. At an average cost of $1,500 a year for each drug, someone without supplementary insurance who takes six different prescription drugs—and this is not rare—would have to spend $9,000 out of pocket. Not many among the old and frail have such deep pockets.

Furthermore, " in one of the more perverse of the pharmaceutical industry's practices, prices are much higher for precisely the people who most need the drugs and can least afford them. The industry charges Medicare recipients without supplementary insurance much more than it does favored customers, such as large HMOs or the Veterans Affairs (VA) system. Because the latter buy in bulk, they can bargain for steep discounts or rebates. People without insurance have no bargaining power; and so they pay the highest prices."[54]

Despite the drug companies attempting to justify the high costs of drugs on the basis of need for research and development funds, this argument raises many more questions than it answers. Why are drug prices in neighboring nations like Canada and Mexico so much lower (30% or more) than in the United States? Moreover:

1. "Just one of every five dollars the drug industry receives goes to drug research.
2. Some drug companies spend about twice as much for advertising and marketing as they spend for research.
3. Drug industry profits are so large they outstrip every other industry's profits by far."[55]

Drug companies are the most profitable industry in America. In 2001, a year that saw a drop in employment rates and a plunge in the stock market, the top 10 U.S. drug companies increased their profits by 33%. This occurred despite the overall profits of Fortune 500 companies declining by 53%, the second-biggest drop in Fortune 500 profits in its 47-year history.

Overall, the United States spends more than $1 trillion for health care annually, much of it to improve drug company profits. The United States is the only advanced democracy without a government-sponsored health care program and possesses more than enough capital to adequately treat all its citizens.

Moreover, prescription drugs are often unsafe. A 1998 study reported in the *Journal of the American Medical Association* (*JAMA*) showed that 106,000 people die each year (300 per day) in American hospitals from medication side effects. That is more deaths than from all plane crashes, but they go unreported by the electronic media because there are no pictures of crash sites, fires, and rescue teams to show on TV.[56]

# Deceptive Advertising

One tenet of capitalism is expansion. Every corporation wishes to produce an increasing amount so that profits likewise will inflate. The problem, of course, is that the public must be convinced to consume this ever larger surplus.[57] One way to create demand is through advertising.

In 2000, advertising expenditures amounted to over $200 billion. A strong argument could be made that advertising expenditures are wasteful in three ways: (1) they create a demand to consume that increases the waste of natural resources; (2) they increase the cost of products because consumers pay all the advertising costs; and (3) the money spent serves no useful purpose (other than profits).

But advertising is a problem to the public in another way: it is sometimes designed to be deceptive. In a fundamental way, all advertising is deceptive because it is designed to manipulate. Symbols are used to make the observer concerned with his or her status, beauty, or age or to associate sex appeal with a certain look. Advertising is deceptive because it creates a desire to consume new products. But the deception we want to consider goes beyond this type of illusion. We are concerned with a more willful form of deception, where the goal is to sell, even through lies.[58]

A retired advertising executive discussed the cardinal principle in U.S. advertising:

> Don't worry whether it's true or not. Will it sell? ... The American people ... are now being had from every bewildering direction. All the way from trying to persuade us to put dubious drug products and questionable foods into our stomachs to urging young men to lay down their lives in Indochina, the key will-it-sell principle and the employed techniques are the same. Caveat emptor has never had more profound significance than today, whether someone is trying to sell us war, God, anti-Communism or a new improved deodorant. Deceit is the accepted order of the hour.[59]

The tendency toward deception in advertising takes two forms, blatantly false advertising and puffery. Let's examine these in turn. The following examples will show how advertising can be outright false:

- The FTC issued a Weight Loss Advertising Report discussing the results of a "review of 300 weight loss ads (disseminated in all major media forms), and staff's comparison of weight loss ads from 1992 with those that ran in 2001."[60] They found that false and misleading claims in weight loss ads are pervasive and have increased during this period. This increase has occurred despite an unprecedented level of FTC enforcement actions over the last decade.
- Coors Light beer had to stop advertising "a taste of the Rockies," as long as its water came from Virginia.[61]

- General Nutrition Centers paid a $2.4 million fine for unsubstantiated health claims involving more than 40 of its products.[62]
- Eggland's Best had to stop advertising its egg substitute as "better than real eggs."[63]
- Diet Centers, Nutri/System, and Physicians Weight Loss Centers were forced to stop advertising their claims concerning losing weight and keeping it off. Studies demonstrate that more than 90% of dieters gain back the weight that they lose.[64]
- Companies commonly use bait-and-switch advertising, although it is a clear violation of FTC rules. The bait involves advertising a product at an extremely low price. The switch is made when customers arrive to buy it; none is available, so the salespersons pressure people to buy other, more expensive articles.
- In the 2004 case *Aspinall v. Philip Morris Companies, Inc.*, the Massachusetts Supreme Court ruled that the mere *purchase* of a deceptively advertised product can satisfy the element of injury for purposes of certifying a class under the Massachusetts Consumer Protection Act, M.G.L. c. 93A. The court's holding will affect companies in numerous industries that advertise products for sale in Massachusetts.[65]
- New York state attorney general Elliott Spitzer found that four western New York auto dealerships and a Louisiana-based firm engaged in auto "scratch-off" prize promotions and other forms of false advertising. The firms paid a total $67,000 in civil penalties.[66]
- "*Rebates* were originally intended to pass *savings* directly from the manufacturer to the consumer. However in the U.S. they have become probably the biggest way to trick shoppers into paying more than the advertised price. Stores advertise a 'sale' price and note only in the fine print that it is not the price at which it is actually sold for, but instead an 'after rebate' price, which also fails to include *sales tax*. Many rebate fulfillment companies have been labeled as trying not to return money to the customers."[67]
- By comparing a sale price to a "regular" price for the same product, advertisers increase the "regular" price, creating the impression that the sale price is very low. The intent is to mislead consumers into thinking that they are saving money by purchasing the "on-sale" item or service. This is especially common in markets with high markups, especially on jewelry, furniture, and automobiles. Some clothing firms have nearly every item on "sale," and some grocery stores advertise "savings" over their regular prices for those using loyalty cards.[68]
- An introductory offer is an offer for a service that is valid for a certain period. After the offer expires, the price or terms of the agreement change, often without further notice to consumers who accepted the offer. One common form of this tactic involves credit cards. A low

interest rate is offered to start, but the rate rises greatly afterward. Enormous increases in rates can be caused by a single late payment or overdraft, and high fees are charged for the late payment or overdraft. Credit card companies in the United States often lure college and university students with such offers and make huge profits from the fees and increased rates.

Introductory offers are also very common for cable TV, satellite TV, and Internet services, especially those bundling more than one service (telephone, Internet, and cable TV). The intent is to get consumers used to receiving the service before the price goes up, so that they will continue on as customers with a much higher profit margin for the service provider.

- Utilizing false descriptive or location terms to increase the perceived value of a product is common, such as advertising "Maine lobsters" when the lobsters are from the Pacific Ocean, or Vidalia onions that are from Texas instead of near Vidalia, Georgia. These practices also involve infringement of trademarks in many cases. United Egg Producers' "Animal Care Certified" logo on egg cartons misled consumers by conveying a higher level of animal care than was actually the case. Both the Better Business Bureau and the Federal Trade Commission found the logo to be deceptive.
- Internet service providers may advertise their service as offering "up to 256 kbps," whereas on average use the speed could be just 20 kbps. The use of "up to" in the description protects them legally, while raising false hopes in customers. Further, the fine print may mention that this figure includes both the download and upload speeds, detracting even more from the customer's usage experience.
- Some products are sold with fillers, which increase the legal weight of the product with something that costs the producer very little compared with the cost of the actual product. For example, chicken meat may be injected with broth or even brine, or TV dinners are filled with gravy or other sauce instead of meat. Canned tuna may also be labeled with a weight that includes the water or vegetable oil, though these are almost always drained off by the customer and are therefore useless. In other cases, packages are underfilled, simply leaving empty space at the top, in products such as coffee, protein powder, and other foods packaged in containers that cannot be seen into until being purchased and opened at home. A particularly deceptive practice involves using the same size of packaging for a smaller amount of product than it used to contain. This deceives consumers into continuing to buy the product, which they expect to contain the same amount as previously. To evade legal problems, the label is changed to reflect the actual new amount, but this is essentially fine print that is easily overlooked. A similar problem with Christmas lights and other light strings is that the length of each set seems to get

shorter each year, despite containing the same number of lights. The length of the set is given in small print, but the number of lights is in large print.[69]

A more subtle form of deceptive advertising is called *puffery*. This term refers to the practice of making exaggerated claims for a product. Although advertisers routinely make such false claims and the result is deception, the law considers such practices to be legal. These unverifiable claims are often made in the form of empty slogans:[70]

"A new kind of family"—ABC Family

"Be the first to know"—CNN International, 2002–present

"It's not TV, it's HBO"—HBO, late 1990s

"No limits"—Showtime (1997–present)

"A better world is our business"—Samsung

"Connecting people"—Nokia

"Ideas for life"—Panasonic

"Imagination at work"—General Electric

"Just what I needed"—Circuit City

"Keeps going and going and going"—Energizer batteries, 1990s

"Like no other"—Sony, 2004

"Live in your world, play in ours"—PlayStation 2

"America's supermarket"—Winn Dixie

"All the right choices"—Foley's

"Always better value"—Dunnes Stores

"Always low prices"—Wal-Mart

"Always lowering prices"—Currys

"Always something exciting"—Foley's

"Ask how, ask now, ask Sherwin Williams"

"Come see the softer side of Sears"

"Design for all"—Target

"Dress for less"—Ross Stores

"Every day's a savings day at Korvette's"

"First to Sears, then to school"—1970s back-to-school ads

"Helping make your life easier"—Albertson's

"Home of fast, friendly, courteous service"—Fry's Electronics

"I don't wanna grow up, I'm a Toys 'R' Us kid"

"Just do it"—Nike, 1988–present

"A diamond is forever"—De Beers Consolidated Mines, 1948–present (by N. W. Ayer & Son)

"Every kiss begins with Kay"—Kay Jewelers[71]

Such claims are false or unsubstantiated. Even though they are considered legal, their intent is to mislead. The goal, as is always the case with advertising, is to use whatever means will sell the product. If that includes trifling with the truth, then so be it.

Even though knowledge concerning puffery in advertising is far from complete, some important facts have emerged from research on this topic:

- People perceive more content in ads than the ads actually contain. Additional values are perceived by consumers and attached to products. For example, one study of sweaters concluded that when sweaters were shown with belts and captions were read by someone with a Scottish accent, consumers were twice as likely to perceive that the sweaters were imported.[72]
- Implied deceptions (puffery claims) are believed more than outright lies. In one study of seventeen puff claims, 70% of respondents felt that the claims were either wholly or partially true.[73]
- Puffery claims are often indistinguishable from factual claims. In another study, a sample of 100 people were placed in a room and presented with both real and puff claims. The researchers found that "many of the puff claims were believed by a large proportion of the respondents. . . . The subjects could not tell that these puffs might not be literally true." Researchers found that the factual claims were believed just as often as the puff claims used in their survey.[74]
- Puffery "has the potential to deceive consumers and, as well, injure the credibility of advertising."[75] In sum, research indicates that a "large proportion of the sample interpret the [puff] claim to suggest superiority."[76] Consumers fed a constant diet of puffery ads may confuse fact and fiction. Moreover, they may actually come to distrust advertising, on the one hand, yet unconsciously be manipulated by it, on the other.[77]

## Fraud

Fraud is committed when one is induced to part with money or valuables through deceit, lies, or misrepresentation. Although the law recognizes fraud as a crime, it has traditionally assumed that fraud directed against a private individual is not a crime because of the principle of caveat emptor. Preston has summarized this principle[78]:

This principle of the marketplace is an open invitation for fraud. Some criminologists have contended that fraud is probably "the most prevalent crime in America."[79] The types of frauds perpetrated on victims involve numerous schemes applied to a wide variety of economic activities, as seen in the following cases.

- In Texas, three former nursing home executives, one an attorney, were charged in a 2007 federal indictment. A federal grand jury issued a 29-count indictment charging the three men "with one count of conspiracy to defraud the Internal Revenue Service (IRS) and the U.S. Department of Health and Human Services (HHS), nine counts of tax evasion, five counts of mail fraud, seven counts of false statements to a government agency and seven counts of false statements relating to health care matters."[80]

- Ruling in the U.S. government's racketeering lawsuit against tobacco companies, U.S. district judge Gladys Kessler struck an important blow for global health by ordering the tobacco company defendants to stop using misleading cigarette marketing terms like *light* and *low-tar* not only in the United States but internationally as well. This ruling applies to defendants in the case, including Philip Morris USA, Altria, R.J. Reynolds, Brown & Williamson, Lorillard, and British American Tobacco. On August 17, 2006, Judge Kessler also found that the tobacco companies had engaged in massive wrongdoing and violated civil racketeering (RICO) laws by lying for decades about the health risks of their products and their marketing to children.[81]

- In 2002 the U.S. Department of Justice, in response to massive corporate frauds involving the bribery of corporate accounting firms, established the Corporate Fraud Task Force. By early 2007 the task force had made more than 1,100 convictions, including[82]: (1) In December 2006, the department obtained guilty verdicts against four senior executives of Enterasys Networks, Inc., for accounting fraud after a 5-week trial in Concord, New Hampshire. (2) Two executives of Comverse Technology, Inc.—its general counsel and chief financial officer—pleaded guilty to backdating stock options. In February 2007, the general counsel of the recruiting firm Monster, Inc., pleaded guilty to charges of conspiracy and fraud arising from his involvement in a scheme to backdate options. (3) In February 2007, in one of the first ever extraditions for an intellectual property offense, the leader of one of the oldest and most renowned Internet software piracy groups was extradited to the United States from Australia. The indictment against Raymond Griffiths charged him with violating the criminal copyright laws of the United States as the leader of an organized criminal group known as DrinkOrDie, one of the oldest software piracy groups on the Internet. Before its dismantling, DrinkOrDie was estimated to have caused the illegal reproduction and distribution of more than $50 million worth of pirated software, movies, games, and music.

- One common corporate fraud is known as "biz ops," companies that sell phony franchise businesses like candy vending machines, Internet kiosks, DVD rental machines, and other income-generating products with promises of high profits from great locations. In 2005–2006, the Justice Department obtained 57 felony convictions in biz ops cases.

- On February 6, 2007, three subsidiaries of Vetco International Ltd. pleaded guilty to violating a federal antibribery law by paying approximately $2.1 million in corrupt payments to Nigerian government officials over a 2-year period. As part of the plea and deferred prosecution agreements, the three subsidiaries paid a total of $26 million in criminal fines, the largest criminal fine to date in an FCPA prosecution by the Justice Department.
- In 2006, Statoil, a Norwegian oil and gas company, made payments of $5.2 million to an Iranian oil official in exchange for assistance in obtaining valuable oil and gas contracts. To resolve this matter, Statoil has acknowledged its criminal conduct and agreed to a $10.5 million criminal penalty and other sanctions. The Schnitzer Steel case involved illegal payments by Schnitzer to both government-owned and private customers in South Korea and China to induce them to purchase scrap metal.
- Many fraudulent schemes are based on the classic pyramid system perfected by Bostonian Charles Ponzi in the 1920s whereby early investors are paid off handsomely with proceeds from sales to later participants. The result is often a rush of new investors, greedy for easy profits. An example of the Ponzi scam was the HomeStake swindle perpetrated by Robert Trippet, which consisted of selling participation rights in the drilling of sometimes hypothetical oil wells. The beauty of this plan was that since oil exploration was involved, it provided a tax shelter for the investors. Thus, the plan especially appealed to the wealthy. As a result, many important persons, including the chair of Citibank, the head of United States Trust, the former chair of Morgan Guarantee Trust, the former chair of General Electric, and entertainers such as Jack Benny, Candice Bergen, Faye Dunaway, Bob Dylan, and Liza Minnelli were swindled out of a good deal of money. John Kenneth Galbraith, the noted economist, in reviewing a book about the HomeStake swindle, said that it should have been titled *How the Rich Swindled Each Other and Themselves*.[83]
- WorldCom artificially inflated its earnings by $3.8 billion, just one of many 2002 scandals that lessened investors' confidence in stock markets. WorldCom's CEO was sued by the New York state attorney general because he and four other telecom executives improperly profited from hot initial public stock offerings given by Salomon Smith Barney in return for investment banking business. On June 27, 2002, the Securities and Exchange Commission (SEC) charged WorldCom with "massive accounting fraud." The civil complaint charges WorldCom with violating antifraud and reporting provisions of the federal securities law. On May 20, 2003, WorldCom Inc. agreed to pay investors $500 million to settle its charges with the SEC.[84]

- Formerly the United States' seventh-largest company, Enron announced in November 2001 that it had overstated its earnings back to 1997 by about $600 million. The company camouflaged a huge debt in a web of loans that were recorded as investment assets in very questionable firms. The company's collapse was the biggest bankruptcy filing in U.S. corporate history.

  In November 2002, former Enron CFO Andrew Fastow pleaded innocent to a 78-count federal indictment charging him with masterminding complex financial schemes while at Enron; he was sentenced to a 6-year prison sentence plus probation. The indictment alleges Fastow and others created schemes to defraud Enron and its shareholders through transactions with off-the-books partnerships that made the company look far more profitable than it was. In March 2003, a federal judge granted Fastow protection from civil lawsuits pending the resolution of his 78-count federal indictment. May 2003 brought more charges for Fastow (in the form of a superseding 109-count indictment), his wife, and seven other former Enron executives. Enron president Kenneth Lay died in July 2006, after being found guilty of fraud, while awaiting sentencing.

- In early June 2002, Tyco accepted the resignation of CEO Dennis Kozlowski, who was later charged for allegedly avoiding payment of more than $1 million in sales taxes on $13.2 million in artwork. Kozlowski resigned in June 2002 after being charged with tax evasion. He pleaded innocent to those charges, as well as charges that he helped loot Tyco of about $600 million. In March 2003, Kozlowski went to Manhattan's State Supreme Court, where he sued Tyco, claiming the company actually owes him money. In 2005, Kozlowski received an 8- to 25-year prison sentence.

- In March 2002, the Pennsylvania-based cable company announced that it had loaned billions of dollars to the founding Rigas family. The family relinquished control of Adelphia, which defaulted on $7 billion in debt and filed for Chapter 11 bankruptcy protection on June 25. In July 2002, company founder John Rigas, two of his sons, and two other former executives were charged with conspiracy, securities fraud, wire fraud, and looting Adelphia out of hundreds of millions of dollars to pay for luxury condos and a golf course. Adelphia has also filed a racketeering suit against Rigas and members of his family. In November 2002, the company's former vice president of finance, James Brown, agreed to testify against the Rigas family. Brown was the first person to plead guilty in the scandal that authorities say cost investors more than $60 billion. In 2005, John Rigas received a 15-year prison sentence. His son Timothy, former Adelphi CEO, was given 20 years in prison.

- The Toronto entertainment company Livent collapsed in 1998 amid allegations of financial impropriety that led to its financial results being restated. Soon after the collapse, the new management of Livent filed a $225 million lawsuit against Garth Drabinsky and Myron Gottlieb, the two Canadians who founded the theater company.

Livent then fired both executives, stating they "fraudulently manipulated" financial records to hide losses of $100 million. They have countersued for $210 million. Livent also filed for bankruptcy protection, citing debts of $334 million. Drabinsky and Gottlieb are facing hearings before the Ontario Securities Commission. Drabinsky is facing charges in New York. Livent shares are now worthless.

- ImClone's cofounder and former CEO Sam Waksal and his daughter, Aliza, were charged with and convicted of insider trading relating to sales of ImClone stock in the days leading up to the release of a federal ruling that rejected the company's new cancer drug. Waksal pleaded guilty in October 2002 to six of 13 counts stemming from large sales of company stock before news broke in December 2001 that regulators would reject ImClone's main experimental cancer drug, Erbitux. In March 2003, Waksal settled civil charges by agreeing to a partial resolution of the insider trading case without admitting the allegations. He consented to pay more than $800,000 from the unlawful sales including prejudgment interest. On June 10, 2003, Waksal was sentenced in U.S. District Court to just over 7 years in federal prison and ordered to pay $4.3 million in fines and restitution. He has the distinction of being the first ex-CEO sentenced to jail in the wave of corporate scandals plaguing U.S. companies since 2001.

## Case Study: The Madoff Scandal

**Bernard Lawrence "Bernie" Madoff** is now incarcerated in federal prison. A former American stock broker, investment adviser, nonexecutive chairman of the NASDAQ stock market, and the admitted operator of the largest Ponzi scheme in history.

In March 2009, Madoff pleaded guilty to 11 *federal crimes* and admitted to turning his *wealth management* business into a massive Ponzi scheme that defrauded thousands of investors of billions of dollars. Several of his investors committed suicide, as did one of his sons.

Madoff said he began the Ponzi scheme in the early 1990s. However, federal investigators believe the fraud began as early as the 1980s, and that the investment operation may never have been legitimate. The amount missing from client accounts, including fabricated gains, was almost $65 billion. The court-appointed trustee estimated actual losses to investors of $18 billion. On June 29, 2009, he was sentenced to 150 years in prison, the maximum allowed.

A prominent Austrian banker, Sonja Kohn, who portrayed herself for 2 years as one of Bernard L. Madoff's biggest victims was accused in

December 2010 of conspiring for 23 years of funneling more than $9 billion into his immense global Ponzi scheme. Some of the money Kohn funneled to Madoff may have come from Russian organized crime syndicates. She is currently in hiding. The accusations were made in a civil lawsuit that sought damages of $19.6 billion—the sum of the cash lost in a fraud that wiped out nearly $65 billion in paper wealth and ruined thousands of investors on almost every rung of the economic ladder.

Madoff founded the Wall Street firm Bernard L. Madoff Investment Securities LLC, a corporation, in 1960, and was its chairman until his arrest on December 11, 2008. The firm was one of the top market maker businesses on Wall Street, which bypassed "specialist" firms by directly executing orders over the counter from retail brokers.

On December 10, 2008, Madoff's sons told authorities that their father had just confessed to them that the asset management arm of his firm was a massive Ponzi scheme, and quoting him as saying it was "one big lie." The following day, FBI agents arrested Madoff and charged him with one count of securities fraud. The *U.S. SEC* had previously conducted investigations into Madoff's business practices, but did not uncover the massive fraud; critics contend that these investigations were very incompetently handled. On December 11, 2010, Madoff's son, Mark, the target of numerous civil lawsuits and embarrassed at seeing his father's name in the news repeatedly, committed suicide.[82]

One such critic is Harry Markopolos,[85] who warned the SEC three times over a 6-year span, with written empirical reports regarding Maroff's Ponzi scheme. According to Markopolos (see NoOneWouldListen.com), several remarkable truths were revealed during his investigation:

- Among Madoff's corporate clients were the Russian Mafyia and South American cocaine cartels.
- The SEC has virtually been captured by the very industry (Wall Street investment houses) it is supposed to regulate. In fact, not a single federal financial regulatory agency—the Federal Deposit Insurance Corporation, the Federal Reserve Bank, the Office of Thrift Supervision, or the Office of the Comptroller of the Currency—is competent to regulate their respective sectors, or they are under the influence of those sectors.
- Several European hedge fund managers, who had invested money with Madoff's firm, knew he was defrauding people, but said nothing about it. Their money was in nontaxable off-shore accounts beyond both the reach of their respective governments and American law.

Martha Stewart, the domestic diva of TV and publishing, came under investigation after she sold nearly 4,000 shares of ImClone on December 27, 2002, a day before prices of the corporation's shares plummeted, when FDA regulators rejected ImClone's application for a new cancer drug. When news of her questionable sale got out, it sent her company's stock plunging 54%, contributing to a 45% third-quarter profit. Stewart relinquished her seat on the board of the New York Stock Exchange and on June 4, 2003, was indicted by a federal grand jury on nine counts of securities fraud and related charges, including conspiracy and obstruction of justice. She then resigned as chairwoman and CEO of Martha Stewart Living Omnimedia. Her stockbroker, former Merrill Lynch employee Peter Bacanovic, was also indicted. Counts against Bacanovic included obstruction of justice and perjury. In March 2004, both defendants were found guilty on all counts. Stewart's appeal was denied, and she served a 5-month jail term, followed by 5 months of home confinement. She was also fined $30,000. She has, since her release, resumed her TV and publishing career.

- In November 2003, several major mutual fund firms, investment banks, and hedge funds were implicated in "market timing" and illegal late trading of mutual fund shares. These activities have enriched an elite group of fund managers and investors at the expense of millions of small investors. The SEC and state regulators in New York and Massachusetts have charged several large firms such as Putnam Investments, Prudential Securities, and Strong Capital Management, as well as some smaller mutual fund companies. Congressional hearings were also held on the mutual fund industry.
- On September 9, 2003, Tenet Healthcare and its former CEO, Jeffrey Barbakow, were the subject of a new U.S. Senate committee on finance investigation into corporate governance practices at the scandal-plagued company. The investigation focused on documents and internal e-mails that were expected to uncover wide-based fraud. In August 2003, Tenet promised to pay a $54 million settlement to the United States and California governments to end criminal and civil suits regarding alleged unnecessary heart surgery procedures at a California hospital. In mid-March 2003, the SEC filed a lawsuit accusing HEALTHSOUTH Corp. and its CEO and chairman, Richard Scrushy, of a $1.4 billion accounting fraud. The SEC alleged that since 1999, at the insistence of Scrushy, HEALTHSOUTH inflated its earnings by at least $1.4 billion so it could meet or exceed Wall Street earnings expectations. CFO William T. Owens later pleaded guilty to federal securities fraud and conspiracy charges and was fired. On March 31, the HEALTHSOUTH board declared the employment agreement with Scrushy "null and void" and fired him as chairman and CEO. In November 2003, the Justice Department indicted Scrushy on more than 85 counts, including fraud and making false corporate statements.
- On August 19, 2003, the SEC fined Deutsche Asset Management $750,000 for failing to disclose to clients that its investment banking

division was representing Hewlett-Packard in the $19 billion merger with Compaq completed more than a year earlier. Deutsche Bank agreed to pay the $750,000 fine but did not admit or deny the SEC's findings.

- In January 2002, Global Crossing filed for Chapter 11 bankruptcy protection, with assets of $22.4 billion and debts totaling $12.4 billion. This was the fourth largest bankruptcy in U.S. history. The company was accused of engaging in misleading transactions and accounting methods which gave the appearance that the company was generating hundreds of millions of dollars in sales and cash revenues that did not actually exist. Gary Winnick, the company's founder and chairman, cashed in $735 million of stock over 4 years, while receiving $10 million in salary/bonuses, consulting fees, and aircraft ownership interest. In October 2002, he promised $25 million to employees who lost money in the company's 401(k) retirement plan.

- In September 2002, the New York state attorney general sued five corporate executives (former WorldCom chief executive Bernard Ebbers, Qwest chairman Philip Anschutz, former Qwest CEO Joseph P. Nacchio, Metromedia Fiber chairman Stephen Garofalo, and former McLeod CEO Clark McLeod) for repayment of funds garnered through profiteering in initial public offerings (IPOs) and phony stock ratings given by Salomon Smith Barney (and, specifically, analyst Jack Grubman) in return for investment banking business. In January 2003, the attorney general reached a "global" settlement with top Wall Street firms. They pledged to pay $1.4 billion to settle federal and state charges. In April 2003, the SEC settled enforcement actions against 10 Wall Street firms and two individual analysts (Henry Blodgett and Jack Grubman) arising from an investigation of research analyst conflicts of interest.

- Former Qwest CEO Joseph Nacchio was sued by the New York state attorney general in September 2002 for improperly profiting from initial public stock offerings given by Salomon Smith Barney in return for investment banking business. In February 2003, federal regulators charged eight former and current midlevel executives of Qwest Communications with helping the phone carrier inflate its financial results by almost $150 million through improper accounting. Qwest founder and director Philip Anschutz was investigated by Congress for possessing advance knowledge of the company's looming financial problems when he sold $213.5 million in Qwest stock in 2002. Qwest announced in September 2002 that it would be restating $950 million in revenue. In February 2003, federal regulators charged eight former and current midlevel executives of Qwest Communications with helping the phone carrier inflate its financial results by almost $150 million through improper accounting.

- Jack Grubman, the Citigroup Salomon Smith Barney telecom analyst, left Citigroup by "mutual agreement" with a $30 million severance package. In April 2003, in a $1.4 billion settlement, Merrill Lynch, Credit Suisse, First Boston, and Citigroup's Salomon Smith Barney unit were charged by the SEC with issuing fraudulent research reports. Grubman specifically was banned from the business for life and fined $15 million. He neither admitted nor denied the charges against him.
- In September 2002, former Sunbeam CEO Al Dunlap agreed to pay the federal government $500,000 to settle charges he oversaw an accounting fraud that led to the collapse of Sunbeam Corp. in the late 1990s. Dunlap also agreed never to serve as an officer or director of a public company again. He neither admitted nor denied wrongdoing under the settlement.

Questionable accounting practices and insider and massive fraud allegations have all affected corporate America since these scandals became public knowledge in 2002 and 2003. Collectively, the 2002–2003 scandals helped cause a $5 trillion loss in stock market values, and cost the public at least $200 billion and 1 million jobs.

## Conclusion

Two issues that have historically concerned Americans are street crime and inflation. Our discussion in this chapter should provide new insight into both of these problems. Street crime, for example, is minuscule in terms of economic costs when compared with the illegal activities by corporations. To cite just one example, the $2 billion to $3 billion lost in the Equity Funding fraud involved more money "than the total losses of all street crimes in the United States for one year."[86]

The primary source of inflation, many argue, is huge governmental expenditures. Of course, these expenditures do affect the inflationary spiral, but the blame lies elsewhere, as well. Ignored by most critics are the sources of inflation found in our corporate economy. In 1982, U.S. consumers spent $1.08 trillion on retail items. Much of that money purchased nothing of value. We have seen that the existence of shared monopolies increases prices by 25%. We have seen that consumers pay all the costs of advertising, which amounted to $66.5 billion in 1982.[87] We have seen that consumers pay inflated prices brought about by price-fixing and other collusive arrangements by so-called competitors. Finally, we have seen that consumers spend billions on products sold under false pretenses, products that do not perform as claimed, products identical to cheaper ones but unavailable or unknown, and the like.

The point is clear: These extra costs to consumers do not bring anything of value back to them. What could be more inflationary than that? Put another way, the corporate economy diverts scarce resources to uses that have little human benefit.

To conclude, Edwin Sutherland, the sociologist who first examined white-collar crime extensively, made several observations relevant to the understanding of such corporate deviant behavior as price-fixing, misleading advertising, and fraud.[88]

1. The criminality of corporations tends to be persistent. Recidivism (repeat offenses) is the norm.
2. The level of illegal behavior is much more extensive than the prosecutions and complaints indicate.
3. Businesspeople who violate the laws designed to regulate business do not typically lose status among their associates. In other words, the business code does not coincide with the legal code. Thus, even when they violate the law, they do not perceive themselves as criminals.


# CRITICAL THINKING EXERCISE 3.1
## The Dehumanization of Women and Crime

Two excellent videos concerning the dehumanization of women in ads are *Killing Us Softly* and *Still Killing Us Softly*. These are available in most college video collections and are also owned by a number of public libraries. Each is about 30 minutes long. Write a brief paper (two to four pages) concerning your reactions to these videos.

You may wish to focus your paper on the following issues:

1. What is the relationship suggested by the video between how women are presented in ads and the victimization of women in crimes such as rape and murder?
2. What messages does advertising send women regarding their independence, beauty, and ability to love their families?
3. What messages does advertising send to men concerning what women want from them?
4. How are men depicted in ads, and what messages do you think men are given by such images?

**118**   CHAPTER 3

# ENDNOTES

1. Wheeler, S. (June 23, 1976). Trends and problems in the sociological study of crime. *Social Problems* 24, 525. This criticism has been made by others, as well. See especially Liazos, A. (Summer 1972). The poverty of the sociology of deviance: Nuts, sluts, and preverts. *Social Problems* 20, 10–20.

2. Clinard, M. B. (1979). *Illegal Corporate Behavior*. Washington, DC: U.S. Department of Justice, Law Enforcement Assistance Administration. See also Clinard, M. B., & Yeager, P. C. (August 1978).Corporate crime: Issues in research. *Criminology, 16*, 255–272.

3. See Sherrill, R. (April 7, 1997). A year in corporate crime. *The Nation*.

4. Enloe, W. (2000). *Effective deterrence for white-collar crime: Perceptions of attorneys specializing in antitrust* (p. 7, master's thesis). San Jose State University.

5. Laufer, W. S. (October 1999). Corporate liability, risk shifting, and the paradox of compliance. *Vanderbilt Law Review, 52*, 1409.

6. Ibid. (p. 1344).

7. Ibid. (p. 1415). During these years, 1996–1998, between 23% and 44% of antitrust offenders received prison sentences.

8. Draffan, G. Primer: Facts and statistics about corporations. *Public Information Network*, PO Box 95316, Seattle WA 98145-2316.

9. Ibid.

10. Enloe (p. 13).

11. Donahue, J. (December 1992). The missing corporate rap sheet: Missing government records of corporate abuses. *Multinational Monitor*, 14–16.

12. Ibid. (p. 19).

13. Marx, K. (1967). *Capital: A critique of political economy*. New York: International Publishers. Originally published in 1866.

14. U.S. Bureau of the Census 1982. (1986). *Census of manufacturers: Concentration ratios in manufacturing* (p. 524). Washington, DC: Government Printing Office; Scherer, R. (October 30, 2003). Mergers and the supersizing of business. *Christian Science Monitor*.

15. Associated Press, October 3, 1980. Some of the material in this section is adapted from Eitzen, D. S., & Zinn, M. B. (1989). *Social problems* (4th ed). Boston: Allyn & Bacon.

16. *Statistical abstract of the United States, 1986* (p. 524). Washington, DC: Government Printing Office.

17. http://www.granneman.com/blog/2006/07/30/corporate-consolidation-reigns-in-american-business-thats-a-problem/, *Harper's* (July 30, 2006); http://yaleglobal.yale.edu/display.article?id=6985 (February 15, 2006); http://onthecommons.org/comment/reply/775, (2005).

18. Etzioni, A. (Winter 1990). Is corporate crime worth the time? *Business and Society Review, 36*, 33.

19. Sherrill, Robert (April 7, 1997) A year in corporate crime, *The Nation*.

20. *New York Times*, March 3, 1996, A-1.

21. Draffan, G. (February 15, 2005). *Corporate mergers and acquisitions*. http://www.endgame.org/mergers.html.

22. Quoted in Green, Moore, & Wasserstein (pp. 13–14).

23. This section on the consequences of shared monopolies is taken primarily from Green, Moore, & Wasserstein (pp. 14–26); and Newfield, J., & Greenfield, J. (1972). *A populist manifesto* (pp. 48–56). New York: Warner Paperback Library.

24. Green, Moore, & Wasserstein (p. 14).

25. DuBoff, R. B. (December 1984). Wealth distribution study causes tinge of discomfort. *In These Times*, 17.

26. Jack Newfield & Jeff Greenfield. (1972) *A Populist Manifesto* (p. 48–56). New York: Warner Paperback Library.

27. Quoted in Ralph Nader, Mark Green, & Joel Seligman, *Taming the Giant Corporation* (p. 216). New York: W. W. Norton.

28. Green, Moore, & Wasserstein (p. 15). See also "The monopoly inflation game." *Dollars and Sense*, January 23, 1977, 12–13.

29. Nader, Green, & Seligman (p. 213).

30. For comparison, see Parenti, M. (1978). *Power and the powerless*. New York: St. Martin's Press.

31. Green, M. J. (March 4, 1972). The high cost of monopoly. *Progressive*, 36 and The Forbes sales 500. *Forbes*, April 25, 1988, 136–137.

32. Currie, E., & Skolnick, J. H. (1988). *America's problems* (2nd ed., p. 86). Glenview, IL: Scott, Foresman.

33. Hay, G. A., & Kelley, D. (April 1974). An empirical survey of price fixing conspiracies. *Journal of Law and Economics 17*, 13–38.

34. The ten worst corporations. *Mother Jones*, January 1997, 30ff.

35. Hay & Kelley (pp. 26–27).

36. Mokhiber, 11; and *USA Today*, September 30, 2002.

37. The following account is taken primarily from three sources: Geis, G. (1978). White collar crime: The heavy electrical equipment cases of 1961. In M. D. Erman & R. J. Lundman (eds.). *Corporate and governmental deviance* (pp. 59–79). New York: Oxford University Press; Smith, R. A. (April 1961).The incredible electrical conspiracy. *Fortune, part I*, 132–37, 170–80; *part II*, May 1961, 161–64, 210–24; and Green, Moore, & Wasserstein (pp. 154–157).

38. Smith (part I, p. 137).

39. For comparison, see *Wall Street Journal*, July 27, 1964, 22. For the account of more recent cases of corporations and their executives receiving little if any punishment for their crimes, see Nathan, R. S. (January 1980). Coddled criminals. *Harper's*, 30–35; Crime in the suites: On the rise. *Newsweek*, December 3, 1979, 114–120; and Mokhiber, R. (1988). *Corporate crime and violence*. San Francisco: Sierra Club Books.

40. Green, Moore, & Wasserstein (p. 152); and *New Republic*, February 20, 1961, 7.

41. Quoted in Smith (part I, p. 133).

42. Ibid. (p. 135).

43. Nader, R., & Green, M. (April 29, 1972). Crime in the suites. *New Republic*, 20–21.

44. For a late 1970s example of a price-fixing violation in the forest products industry, see Briggs, J. A. (June 25, 1979). For whom does the bell toll? *Forbes*, 33–36.

45. For comparison, see Cross, J. (1976). *The supermarket trap* (rev. ed., pp. 119, 124). Bloomington: Indiana University Press; and Schnapper, E. (1974). Consumer legislation and the poor. In D. A. Aaker & G. S. Day (eds.). *Consumerism* (2nd ed., p. 87). New York: Free Press.

46. Jacobs, P. (1979). Keeping the poor poor. In J. H. Skolnick & E. Currie (eds.). *Crisis in American institutions* (4th ed., p. 96). Boston: Little, Brown.

47. Cross (p. 122).

48. http://www.davidcorn.com/archives/2005/08/with_hurrican_k.php, *David Corn.Com* (August 31, 2005).

49. Drake, D., & Uhlman, M. (1993). *Making drugs making money* (pp. 3, 8, 21–22). Kansas City, MO: Andrews & McMeel.

50. Konner, M. (1993). *Dear America* (p. 54). Reading, MA: Addison-Wesley.

51. Ibid. (pp. 54–55).

52. *20/20*, ABC News.

53. Ibid. (pp. 19–20) (transcript).

54. Angell, M. (July 15, 2004). The truth about the drug companies. *New York Review of Books*, http://www.nybooks.com/articles/17244.

55. *healingdaily.com*, http://www.healingdaily.com/conditions/pharmaceutical-companies.htm (2003).

56. Ibid. See Jean Kilbourne's excellent critique (1999). *Can't buy my love: How advertising changes the way we think and feel*. New York: Touchstone.

57. Freeman, H. (February 1977). On consuming the surplus. *Progressive, 41*, 20–21.

58. For an elaboration of the role of television in the manipulation of people, see Goldsen, R. K. (1975). *The show and tell machine: How television works and works you over.* New York: Dial Press.

59. Cohane, J. P. (1978). The American predicament: Truth no longer counts. In M. R. Haskell & L. Yablonsky (eds.). *Criminology: Crime and criminality* (2nd ed., p. 172). Chicago: Rand McNally (originally appeared in *Los Angeles Times,* October 1, 1972).

60. Federal Trade Commission, http://www.ftc.gov/speeches/swindle/030428aggressive. htm (April 28, 2003).

61. *Los Angeles Times,* August 20, 1992, D-2.

62. *New York Times,* April 29, 1994, C-2.

63. *Wall Street Journal,* February 11, 1994, B-6.

64. *Washington Post,* September 30, 1993, D-11.

65. *McDermott Newsletter,* http://www.mwe.com/index.cfm/fuseaction/publications. nldetail/object_id/38a7d2e2-5653-4f7c-8e1b-b81f3b979f77.cfm (August 27, 2004).

66. Office of the New York State Attorney General, http://www.oag.state.ny.us/press/2006/ aug/aug18a_06.html (August 18, 2006).

67. Wikipedia, http://en.wikipedia.org/wiki/False_advertising (March 10, 2007).

68. Ibid.

69. Ibid.

70. Preston, I. L. (1975). *The great American blow-up: Puffery in advertising and selling* (pp. 18–20). Madison: University of Wisconsin Press; and Rotfeld, H. J., & Preston, L. (1981). The potential impact of research on advertising law. *Journal of Advertising Research, 21,* 9–16.

71. List of Advertising Slogans. *Wikipedia.* http://en.wikipedia.org/wiki/List of advertising slogans (March 14, 2007).

72. Rotfeld & Preston.

73. Rotfeld, H. J., & Rotzall, K. B. (1980). Is advertising puffery believed? *Journal of Advertising Research, 9,* 16–20.

74. Wyckham, R. G. (February/March 1987). Implied superiority claims. *Journal of Advertising Research, 27,* 54–63.

75. Ibid. (p. 55).

76. Hemmelstein, H. (1984). *Understanding television* (pp. 68, 271). New York: Praeger.

77. Rotfeld & Preston (p. 10).

78. Preston (pp. 32–33).

79. Sutherland, E. H., & Cressey, D. R. (1974). *Criminology* (9th ed., p. 42). Philadelphia: J. B. Lippincott.

80. *North Texas E-News,* http://www.ntxe-news.com/artman/publish/article_41267. shtml (March 16, 2007).

81. Campaign for Tobacco-Free Kids. http://www.emaxhealth.com/58/10277.html (March 2007).

82. http://en.wikipedia.org/wiki/Bernard_Madoff (26 Oct. 2010). Henriques, D., & Lattman, P. (December 10, 2010). Madoff trustee seeks $19.6 billion from Austrian banker. 12:22 pm Bloomberg News.Com; http://www.huffingtonpost.com/2010/12/11/mark-madoff-suicide-hanged_n_795342.html.

83. Galbraith, J. K. (December 1977). Crime and no punishment. *Esquire,* 102–106. See also McC lintick, D. (1976).The biggest Ponzi scheme: A reporter's journal. In D. Moffett (ed.). *Swindled* (pp. 9–126). New York: DowJones Books.

84. Markopolis, Harry. (2010). No one would listen.com

85. The ensuing discussion is based on the following sources: Simon, D. R. (2004). *Tony Soprano's America: The criminal side of the American dream* (pp. 48–54). New York: Westview:; http://www.forbes.com/2002/07/25/accountingtracker.html; Lyman, M. D., & Potter, G. (2004). *Organized crime* (3rd ed., pp. 444–446). Upper Saddle River, NJ: Prentice-Hall; http://money.cnn.com/2004/07/16/news/newsmakers/martha_ sentencing/.

86.  Johnson, J. M., & Douglas, J. D. (Eds.). (1978). *Crime at the top: Deviance in business and the professions* (p. 151). Philadelphia: J. B. Lippincott.

87.  Bureau of the Census. (1983). *Statistical abstract of the United States, 1984* (pp. xxvi, 567). Washington, DC: Government Printing Office.

88.  The following is taken from Sutherland, E. H. (1961). *White collar crime* (pp. 21–33). New York: Holt, Rinehart and Winston.

# 4

# Corporate Deviance: Human Jeopardy

This chapter addresses the corporate disregard for the welfare of people, which involves the abuse of consumers, workers, and society itself. Our thesis is that the profit-maximizing behaviors practiced by corporations under monopoly capitalism are hazardous to our individual and collective health and therefore constitute another manifestation of elite deviance. The first part of this chapter examines four manifestations of corporate deviance that jeopardize individual health: unsafe products, food pollution, tobacco products, and dangerous working conditions. The second part focuses on two problems that society faces from various corporate activities: the waste of natural resources and pollution of the environment.

## Individual Jeopardy

### Unsafe Products

Commonly, the concern over violence in society is directed toward murder, rape, child abuse, and riots. We do not include in the context of violence the harm inflicted on people by unsafe products. The National Commission on Product Safety has revealed that 20 million Americans are injured in the home as a result of incidents connected with consumer products. "Of the total, 110,000 are permanently disabled and 30,000 are killed. A significant number could have been spared if more attention had been paid to hazard reduction."[1] The costs from deaths, injuries, and property damage were recently estimated by the Consumer Product Safety Commission at $700 billion annually.

The U.S. Consumer Product Safety Commission (CPSC) reports that several bad records in consumer product safety areas were set during fiscal year 2005, including:

- Most recalls of defective consumer products
- Most civil penalties handed out for industry failure to report hazardous products

Product Recalls Manufacturers voluntarily recalled 397 products during fiscal 2005, the highest number of voluntary recalls filed with CPSC in 10 years, including the highest annual total ever for products not covered by a mandatory safety standard.

- In 2005, new records for the number of recalls involving 15 hazardous all-terrain vehicles (ATVs) and 10 rechargeable batteries were set.
- There were record civil penalties imposed for failure to report hazards.
- Six different manufacturers failed to report known defective products to CPSC during 2005 and paid a record $8.8 million in total fines for their "forgetfulness."

In 2007, there was a series of product recalls of goods imported from China. Recalled, among many other items, were tainted pet food, toothpaste containing antifreeze, and millions of Mattel toys laced with lead-based paint. Some industry experts, like independent toy industry consultant Chris Byrne, argued that U.S. manufacturers that import these goods are more culpable than the Chinese suppliers for allowing unsafe imports into America.[2]

Considerable evidence points to numerous unsafe products, from clothing to toys to tires, but nowhere has the poor corporate safety record been more visible than in the auto industry. The indictment against this industry involves two basic charges: (1) faulty design and (2) working against governmental and consumer efforts to add safety devices as basic equipment.

*The Auto Industry.*    In 1929, the president of Du Pont tried to induce the president of General Motors (GM) to use safety glass in Chevrolets, as Ford was already doing. The president of GM felt that this addition was too costly and would therefore hinder sales. In his reply to Du Pont, he said, "I would very much rather spend the same amount of money in improving our car in other ways because I think, from the standpoint of selfish business, it would be a very much better investment. You can say, perhaps, that I am selfish, but business is selfish. We are not a charitable institution; we are trying to make a profit for our stockholders."[3]

This example shows how the profit motive superseded the possibility of preventing deaths and serious injuries. Unfortunately, this is not an isolated instance in the auto industry. We will review two representative cases, one involving GM and the other, Ford.

Ralph Nader attacked GM's Corvair in *Unsafe at Any Speed* (1972), showing how that car had many dangerous defects, including a heater that gave off carbon monoxide and an instability that increased its likelihood of overturning.[4] GM's response to this indictment was to attack his credibility and hide evidence supporting his allegations.[5]

Throughout much of the 1970s, the fastest-selling domestic subcompact was Ford's Pinto. From the very beginning, however, the Pinto was flawed by a fuel system that ruptured easily in rear-end collisions.[6] Preproduction crash tests established this problem, but since the assembly-line machinery had already been tooled, Ford decided to manufacture the car as it was, despite the fact that it could produce a much safer gas tank. This decision was made partly because the Pinto was on a tight production schedule; Ford was trying to enter the lucrative subcompact market dominated by Volkswagen as quickly as possible. The time span from the conception of the Pinto to production was targeted at 25 months, when the normal time for a new car was 43 months. Also involved in the decision to go with the original gas tank were styling considerations and the effort to maximize trunk space. The concern for profits over human considerations was clearly evident in Ford's reluctance to change the design of the Pinto as fatalities and injuries occurred because of the faulty gas tank. Although the company calculated that it would cost only $11 to make each car safe, it decided that this was too costly. Ford reasoned that 180 burn deaths, 180 serious burn injuries, and 2,100 burned vehicles would cost $49.5 million (each death was figured at $200,000). But doing a recall of all Pintos and making each $11 repair would amount to $137 million (see Table 4.1).

In addition to the decision to leave the Pinto alone, Ford lobbied in Washington to convince government regulatory agencies and Congress that auto accidents are caused not by cars but by (1) people and (2) highway conditions. This philosophy is rather like blaming a robbery on the victim. Well, what did you expect? You were carrying money, weren't you? It is

**TABLE 4.1**   *$11 vs. a Burn Death: Benefits and Costs Relating to Fuel Leakage Associated with the Static Rollover Test Portion of FMVSS 208*

| Benefits | | Costs | |
|---|---|---|---|
| Savings: | 180 burn deaths<br>180 serious burn injuries<br>2,100 burned vehicles | Sales: | 11 million cars<br>1.5 million light trucks |
| Unit Cost: | $200,000 per death<br>$67,000 per injury<br>$700 per vehicle | Unit Cost: | $11 per car<br>$11 per truck |
| Total Benefit: | 180 × ($200,000)<br>+ 180 × ($67,000)<br>+ 2,100 × ($700)<br>= $49.5 million | Total Cost: | 11,000,000 × ($11)<br>+ 1,500,000 × ($11)<br>= $137 million |

Source: Ford Motor Company internal memorandum, "Fatalities Associated with Crash-Induced Fuel Leakage and Fires," cited in Mark Dowie, "Pinto Madness," *Mother Jones* 2 (September/October 1977), 24. © *Mother Jones*. Used with permission.

an extraordinary experience to hear automotive "safety engineers" talk for hours without ever mentioning cars. They will advocate spending billions educating youngsters, punishing drunks, and redesigning street signs. Listening to them, you can momentarily begin to think that it is easier to control 100 million drivers than a handful of manufacturers. They show movies about guardrail design and advocate the clear-cutting of trees 100 feet back from every highway in the nation. If a car is unsafe, they argue, it is because its owner doesn't properly drive it. Or, perhaps, maintain it.[7]

Meanwhile, fiery crashes involving Pintos occurred with some regularity. Liability suits against Ford increased, with judgments routinely found against the company. In 1978, a jury in California awarded $127.8 million, including $125 million in punitive damages, to a teenager badly burned when his 1972 Pinto burst into flames after being hit in the rear by a car traveling at 35 miles per hour.[8]

In that same year, 10 years after the government had begun investigating the Pinto problem, the Department of Transportation finally announced that its tests showed conclusively that the Pinto was unsafe and ordered a recall of all 1971 to 1976 Pintos. One critic of Ford's defiance of human considerations made this telling observation: "One wonders how long Ford Motor Company would continue to market lethal cars were Henry Ford II and Lee Iacocca [the top Ford officials at the time] serving twenty-year terms in Leavenworth for consumer homicide."[9]

Vehicle manufacturers do not like government recalls for obvious reasons. Faulty vehicles are expensive to repair. They can also cause scandals if defective products cause injuries and deaths. Finally, defects may ruin a vehicle's reputation, resulting in reduced sales. In April, 2010, Toyota faced "the National Highway Traffic and Safety Administration's (NHTSA) maximum penalty of $16.375 million... Specifically, the NHTSA has a problem with Toyota failing to tell the agency about the 'sticky pedal' problem for at least 4 months. This maximum fine might also be taken as notice to all other automakers doing business that the NHTSA now has more authority." The pedal has been blamed for several accidents and a undetermined number of deaths.

"We now have proof that Toyota failed to live up to its legal obligations," said *Transportation* Secretary Ray LaHood. "Worse yet, they knowingly hid a dangerous defect for months from U.S. officials and did not take action to protect millions of drivers and their families. For those reasons, we are seeking the maximum penalty possible under current laws."[10] This is part of the story in the decline of both Ford Motor Company and Chrysler.

- In March 2007, Ford announced a recall of 109,664 Crown Victoria police cars because of cracks that can develop in the police cruiser wheels, causing rapid air loss during high-speed pursuits. The cracks have been reported in a small percentage of the steel wheels on 2003 to 2005 Ford Crown Victoria police interceptors. The wheels were covered by a Ford extended warranty program, according to a company executive.

Ford notified the National Highway Traffic Safety Administration (NHTSA) of the problem, stating that the cracks can form near the weld line that connects the rim to the wheel disk. Ford dealers inspected and replaced the wheels and the spare as needed. The Crown Victoria police interceptors recalled were built from October 10, 2001, to December 8, 2004. This is the second Ford recall involving wheels on the police interceptor. In August 2003, the company recalled wheels on the cars and extended the wheel warranties. Police departments have reported two crashes that they attributed to the wheel problem, according to a Ford spokesman, but the automaker is disputing the reports. No one was injured in either crash. A number of police departments have filed suits against Ford.

- In March 2007, Ford Motor Company recalled 155,000 pickup trucks and sport utility vehicles, including 2003 models of its F-150, F-250, F-350, F-450, and F-550 Super Duty truck, the Ford Excursion SUV, and the Lincoln Blackwood pickup. A faulty cruise-control switch suspected of causing fires in older model Ford trucks is the reason for the latest recall. The F-150 pickup is the top-selling vehicle in the United States. F-Series trucks have faced declining sales in recent months, however. Sales for the F-150 pickup were down almost 12% in 2006 to nearly 800,000 vehicles. Ford recalled 5.8 million vehicles in 2006 after a lengthy investigation by the NHTSA because of engine fires linked to the cruise-control systems in trucks, SUVs, and vans. The investigation concluded that brake fluid could leak through the cruise control's deactivation switch into electrical components and cause corrosion that might lead to overheating and fire.

- In late 2006, Chrysler Group recalled more than 489,000 vehicles, including some models of the Jeep Liberty, the Dodge Durango, and the new Dodge Avenger sedan. Chrysler is recalling 328,424 Durango SUVs because of the risk of overheating linked to an integrated circuit in the vehicle's instrument cluster. The recall covered 2004 to 2006 model year Durango SUVs, according to Chrysler. In 2007, the automaker recalled 2008 model Dodge Avenger sedans because of a problem with the door latches on the new cars. And Chrysler recalled 149,605 Jeep Liberty vehicles, made between 2006 and 2007, because of air-conditioning glitches.

The automobile industry has traditionally resisted new safety devices because the added cost might hurt sales.[11] Following tests conducted by the government and the insurance industry in the late 1950s, the government ruled that lap belts must be installed in all new cars built after January 1, 1965. The auto industry resisted (as it has since resisted other requirements such as lap-and-shoulder belts, ignition interlocks, and buzzers), despite clear evidence that these devices would be effective in saving lives: "between 1968 and 1977, the stock of cars on the road grew from 83 million to 112 million, an increase of 35 percent. Over the same period traffic fatalities declined 6 percent."[12]

As lap belts are effective only when used and relatively few were being used at the time, the government reasoned that safety could be improved significantly if a passive restraint such as the air bag were included as standard equipment. A study by Allstate Insurance concluded that air bags would reduce occupant crash deaths by 65%. Had all cars been so equipped in 1975, 9,500 fewer persons would have died in car crashes in that year instead of the 27,200 who did. Additionally, 104,000 serious injuries could have been prevented each year.[13]

Recent research indicates that General Motors, Standard Oil (now Exxon), and Du Pont colluded for decades to make and market lead-containing gasoline, a deadly poison, despite the existence of safe alternatives. Abetted by the U.S. government, these corporations suppressed the scientific knowledge that lead kills. Today lead-containing gasoline is still sold in poor nations all over the world.[14]

*Health Products.*   Corporations have marketed numerous products to promote health that are known to be dangerous. In 2005, the U.S. Food and Drug Administration (FDA) announced plans to create an independent monitoring board to oversee the safety of prescription drugs. This is because the FDA delayed issuing labels on antidepressants even though research indicated they can cause suicidal tendencies in children and teens. The FDA also approved Vioxx and Celebrex, even though studies linked them to strokes and heart attacks. Estimates are that the two drugs may be responsible for more than 55,000 deaths.[15]

## Food Pollution

The food industry is obviously big business. In this section, we examine how the food industry, in its search for more profits, often disregards the health of consumers, which constitutes deviance. We explore four areas in which human considerations are often secondary to profit: (1) the sale of adulterated products, (2) the extensive use of chemical additives, (3) the increased use of sugar and fats, and (4) the sale of products known to be harmful.

*Adulterated Products.*   We will use the meat industry as our illustration of blatant disregard for the health of consumers. Upton Sinclair's exposé of the Chicago stockyards and meatpacking houses around 1900 showed how spoiled meat was sold, how dangerous ingredients (such as rats and dung) were included in sausage, and how rats overran piles of meat stored under leaking roofs.[16] President Theodore Roosevelt commissioned an investigation of Chicago meat packers, and, as a result, the Meat Inspection Act of 1906 required that meat sold in interstate commerce had to be inspected according to federal standards. However, meat processed and sold within a state was not subject to the law, thus omitting as late as 1967 nearly 15% of the meat slaughtered and 25% of all meat processed in the United States.

As a result,

> Surveys of packing houses in Delaware, Virginia, and North Carolina found the following tidbits in the meat: animal hair, sawdust, flies, abscessed pork livers, and snuff spit out by the meat workers. To add even further flavoring, packing houses whose meat did not cross state lines could use 4-D meat (dead, dying, diseased, and disabled) and chemical additives that would not pass federal inspection. Such plants were not all minor operations; some were run by the giants Armour, Swift, and Wilson.[17]

In 1967, the Wholesome Meat Act was passed, specifying that state inspection standards must at least match federal standards. This was accomplished in 1971, but there have been continuing violations. One problem is meat that is returned by a retailer to a packer as unsatisfactory and is then resold as number two meat to another customer if it meets standards of wholesomeness. As an example of how this can be abused, consider the following occurrence in a Los Angeles Hormel plant.

> When the original customers returned the meat to Hormel, they used the following terms to describe it: "moldy liver loaf, sour party hams, leaking bologna, discolored bacon, off-condition hams, and slick and slimy spareribs." Hormel renewed these products with cosmetic measures (reconditioning, trimming, and washing). Spareribs returned for sliminess, discoloration, and stickiness were rejuvenated through curing and smoking, renamed Windsor Loins, and sold in ghetto stores for more than fresh pork chops.[18]

This Hormel abuse occurred because the U.S. Department of Agriculture inspector, who was paid $6,000 annually by Hormel for overtime, looked the other way.[19]

Meat packers are also deceptive about what is included in their products. The labels on packages are not always complete. Consider, for instance, the ingredients of the hot dog.

> The hot dog . . . by law can contain 69 percent water, salt, spices, corn syrup and cereal and 15 percent chicken; that still leaves a little room for goat meat, pigs' ears, eyes, stomachs, snouts, udders, bladders and esophagus—all legally okay. There is no more all-American way to take a break at the old ball game than to have water and pigs' snouts on a bun, but you might prefer to go heavier on the mustard from now on.[20]

Upton Sinclair's lurid description of the 1900s-era Chicago slaughterhouses fits some situations even today. In 1984, Nebraska Beef Processors and its Colorado subsidiary, Cattle King Packing Company, the largest supplier of ground meat to school lunch programs and also a major supplier of meat to the Department of Defense, supermarkets, and fast-food chains, was found guilty of (1) regularly bringing dead animals into its slaughterhouses and mixing rotten meat into its hamburgers, (2) labeling old meat with phony dates, and (3) deceiving U.S. Department of Agriculture inspectors by matching diseased carcasses with the healthy heads from larger cows.[21]

The Nebraska Beef–Cattle King scandal was not an isolated case. Two additional examples make this point. In 1979, a New Jersey firm was convicted of making pork sausage with an unauthorized chemical that masks discoloration of spoiled meat. And in 1982 a California company used walkie-talkies to avoid inspectors while doctoring rotten sausage. Some 500 million salmonella-tainted eggs from two large Iowa farms were recalled in 2010. Lax oversight by the FDA has made the public even more distrustful of the entire egg industry.[22]

*Extensive Use of Chemical Additives.*   The profits from the food industry come mainly from processing farm goods by fortifying, enriching, and reformulating them to produce goods that look appealing, have the right taste and aroma, and will not spoil. More than 1,500 food additives have approved use as flavors, colors, thickeners, preservatives, and other agents for controlling the properties of food. Let's briefly look at some of these additives.[23]

- Sodium nitrates and nitrites are added to keep meat products appearing blood red. Nitrates are also used to preserve smoked fish.
- A variety of preservatives is used to prevent the spoilage of bread, cereals, margarine, fish, confections, jellies, and soft drinks. The most commonly used are butylated hydroxytoluene (BHT), butylated hydroxyanisole ( BHA), diethylstilbestro (DES), sodium benzoate, and benzoic acid.
- About 95% of the color in the food we eat is the result of added synthetic colors. The use of red dye number 2 was prohibited by the government when it was found to cause cancer in mice, although it is still allowed in maraschino cherries because it is assumed that no one will eat more than one or two at a time.
- Flour, that all-purpose staple, is bleached and conditioned by a number of potent poisons: hydrogen acetone, benzyl peroxide, chlorine dioxide, nitrogen oxide, and nitrosyl chloride. Also added to flour are such strengtheners as potassium bromate and ammonium presulfate.

An indirect additive that affects the health of consumers is one that is fed to animals. DES, an artificial female sex hormone, fattens about 75% of the beef cattle in the United States. This hormone is added because it causes dramatic weight gain on less feed. It has been outlawed for use with poultry, although hens are fed arsenic because it makes them lay more eggs.

Sugar substitutes are another type of food additive that has questionable health consequences. Cyclamates were banned in 1970 after tests linked them to various types of cancer. And saccharin, another additive, has been shown to be dangerous but has not been banned; Congress has only decreed that food containing saccharin must carry warning labels. The latest sugar substitute, aspartame (or Nutrasweet), is also believed by some scientists to pose a health danger to some 50 million regular users.

However, no ban or warning has been issued for products containing Nutrasweet. The per capita consumption of the various noncaloric sweeteners has increased from the sugar-sweetness equivalent of 2.2 pounds in 1960 to 20.0 pounds in 1988.[24]

According to a growing number of scientists, aspartame is the most dangerous substance added to foods. Aspartame currently accounts for more than 75% of the adverse reactions to food additives reported to the FDA. Many of these reactions are very serious.[25] Some of the 90 different documented symptoms listed in a 1994 Heath and Human Services report as being caused by aspartame include the following:[26]

| | |
|---|---|
| Headaches and migraines | Dizziness |
| Seizures resulting in death | Nausea |
| Numbness | Muscle spasms |
| Weight gain | Rashes |
| Depression | Fatigue |
| Irritability | Tachycardia |
| Insomnia | Vision problems |
| Hearing loss | Heart palpitations |
| Breathing difficulties | Anxiety attacks |
| Slurred speech | Loss of taste |
| Tinnitus | Vertigo |
| Memory loss | Joint pain |
| Brain tumors | Multiple sclerosis |
| Epilepsy | Chronic fatigue syndrome |
| Parkinson's disease | Alzheimer's |
| Mental retardation | Lymphoma |
| Birth defects | Fibromyalgia |
| Diabetes | |

Aspartame is 10% methanol, a form of alcohol that can be a deadly poison. Symptoms from methanol poisoning include headaches, ear ringing, dizziness, nausea, gastrointestinal disturbances, weakness, chills, memory lapses, numbness and extremity pains, behavioral disturbances, and neuritis. The most well-known problems from methanol poisoning are vision problems, which can range from blurred vision to blindness.

Even the air force and navy magazines, such as *Flying Safety* and *Navy Physiology,* have warned in articles about the hazards of aspartame's cumulative deleterious effects, which include the greater likelihood of birth defects and the danger to pilots of seizures and vertigo.[27]

There is a great deal of controversy among scientists about the effects of additives in our diet. "Altogether, laboratory tests have produced evidence that some 1,400 substances, drugs, food additives, pesticides, industrial chemicals, cosmetics, might cause cancer. But there are only a few chemicals which all the experts see as linked to human cancer."[28] Typically, government scientists disagree with the scientists hired by industry.[29] Several considerations, though, should make us cautious about what we eat.

First, many of the additives are poisons. The quantities in food may be minute, but just what are the tolerance levels? Is any poison, in any amount, appropriate in food? Is there the possibility of residue buildup in vital organs?

Second, what happens to laboratory animals fed relatively large quantities of these additives? They are poisoned, get cancer, and suffer from other maladies induced by the additives.

Finally, what happens with the interaction of these additives on humans? Scientists may be able to test the effects of a few chemicals, but what about the hundreds of thousands of possible combinations? In a slice of bread, for example, there can be as many as 93 different additives. The danger is that it takes years, maybe 20 or 30, of eating a particular diet for an individual to develop cancer. Since most of the additives are relatively new, we do not know what they may eventually cause. We do know that the average American has increased his or her yearly intake of food additives from 3 pounds in 1965 to about 5 pounds in 1977.[30] And cancer rates continue to rise.

Why, then, do companies insist on adding these potentially harmful chemicals to our food? One possibility is that consumers demand more variety and convenience. But, more important, the food industry has found that processing synthetic foods is very profitable. As one food marketer remarked, "The profit margin on food additives is fantastically good, much better than the profit margins on basic, traditional foods."[31] Hightower has shown how this works:

> It gets down to this: Processing and packaging of food are becoming more important pricing factors than the food itself. Why would food corporations rather sell highly processed and packaged food than the much simpler matter of selling basics? Because processing and packaging spell profits.
>
> First, the more you do to a product, the more chances there are to build in profit margins—Heinz can sell tomatoes for a profit, or it can bottle the tomatoes for a bigger profit, or it can process the tomatoes into ketchup for still more profit, or it can add spices to the ketchup and sell it as barbeque sauce for a fat profit, or it can add flavors and meat tenderizer to the barbeque sauce for the fattest profit of all.
>
> Second, processing and packaging allow artificial differentiation of one company's product from that of another—in other words, selling on the basis of brand names. Potatoes can be sold in bulk, or they can be put in a sack and labeled Sun Giant, which will bring a higher price and more profit.

Third, processing and packaging allow the use of additives to keep the same item on the shelf much longer and they allow for shipment over long distances, thus expanding the geographic reach of a corporation.

Fourth, processing and packaging separate consumers from the price of raw food, allowing oligopolistic middlemen to hold up the consumer price of their products even when the farm price falls. When the spinach crop is so abundant that spinach prices tumble at the farm level, the supermarket price of Stouffer's frozen spinach souffle does not go down.[32]

What's more, American corporations, in their quest for profits, have knowingly marketed defective medical devices, lethal drugs, carcinogens, toxic pesticides, and other harmful products overseas when they have been banned for sale in the United States. (A more detailed discussion of such practices is found in Chapter 5.)

*Sugar and Fat Consumption.*    Consumers have begun to question the types of food provided by the food industry and the advertising efforts to push certain questionable items. In particular, we will address how the food industry has promoted the consumption of sugar and fats. In the previous section, we noted the problem with chemical additives. However, we did not discuss the foremost food additive—sugar. The introduction of processed foods has increased the annual amount of sweeteners consumed (refined sugar, corn sweeteners, and noncaloric sweeteners) from 122 pounds per capita in 1984 to 152 pounds in 2003, including 46 gallons of sugared soft drinks.[33]

A 1991 study by the Center for Science in the Public Interest concluded that Saturday morning children's television (TV) programs were loaded with commercials for foods high in sugar and fat, including drinks, chips, salty canned pastas, and fast food.[34]

In 2004, documentary maker Morgan Spurlock researched the American way of eating. His findings are supported by other studies:

- Ominously, 37% of American children and adolescents are carrying too much fat, and two out of every three adults are overweight or obese. Soft drink consumption among teens (aged 10 through 17) has doubled since 1984. Experiments with sugar in animals found its effects addictive, complete with withdrawal symptoms. People with high sugar intake have low intake of key nutrients (especially essential minerals). Americans spend $32 billion on snacks. Snacks are associated with obesity.
- Only one in four Americans exercises regularly. The percentage of overweight children in the United States has doubled in the last two decades. Physical education programs have been cut at many schools around the nation, but unhealthy lunches and vending machines loaded with junk food remain. Collectively, Americans eat 54 billion meals outside their homes annually at a cost of $2,116 per family. The more meals children eat in restaurants, the higher their calorie intake, the lower their consumption of fruit and vegetables, and the higher their consumption of fried foods and soft drinks.

- Spurlock's film presents the health-depleting qualities of fast food. He ate three times a day at McDonald's and gained a pound a day. His cholesterol level increased significantly, his liver became pathological, and his sex drive declined dramatically. His interview with the son of the owner of Baskin Robbins contains a confession that both his father and his uncle (Baskin) died of heart disease when they were around 50 years old. This was due to eating high-fat ice cream regularly.[35]
- Spurlock shows pictures of famous personalities to children who look to be about 6 years old. They could all identify Ronald McDonald and George Washington but were stumped by a picture of Jesus.

The use of sugars presents four health dangers. First, dental disease, such as cavities and gum problems, is clearly exacerbated by sugar. Another problem is that refined sugar, although an energy source, offers little nutritional value. Not only does it deprive the body of essential nutrients found in complex carbohydrates, but it actually increases the body's need for certain vitamins. Third, there appears to be a relationship between the proportion of refined sugar calories in the diet and the incidence of diabetes. Finally, there is the problem of obesity.

Another trend in the U.S. diet is the increased consumption of fats. From 1960 to 1989, the average annual amount of fat consumed per person rose from 45.1 to 60.7 pounds.[36] One source of this fat for modern Americans is the potato chip. Potato chips are 40% fat, compared with 0.1% fat in baked potatoes.[37] Food processors push us to eat potato chips rather than fresh potatoes because the profit is 1,100% more.[38] In 1977, the Senate Select Committee on Nutrition recommended that Americans reduce their consumption of fats by 40% because fat consumption leads to problems of obesity, cancer (breast and colon), and heart disease.[39] Currently 60% of American adults are obese (defined as weighing at least 20% more than normal weight).

***Enticing Children.*** The increased consumption of additives, sugar, and fats in food by children is a special health concern. Children are an important market, and food producers have spent multimillions of dollars in advertising aimed at them. Obviously, these corporations believe that their advertising influences the interests, needs, and demands of children. This belief is backed by research findings that show that children are susceptible to this influence. One study of youngsters in grades one through five found that 75% had asked their mothers to purchase the cereals that they had seen on TV. In another study, 80% of the mothers of children aged 2 to 6 expressed the conviction that TV ads caused their children to ask for certain products.[40]

The nutritional problem emanating from the TV advertising blitz aimed at children is that the most advertised food products are sugar-coated cereals, candies, and other sweet snack foods. One study, for example, found that 96% of all food advertising on Saturday and Sunday children's TV programs was for sweets.[41] This report by the Federal Trade Commission (FTC) shows that these advertisements are effective, for several reasons:

(a) [C]hildren's requests for specific, brand-name cereals and snack-foods are frequently, if not usually, honored by their parents; (b) very high proportions of children are able to name specific (heavily advertised) brands as their favorites; (c) when asked to list acceptable snacks, high proportions of children mention cookies, candy, cake, and ice cream, including specific (heavily advertised) products; (d) U.S. consumption of snack desserts has increased markedly since 1962, and significant proportions of the purchases are made by children.[42]

The TV advertising directed at children is effective because the advertisers have done their research. Social science techniques have been used by motivation researchers in laboratory situations to determine how children of various ages react to different visual and auditory stimuli. Children are watched through two-way mirrors, their behavior is photographed, and their autonomic responses (e.g., eye pupil dilation) are recorded to see what sustains their interest, their subconscious involvement, and the degree of pleasure that they experience.[43] Thus, advertisers have found that if one can associate fun, power, or a fascinating animated character with a product, children will want that product.

The staff of the FTC has argued that all TV commercials aimed at children are inherently unfair and deceptive. The young, they contend, are unable to be rational consumers. Therefore, in 1978, the commission proposed that (1) there be a ban on all ads for children under age 8, (2) a ban on all ads for highly sugared foods for those under 11 be enforced, and (3) there be a requirement for nutritional counter-ads to be paid for by industry.

This stance has been met with derision from the advertising and corporate industries. In hearings conducted by the FTC, advertisers and manufacturers argued against the evils of government regulation. The attorney for Mattel, a major manufacturer of children's toys, testified, "Our position, simply stated, is that the proposed ban is unconstitutional, economically injurious and unnecessary."[44] A spokesman for the National Association of Broadcasters also argued that self-regulation by the industry has worked: "Industry self-regulation has in fact been successful and now provides the mechanisms for effective regulation of advertising to children."[45] Also at the hearings, the counsel for the Kellogg Company said that "in an American democratic capitalistic society we must all learn, top to bottom, to care for ourselves. And the last thing we need in the next twenty years is a national nanny."[46]

These arguments have been countered by others. A child psychologist agreed with the FTC ban, saying, "I'm angry. In fact, I'm mad as hell. I'm furious that the most powerful communications system and the most powerfully and persuasive educational device that has ever existed in human history is being used systematically to mislead and lie to children." Friedlander added that children under the ages of 6 to 8 "are absolutely unable to understand and defend themselves against the ulterior motives of our business system."[47]

Bill Moyers, after confessing a bias for the necessity of advertising in general, ended his TV program with these words:

> It's astonishing to me that advertising to young children is even a matter of debate; that high-powered people with enormous skills and resources should have unbridled access to the minds of young children is no less absurd because those who profit from it consider it a sacrosanct right. If the government wanted to shower 20,000 propaganda messages a year on our children [the average number of advertisements seen annually by a child in the United States], we would take to the barricades and throw the scoundrels out. Yet the words of an advertising executive are treated as constitutional writ when he tells the FTC: "Children, like everyone else, must learn the marketplace. Even if a child is deceived by an ad at age four, what harm is done? Even if a child perceives children in advertisements as friends and not actors, selling them something, where's the harm? . . . " In the end, this debate is between two views of human nature. One treats young children as feeling, wondering, and wondrous beings to be handled with care because they're fragile; the other treats them as members of a vast collective to be hustled. We shall know a great deal about our society when we know, in this battle, which view prevails.[48]

## The Tobacco Industry

Although a number of industries have been guilty of manufacturing, advertising, and selling harmful products, we will consider only the tobacco industry. In 1979, 15 years after the surgeon general's first warning that smoking is linked to lung cancer and other ills, the secretary of health, education, and welfare issued the new surgeon general's report on the health hazards of smoking cigarettes.

Each day, in the United States more than 3,000 youths will begin to smoke, making themselves vulnerable to a host of cancers—lung, mouth, pharynx, larynx, esophagus, pancreas, cervix, kidney, and bladder—as well as heart disease and a host of other dangerous diseases. Among those who continue to smoke, approximately one-half will die prematurely, losing an average of 20 to 25 years of their life expectancy. And an estimated 450,000 people in the United States will die this year alone from tobacco-related diseases—the *most preventable and costly cause of death in America.* The global picture is even more worse: more than 1 billion people smoke worldwide, and an estimated 3 million die annually from tobacco-related diseases. By 2025, the number of tobacco-related deaths is expected to reach 10 million per year.

A recent American Cancer Society investigation notes that a woman's risk of contracting and dying of breast cancer increases by 25% if she smokes. The breast cancer risk increases in direct proportion to the number of cigarettes smoked per day and the total number of years smoked. Women smokers who consume two packs per day have a 75% chance of dying of breast cancer.

- Women who smoke cigarettes tend also to be estrogen-deficient. These smokers experience early menopause and an increased risk of some osteoporotic fractures. Nor are the negative effects of smoking limited to tissues having direct smoke contact. Smokers suffer increased risks of cancer of the esophagus, kidneys, and bladder, presumably from swallowed or absorbed cigarette products.

Nonsmoking women who are around smokers as little as 1 hour a day can almost triple their risk of contracting breast cancer, the second-highest cause of death among American women, and the highest cause of death among middle-aged women.

A research team from the University Hospital in Geneva, Switzerland, who defined smoking as a *mental disorder* (whose chief symptom is dangerousness to self and others), and studies the exposure to smoke of nearly 1,300 women concluded:

- As few as one to 10 cigarettes a day was enough to double a woman's risk of breast cancer.
- Consuming 10 to 19 cigarettes a day increases breast cancer risk almost fivefold.
- Women exposed to toxic tobacco smoke for 1 hour per day for 12 consecutive months nearly tripled their risk of contracting breast cancer.
- More women die of breast cancer than from any other cancer.[49]

No medical group or scientific group in the world has disputed the conclusion that smoking is very injurious to health, yet the tobacco industry continues to push its products (buttressed, we might add, by government subsidies). In 1988, the tobacco industry spent an estimated $2.5 billion promoting its products, much of it aimed at portraying smoking as a youthful and attractive habit. In this regard, the FTC has characterized cigarette advertising as follows: "Cigarette ads associate smoking with good health, youthful vigor, social and professional success and other attractive ideas . . . that are both worthy of emulation and distant from concerns relating to health. . . . Thus the cigarette is portrayed as an integral part of youth, happiness, attractiveness, personal success, and an active, vigorous life style."[50]

In addition to regular advertising, the tobacco industry has countered the antismoking campaign in several ways, each of which indicates disregard for the health of consumers. First, the industry has refused to accept the evidence against smoking, especially passive smoking. It argues that the links between smoking and various diseases are merely inferences from statistics. As Bill Dwyer of the Tobacco Institute has said, "Statistics are like a bikini bathing suit: what they reveal is interesting; what they conceal is vital."[51] Representatives of the industry argue in the media and in speeches before civic groups that they don't encourage anyone to smoke.

A second tactic used by the tobacco industry has been to shore up its power in Washington through extensive lobbying efforts and contributions to the political campaigns of key decision makers.

A more subtle strategy is giving and withholding advertising money to publications, depending on their editorial treatment of the tobacco issue.[52] Although several publications (e.g., *Reader's Digest, Good House-keeping,* and *the New Yorker*) do not accept cigarette advertising based on principle, most do. As a result, many publications depend on these revenues and thus do not wish to anger their sponsors by running articles critical of tobacco. *Time* and *Newsweek*, for example, have published supplements on health topics in cooperation with prestigious medical organizations such as the American Medical Association; however, most of the physician-prepared materials on smoking were edited out.[53] Tobacco companies have targeted women in particular as potential smokers and stepped up advertising in women's magazines. In response, these magazines have shown near silence on the dangers of cigarettes. A study by the American Council on Science and Health found the following with respect to women's magazines:

> *Cosmopolitan,* which receives $5.5 million a year in cigarette advertising (nearly ten percent of its total revenue), devoted only 2.3 percent of its total health coverage to smoking ("although smoking was noted as a risk factor in heart disease, it was never mentioned in private or in reference to lung cancer"). *Mademoiselle,* which receives $1 million in cigarette advertising (seven percent of its total revenue), devoted less than two percent of its health coverage to smoking ("unreliable source of information about the hazards of smoking. Used editorial ploys to deemphasize smoking, gave misinformation, and excluded smoking from mention on relevant health topics altogether. One of the worst"). . . . *Redbook,* which receives $7.5 million in cigarette advertising (sixteen percent of its total revenue), ran eighty health-related articles, but not one of them on smoking.[54]

These magazines seem to shy away from articles against tobacco use because they are afraid of losing advertising revenues from tobacco companies. Actually, these publications are afraid of more that just lost revenues. The tobacco companies are parts of huge conglomerates, and if all the companies in the conglomerates withheld their advertising dollars, the magazines and newspapers would be in serious financial trouble. Economic power clearly explains why a society permits and even encourages the production, distribution, and sale of a dangerous drug.

Another strategy used by tobacco companies to increase sales in the face of antismoking pressures is to target marketing toward those categories of people most likely to smoke—the young, women in their early 20s, blue-collar men, and racial and ethnic minorities. African Americans and Hispanics, for example, have been the special targets of cigarette promotion.

- Cigarettes are heavily advertised in black-oriented magazines such as *Ebony, Jet,* and *Essence.* Billboards advertising cigarettes are used in black communities four to five times more often than in white communities. Smoking rates among African Americans increased from 26% to 29% in the 1990s, but smoking rates among whites stayed constant at 25.5%.
- African American men are 30% more likely than white males to die from smoking-related diseases, and blacks who give up smoking are more likely than whites to start smoking again.[55]
- Of the top 10 companies advertising in Hispanic markets, two are cigarette companies (Philip Morris was number one, and R. J. Reynolds was number 10).
- In 1989, the Canadian government charged that Imperial Tobacco Ltd. (which owns Brown and Williamson in the United States) and RJR-MacDonald (owned by U.S. conglomerate RJR Nabisco) deliberately attempted to hook children aged 18 and under through their advertising. Evidence was produced documenting tobacco firms' marketing plans for young smokers, which attempted to change youths' attitudes on smoking and health. Documents also made clear attempts at convincing French-speaking Canadian youths aged 12 to 17 to begin smoking filtered and so-called light cigarettes.
- It has been estimated by the United Nations that over 500 million died from smoking-related illnesses in the 20th century. Cigarettes are very heavily advertised in Asia, Africa, and Latin America due to a lack of the legal restrictions faced by tobacco producers in other parts of the world, such as North America and Europe (e.g., warning labels).[56] Tobacco companies hope to expand their market overseas, particularly in developing countries, which present a growing market. Philip Morris, for example, sells more than 175 brands in 160 countries, and its foreign sales have grown rapidly.[57] The foreign market also provides companies with a market for the high-tar brands that are losing sales in the United States. The problem with all this, of course, is that

the tobacco firms are promoting the use of a known health hazard for their own profit.

Finally, in 1997, a federal judge ruled that the FDA has some authority to regulate sales and labeling on cigarettes but cannot regulate the promotion and advertising of tobacco products.[58] Moreover, in a separate agreement between the Liggett Company and a number of state attorneys general around the nation, the tobacco company agreed to the following:

To admit that smoking is addictive and that the tobacco industry withheld such information from the public

To admit that cigarettes cause lung cancer and heart problems

To admit that cigarette advertising has targeted children

To pay 25% of its profits for the next 25 years ($750 million in total) to combat the medical and other costs of smoking

To agree to put on its packages that nicotine is addictive and can cause lung cancer[59]

Unfortunately, this settlement will do very little to punish the tobacco companies in any way. The profit forfeiture will be paid for by smokers, who will pay 50 cents more per pack to slowly kill themselves and those around them. Moreover, tobacco advertising is still largely protected by the First Amendment right to free speech.

## Dangerous Working Conditions

In a capitalist economy, workers represent a cost to profit-seeking corporations. The lower that management can keep labor costs, the greater its profits. Historically, this has meant that workers labored for low wages, for inferior or nonexistent fringe benefits such as health care, and in unhealthy environments. The labor movement early in this century gathered momentum because of the abuse experienced by workers.

After a long and sometimes violent struggle, unions were successful in raising wages, adding fringe benefits, and making conditions safer. But owners were slow to change, and worker safety was (and continues to be) one of the most difficult issues. Many owners of mills, mines, and factories continue to consider the safety of their workers a low-priority item, presumably because of the high cost.

The mining industry provides an excellent example of this neglect. In numerous instances, mining disasters have occurred after repeated government warnings. Thousands of miners die from mining accidents each year, especially in the process of *coal mining* and *hard rock mining*. Most of the deaths today occur in developing countries, especially *China*, and rural parts of developed countries. In August 2010, a handheld meter found deep inside the Upper Big Branch mine in West Virginia detected explosive levels of methane before a blast killed 29 miners. More than two dozen coal miners died in workplace accidents in 2006. The year began with a terrible workplace tragedy, the explosion at the Sago Mine in West Virginia that claimed the lives of 12 miners.

As oil prices increase, pressure increases to produce more coal. The Bush administration put coal miners in danger by killing 17 Mine Safety and Health Administration (MSHA) safety rules, including measures on mine rescue teams and emergency oxygen. These very rules could have helped the Sago miners. The administration also weakened mine ventilation standards and allowed coal conveyor belt shafts to be used as a source of air, a dangerous practice prohibited by the Mine Act.

President Bush has put mining executives in charge of the MSHA. His administration has failed to punish mining companies for safety violations. Historically, mining scandals bring calls for reform.

Currently two proposed congressional bills (H.R. 4695/S. 2231 and S. 2308) would protect coal miners by:

- Requiring immediate notification of accidents and rapid emergency response
- Requiring new, stronger standards on mine rescue teams, communications, tracking devices, and oxygen availability for mine emergencies
- Setting mandatory minimum penalties for egregious and repeated violations
- Prohibiting the use of conveyor belts to ventilate work areas.[60]

In addition to mining disasters, coal miners face the long-term consequences of breathing coal dust. The United Mine Workers has estimated that 11 coal miners die every day from miner's asthma, silicosis, and "black lung," an incurable respiratory disease that has killed at least 100,000 American coal miners. The typical corporate response to black lung is to blame the victim, arguing that respiratory problems are a consequence of the miner's lifestyle or genetics and not the condition of the mine (which would make mining corporations liable).

The coal companies have sometimes used two other tactics: (1) when required to provide the government with dust samples, they have submitted fraudulent samples; and (2) they have ignored the federally permissible coal dust concentration limits. In the latter instance, companies pay slap-on-the-wrist fines; in 1983, the average fine for this offense was $117 per company. In the end, paying the fines is cheaper than providing workers with a relatively safe working environment.

The mining industry illustrates the two major dangers of the workplace: injuries from on-the-job accidents and exposure to toxic chemicals at work that have long-term negative effects. On-the-job accidents annually cause 3.3 million injuries requiring hospital treatment. Exposure to toxic chemicals causes at least 100,000 worker deaths each year and 390,000 new cases of occupational diseases.[61] The death toll from corporate crime represents six times the number of homicide victims. We will focus on this latter type of workplace hazard.

The dangers today are invisible contaminants such as nuclear radiation, chemical compounds, dust, and asbestos fibers in the air. Because of increased production and use of synthetic chemicals in industry over recent decades, the level of danger from these contaminants is increasing. Just in the microelectronics industry, for example, 5,000 chemicals (solvents, acids, and gases) are used, and, of these, about 500 are rated as dangerous.[62]

Since the passage of the 1970 Occupational Safety and Health Act, it has been a misdemeanor to cause the death of a worker by intentionally violating safety laws. The maximum prison term under the act is 6 months, and in 1990 fines were raised from $10,000 to $70,000 per incident, a pittance in corporate America. The Occupational Safety and Health Administration (OSHA) also possesses the ability to refer cases to federal and state prosecutors. In more than 30 years, OSHA has proposed fines of $1 million or more only three times.[63]

OSHA's charter deals with prevention, not punishment. It employs only 2,200 inspectors in more than 200 offices to inspect 7.1 million work sites employing 115 million people. In 2003, the agency conducted 40,000 inspections and discovered 83,000 safety violations, including 2,152 repeat violations. Almost 60,000 of the violations were considered "serious" and resulted in $82 million in fines.[64]

In April 2010, a Horizon Deep Water oil well, leased by British Petroleum, exploded in the Gulf of Mexico, killing 11 oil workers and spilling over 315 million gallons of crude oil into the Gulf. Fears arose that some of the oil may make its way into the Gulf Stream, up the East Coast of the United States, and even to the North Atlantic Coastal regions of United Kingdom. Thousands of sea creatures and birds were killed by the spill, and hundreds of Gulf Coast residents lost their livelihoods.

"Initially BP downplayed the incident; CEO Tony Hayward called the amount of oil and dispersant "relatively tiny" in comparison with the "very big ocean..." Hayward also initially stated that the environmental impact of the Gulf spill would likely be "very very modest." Later, he said that the spill was a disruption to Gulf Coast residents and himself adding, "You know, I'd like my life back." He later apologized for his statements. BP's chief operating officer Doug Suttles contradicted the underwater plume discussion noting, "It may be down to how you define what a plume is here... The oil that has been found is in very minute quantities." On June 16 BP Chairman Carl-Henric Svanberg speaking to reporters after meeting with President Obama at the White House said, "I hear comments sometimes that large oil companies are greedy companies who don't care. But that is not the case in BP. We care about the small people . . ."

On April 22, the United States Coast Guard and the Minerals Management Service launched an investigation of the possible causes of the explosion. On May 11, the Obama administration requested the National Academy of Engineering conduct an independent technical investigation to determine the root causes of the disaster so that corrective steps could be taken to address the mechanical failures underlying the accident. On May 22, President Obama announced that he had issued Executive Order 13543 establishing the bipartisan National Commission on the BP Deepwater Horizon Oil Spill and Offshore Drilling, with former Florida Governor and Senator Bob Graham and former Environmental Protection Agency Administrator William K. Reilly serving as cochairs. The purpose of the commission is to "consider the root causes of the disaster and offer options on safety and environmental precautions." On June 1 U.S. Attorney General Eric Holder announced that he has opened a criminal investigation of the BP oil spill. "There are a wide range of possible violations, and we will closely examine the actions of those involved in this spill," Holder said.

On April 30, the United States House Committee on Energy and Commerce asked Halliburton to brief it as well as provide any documents it might have related to its work on the Macondo well. Attention has focused on the cementing procedure and the blowout preventer, which failed to fully engage. According to Doug Brown's, the chief mechanic on the Deepwater Horizon, testimony on May 26 at the joint U.S. Coast Guard and Minerals Management Service hearing, a BP representative overruled Transocean employees and insisted on displacing protective drilling mud with seawater just hours before the explosion. One of the BP representatives on the board responsible for making the final decision, Robert Kaluza, refused to testify on the Fifth Amendment grounds that he might incriminate himself; Donald Vidrine, another BP representative, cited medical reasons for his inability to testify, as did James Mansfield, Transocean's assistant marine engineer on board . . .

In a June 18 statement, Jim Hackett, the CEO of Anadarko Petroleum Corporation, said research "indicates BP operated unsafely and failed to monitor and react to several critical warning signs during the drilling. . . . BP's behavior and actions likely represent gross negligence or willful misconduct." BP responded by strongly disagreeing with the Anadarko statement and said that, despite being contractually liable for sharing clean-up costs, Anadarko is "refusing to accept responsibility for oil spill removal costs and damages."[65]

"Two weeks after BP's Macondo well blew out in the Gulf of Mexico, the federal government's Minerals Management Service finalized a regulation intended to control the undersea pressures that threaten deepwater drilling operations."

MMS did not write the rule. As it had dozens of times before, the agency-adopted language provided by the oil industry's trade group, the

American Petroleum Institute, and incorporated it into the Federal Register. As of November 2010, BP has paid $40 billion to clean up the spill and compensate those injured by it. Yet, in the quarter ending September 30, 2010, BP still managed a profit of $1.75 billion.

MMS received two favorable public comments about the regulation: one from the Offshore Operators Committee, an industry group, and the other from BP. The regulation stated: "BP, a large oil and gas company, expressed the importance of this rule and how they have been involved with MMS and industry to develop the industry standard.

The fact that BP—which has come under withering criticism for how it managed mounting pressure in the Macondo well—took partial credit for crafting the rule is not surprising. MMS has adopted at least 78 industry-generated standards as federal regulations, American Petroleum Institute records show."[66]

- It has been 33 years since Montana passed its strip mine reclamation law, and 29 since the federal law was passed. A total of 216 acres have been deemed fully reclaimed.
- In 2001, the federal government found that "the Montana program is not effective in having all disturbed lands reclaimed to the approved post-mining land use contemporaneously."[67]
- In 2004, the Interior Department lessened an important environmental safeguard by permitting strip-mining operations to reduce more mountaintops to heaps of rubble.

Dwight Evans is vice president of Southern Company, an electric firm that gave more than $200,000 to Bush's 2004 reelection campaign. But John Walke, director of the Clean Air Project at the Natural Resources Defense Council, said the electricity power sector is the biggest producer "of global warming pollution, toxic mercury pollution, smog and soot in America. And more than any other industry, they have received tremendous benefits from the Bush administration."[68]

Environmental groups insist that many Bush administration officials, in addition to Bush himself and Vice President Cheney, have ties to the oil industry, automotive industry, and other groups that have fought against environmental protections. Numerous energy industry officials were also members of Cheney's super secret Energy Policy Council.

In December 2003, Bush signed the Healthy Forests Initiative, a plan that has been criticized as a giveaway to timber companies. The act is based on the assumption that logging by the timber industry will reduce forest fires. This notion is contradicted by scientific research, which has amassed evidence that logging can increase fire risk. Bush's real goal is to "cut the public out of the public lands management decision making process and to give logging companies virtually free access to our National Forests."[69]

The Great Lakes Legacy Act of 2002 authorizes the federal government to begin cleaning up pollution and contaminated sediment in the Great Lakes, and the Brownfields legislation of 2002 allegedly accelerates the cleanup of abandoned industrial sites, or Brownfields, to better protect public health, create jobs, and revitalize communities.

Bush's Clear Skies Act, critics charge, allows utilities to pollute more than they do currently. During his first presidential bid, Bush stated he supported the Kyoto Protocol global warming treaty, but once in office he reversed that position, saying it would harm the U.S. economy. However, Bush claims his reason for not supporting the Kyoto Protocol is that it unfairly targets the United States while being unduly lenient with developing countries, especially China and India. Bush stated, "The world's second-largest emitter of greenhouse gases is China. Yet, China was entirely exempted from the requirements of the Kyoto Protocol." He has also questioned the science behind the global warming phenomenon, insisting that more research be done to determine its validity.[70]

Of the 38 million workers in manufacturing industries, 1.7 million are exposed to a potential carcinogen each year. Workplace carcinogens are believed to cause an estimated 23% to 38% of all deaths resulting from cancer each year.[71]

Moreover, exposure to certain chemicals has negative consequences for reproduction.

> The government estimates that 15 million to 20 million jobs in the United States expose workers to chemicals that might cause reproductive injury. According to the National Institute for Occupational Safety and Health (NIOSH), 9 million workers are exposed to radio frequency/microwave radiation, which causes embryonic death and impaired fertility in animals; at least 500,000 workers are exposed to glycol ethers, known to cause testicular atrophy and birth defects in animals; and some 200,000 hospital and industrial employees work with anesthetic gases and ethylene oxide, both linked to miscarriage in humans.[72]

Consider the following examples of the specific risks of continued exposure in certain industries.

- Workers in the dyestuffs industry (working with aromatic hydrocarbons) have about 30 times the risk of the general population of dying from bladder cancer.[73]
- The wives of men who work with vinyl chloride are twice as likely as other women to have miscarriages or stillbirths.[74]
- In 1978, Occidental Chemical Company workers handling the pesticide DBCP were found to be sterile as a result of the exposure, substantiating a 1961 study by Dow Chemical that indicated that DBCP caused sterility in rats.[75]

- A 1976 government study determined that if 129,000 workers were exposed to the current legal level of cotton-dust exposure, over a period of time, 23,497 would likely become byssinotics (victims of "brown lung").[76]
- Starting with 632 asbestos workers in 1943, one researcher determined each of their fates after 20 years of employment. By 1973, 444 were dead, a rate 50% greater than for the average white male. The rate for lung cancer was 700% greater than expected, and the rate for all types of cancers was four times as great.[77]

The case of Karen Silkwood is a well-known illustration of industry's disregard for the safety of its employees. Silkwood, a plutonium plant worker, charged that the Kerr-McGee plant in which she worked was unsafe and that she was contaminated by plutonium radiation exposure. After her death in a somewhat questionable car accident, Silkwood's family sued Kerr-McGee. During the trial, Kerr-McGee employees testified that they were provided little or no training on the health hazards involved in handling plutonium. They were never told that radiation exposure could induce cancer. Attorneys for Kerr-McGee argued in court, however, that there had been no documented case of plutonium cancer in humans. This was countered by the testimony of John Gofman, one of the first physicists to isolate plutonium, who said that Silkwood had an instant "guarantee of cancer based on her exposure."[78]

Industry has historically ignored data or stalled through court actions rather than make its plants safer. Two examples forcefully make this point.

In 1970, an Italian toxicologist reported that long-term intermittent exposure of rats to vinyl chloride in air resulted in several types of cancer.[79] This was the first test on possible carcinogenicity in the plastics industry. In 1972, these earlier findings were confirmed by a major study supported by British, Belgian, and French firms. Cancer was found at the lowest level tested, 50 parts per million (ppm). (At that time, the permissible exposure level for U.S. workers was 500 ppm.) Representatives of U.S. industry were given the full details of these studies in January 1973 but entered into an agreement with the European consortium not to disclose the information without prior consent. The U.S. organization involved in this agreement, the Manufacturing Chemists Association, failed to disclose the dangers of vinyl chloride, despite a request from a government agency for all available data on the toxic effects of vinyl chloride. The data were finally revealed to the government 15 months later, after three workers exposed to vinyl chloride at a B. F. Goodrich plant died of angiosarcoma of the liver. According to a special committee report of the American Association for the Advancement of Science, the Manufacturing Chemists Association had deliberately deceived the government and "because of the suppression of these data, tens of thousands of workers were exposed without warning, for perhaps some two years, to toxic concentrations of vinyl chloride."[80]

Unlike vinyl chloride, the health dangers of asbestos have long been known. The link with asbestosis, a crippling lung disease, was established in 1900, and the relationship between asbestos and lung cancer was first noted in 1935. Studies of asbestos insulation workers in subsequent years have revealed a death rate from lung cancer seven times above normal and a death rate from all causes three times that of the general population.[81]

Despite these facts, asbestos workers have been consistently uninformed about the serious health hazards associated with working in that industry. In a Johns-Manville plant, for example, company doctors diagnosed lung disease in workers yet never told them that their lung problems were related to asbestos.

Plants have also been lax about meeting government standards for exposure. The maximum exposure level set by the government was 12 fibers per cubic meter for plants that had government contracts. An inspection of an asbestos plant in Tyler, Texas, revealed, for instance, that 117 of 138 samples in the plant exceeded the limit. The government fined the owner of the plant, Pittsburgh Corning, a total of $210 for these violations.

When the hazards of working with asbestos became more generally known, the industry reacted by sponsoring research to disprove the dangers of asbestos. One such industry study was faulty on at least two counts. First, it used researchers who had long been consultants to industry and therefore might be suspect for their lack of objectivity. Second, the study examined workers who had worked a relatively short time. Since lung cancer has a latency period of 20 years or so, the use of short-term workers in the study had the effect of whitewashing the real situation.[82]

The lack of concern for the safety of workers in the plastics and asbestos industries is typical of other industries, as well. Safety regulations for cotton dust have been opposed by the textile industry. As usual, industry argued that it would cost billions to clean up the mills, jobs would be lost, and prices to consumers would rise dramatically. Similarly, copper refiners have resisted rigorous safety regulations. For example, a study of mortality among Tacoma, Washington, smelter workers found the death rate from lung cancer to be between three and four times higher than normal and 10 times as high for workers exposed to the highest toxic concentrations. Moreover, a study found that children within a half mile of the smelter had absorbed as much arsenic as the workers themselves.[83] Despite these findings, the owner of the smelter in Tacoma, ASARCO, led an industry-wide campaign against the government's new standards. Again, the company offered the familiar argument that the costs of compliance would be $100 million, adding 15 cents to the now 72 cents needed to produce a pound of copper.

This raises the critical question: At what point are profits more important than human lives? Speaking of the cotton industry, which is representative of other major industries, one observer has argued as follows:

> In a society in which profits did not take precedence over people, . . . the finer points of byssinosis [brown lung disease] would have been considered tangential long ago and the road to its prevention would now be clear: Better air filtration systems would have been installed and other capital expenditures made. But in the United States, where society is tuned to a different chord, the present delay over preventive measures, like the oblivion which preceded it, is rooted not in science and technology but in economics and politics—in the callous traditions of the cotton industry and in government's compromising ways.[84]

Finally, we should ask: What is a crime? Is it not when a victim is hurt (physically, emotionally, or financially) by the willful act of another? When 100,000 Americans die annually from occupationally related diseases, is that a crime?

Officially, these deaths and the human suffering induced by willful neglect for worker safety are not considered crimes. (See Chapter 1 for a discussion of criminal versus noncriminal deviance.) One observer, Joel Swartz, has argued that these deaths should be considered criminal—as murders.

> By any legitimate criteria corporate executives who willfully make a decision to expose workers to a dangerous substance which eventually causes the death of some of the workers should be considered murderers. Yet no executive has ever served even a day in jail for such a practice, and most probably are well rewarded for having saved the company money. The regulatory apparatus that is complicit with such practices should of course be considered an accomplice.[85]

But the guilt does not stop with corporate executives, as Swartz goes on to argue.

> In the long run it is not the outright deception, dishonesty and cunning of corporate executives, doctors and bureaucrats which is responsible for the problem. Rather, the general functioning of the system is at the heart of the problem. . . . The tremendous toll in occupational illnesses results from the oppression of one class by another. The people who own corporations try to exact as much wealth as they can from the workers. Improvements in working conditions to eliminate health hazards would eat into the profits that could be exacted. . . . In particular the asbestos industry would rather spend millions of dollars trying to prove that asbestos is safe, than spend the money necessary to eliminate exposures. In oil refineries many of the exposures to chemicals result from inadequate maintenance of plant equipment. Maintenance costs come to 15 percent of total refinery costs, but these costs are considered controllable. In other words, skipping on maintenance is a good way to cut costs. Only the worker suffers.

Another reason that the system causes occupational illnesses is the pressure it applies for expansion, especially in certain industries such as chemicals and plastics. The chemical industry, especially, is able to reap high profits by rapidly introducing new chemicals. . . . Thus demands that chemicals be adequately tested before use, and the possibilities that new chemicals found to be dangerous might be banned, constitute a tremendous threat to the industry. . . . The ultimate reason for the problem is the drive of corporations to extract as much profit as possible from the workers. But to continue to function this system requires constant efforts by people from corporate executives to scientists to bureaucrats. These efforts result in a staggering toll in death and disease which should qualify the perpetrators as criminals by any reasonable human standards. But the system, functioning the way it is, rewards certain criminals very handsomely. The ultimate success in the battle to improve health and safety conditions will require getting rid of these criminals and the system which enables them to operate.[86]

# Collective Jeopardy

The first part of this chapter focused on the hazards that individuals face at work or from the products that they purchase. In this section, we broaden our scope somewhat. Here the victims of corporate deviance are not individuals per se but the collectivities of people who comprise individual communities, U.S. society, and even the world. The discussion will center on three broad areas of this collective jeopardy—wasting natural resources, polluting the environment, and global warming.

Perhaps the most important issue in environmental crime is global warming. Global warming occurs when so-called greenhouse gases such as carbon dioxide ($CO_2$) are released into the atmosphere, largely from vehicle emissions and industrial factories. The emissions form a sort of shield that traps heat in the atmosphere and increases the earth's temperature. This causes numerous unwanted conditions such as intense hurricanes, the melting of glaciers, and a rise in the oceans' water levels. The potential is that many of the world's coastal cities will be under water within a matter of decades.

Global warming, like all types of crime, has myths and misconceptions attached to it. The issue itself is a great example of Chomsky and Herman's notion of how news gets filtered via propagandistic myths (see Chapter 1 for description). The myths about global warming have been constructed by powerful economic and political interests.[87]

- **Myth:** There is disagreement among scientists concerning whether humans are actively causing global warming.
- **Fact:** A random sample of 928 peer-reviewed articles in scientific journals found that of those articles that dealt with global warming, 90% concluded that humans played a vital role in causing it. In fact,

the misinformation that humans played no role in the problem has been deliberately created by a well-funded campaign sponsored by Exxon, Mobil and other oil, coal, and utility firms in their efforts to continue the unrestrained polluting of the atmosphere. The group's effort has been to convince the public that global warming is merely a theory.

Another study of newspaper articles about global warming found that during the past 14 years in America's most influential newspapers (the *New York Times*, *Wall Street Journal*, *Washington Post*, and *Los Angeles Times*) over half of the articles published gave global warming equal status to the scientifically disconfirmed notion that people play no role in causing it.[88]

- The Bush administration attempted to censor whistle-blowing scientists who work for the government. NASA's James Hansen tried to warn about the dangers of global warming. The Bush White House hired lobbyist James Cooney in 2001. Even though Cooney lacked scientific training of any kind, he was placed in charge of editing and censoring the official pronouncements on global warming by the EPA and other agencies of the federal government. A White House memo leaked to the *New York Times* by a whistle-blower inside the EPA demonstrated that Cooney had deleted any mention of global warming's dangers. Thereafter, Cooney resigned his post and took a position at Exxon Mobil.
- **Myth:** Many things impact climatic changes, so there is no need to center worry on CO2 and other greenhouse gases.
- **Fact:** At no point in the past 650,000 years did $CO_2$ rise above 300 ppm until industrialization. Scientists project that over the next 45 years $CO_2$ levels will reach 600 ppm, causing increasing numbers of hurricanes, floods, droughts, and other climatic disruptions. The hottest year on record was 2005, and 20 of the last 25 hottest years have occurred in the last 25 years. More great weather and flood disasters (hurricanes, heat waves, etc.) have happened since 1998 than in the last 40 years combined.
- **Myth:** Climatic changes occur naturally over time, so any changes we are now witnessing are merely part of a natural cycle.
- **Fact:** In 2004–2005 the world experienced a record number of hurricanes, floods, and heat waves. The Arctic ice cap is relatively thin and melting rapidly and may soon completely disappear. Polar bears are now drowning in significant numbers. In fact, scientists believe we are facing a mass extinction crisis with an extinction rate 1,000 times the normal rate. In the Amazon rain forest, many species are becoming extinct, and this ads more $CO_2$ to the atmosphere. This is because the forest is disappearing due to logging and building. Trees reduce $CO_2$ and increase oxygen levels. Thirty percent of the $CO_2$ released into the

atmosphere each year is due to the burning of trees and bushes for sub-sistence agriculture and wood fires used for cooking.[89]

- **Myth:** The hole in the ozone layer causes global warming.
- **Fact:** The ozone layer is part of the upper atmosphere, containing a high concentration of ozone gas, which shields the earth from radiation. It is caused by the emission of man-made chemicals called chlorofluoro-carbons, which have been banned by the Montreal Protocol agreement. The hole causes increased radiation to reach the planet's surface, caus-ing increased cases of skin cancer and other problems. Global warming could slow the natural repairing of the earth's environment by cooling the stratosphere.[90]

## Wasting Resources

Since earth's creation billions of years ago, the ecosystem has worked intrade-pendently, relatively undisturbed by the impact of human beings. But recent developments have begun to disturb the delicate balance of nature. Explo-sive population growth, modern technology, and high rates of consumption have combined to pollute the environment and deplete resources. We will focus on the waste of resources.

A most pressing concern for humanity is the accelerated rate of the con-sumption of nonrenewable resources. Obviously, the amounts of available metals and fuels (except for wood and sun) are finite. And the greater the number of people, the faster these resources will be consumed. If technol-ogy is added to the equation, the result is a further increase in the ratio of resource depletion.

Mineral resources have remained relatively untouched until the past 100 years or so. Total mineral production during the past 30 years was greater than that from the beginning of the Bronze Age until World War II. In 1976, the U.S. Bureau of Mines estimated that world consumption of alumi-num would be twice today's level in 9 years, that use of iron will double in a decade and a half, and that demand for zinc will double in 17 years.[91]

The problem is exacerbated when these resources are not evenly dis-tributed. The indigenous reserves of minerals and fuel of those countries that industrialized first are being exhausted. And these are the very nations in which the demand is greatest. Western Europe must now import nearly all the copper, phosphate, tin, nickel, manganese ore, and chrome ore that it uses. In 1950, the United States depended on foreign sources for 50% or more of four of the 13 basic minerals; by the year 2000, it relied on imports for at least 50% of 12 of these 13 minerals.

Except for coal, the major deposits of raw materials are found in the poor and developing nations of the world, yet because of high technol-ogy, most of these resources are consumed by only about one-fourth of the world's population. Because these resources are rapidly diminishing (except for coal), severe shortages and dislocations will occur. The well-endowed countries will raise prices and be able to trade their surpluses for other needed resources. The high-technology countries (and therefore those with the greatest appetite for natural resources) will not be hurt in the short run because they will be able to purchase necessary resources.

In the long term, however, the technological societies will suffer for at least three reasons. First, as resources are exhausted (and if not replaced by adequate synthetics or renewable fuels such as the sun, wind, and tides), these societies will be forced to reduce their productivity, resulting in economic dislocations and dissatisfactions. Second, discontentment will also be found in resource-rich nations. Although they will benefit monetarily, they will no doubt feel exploited eventually as their resources are dissipated. Certainly, these countries will insist on even higher prices for their resources as they near depletion, which will increase the probability of hostile acts by wealthy nations against resource-rich nations.

A third source of international unrest brought about by the disproportionate use of limited resources by the wealthy nations will be from the have-not nations. The gap between the haves and the have-nots will continue to widen as the rich get the benefit of more resources and whatever gains are accomplished by the have-nots are canceled by rapid population growth. The result from such a situation is the heightened likelihood of hostile outbreaks between the rich and poor nations as the latter become more and more desperate in their need for resources.

The United States is the largest per capita consumer of the world's resources. One example makes the point: the United States, with only 5% of the world's population, consumes 30% of the world's energy resources. The enormous U.S. consumption of energy and raw materials is a huge drain on U.S. and world storehouses.

Why do we consume so much? Although there are many reasons, we will focus on the primary one: the American economic system, a system based on profits, the quest for which is never satiated. Companies must grow. More sales mean more profits. Sales are increased through advertising, product differentiation, new products, and creative packaging. Advertising creates previously nonexistent demand for products. The introduction of new products makes the old ones obsolete. Product differentiation (many models with different features) is redundant and wasteful, but it increases sales. The automobile industry is an excellent illustration of both product differentiation and planned obsolescence. Minor styling changes for each model year, with massive accompanying advertising campaigns, have the effect of making all older cars obsolete, at least in the minds of consumers.

Writing in 1960, Vance Packard warned of the waste demanded by our economic system.[92] Progress through growth in profits is maximized by consumers who purchase products because they feel the need to replace old ones when they are used up or outmoded. This supposed need is promoted by manufacturers who produce goods that do not last long or who alter styles so that consumers actually discard usable items. These two marketing strategies—creating obsolescence through poor quality and through desirability—produce growing profits. But both strategies are fundamentally based on waste, a societal problem that cannot continue indefinitely.

One type of obsolescence is positive: the introduction of a new product that outperforms its predecessor. However, even this type can be orchestrated to increase waste and profit. The technology may exist for a major breakthrough, but the manufacturer or industry may choose to bring out a series of modifications that eventually lead to the state of the art. The rationale for this procedure is to saturate the potential market with the stepped-up technology, move to the next stage of development, and so on until the major breakthrough is attained. In this way, the consumer purchases a number of products rather than immediately purchasing the ultimate. The history of the personal computer, iPod, cell phone, and wide-screen TV provides a good illustration of this marketing principle.[93]

The waste of our throwaway age is easy to see. Beverages are packaged in convenient disposable cans. Meat can be purchased in disposable aluminum frying pans, to be thrown away after one use. TV dinners are warmed and eaten in the same containers. We can purchase disposable cigarette lighters and cameras and plastic razors with built-in blades. What's more, we junk 7 million cars annually, as well as 10 million tons of iron and steel. These are but a small sample of the products that are quickly used and destroyed.

To maximize profits, one must minimize costs. Among other things, this search for profits results in abusing the environment. Consider the role of the profit motive in raping the land, which is the ultimate waste of resources.

## Polluting the Environment

The assault on the environment is the result of an ever-larger population, higher rates of consumption, and an increasing reliance on technology. These are worldwide trends. "Not only are more societies acquiring more efficient tools wherewith to exploit the earth; nearly everywhere, there are increasing numbers to do the exploiting, and befoul the air, water, and land in the process."[94] As an example, let's look at one major consequence of the increased use of technology: heat pollution.

Thermal pollution takes two basic forms: waste heat from the generation of electric power that (1) raises the temperature of the water (affecting fish and plant life in waters) and (2) increases heat in the atmosphere.

Obviously, a rapidly expanding population increases the demands for more electricity and more industrial output, thereby adding to the creation of heat. Moreover, the addition of 70 to 80 million people each year (the current world rate) adds heat to the atmosphere just by the metabolism of these bodies.

There is a countervailing force, however, that is believed to have a cooling effect. It, too, comes from pollution: airborne dust, which has increased in every daily activity from suburban driving to farming the soil.

> Periods of global cooling have been recorded over the past two centuries after major volcanic eruptions spewed tons of dust particles into the air. Meteorologist Helmut Landsberg estimates that, along with world population, the amount of dust in the atmosphere has doubled since the 1930s, despite the absence of major volcanic eruptions. Some scientists fear that increased amounts of atmospheric dust may act as insulation, reflecting the sun's rays away from the earth and lowering temperatures.[95]

So, technology creates in its wake two forces, one that screens the sun out and another that traps the heat in. Although both effects are negative for human life as we know it, the exact impact of these forces is not fully understood. Clearly, climate will be affected, but we are unsure of exactly how. What is known is that when modern technology tampers with the climate, it produces negative consequences.

Heat pollution, however, is only one form of pollution. In the short term, it is the least hazardous. Pollution comes in many forms. We use fossil fuel transportation, burn wood in our fireplaces, use aerosol sprays, kill weeds with pesticides, and throw away junk. Indirectly, we pollute when we use electricity, heat our homes with natural gas, and use the thousands of products created by industry.

*Wildlife.*   In 1993, *National Wildlife* magazine published the 25th in its series of annual reports on the environment. According to the report, conflict continued to increase in 1992 over whether economic or ecological concerns should be of primary importance in the allocation of America's natural resources. The continued sluggishness of the U.S. economy rendered this debate increasingly political as the environment once again became a theme in the presidential election.

The Endangered Species Act expired in 1992, and while it would continue to be enforced, the controversy surrounding reauthorizing the law centered on a few publicized conflicts between economic development and species survival. One example was provided by a controversy in the Southeast over the use of turtle excluder devices (TEDs), which allow endangered sea turtles to escape from shrimping nets. In December, the National Marine Fisheries Service extended mandatory use of TEDs to year-round, despite industry fears that the devices might reduce catches. Meanwhile, the decline in duck populations, a traditional indicator of the health of North America's ecosystems, was the worst recorded since the 1930s. This decline prompted calls for increased protection, that is, decreased development, of wetlands, which play roles in the life cycles of ducks and many other endangered and threatened animals.

A 2005 EPA report concluded that over the next 30 years, the United States might have to clean up as many as 350,000 Superfund sites at a cost of up to $250 billion. Currently, there are 600,000 known or suspected hazardous waste sites scattered across America. More than 1,200 of the worst sites have been identified by the federal government as serious threats to human health and are listed as federal Superfund sites. The EPA has announced that the pace of cleaning up the 1,200 worst sites will soon slow down because the Superfund is now empty. This means the taxpayers, not the responsible industrial corporations, will foot the cleanup bill.

- One in four Americans—65 million people—lives within four miles of a Superfund site.
- Fifty percent of the U.S. population relies on groundwater for its drinking water. Groundwater pollution is a problem at more than 85% of Superfund sites.
- A California study found children born to mothers living within a quarter-mile of a Superfund site had a higher risk of birth defects, such as heart defects and neurological problems.[96]

But what influences our consumer choices? Do we have a choice to travel by mass transit? Do we have a choice to buy products transported by truck or rail (railroads are much less polluting because they are more efficient)? Do we have a choice to use soap instead of detergent? The role of the corporations in limiting our consumer choices is an especially instructive way to understand how a laissez-faire economic system works to the ultimate detriment of people and society.

In a capitalist system, private businesses make decisions based on making profit. This places the environment in jeopardy. Best and Connolly have shown how corporate decision makers choose alternatives that have negative impacts on the ecology.[97] They describe the logic of capitalism in the following:

> Under such circumstances [capitalism] it is quite irrational for any individual producer or consumer to accept the higher costs involved in curtailing various assaults on the environment. Thus a company that purified the water used in production before disposing it into streams would add to its own costs, fail to benefit from the purified water flowing downstream, and weaken its competitive market position with respect to those companies unwilling to institute purified procedures. Since it is reasonable to assume that other companies in a market system will not voluntarily weaken their position in this way, it is

irrational for any single company to choose to do so. . . . Thus a range of practices which [is] desirable from the vantage point of the public [is] irrational from the vantage point of any particular consumer or producer. And a range of policies which [is] rational from the vantage point of individual consumers and producers [is] destructive of the collective interest in preserving nonrenewable productive resources and in maintaining the environment's capacity to assimilate wastes.[98]

Why, for example, does the United States depend on an irrational transportation system? If mass transit for commuting replaced the automobile in our urban centers, 50% of the fuel now consumed by cars would be saved. Best and Connolly argue that the automobile industry has intervened to suppress a viable mass transit alternative. In the mid-1920s, GM, sometimes with Standard Oil and Firestone, purchased control of electric trolley and transit systems in 44 urban areas. After purchase, the electric rail systems were dismantled and replaced by diesel-powered bus systems supplied by GM. When the systems were subsequently sold, part of the contract stated that no new equipment could be purchased that used a fuel other than gas. GM favored the diesel bus because its life was 28% shorter than its electric counterpart, resulting in more profit for the company. Standard Oil and Firestone obviously benefited from such an arrangement.[99] The results are well known: we are dependent on gasoline for transportation, and our cities are smothered in toxic emissions of carbon monoxide, lead, and other deadly chemical combinations from internalcombustion engines.

Other examples come from the substitution of synthetic for organic materials. Industry decided to displace soap with synthetic detergents because the profit margin increased from 30% of sales to 52%.[100] The decision was made not by consumers but by management. These decisions and others (e.g., the change from wool and cotton to synthetic fibers; plastics substituted for leather, rubber, and wood; and synthetic fertilizers replacing organic fertilizers) have often been incompatible with good ecology because the new chemicals are sometimes toxic and/or nonbiodegradable.

Remember, citizens, as voters and consumers, were not involved in these decisions to shift from organic to synthetic products. Rather, the decisions were made for them and, it turns out, against their long-term interests by companies searching for more lucrative profits. Barry Commoner has claimed that these new technologies have invariably been more polluting but were introduced nonetheless because they yielded higher profits than the older, less polluting displaced technologies. Moreover, the costs to the consumers are borne in the increased health hazards and in the cost for cleaning up the environment.

Environmental pollution is connected to the economics of the private enterprise system in two ways. First, pollution tends to become intensified by the displacement of older productive techniques by new ecologically faulty, but more profitable technologies. Thus, in these cases, pollution is an unintended concomitant of the natural drive of the economic system to introduce new technologies that increase productivity. Second, the costs of environmental degradation are chiefly borne not by the producer, but by society as a whole, in the form of "externalities." A business enterprise that pollutes the environment is therefore being subsidized by society; to this extent, the enterprise, though free, is not wholly private.[101]

Pollution, as we have seen, is a direct consequence of an economic system in which the profit motive supersedes the concern for the environment. This is clearly seen when corporations are unwilling to comply with government regulations and to pay damages for ecological disasters such as oil spills. In 1999, Russell Mokhiber published an article about the 100 most serious corporate crime cases of the 1990s. The environmental crime cases are especially instructive. Of the 100 cases discussed, 38 were environmental, the most of any category. When a corporation such as Royal Caribbean was charged with dumping oil and other hazardous wastes (some mixed with ordinary garbage) into U.S. harbors and coastal areas, the firm hired a former U.S. attorney general and two former members of the U.S. Department of Justice's Environmental Crimes Section to defend itself. Nevertheless, in the end, Royal Caribbean lost and was fined $18 million, the largest fine ever levied against a cruise line in connection with polluting American waters.[102]

- In 1991, Exxon pled guilty to spilling 11 million gallons of crude oil in Prince William Sound, Alaska, fouling 700 miles of Alaska shoreline. The corporation paid a $125 million fine.
- In 1996, the Summerville Mining Company was fined $20 million on 40 counts of violating the Clean Water Act and other federal statutes in connection with spraying cyanide into ponds as part of a process used in mining gold.
- In 1998, the Louisiana-Pacific Corporation was fined $37 million and convicted of 18 felony counts, including conspiring to violate the Clean Air Act, lying to the Colorado Department of Public Health, and submitting nonrepresentative samples to the American Plywood Association.
- In 1996, the Iroquois Pipeline Operating Company was fined $15 million for violations of the Clean Water Act. The case stemmed from the construction of a 370-mile pipeline from Canada through upstate New York and Connecticut to Long Island. Damage was done to more than 200 streams and was not cleaned up.
- In 1999, the Colonial Pipeline Company was fined $7 million after pleading guilty to spilling 1 million gallons of oil into the Reedy River in South Carolina, killing approximately 35,000 fish.
- In 1996, Rockwell International Corporation paid a $6.5 million fine in connection with charges following a 1994 explosion at its Santa Susana

Field Laboratory in Simi Hills, California. The explosion was the result of illegally stored and disposed-of hazardous waste and killed two scientists.

- In 1991, the Aluminum Company of America paid a $3.75 million fine and $7.5 million in other damages for hazardous waste violation, at the time the largest fine ever assessed for hazardous waste violation.

- In 1992, Bristol-Myers Squibb, one of the world's largest pharmaceutical companies, paid $3 million for discharging pollutants into area waters around Syracuse, New York. The company also agreed to build a pretreatment plant that cost $10 million.

- In 1997, another major drug firm, Warner-Lambert, paid a $3 million fine for falsifying reports on the level of pollutants it was releasing into a drainage channel that feeds the Cibuco River in Puerto Rico. The firm paid an additional $670,000 in civil penalties for routinely releasing excessive pollutants.

- In 1996, International Paper's subsidiary Arizona Chemical paid $2.5 million and $1.5 million in restitution fines for violations of the Clean Water Act. The violations occurred when the firm manipulated the waste treatment system's sampling procedure so that more favorable results could be reported.

- In 1995, the Conrail Corporation pled guilty to six felony counts of violating federal environmental laws by knowingly discharging harmful quantities of grease and oil into New England's Charles River. Conrail paid a $2.5 million fine for causing an oil slick hundreds of yards long.

- In 1998, HAL Beheer BV, owner of the Holland America cruise line, was fined $2 million and placed on 5 years' probation for dumping untreated bilge water into coastal waters within three miles of U.S. shores. The firm also pled guilty to failing to keep proper records of oily mixture discharge.

- In 1998, Browning-Ferris, Inc., paid a $1.5 million fine for discharging contaminated wastewater from its medical waste facility in Washington, D.C., in violation of the Clean Water Act.

- In 1994, the United Oil of California Corporation, a major oil company, pled no contest to three pollution charges and paid a $1.5 million fine for leaking petroleum thinner into the ocean groundwater at a southern California oil field.

- In 1990, Eastman Kodak, a leading photo corporation, pled guilty to state charges of unlawful dealing in hazardous waste and paid a $1 million fine. The company spilled some 5,100 gallons of methylene chloride and failed to notify government officials of the spill. Neighborhood groups fighting Eastman were disappointed with the fine, claiming that it was the equivalent of an individual getting a ticket for jaywalking.[103]

The environmental crime patterns of the 1990s reveal that most of these offenses were not accidents; they were deliberate. In a number of cases, conspiracies were engaged in to cover up what took place. Second, for the most part, the fines imposed were meager compared with the multibillion-dollar resources of the corporations involved. Third, in none of the cases discussed did anyone go to prison. Probation was the most serious punishment levied, besides a fine. Finally, serious damage to the local environments was done in many cases, especially concerning the pollution of lakes, rivers, and oceans.

The government thus has enacted laws to curb pollution, but they are very mild. Turner has listed the defects in these conservation laws.

1. The laws are often phrased in ambiguous language, making prosecution difficult.
2. The laws typically mandate weak civil penalties and hardly ever carry criminal penalties.
3. The vast majority of the laws do not attack the sources of pollutants but rather require treatment of pollutants after they have been created.
4. Many state antipollution laws are enacted with "grandfather clauses" that allow established companies to continue their harmful activities.[104]

The mildness of the pollution laws and their enforcement indicates the power of the powerful to continue their disregard for people and nature in their search for profits. The government could take a much firmer stance if it chose to do so. Suppose, for example, that the situation were reversed: "Can you possibly reverse this situation and imagine the poor polluting the streams used by the rich, and then not only getting away with it and avoiding arrest, but also being paid by the rich through the government to clean up their own pollution?"[105]

In such a case, how would the poor be treated? The answer is obvious: the powerful would punish them severely and immediately curb their illegal behaviors. The implication is that whoever has the power can use it to his or her own benefit, disregarding the masses and nature.

## Conclusion

This chapter has shown conclusively the fundamental flaw of capitalism. Corporations are formed to seek and maximize profits. All too often, the result is a blatant disregard for human and humane considerations. It is too simplistic to say that corporations are solely responsible for these dangers to individuals and society. In many cases, consumers insist on convenience rather than safety. They would rather smoke or drink diet cola with aspartame than have the government demand that they quit. Moreover, consumers typically would rather take an unknown risk than pay higher prices for products, which would pay for the cost of cleaning up the pollution. So, too, workers would rather work in an unsafe plant than be unemployed. But, for the most part, these attitudes are shaped by corporate advertising and corporate extortion (threatened higher prices and unemployment if changes are enforced). Also, corporations are guilty of efforts to persuade us that the dangers are nonexistent or minimal when the scientific evidence is irrefutable. They also do everything possible to block efforts by the government and consumer groups to thwart their corporate policies. For example, despite evidence that many forms of cancer are environmentally related, corporations have refused to alter their behavior. Instead, they counterattack in two characteristic ways.

> Monsanto Chemical Co ... has embarked on a costly advertising campaign to persuade us that chemical products are essential to our way of life. More than 100 industrial corporations have banded together to form the American Industrial Health Council, a lobby that is spending more than $1 million a year to combat the stricter carcinogen controls proposed by the Occupational Safety and Health Administration (OSHA).[106]

The probusiness approach argues that risks are inherent in living. But the consumer is the ultimate arbiter. He or she may choose. If the consumer does not buy dangerous or wasteful products, then industry will provide alternative products to suit his or her wishes.[107] Likewise, the worker in an asbestos plant or a cotton mill can change jobs if he or she feels that the current job is unsafe. Companies continue to argue that what goes on in the marketplace is not within the domain of government. We argue, to the contrary, that the government must serve a watchdog function. We also argue that individuals do not have the simple options that the corporations suggest. We buy the products that are available. Our attitudes are shaped by advertising. Employees cannot shift from one job to another in the hopes of finding safer conditions when most of the plants in the industry for which they are trained have similar problems and when the unemployment rate is high.

The dangers pointed out in this chapter direct attention to the fundamental irrationality of our economic system. When the pursuit of profits supersedes the health of workers and consumers, when corporate decisions encourage enormous waste and pollution, then the economic system is wrong and will ultimately fail.

## CRITICAL THINKING EXERCISE 4.1
### Business Crime and Punishment in America

The *Wall Street Journal* calls itself "the daily diary of the American Dream." As argued in Chapter 2, the values connected with the American dream, as well as a lack of opportunity, encourage a great deal of criminal behavior, including crimes among corporations. Using recent issues of the *Wall Street*

*Journal,* do a content analysis of the amount of corporate and employee crime. In your analysis, answer the following questions:

1. What is the most common crime committed by corporations?
2. What percentage of the articles mention prison as part of the sentence imposed on convicted executives and employees?
3. What is the average fine imposed on corporations? On employees?
4. Who are the most frequent victims of corporate criminals? The public? The government? Women? Children? Minorities?

What do the results of your study indicate about the way corporate and white-collar employees are treated by the criminal justice system?

## ENDNOTES

1. National Commission on Product Safety. (1974). Perspectives on product safety. In D. A. Aaker & G. S. Day (eds.). *Consumerism: search for the consumer interest* (pp. 321–322). New York: Free Press. See also Etzioni, A. (1975 November). Mindless capitalism, an unyielding elite. *Human Behavior, 4,* 10–12; and Nader, R. (ed.). (1973). *The consumer and corporate accountability* (p. 51). New York: Harcourt Brace Jovanovich.

2. 2005 Bad Year for Consumer Safety, CPSC Reports. http://usgovinfo.about.com/od/consumerawareness/a/cpscbadyear.htm (November 14, 2006); CNNMoney.com August 2, 2007.

3. Quoted in Mintz, M., & Cohen, J. S. Crime in the suites (p. 79). In Nader R. (ed1972.).

4. Nader, R. (1972). *Unsafe at any speed: The designed-in dangers of the American automobile.* New York: Bantam.

5. Mintz, M. Confessions of a GM engineer (pp. 301–309). In Nader R. (ed.). For a similar situation among tire manufacturers, see Forewarnings of fatal laws. *Time,* June 25, 1979, 5–61.

6. The following is taken from Dowie, M. Pinto madness. In J. Skolnick & E. Currie (eds). *Crisis in American institutions* (4th ed., pp. 23–40). Boston: Little, Brown (originally appeared in *Mother Jones* 2, September/October 1977, 24–25).

7. Ibid. (p. 30). This is the argument made in Guzzardi, Jr., W. (April 1979). The mindless pursuit of safety. *Fortune,* 54–64.

8. Cullen, F. T., Maakestad, W. J., & Cavender, G. (1987). *Corporate crime under attack: The Ford Pinto case and beyond.* Cincinnati, OH: Anderson. See also Mokhiber, R. (1988). *Corporate crime and violence* (pp. 373–382). San Francisco: Sierra Club Books.

9. Dowie (p. 39).

10. http://www.autoblog.com/2010/04/05/report-nhtsa-to-seek-16m-fine-against-toyota-for-recall-scandal. The following discussion is based on http://www.consumeraffairs.com/news04/2007/03/ford_police_recall.html (March 7, 2007); http://www.consumeraffairs.com/news04/2007/03/ford_recall_2003.html (March 17, 2007); http://www.consumeraffairs.com/recalls04/2006/ford_five_hundred.html (March 10, 2007).

11. The following is taken from Harris, F. R. (1973). The politics of corporate power. In R. Nader & M. J. Green (eds.). *Corporate power in America* (pp. 27–29). New York: Grossman; and Detroit fights airbags. *Dollars and Sense,* July/August 1978, 6–7.

12. Detroit Fights Airbags (p. 6).

13. Ibid. (p. 7).

14. Kitman, J. L. (March 20, 2000). The secret history of lead. *Nation, 270,* 11–44.

15. Pugh, T. (15 February 2005). FDA to monitor prescription drugs. *Kansas City Star.*

16. Sinclair, U. (1960). *The jungle* (first published in 1905 reprint). New York: New American Library.

17.  McCaghy, C. H. (1976). *Deviant behavior: Crime, conflict, and interest groups* (p. 215). New York: Macmillan.

18.  Wellford, H. (1972). *Sowing the wind: A report from Ralph Nader's center for study of responsive law on food safety and the chemical harvest* (p. 69). New York: Grossman.

19.  McCaghy (p. 216).

20.  Sherrill, R. (March 4, 1973). Cited in McCaghy, 216 (originally appeared in *New York Times Book Review*, 3). See also Marine, G., & Van Allen, J. (1972). *Food pollution: The violation of our inner ecology* (Chapter 2). New York: Holt, Rinehart and Winston; and Cross, L. (1976). *The supermarket trap: The consumer and the food industry* (rev. ed.). (Chapter 9). Bloomington: Indiana University Press.

21.  Karlen, N. (September 24, 1984). A 'Mystery Meat' scandal. *Newsweek*, 29; and Thomas, M. (January 31, 1984). Ex–Cattle King worker acknowledges fraud. *Denver Post*, 1, 11.

22.  Suddath, C. (6 Sept., 2010). Food recalls. *Time*, 19.

23.  The following discussion of additives is taken primarily from Zwerdling, D. (1978). Food pollution. In R. C. Edwards, M. Reich, & T. E. Weisskopf (eds.). *The capitalist system* (2nd ed., pp. 19–24). Englewood Cliffs, NJ: Prentice Hall. See also Verrett, J., & Carper, J. (1975). *Eating may be hazardous to your health*. Garden City, NY: Doubleday.

24.  Government Printing Office. (1986). *Statistical abstract of the United States, 1987* (p. 110). Washington, DC: Government Printing Office.

25.  Department of Health and Human Services. (February 25 and 28, 1994). *Report on all adverse reactions in the adverse reaction monitoring system*. Department of Health and Human Services.

26.  Safety of amino acids. Life Sciences Research Office, FASEB, FDA Contract No. 223–88–2124, Task Order No. 8; and Hearing before the Committee on Labor and Human Resources, United States Senate, First Session on Examining the Health and Safety Concerns of Nutrasweet (Aspartame), November 3, 1987.

27.  U.S. Air Force. (1992). Aspartame alert. *Flying Safety, 48*(5), 20–21. See also Aspartame (NutraSweet) Toxicity Home Page: http://www.tiac.net/users/mgold/aspartame/aspartame.html for full discussion and documentation.

28.  Miller, J. (December 1975). Testing for seeds of destruction. *Progressive, 39*, 37–40. See also Spark, R. F. (June 3, 1978). Legislating against cancer. *New Republic*, 16–19.

29.  It is even possible that financial ties to huge food corporations may shade the so-called expert testimony of nutritionists, as argued by Rosenthal, B., Jacobson, M., & Bohm, M. (November 1976). Professors on the take. *Progressive, 40*, 42–47.

30.  The 1965 data are from Marine and Van Allen, 38; 1977 data are from Drummond, H. (April 1977). Add poison for flavor and freshness. *Mother Jones, 2*, 13.

31.  Quoted in Zwerdling (p. 20).

32.  From Hightower, J. (1975). *Eat your heart out: Food profiteering in America*. New York: Crown Publisher, Inc.

33.  *Statistical Abstract of the United States, 1987*, 110.

34.  *Detroit Free Press*, June 7, 1991, 1-F, 6-F.

35.  http://www.supersizeme.com/home.aspx?page=aboutmovie; Kelly Brownell, *Food Fight* (New York: McGraw-Hill, 2004), 29ff.

36.  Government Printing Office (1977). *Dietary goals for the United States* (2nd ed., pp. 35, 39). Washington, DC: Government Printing Office.

37.  U.S. Senate. *Select committee on nutrition and human needs, 35*, 19.

38.  Hightower (p. 631).

39.  U.S. Senate. *Select committee on nutrition and human needs, 35*–48. See also the documentary Spurlock M. (2005). *Supersize me*. HartShop Video LLC, for a discussion of these issues.

40.  Elias, M. (April 1974). How to win friends and influence kids on television (and incidentally sell a few toys and munchies at the same time). *Human Behavior, 4*, 20. For an extensive review of research, see National Science Foundation. (1976). *The effects of television*. Washington, DC: Government Printing Office.

41.  Federal Trade Commission. (1978). *Staff report on television advertising to children* (p. 57). Washington, DC: Government Printing Office.

42. Summarized in U.S. Commission on Civil Rights. (1979). *Window dressing on the set: An update* (p. 49). Washington, DC: Government Printing Office.

43. Elias (pp. 16–23).

44. Weinstock, M. (January 22, 1979), quoted in *Broadcasting, 96*, 25.

45. Summers, J. (March 26, 1979), quoted in *Broadcasting, 96*, 84.

46. Furth, F. (April 30, 1979), quoted in Keep out of the reach of children. *Bill Moyers' Journal* (p. 3 of transcript).

47. Friedlander, B. (April 2, 1979), quoted in *Broadcasting, 96*, 64.

48. *Bill Moyers' Journal,* 11. "Keep Out of the Reach of Children: Bill Moyers' Journal," April 30, 1979.

49. Morabia, A., Bernstein, M., Heritier, S., & Khatchatrian, N. (May 1, 1996). Relation of breast cancer with passive and active exposure to tobacco smoke. *American Journal of Epidemiology, 143*, 918–928; Breast Cancer.Org (February 12, 2004); Calle, E. E., Miracle-McMahill, H. J., Thun, M. J., & Heath, Jr., C. W. (May 15, 1994). Cigarette smoking and risk of fatal breast cancer. *American Journal of Epidemiology, 139*, 1001.

50. Cited in Darmstadter, R. (Fall 1983). Snuff and chaw: The tobacco industry plugs nicotine by osmosis. *Business and Society Review, 47*. Copyright © 1983, Warren Gorham & Lamont, 210 South Street, Boston, MA 02111. All rights reserved.

51. Blair, G. (January 1979). Why Dick can't stop smoking: The politics behind our national addiction. *Mother Jones, 4*, 36.

52. The following is adapted from Stanley Eitzen, D., & Baca Zinn, M. (1989). *Social problems* (4th ed., pp. 588–589). Boston: Allyn & Bacon.

53. Schudson, M. (December 15, 1987). The smoking gun: A nation at risk. *In These Times, 9*, 18.

54. Taylor, P. (1985). *The smoke ring: Tobacco and multinational politics* (pp. 57–58). New York: New American Library.

55. Darmstadter (p. 24).

56. Ibid. (pp. 24–25).

57. These examples are taken from White, L. C. (1988). *Merchants of death: The American tobacco industry* (pp. 129–131). New York: William Morrow. See also Mintz, M. (May 1991). Marketing tobacco to children. *Progressive, 5*, 24–29.

58. Eckholm, E. (July 1978). Four trillion cigarettes. *Progressive, 42*, 26; White, 199–200.

59. Reuters, March 29 and April 25, 1997: *Detroit Fights Airbags*, (1978) Dollars and Sense (July/August): 6–7.

60. Working Families e-Activist Network, peoplepower@aflcio.org; http://en.wikipedia.org/wiki/2006_Sago_Mine_disaster (March 14, 2007).

61. Claybrook, J. (1984). *Retreat from safety: Reagan's attack on America's health* (p. 78). New York: Pantheon; and Kappeler, V., & Potter, G. (2006). *The mythology of crime and criminal justice* (4th ed., p. 150). Long Grove, IL: Waveland Press.

62. Economic Affairs Bureau. (1985). High tech and health. In *Diagnosis: Capitalism, by dollars & sense* (p. 15). Somerville, MA: Economic Affairs Bureau.

63. Kappeler & Potter. (2005). *The Mythology of Crime and Criminal Justice* (4th ed., p. 157). Longwood, IL: Waveland Press.

64. Ibid.

65. http://en.wikipedia.org/wiki/Deepwater_Horizon_oil_spill (4 November, 2010)

66. http://www.washingtonpost.com/wpdyn/content/article/2010/08/24/AR2010082406754.html

67. Slater, (August 30, 2004). Energy firms buy Bush favors, critics charge. *Common Dreams.org*, http://www.commondreams.org/headlines04/0830-05.htm.

68. The Sierra Club. http://www.sierraclub.org/forests/fires/healthyforests_initiative.asp (May 2003).

69. Domestic Policy of the George W. Bush Administration. *Wikipedia*, http://en.wikipedia.org/wiki/Domestic_policy_of_the_George_W._Bush_administration (March 18, 2007).

70. Ibid.

71. Marshall, C. (April 25, 1987). An excuse for workplace hazards. *Nation*, 532.

72. Cole, P., & Goldman, M. B. (1975). Occupation. In J. F. Fraumeni Jr. (ed.). *Persons at high risk of cancer* (p. 171). New York: Academic Press.

73. Press. E. (May 31, 1999). Texaco on trial. *Nation*, 11–12, 16.

74. McGhee, D. (October 1977). Workplace hazards: No women need apply. *Progressive, 41, 25.*

75. Ben-Horin, D. (May 1979). The sterility scandal. *Mother Jones, 4,* 51–63.

76. Schinto, J. (August 1977). The breathless cotton workers. *Progressive, 41,* 29.

77. Reported in Epstein, S. S. (1978). *The politics of cancer* (pp. 84–86). San Francisco: Sierra Club Books. See also Zeldin, L. (October 1978). The asbestos menace. *Progressive, 42,* 12.

78. Reported in Silkwood Vindicated. *Newsweek,* May 28, 1979, *40,* 102–6.

79. Epstein (pp. 10–12).

80. Edsall, J. T. (1975). Report of the AAAS Committee on Scientific Freedom and Responsibility. *Science, 188,* 687–693 (reported in Epstein, 103–104).

81. See Doll, R. (1955). *British Journal of Industrial Medicine, 12,* 81.

82. The following account is taken primarily from Swartz, J. (). Silent killers at work. *Crime and Social Justice,* P.O. Box 4373, Berkeley, CA, 94704.

83. Williams, R. M. (January 20, 1979). Arsenic and old factories. *Saturday Review,* 26.

84. Schinto (p. 28), "The Breathless Cotton Workers," *Progressive 41,* August 1977, 29. For a description of how the government has waffled in this area, see "Brown Lung Compromise," *Progressive, 42,* August 1978, 13.

85. Swartz, J. (p. 18). Silent Killers at Work. *Crime and Social Justice,* P.O. Box 4373, Berkeley, CA, 94704.

86. Swartz, J. Silent Killers at Work. *Crime and Social Justice,* P.O. Box 4373, Berkeley, CA, 94704.

87. The following discussion is based on Gore, A. (2006). *An inconvenient truth.* New York: Rodale.

88. Ibid. (pp. 262–264).

89. Ibid. (p. 227).

90. Ibid. (p. 313).

91. Brown, L. R., McGrath, P. L., & Stokes, B. (1976). *Twenty two dimensions of the population problem.* Worldwatch Paper 5. (p. 58). Washington, DC: Worldwatch Institute.

92. Packard, V. (1960). *The waste makers.* New York: David McKay.

93. Ibid. (pp. 55–56).

94. Sprout, H., & Sprout, M. (1978). *The context of environmental politics* (p. 17). Lexington: University Press of Kentucky.

95. McGrath, B., & Stokes (pp. 35–36). Brown, L. R., McGrath, P. L., & Stokes, B., (1976). *Twenty Two Dimensions of the Population Problem.* Worldwatch Paper 5. (p. 58). Washington, DC: Worldwatch Institute.

96. *USA Today,* February 16, 2005; and http://www.BeSafe.com, February 17, 2005.

97. Best, M. H., & Connolly, W. E. (1978). Nature and its largest parasite. In R. C. Edwards et al. (eds.). *The capitalist system* (2nd ed., p. 419). Englewood Cliffs, NJ: Prentice Hall.

98. Best, M. H., & Connolly, W. E. (1978) *Nature and Its Largest Parasite.* In R. C. Edwards et al. (eds.). *The Capitalist System* (2nd ed., pp. 420–421). Englewood Cliffs, NJ: Prentice Hall.

99. Commoner, B. (1971). The economic meaning of ecology. In J. H. Skolnick & E. Currie (eds.). *Crisis in American institutions* (4th ed., p. 285). Boston: Little, Brown, excerpted from *The closing circle.* New York: Knopf, 1971.

100. Ibid. (p. 291).

101. Commoner, B. (1971). The Closing Circle, Bantam Books.

102. The above examples are taken from two speeches by Ralph Nader at Colorado State University, May 1970 and November 1977.

103.   Mokhiber, R. (1988). *Corporate Crime and Violence* (pp. 248–57). San Francisco: Sierra Club Books.

104.   Turner, J. H. (1977). *Social problems in America* (pp. 419–420). New York: Harper & Row.

105.   Henslin, J. M., & Reynolds, L. T. (1976). *Social problems in American society* (2nd ed., 220–). Boston: Holbrook.

106.   The politics of cancer. *Progressive, 43*, May 1979, 9.

107.   See Guzzardi (pp. 54–64); and Diseased regulation. *Forbes*, February 19, 1979, 34.

# CHAPTER

# 5

# National Defense, Multinational Corporations, and Human Rights

This chapter focuses on the international dimensions of deviance by economic and political elites. We examine three types of acts: (1) unethical or illegal practices relating to U.S. defense policy, (2) the conduct of multinational corporations (MNCs) abroad, and (3) violations of human rights by nations supported by the United States.

We begin with a discussion of the military-industrial complex. Consider the following recent examples:

On September 11, 2001, the world received a glimpse of the new global crime problem. The planes that crashed into the World Trade Center and the Pentagon were part of a narcoterrorist conspiracy involving terrorists from al-Qaeda, protected by Afghanistan's Taliban government, and financed by the heroin trade (90% of the world's heroin comes from Afghanistan and is distributed by Russian organized crime syndicates).[1] This combination of terrorist groups, organized crime syndicates that traffic in drugs and arms, and governments that protect these interests is relatively new in the annals of crime and has already become a leading crime problem of the 21st century.

The story of this combination of interests does not end here. It also seems that the U.S. government had dealings with some of the leaders of al-Qaeda, as well as advanced warnings of the 9/11 attack.

- In 1998, a Central Intelligence Agency (CIA) operative in Saudi Arabia warned the U.S. government of the dangers of al-Qaeda and provided CIA personnel in Saudi Arabia with the names of al-Qaeda members, many of whom ended up taking part in the 9/11 incidents.
- In May 2001, the U.S. State Department gave the Taliban $43 million in economic aid for Afghan farmers.
- In June 2001, German intelligence warned U.S. officials of an impending attack in the United States by al-Qaeda terrorists. During the same month, the Bush administration told the FBI to back off investigations of Bin Laden family activities in the United States.
- In July 2001, al-Qaeda leader Osama Bin Laden was treated at an American hospital in Dubai and interviewed by CIA officials.
- In August 2001, the FBI arrested a member of al-Qaeda who had been taking flying lessons in the United States. Russian president Vladmir Putin

also warned American officials of an upcoming attack by al-Qaeda terrorists.

- On September 11, 2001, the Israeli corporation Odigo warned American officials of an impending al-Qaeda attack 2 hours before the bombings of the World Trade Center and Pentagon.[2]
- The Bush and Bin Laden families have been very close friends for more than 30 years. Members of the Bin Laden family were allowed by the U.S. government to fly home to Saudi Arabia from the United States in the days following 9/11, whereas all other commercial air traffic remained grounded. A report on these incidents was prepared by the Bush administration, but was classified secret, and thus far the administration has refused to release it.
- Documents from the Cheney energy task force dated March 2001, released under the Freedom of Information Act, confirm that the task force's documents included maps of oil fields and charts of proposed oil and gas development projects in Iraq, Saudi Arabia, and the United Arab Emirates. Rather than a war on terrorism, these documents confirmed the Bush administration's real foreign policy objectives concerned the increasing of petroleum supplies abroad to American markets.[3]

Subsequent to the September 11 attacks, the United States went to war with Afghanistan's Taliban, allying with the Afghan Northern Alliance rebels. Today, the Northern Alliance has increased opium production and is trafficking in heroin. Following the war in Afghanistan, the Bush administration chose to go to war with Saddam Hussein's Iraq in 2003. Contrary to the claims of Bush officials concerning reasons for the war, there were never any weapons of mass destruction (WMDs) discovered in Iraq, either by United Nations inspectors or by Bush's own investigative team. Moreover, no link between Iraq and al-Qaeda was ever established, and there is no evidence that Hussein was linked to the 9/11 terrorist attacks. Sadly, some 70% of the American public were persuaded to support the Iraq war premised by the belief that all of the above claims were proven facts.[4]

Meanwhile, a commission appointed to investigate the 9/11 attacks was obstructed by the Bush administration. Thanks to the relatives of the 9/11 victims, the Bush White House was pressured into the investigation.[5]

We are now living in a new era when it comes to waste, fraud, and abuse within the Department of Defense, foreign aid, and black operations within the intelligence community. Although most defense contracting fraud used to involve cost overruns and kickbacks on weapons systems contracts, this is no longer the basic problem. What has become a systemic issue is that so many things the Pentagon used to do using military personnel are now completed via the use of private corporations. Second, countries such as Iraq, Afghanistan, and Pakistan suffer from corruption scandals on an almost weekly basis.

- Regarding Iraq, there is corruption from the lowest to the very highest levels of the government. Border guards charge up to $1,500 for trucks with produce to enter the country. Some trucks are held at the border for days until the guards are paid. A common way to become a border guard or regular police officer is to pay a bribe, up to $5,000. A car license can cost up to $3,000. The pocketing of money is often passed to elected officials. On March 18, 2010, the Board of Supreme Audit, an anticorruption agency, said that the Salahaddin provincial council had been stealing money from the local government.
- There are more serious examples of institutionalized corruption. In May 2009 the *Trade Minister resigned*. He, along with his two brothers and nephew, was accused of taking kickbacks and embezzling money. The Trade Minister was in control of the country's *$5.3 billion food ration system*, the largest in the world. The Ministry was also in charge of importing grain, seeds, and construction materials, all ripe for graft. The trouble with the Ministry began when $8 million worth of expired products were found in a warehouse in Muthanna that were meant for the food ration system. Later arrest warrants were issued for the Minister and his family members. Afterward documents were discovered showing that $4 billion was missing from the Ministry in 2009, and it could go as high as $8 billion over 4 years. Another scam involved purchasing contaminated milk from China. This was a conspiracy where officials would buy old food for cheap and charge the ministry full price and keep the difference. Another plot involved employees buying food and selling it on the black market, then replacing the stolen food with cheap substitutes. Yet another conspiracy involved the Ministry working with merchants to buy products for twice their price, and then splitting the difference. An investigation by parliament found that only half of those eligible for their food rations were getting them completely as a result of the corruption within the Trade Ministry.

The Defense Ministry took bribes as part of contracts to buy foreign aircraft. The parliament is also looking into how the Interior Ministry bought bomb detecting wands from a British company for $85 million that don't work, and were priced far above their going rate.

Ministers and other top officials can stop cases. The 2008 Amnesty Law that was supposed to help with reconciliation has a clause in it that covers graft and fraud. This led to 1,552 cases being dropped in 2009. Forty-eight cases from the Ministry of Trade, 145 cases from the Ministry of Defense, and 528 cases from the Ministry of Interior were all exempted by this law last year.[6]

There have also been scandals related to Iraqi reconstruction.

The agency in charge of investigating fraud in the spending of Pentagon funds in Iraq actually "quietly left" the country in 2004. The Knight Ridder Washington Bureau reports that both government and public experts say this decision has left large gaps in how more than $140 billion was spent. Experts say the other agencies now doing the audits do not have the expertise, access, and authority that the inspector general has—and do not make their reports public. That means that much of the money being spent in Iraq does not get public attention, inviting possible waste, fraud, and abuse.

The annual *Transparency International Global Corruption Report* for 2005 showed that Iraq is the most corrupt country in the Middle East, and this corruption has been one of the main obstacles in reestablishing stability in Iraq. Iraqi businessmen complain about bribery affecting virtually all government operations. Contractors alleged that inspectors checking up on the refurbishment of schools by Iraqi companies in September 2003 were bribed to turn a blind eye to shoddy or unfinished work. CNN reported that large-scale corruption in Iraq's ministries, particularly the defense ministry, "has led to one of the biggest thefts in history with more than $1 billion going missing," according to Iraq's finance minister. Some of the worst allegations of impropriety concern the purchasing of military equipment by the defense ministry under the previous government, including more than $230 million spent on 28-year-old secondhand Polish helicopters. Nearly 100% of the defense ministry's procurement budget has been stolen. Philip Giraldi (a former CIA officer and a partner in Cannistraro Associates, an international security consultancy) charged that billions of dollars have disappeared in Iraq, and that the U.S.-dominated Coalition Provisional Authority (CPA), which was in charge in Iraq until 2004, bears the primary responsibility for what has happened. The CPA may be the most corrupt administration in history. At least $20 billion that belonged to the Iraqi people has been wasted, together with hundreds of millions of U.S. taxpayer dollars. Exactly how many billions of additional dollars were stolen, given away, or "lost" will never be known. This is due to a deliberate decision by the CPA not to audit oil exports, which leaves revenue generated in 2003 and 2004 unmeasurable. One estimate is that there was as much as $4 billion from illegal oil exports, due to fraud and black marketeering. British sources claim that contracts not handed out to cronies were sold to the highest bidder, with bribes as high as $300,000 being demanded for particularly lucrative reconstruction contracts.[7]

Stuart W. Bowen Jr., Special Inspector General for Iraq Reconstruction (SIGIR), told Congress in 2005 that there is a "reconstruction gap" in Iraq regarding $18 billion provided by Congress to rebuild Iraq's infrastructure.

- By March 2007, about $10 billion has been squandered by the U.S. government on Iraq reconstruction aid because of contractor overcharges and unsupported expenses. Fining companies a million dollars, said Senator Arlen Specter (R-PA), can simply amount to "an inexpensive license to cheat the taxpayers." According to army spokesman Dave Foster, eight individuals or companies have been restricted from obtaining army contracts, and eight others have been disbarred for obtaining army business. As of January 30, 2007, 16 companies or individuals have been suspended from acquiring army contracts due to allegations of fraud and misconduct in Iraq reconstruction contracts. Iraqi officials are also investigating as many as 2,000 cases of fraud, amounting to about $8 billion in unaccounted-for Iraqi construction funds. So far, he said, 16 people have been convicted in connection with fraud, kickbacks, or other contracting violations.

- On February 7, 2007, four family members of employees killed in Fallujah testified about what they view as profiteering by Blackwater USA, including the company's alleged failure to provide armored vehicles and other critical safety equipment. The Oversight and Government Reform Committee examined the costs of Blackwater's security operations to the taxpayer and the adequacy of federal oversight of Blackwater and other security contractors.[8]

In April 2003, when the Bush administration declared war on Hussein's regime, it charged that Iraq possessed numerous WMDs. Yet, a January 2004 report issued by the Carnegie Endowment for International Peace severely criticized Bush's claims on several grounds:

- Iraq's programs did not "pose an immediate threat to the United States, to the region or to global security."
- The extent of the threat of chemical and nuclear weapons was largely unknown at the time.
- The uncertainties were even greater regarding biological weapons.
- The shifts between prior intelligence assessments and an October 2002 national intelligence estimate "suggest that the intelligence community appears to have been unduly influenced by policy maker's views sometime in 2002."
- Iraq's nuclear weapons program had been suspended for several years. Iraq focused on preserving a dual-use chemical and probably biological weapons capability, not weapons production. Iraq's nerve agents had lost most of their lethal effects as early as 1991.
- Operations Desert Storm and Desert Fox, UN inspection teams, and sanctions effectively destroyed Iraq's large-scale chemical weapons production capabilities.
- "There was and is no solid evidence of a cooperative relationship between Saddam's government and Al-Qaeda."[9]
- The American and British intelligence services misestimated the number of Iraq's chemical and biological weapons.
- No solid evidence exists that Iraq transferred WMDs to terrorists, but much evidence to the contrary does exist.
- There were at least two options preferable to war that could have been utilized without international support: allowing UN inspections to continue until obstructed or completed, or imposing a tougher program of forced inspections on Iraq. In 2010, a memo was discovered

showing that George W. Bush planned to invade Iraq before he was even nominated for President in 2000, and the World Trade Center bombing merely served as a convenient excuse to do so.[10]

In early May 2004 the *New Yorker* obtained the report written by Major General Antonio M. Taguba (not meant for public release). Taguba found that between October and December 2003 there were numerous instances of wanton criminal abuses at Abu Ghraib prison where Iraqi detainees were being held. These illegal abuses of detainees were committed by soldiers of the 372nd Military Police Company and by members of the American intelligence community. General Taguba's report listed numerous wrongdoings:

- Breaking chemical lights and pouring phosphoric liquid on detainees;
- Pouring cold water on naked detainees;
- Beating detainees with a broom handle and a chair;
- Threatening male detainees with rape;
- Allowing a military police guard to stitch the wound of a detainee who was injured after being slammed against the wall of his cell;
- Sodomizing a detainee with a chemical light and perhaps a broomstick;
- Using military working dogs to frighten and intimidate detainees with threats of attack, and in one instance actually bite a detainee.

Several photographs confirming these abuses were broadcast on CBS's *60 Minutes 2* the week before the *New Yorker* published its story.[11]

One week after publishing the initial story of prisoner abuses, the *New Yorker* obtained a secret memo indicating that Secretary of Defense Donald Rumsfeld had authorized expanding a secret program that encouraged the physical torture and sexual humiliation of prisoners to gather intelligence about the growing opposition in Iraq. The program was allegedly approved by then national security adviser Condoleezza Rice. President Bush was also notified of the program's expansion. The Defense Department responded by claiming that it always followed the rules of the Geneva Convention concerning the humane treatment of war prisoners, and denied the torture of Iraqi prisoners was an intended policy.[12]

In Afghanistan, and Iraq cases of suspected fraud and other wrongdoing by U.S. troops and contractors overseeing reconstruction and relief projects in both countries were up dramatically in 2010. The Defense Department's inspector general for investigations, says his agency is investigating 223 cases—18% more than a year ago. Investigators have charged an Army officer with pocketing cash meant to pay Iraqi civilian militiamen, contractors offering an Army officer $1 million for the inside track on a road project in Afghanistan, and three contractors for an alleged conspiracy to steal hundreds of thousands of dollars worth of fuel from a U.S. base in Baghdad.

Army Maj. John Cockerham was sentenced in December to 17 and one-half years in prison for accepting $9 million in bribes for contracts to sell water and other supplies to the U.S. military.

In Afghanistan, now called "Corruptistan" by some reporters where U.S. spending on reconstruction will soon surpass the $50 billion spent in Iraq, the U.S. government is bolstering its investigative presence. The Inspector General office has a staff of 15 and plans to expand to 32 by October. "In this grotesque carnival, the U.S. military's contractors are forced to pay suspected insurgents to protect American supply routes. It is an accepted fact of the military logistics operation in Afghanistan that the U.S. government funds the very forces American troops are fighting. And it is a deadly irony, because these funds add up to a huge amount of money for the Taliban (Islamic Terrorists)."[13]

In Iraq, investigators have opened 67 fraud cases in 2010, according to the SIGIR. In Afghanistan, it's 42 cases this year versus four last year. Stuart Bowen, who heads The Special Inspector General for Afghanistan Reconstruction SIGIR, says more tipsters are coming forward.

> Afghanistan in 2009 was "rated by Transparency International as the second-most corrupt nation in the world, with public sector corruption worsening for the second consecutive year."[14]

- New Jersey-based Louis Berger Group, which has overseen the construction of roads, power plants, and schools across Afghanistan, acknowledged that it had knowingly and systematically overcharged the U.S. government and agreed to pay $69.3 million in criminal and civil penalties.[15]

Afghanistan's president, Hamid Karzai, has admitted receiving "some $500 million in foreign assistance in the last few years from the U.S.'s sworn enemy, Iran, delivered in bags and cash." Hundreds of U.S. diplomatic cables obtained by WikiLeaks paint a picture of corruption in Afghanistan at every level of government and society. Cables from the U.S. ambassador in Kabul portray President Karzai as paranoid, with an "inability to grasp the most rudimentary principles of state-building."

Many of the cables were sent from the U.S. Embassy in Kabul over the past 2 years. The *New York Times*, which had advance access to the estimated 250,000 documents leaked to WikiLeaks, reported the documents showed corruption's "pervasive nature, its overwhelming scale, and the dispiriting challenge it poses to American officials." The only member of the Afghan cabinet not accused of accepting bribes in these cables is the Minister of Agriculture.[16]

Finally, there is Pakistan, America's close ally.[17] There is a top secret war going on in Pakistan, and much of it is not even being fought by U.S. soldiers. At a covert top secret operating base run by the U.S. Joint Special

Operations Command (JSOC) in the Pakistani city of Karachi, members of an elite division of the Blackwater corporation operate a top secret program in which they plan assassinations of suspected Taliban and al-Qaeda operatives inside and outside Pakistan. The Blackwater agents also gather intelligence, including targets that guide secret U.S. military drones to the well-documented CIA predator strikes, according to a well-placed source within the U.S. military intelligence apparatus.[18]

> A 2010 report by the International Crisis Group (ICG), titled "Reforming Pakistan's Civil Service," analyzed the structure and functioning of Pakistan's civil bureaucracy concluded that corruption is so widespread among Pakistan's civil service that there is a likelihood of a military coup d'etat.[19]

In summer, 2010, floods in Pakistan may have killed or displaced as many as 20 million people. Yet, "Pakistanis are scandalized and embarrassed that their politicians, bureaucrats and generals have fostered so much corruption for so long that nobody trusts them to deal fairly with the victims of this summer's historic floods. Yet early actions indicate the skeptics are right; feudal landlords and politicians have been accused, according to news reports, of breaching levees to save their lands or diverting relief goods to their constituents."[20]

> It is sad to consider the fact that secret wars that involve supporting corrupt regimes is nothing new in American history. As we shall see, this has become an institutionalized aspect of America's foreign policy no matter which party occupies the White House.[21]

The conclusions scholars and social critics have drawn from these and other examples of America's secret wars supporting corrupt dictatorships in cultures it doesn't understand possess immense consequences, implications so serious that they may result in the economic, political, and moral decline in the United States as we know it:

1. The power to officially declare war under the U.S. Constitution rests with Congress, as does funding wars once they are declared. Yet, the U.S. Congress has not officially declared war since the Japanese attacked Pearl Harbor in 1941. We are nevertheless nearly perpetually involved in "police actions," "liberations," "nation-building projects," and "humanitarian relief efforts" everywhere around the globe that begin secretly, and end up costing American lives and trillions of American dollars.[22]
2. American presidents no longer decide to ask Congress for declarations of war. Wars are either ongoing when they take office or already planned in advance by powers inside the so-called National Security Establishment long before they take office.[23]

3. Spending trillions of dollars on useless wars abroad while poverty, unemployment, and infrastructure (roads, bridges, the electric grid) collapse at home is a sure equation for permanent national decline. History is very clear, states Arianna Huffington, that most great civilizations have declined from within, creating national suicide, rather from being invaded from abroad.[24]

There was a time, shortly after World War II's end, when America accounted for two-thirds of the world's trade exports. Now the United States not only has a huge negative trade balance with the rest of the world, it has managed to make manufacturing jobs one of its chief exports: Over 5.8 million manufacturing jobs have been transferred overseas since 2000, and with them has gone a substantial portion of the middle class and the labor movement.[25]

So how did all this come about, this permanent warfare state, the perpetual support of corrupt and brutal dictatorial regimes, and the unconstitutional loss of Congress' ability to declare war? In 2010 alone the wars in Iraq, Afghanistan, and Pakistan cost the nation $180 billion, and the fiscal year 2010 defense budget was $663.8 billion, more money than the next highest 27 nations combined spend on defense. It has been said many times that those who do not learn from the past are doomed to repeat it. So let us see what can be learned from a short review of the evolution of America's so-called "military-industrial complex."

# The Military-Industrial Complex

## The Defense Establishment and Its Origins

In 1945, the United States emerged victorious from World War II, its economy and military forces intact. There was, at that time, a crucial need to help rebuild the war-torn economies of Western Europe. In addition, the communist revolution in China (1949) pointed out the necessity of preventing newly independent third world nations from entering the communist orbit. Thus, from 1945 to 1975, $170 billion in loans and grants were made by the United States to friendly nations all over the world.[26] In return for such aid, recipients agreed to adopt the dollar as the standard currency of exchange and to give U.S. firms certain advantageous trade and investment opportunities.

Those nations agreeing to accept U.S. aid were to be protected by a worldwide U.S. military network. As of 1988, the United States possessed some 360 military bases in 40 countries, with more than one-third of U.S. military personnel stationed overseas.[27] Since World War II, U.S. troops and naval forces have been involved in 215 so-called shows of force and have intervened militarily in Korea, Lebanon, the Dominican Republic, Vietnam, and most recently Grenada, Nicaragua (through employment of mercenary

Contras), the Persian Gulf, and Bosnia.[28] Militarily, the United States has provided what the Douglas Aircraft Company, in a report for the Army Research Office, called the "Pax Americana" (the American peace).[29]

These strategies have resulted in an unprecedented situation: between 1945 and 1977, the United States spent an astounding $1,500 billion on defense.[30] During the Reagan years alone (1981–1989), an additional $1 trillion was spent on defense. The defense budget for fiscal 1996 was $265 billion, $7 billion more than the Pentagon had requested. This is 37% of the world's entire defense budget. Actually, if one includes the hidden military expenses in other departmental budgets, such as the Energy Department's fuel for nuclear weapons, the military portion of the NASA budget, and the interest for past military budgets, total expenditures are closer to $494 billion ($1.3 billion a day).[31] These expenditures, together with the nearly worldwide deployment of U.S. military forces, have created a huge permanent military establishment.

In fact, on January 13, 1961, outgoing president Eisenhower warned of the consequences of the military-industrial complex in his farewell address:

> In the councils of government, we must guard against the acquisition of unwarranted influence, whether sought or unsought, by the military-industrial complex. . . . We must never let the weight of this combination endanger our liberties or democratic processes. We should take nothing for granted. Only an alert and knowledgeable citizenry can compel the proper meshing of the huge industrial and military machinery of defense with our peaceful methods and goals, so that security and liberty can prosper together.[32]

Despite Eisenhower's warning, the military-industrial complex has continued to increase in both size and influence. Moreover, the nature of the complex is poorly understood by the public. It is not a malevolent conspiracy, as some believe, but an interrelated "community of interests."[33] It is really a MITLAMP (military-industrial-technological-labor-academic-managerial-political) complex:

1. The military sector consists of some 1.5 million active-duty military personnel; their current pay and allowances constitute about 30% of the defense budget.[34] In addition, in 1992, military retirees and veterans received payment of approximately $16,145,203,000. Finally, in 1992, more than $34 billion was budgeted for the Veterans Administration (VA), which wields considerable political pressure.[35]

2. The industrial segment consists of more than 100 defense contractors whose economic base consists of the weapons portion of the defense budget. In 1973, 3,233 retired officers worked for such companies. And between 1979 and 1983, 1,455 additional officers above the rank of colonel accepted positions with defense contractors (along with 335 civilian Pentagon employees with equivalent rank and 31 National Aeronautics and Space Administration [NASA] employees).[36]

3. The labor component of the complex consists of part of the Pentagon workforce, 5% of whom are directly involved and 16% of whom are indirectly involved in military matters.
4. The academic division of the MITLAMP complex consists of university departments involved in Pentagon-funded research on various U.S. campuses. In 1992, 12 universities received more than $10 million each in grants from the Department of Defense. Two universities, Johns Hopkins and the Massachusetts Institute of Technology (MIT), received more than $406 and $389 million, respectively.[37]
5. The managerial component consists of the 7.8% of U.S. managers who are directly involved in administering the intellectual, scientific, technological, and workforce requirements essential to MITLAMP goals. Another 9% of the managerial contingent is indirectly employed in such administration.
6. Finally, the political component of the MITLAMP complex consists of Congress members whose districts contain military facilities and/or employers receiving defense contracts. Such members often sit on congressional committees (such as the Senate and House Armed Services committees) that oversee the Pentagon budget.

At the apex of the military-industrial complex stand the National Security Managers, a group of politicians, civil servants, and businesspersons who tend to rotate among various posts in the Pentagon, Department of State, Atomic Energy Commission, National Security Agency, and CIA, the agencies that administer foreign aid and certain national and international police training programs, the White House, and big business. Such people (as was mentioned in Chapter 1) sit on the boards of trustees of the universities that receive the bulk of defense-related research funds and compose the directors of leading foundations that fund the think tanks and elite associations that regularly make policy recommendations to the executive branch of the federal government, as discussed in Chapter 1. Not surprisingly, the corporations that receive the most financial benefit from defense contracting are the same MNCs whose overseas holdings are protected by the military-counterinsurgency umbrella provided by the U.S. worldwide military establishment.

Another way to view the military-industrial complex is as a triangle. One leg of the structure is the military itself, consisting of 1 million civilian and 2 million military employees. A second leg consists of major corporations involved in defense contracting. Out of 30,000 firms engaged in prime contracting, the top 25 are awarded more than 50% of all defense weapons business. The third leg of the triangle consists of the politicians and their constituencies (districts) that are economically dependent on military bases and/or defense contractors. Here, 10 states receive almost two-thirds of the prime contracts awarded for weapons procurement, with California receiving between one-fifth and one-quarter of all Pentagon money each year throughout the 1980s. Moreover, 10 states receive more than half of all funds spent on military bases and personnel. Finally, almost 3 million private-sector employees work in defense industries, making politicians representing such districts extremely sensitive to the tax bases and local incomes involved.[38]

Among the firms garnering the lion's share of defense contracts are corporate giants such as General Dynamics, McDonnell-Douglas, Lockheed, Rockwell, General Electric, Boeing, United Technologies, Raytheon, Westinghouse, IBM, RCA, Ford, General Motors, and Exxon. Eight of the top 10 contractors in 1963 were still among the top 10 in 1992, and two others were still in the top 15. Among the top fifty contractors were oil companies (Shell and Exxon), telephone firms (AT&T and ITT), universities (MIT and Johns Hopkins), and a health care firm (Foundation Health). Thus, many firms not usually thought of as weapons makers have a large stake in defense contracting.[39]

The weapons industry is notoriously noncompetitive; inefficiency, cost overruns, waste, and corruption are rampant. Purchases of $7,000 coffeepots, $900 Allen wrenches, $700 toilet seats, and $400 hammers have been well documented. In addition, as of 1994, government investigations of contract abuse were initiated against 70% of the Pentagon's top 100 contractors, and fines for that year totaled a record $1.2 billion.[40]

Perhaps most disturbing is the quality of what is produced: "During the 1980s, nearly every major weapons system [was] plagued with performance shortcomings and cost overruns—including the Bradley fighting vehicle, the DIVAD gun, the Viper missile, the F-18 fighter and attack submarines, and the B-1B, Stealth, and F-15 aircraft."[41]

*Case Study: The Pentagon's Black Budget.*   On the campaign trail in 1979, President Reagan dismissed notions of a military-industrial complex as paranoid and fictitious. But, in fact, not only is there a military-industrial complex, but there is also a good deal of secretive deviance institutionalized within it. Much but by no means all of this behavior stems from the fact that a good deal of what happens within military and intelligence agencies is labeled secret and thus sealed from both congressional and public views.

Perhaps the clearest example of the deviance stemming from excessive secrecy has been uncorked by Pulitzer Prize–winning journalist Tim Weiner. In his book *Blank Check,* he describes a "black" or secret budget. So-called black funds originated in World War II with the Manhattan Project, which created the atomic bomb used on Japan in 1945. After the war came the creation of the national security state, the CIA, the National Security Council (NSC), and numerous other intelligence organizations within the armed services. These agencies justified continuation of the secret budget by lying to Congress about the level of Soviet military spending. The net result was to hide control over the nation's nuclear strategy from Congress and the American people. The budget is controlled by only three people: the president, the secretary of defense, and the director of the CIA. Items can be hidden from public view under titles like Special Programs and Selected Activities.

Since its beginnings, the black budget has continually been expanded; in 1990, it was estimated at $36 billion. Hidden within it is money for numerous questionable weapons projects, as well as money for the cover-up of a variety of covert, sometimes criminal operations. Weiner has chronicled a number of examples.

- MILSTAR, a proposed $20 billion top-secret satellite project, was designed to coordinate a 6-month nuclear war with the Soviet Union. Given that the cold war has been declared "won" by the first Bush administration and that the USSR has been dissolved, justification for this proposed overpriced system is puzzling. Now that Congress has finally learned of the MILSTAR plans, perhaps some hard questions can be asked.
- The B-2 stealth bomber has become the costliest airplane in U.S. history. The stealth's initial cost was estimated at $22 billion in 1981 and was finally pegged at more than $68 billion ($820 million per plane) in 1991. The B-2's development is laced with incidents of crime.

  1. In 1985, the stealth's manufacturer, Northrop, hired William Reinke as chief engineer. Reinke promptly set up his own firm, RE Engineering, and awarded it $600,000 in subcontracts from Northrop. Before being sentenced to 5 years in prison for fraud, Reinke sold Northrop $20 Radio Shack headphones for $90 and $1.24 cables for $4.50.
  2. Ron Brousseau, Northrop's buyer of stealth parts, was concerned about his retirement fund. He demanded and received a 5% kickback from subcontractors, a practice so common in the defense industry that it has been nicknamed the "nickel job." Brousseau also assisted subcontractors in a "courtesy-bidding" (price-fixing) scheme, wherein different firms take turns being low bidders on contracts, creating the illusion of competition. Brousseau was sentenced to a 3-year prison term for fraud.

- The Northrop Corporation itself was involved in numerous illegalities regarding the Stealth and other projects.

  1. Northrop overcharged the government $400 million for the stealth and was indicted for fraud and conspiracy. Northrop's chairman, William Jones, resigned in disgrace.
  2. In May 1991, Northrop agreed to a unique $18 million settlement with its shareholders. The payments were made in response to a suit by shareholders challenging the conduct of corporate officials who had become enmeshed in wrongdoing or controversy. Among the

breaches of duties cited were the following:

The cruise missile scandal, in which Northrop pleaded guilty to criminal fraud for falsifying missile test results (funds for the cruise were a black item in the Pentagon budget)

The MX missile guidance system, the subject of a Department of Justice civil suit brought in 1990

The Tacit Rainbow missile project, terminated by the air force following years of problems

The Harrier jet stabilizer, the subject of a heated congressional hearing in 1990

- Voishan, the company that provided fasteners for the stealth bomber, defrauded the government by providing defective parts "approved" by a fictitious inspector.

Aside from questionable and sometimes illegal projects, the black aspect of the Pentagon budget has also involved covert operations, knowledge of which was unconstitutionally hidden from congressional oversight.

- After the failed hostage rescue in Iran in 1981, a secret operations unit continued activities, funded by a secret budget funneled from other projects approved by Congress. Funds totaling $320 million were utilized for these operations, code-named Yellow Fruit, but a great deal of the money was illegally misspent on activities including vacations, prostitutes' services, drugs, clothing, and high-tech equipment. As a result of the fraud connected with Operation Yellow Fruit, only 10 to 20% of the $320 million was actually spent on covert operations. Three U.S. army officers responsible for the funds were sentenced to prison terms ranging from 18 months to 10 years and fined $5,000 to $50,000 in the first secret court-martial held by the U.S. army since the Vietnam era.[42]
- In another black operation between 1986 and 1991, the CIA secretly aided Afghan rebels who were fighting Soviet troops. The CIA also prompted China, Saudi Arabia, and Iran to provide aid. Some of the arms provided to the Afghans were sold to Pakistan in acts of self-enrichment, and some of the funds earmarked for the Afghans were diverted to the Contras in violation of the Boland Amendment.
- In 1984, the CIA received Palestinian arms captured by Israel and provided them illegally to the Nicaraguan Contras. In one of the CIA deals, Israel received CIA weapons credits for sending captured arms to the Contras. Israel would then sell a like amount of arms to China, which would promptly export an equal sum of weapons to a CIA dummy corporation. In turn, the CIA would funnel the secret arsenal to Iran and/or the Contras. Other weapons were stockpiled for Afghan use, not in fighting the Soviets but in the bloody civil war that followed the Soviet withdrawal in 1990.

## Consequences of Defense Policies

Defense contracting fraud (as well as waste and abuse) has a long and notorious history. Contemporary defense contracting fraud grew in the aftermath of World War II when the United States decided to permanently retain its war apparatus. Likewise, the amount of fraud involved has increased in virtually every decade since the 1940s, as have relationships between defense contractors, Pentagon employees, and Washington politicians. Consider some recent examples.

- Between 1980 and 1992 every one of the top 10 defense contractors was convicted of or confessed to defrauding the government.

A Project on Government Oversight (PGO) study found that in one 4-year period, October 1989 to February 1994, 85 instances of fraud, waste, and abuse in weapons contracting occurred.

- The largest investigation of Pentagon fraud between 1986 and 1990, Operation Ill Wind, began when Pentagon official John Marlowe was caught molesting little girls. He plea-bargained to avoid jail and, in the next few years, secretly recorded hundreds of conversations with weapons contractors. There is no way of knowing how much Ill Wind's crimes cost. The investigation itself cost $20 million. More than 90 companies were convicted of felonies, including eight of the military's 15 largest contractors. Assistant navy secretary Melvyn Paisley was sentenced to 4 years in prison for taking bribes and diverting work to a firm he secretly controlled with a partner. By 1994, nearly 70 of the Pentagon's 100 largest contractors were being investigated. By 2002, the DOD could not account for some $2.3 trillion in taxpayer moneys.[43]
- Boeing was involved in a huge tanker plane scandal in 2003. The corporation sought a $27 billion contract from the Pentagon to lease unneeded 767s that refuel fighter planes in midair. Boeing hired Darleen Druyan, a Pentagon procurement official who gave the contract to the company, shortly after she was offered a position at Boeing. In 2004, Druyan pleaded guilty to conspiring to defraud the federal government. In a supplemental plea, Druyan admitted that she "agreed to a higher price for the aircraft than she believed was appropriate." This was as a "parting gift" to Boeing, she told government prosecutors. She also provided to Boeing proprietary information from another aircraft manufacturer. Numerous Bush administration officials were involved. Boeing also possessed ties to White House chief of staff Andrew Card, who, acting under the direction of President Bush, intervened on Boeing's behalf with the air force and Office of Management and Budget. House Speaker

Dennis Hastert and Congressman Norm Dicks spoke directly with President Bush on Boeing's behalf, and Bush named Andrew Card as the administration's leader on the deal. Senior civilian Pentagon official, air force acquisitions officer Marvin Sambur, intervened on Boeing's behalf, urging immediate signing of the contract as a way of preempting the scandal from squelching the deal.[44]

Halliburton, Dick Cheney's former company, became embroiled in several scandals in the last quarter of 2004:

- Swiss authorities shut down bank accounts allegedly used by Halliburton for bribing the Nigerian government;
- A high-level army whistle-blower claimed that army officials illegally favored Halliburton in contracting decisions—sparking an FBI investigation;
- Accusations emerged that company officials demanded bribes from subcontractors in Kuwait;
- In filings with the Securities and Exchange Commission, Halliburton admitted it may have paid bribes in Nigeria;
- An audit by the inspector general for the U.S. occupation authority in Iraq found that Halliburton could not account for over a third of the items it handled (worth some $1.8 billion) in Kuwait while working for the occupation authorities.[45]

Documents declassified in 1993 demonstrate that the military-industrial complex "systematically and repeatedly lied to Congress and the public to frighten them into an ever-larger military. . . . The military has sucked away public investment, both dollars and talent, from many of the areas now so deeply in need—education, health care, public infrastructure, social services and research and development for civilian economic enterprise."

Meanwhile, the waste, fraud, and abuse inherent in the militarized economy continue apace.

- There is now $90 billion in surplus equipment in Pentagon warehouses, about $30 billion in excess of what would be needed if World War III broke out.
- The air force had $5 million in unneeded engine blades, and an air force computer routinely misclassifies onetime orders as needed recurrently, causing repeated reorders of items needed one time. Three hundred aircraft engines had to be scrapped because of improper storage. The army spent $35.9 million for replacement of equipment that was repairable.
- Even the Pentagon admits that the Sea Wolf submarine ($2.8 billion) and a new aircraft carrier ($4.5 billion) are unneeded. The systems are being built just to keep defense workers employed.[46]

## The New Global Economy

- The Indonesian government diverted millions of dollars in World Bank aid money to finance the establishment of the militia groups that laid waste to East Timor in 1999, Australian television claims. At least $59 million of World Bank aid money was used to fund militia activities in East Timor.[47]
- Art dealers were furious when rumors appeared that incriminating evidence of collusion existed between two of the world's leading multinational auction houses, Christie's and Sotheby's.[48] In January 2000, Christie's admitted handing over evidence to the antitrust division of the U.S. Justice Department of possible collusion between the two rivals.
- "Swiss authorities investigating a Russian money-laundering affair have issued an international arrest warrant for former top Kremlin official Pavel Borodin, who was a key aide to Boris Yeltsin before the former Russian president resigned unexpectedly." The charges are part of an investigation into alleged payoffs to Russian government officials by Swiss-based construction firm Mabetex.[49]
- British American Tobacco (BAT), the world's second-largest cigarette company, established a black market in its own products in China and across Asia, according to company documents. One set of papers, released by British health campaigners, showed how in 1993 the firm, alarmed by advances made by its competitor Philip Morris, actively planned to circumvent the China state tobacco monopoly, stating that "alternative routes of distribution of unofficial imports need to be examined, evaluated and, if appropriate, maximised."[50] In another document of about the same time, the firm's American subsidiary, Brown and Williamson, told its UK headquarters that the best growth prospects in China were in the black market. BAT managed and supplied smugglers with its cigarettes and condoned their activities. Likewise, in February 2000, a group of class-action lawyers announced in New York that they planned to file an antitrust lawsuit accusing cigarette makers of illegally fixing prices since the 1980s and of meeting secretly to make illegal agreements on wholesale prices. One of the companies named is BAT's American subsidiary, Brown and Williamson Tobacco Corporation.
- U.S. defense contractor Lockheed Martin announced in 1999 that it would give South Korea aircraft parts, military software, and instrumentation equipment worth about $25 million as compensation for overcharging the South Korean government on purchases of eight P-3C antisubmarine aircraft. Daewoo, a large Korean corporation, blew the whistle on Lockheed because Lockheed failed to share the profits as promised.[51]

Moreover, the collapse of the former Soviet Union has resulted in the first truly global capitalist economic system. Among the characteristics of this new global economy are the following:

1. The internationalization of business, by which anything can be made anywhere on earth and sold everywhere. The result is that MNCs and finance capital now know no boundaries.
2. A great shift from manufacturing industries to service industries, such as computers, management, and finance.
3. A dramatic population shift in which tens of millions of people from the poor third world nations of Asia, Africa, and Latin America migrate to prosperous first world nations of North America and Europe.
4. Growing economic inequality both within and between nations. Per capita incomes in third world nations now range from $500 to $2,000 per year, whereas those of first world nations typically average around $23,000.[52] This means, among other things, that labor costs in poor nations are a mere fraction of what they are in rich nations.[53]

The new global economy has also created new opportunities for deviant behavior on a massive scale.

## Deviance and Multinational Corporations

The U.S. economy, with its needs for investment outlets, cheap labor, and access to scarce raw materials, has created an environment in which certain types of deviance tend to occur. In Haiti, for example, it is common for workers to earn 67 cents to $1.67 per day working in multinational clothing factories.

- "At Quality Garments S.A., a clothing contractor in the SONAPI Industrial Park, the factory is hot, dimly lit, crowded. . . . There is no ventilation. . . . For their labor, the workers are in many cases paid as little as 15 gourdes per day, or 12 cents per hour, well below the legal minimum wage of 30 cents per hour."[54] The same exploitive conditions prevail at other factories:

    Seamfast Manufacturing, which produces dresses for Ventura Ltd. under the Ventura label, sold at K-Mart and J. C. Penney, and Universal Manufacturing; and at Chancerelles S.A., a subsidiary of Fine Form USA, which produces bras and underpants for Elsie Undergarments of Hialeah, Florida. The garments are sold under the Shuly's and Elsie labels at J. C. Penney and smaller retailers.

    National Sewing Contractors, which produces Disney pajamas, which are sold under the Sister Sister label at Wal-Mart, K-Mart, J. C. Penney, and Kids 'R' Us.

    Excel Apparel Exports, which produces women's underwear for the Hanes division of Sara Lee Corporation, under the Hanes Her Way label sold at Wal-Mart. The plant also produces women's slips sold at Dillard Department Stores and nightwear for Movie Star, to be sold at Sears and Bradlees.

- Alpha Sewing, which produces industrial gloves for Ansell Edmont of Coshocton, Ohio, claims that it is the world's largest manufacturer of safety gloves and protective clothing, but the workers at Alpha Sewing lack the most basic safety protection. They produce Ansell Edmont's Vinyl-Impregnated Super-Flexible STD gloves with bare hands while working with polyvinylchloride (PVC), which removes layers of skin.
- At Classic Apparel, which produces sports team merchandise for H. H. Cutler, workers attach "Made in USA" labels to clothes made in a Haitian factory and sold as American goods in Wal-Mart. Wal-Mart has a policy of selling goods made in America. But a 2002 *Dateline NBC* investigation found that goods sewn by children in Bangladesh for Wal-Mart were labeled "Made in USA." Wal-Mart promised to investigate the situation. Over half of the nearly 50 assembly plants producing in Haiti for the U.S. market are paying less than the legal minimum wage, and while the U.S. Agency for International Development (AID) gave $215 million in 1995 for economic development to Haiti, the United States has opposed raising the Haitian minimum wage to $2.40 a day.

In recent decades, deviance by MNCs has included illegal payments to foreign governments and the exporting of hazardous goods. By the late 1970s, a practice known as *corporate dumping* had aroused a good deal of concern among public-interest groups and government agencies. The practice involves exporting goods that have been either banned or not approved for sale in the United States.

Most often, the greatest market for such unsafe products is among the poor of the third world. Hazardous products are often legal in such countries. And because many of the poor in these nations are illiterate, they are often unaware of the hazards involved with the use of these products.

Examples of the products involved in corporate dumping are growing at a rapid pace.

An undisclosed number of farmers and over 1,000 water buffaloes died suddenly in Egypt after being exposed to leptophos, a chemical pesticide, which was never registered for domestic use by the Environmental Protection Agency (EPA), but was exported to at least 30 countries.

After the Dalkon Shield intrauterine device killed at least 17 women in the United States, the manufacturer withdrew it from the domestic market. It was sold overseas after the American recall and is still in common use in some countries.

No one knows how many children may develop cancer since several million children's garments treated with a carcinogenic fire retardant called Tris were shipped overseas after being forced off the domestic market by the Consumer Product Safety Commission (CPSC).

Lomotil, an effective antidiarrhea medicine sold only by prescription in the United States because it is fatal in amounts just slightly over the recommended doses, was sold over the counter in Sudan, in packages proclaiming it was used by astronauts during Gemini and Apollo space flights and [was] recommended for use by children as young as 12 months.

Winstrol, a synthetic male hormone, which was found to stunt the growth of American children, is freely available in Brazil, where it is recommended as an appetite stimulant for children.

Depo-Provera, an injectable contraceptive banned for such use in the United States because it caused malignant tumors in beagles and monkeys, is sold by the Upjohn Co. in 70 other countries, where it is widely used in U.S.-sponsored population control programs.

450,000 baby pacifiers of the type that has caused choking deaths have been exported by at least five manufacturers since a ban was proposed by the CPSC. 120,000 teething rings that did not meet recently established CPSC standards were declared for export and are on sale right now in Australia.[55]

For decades, American corporations have been exporting chemicals, especially pesticides, proved to be poisonous to the health of third world peoples, and Congress has done little to stop this dumping. In 1981, President Carter issued an executive order restricting the export of substances banned for sale in the United States, but President Reagan rescinded it shortly after taking office. The American chemical industry produces about $30 billion worth of poisons each year, and about one of seven third world agricultural workers suffer acute pesticide poisoning each year. Nearly 99% of deaths from pesticide exposure occur in the third world, in children with cancers and other chronic diseases.

Toxic industrial waste is also deposited in developing nations. Four international treaties banned this practice, with the Basel Convention (which became law in 1992) considered the most important. The Basel Convention bans all hazardous waste exports from developed nations to developing ones. However, there are many loopholes, including the toxic chemicals contained in components of computers and cell phones. Most nations have ratified the treaty, with the United States being one of the few exceptions.[56]

In 1990, Congress voted to outlaw export of the pesticide DCBP, but lobbying by pesticide interests, including companies such as Shell Oil, Occidental Petroleum, and Dow Chemical, left the measure hung up in a conference committee.

The fact remains that DCBP causes 20,000 deaths per year among Latin American plantation workers who cannot read warning labels; other effects include sterility, breathing problems, convulsions, nerve damage, and blindness. American workers sued Occidental in 1977, claiming that DCBP had made them sterile, and won a $2.3 million settlement. Although DCBP is no longer manufactured in the United States, other dangerous pesticides, such as chlordane (a potent carcinogen) and heptachlor (a suspected carcinogen), both manufactured by Velsicol, continue to be exported. In fact, 1.5 to

2 million pounds are exported per year, despite a ban on these products by 48 nations.[57]

## Government Policy

In some cases, corporate dumping has been aided by government policy. In one instance, the population office of AID purchased hundreds of shoe-box-sized cartons of unsterilized Dalkon Shields for distribution in the third world. The birth control device, which causes uterine infections, blood poisoning, spontaneous abortion in pregnant women, and perforation of the uterus, was sold to AID at a 48% discount because of its unsterile condition.[58] The device was distributed in 42 nations, largely in the third world. Moreover, insufficient information concerning the use and hazards of the shield accompanied the shipment.

Some companies dump workplace hazards as well as hazardous products in poor nations. One example is the case of asbestos, a cancer-causing agent. Thanks to the Occupational Carcinogens Control Act of 1976, fines of $1,000 for violations and $5,000 for repeat violations are provided for U.S. manufacturers that expose workers to carcinogenic agents. However, no such regulations protect foreign workers from contracting cancer from asbestos fibers. On the contrary, Mexican law merely provides a light fine ($45 to $90) for failure to warn workers that they are working around a health hazard. As a result, U.S. asbestos makers increasingly locate plants in Mexico and other third world nations with lax workplace hazard laws (e.g., Brazil) and are now producing quantities of asbestos there.[59]

Corporate dumping is undesirable for two main reasons. First, it poses serious health hazards to the poor and uninformed consumers of the third world. In the long run, this contributes to the anti-Americanism of many nonaligned nations. Second, many types of corporate dumping produce a boomerang effect. That is, some of the hazardous products sold abroad by U.S. companies are often used in the manufacture of goods that are exported to the United States and other developed nations.

> The "vast majority" of the nearly one billion pounds of pesticides used each year in the Third World is applied to crops that are then exported back to the U.S. and other rich countries. . . . This fact undercuts the industry's main argument defending pesticide dumping. "We see nothing wrong with helping the hungry world eat," is the way a Velsicol Chemical Company executive puts it. Yet, the entire dumping process bypasses the local population's need for food. The example in which DCBP manufactured by Amvac is imported into Central America by Castle Cooke to grow fruit destined for U.S. dinner tables is a case in point.[60]

The boomerang effect of corporate dumping may represent the breeding ground of yet another major scandal regarding the practices of MNCs and certain U.S. government agencies in the third world.

## Dumping Toxic Waste

Many third world nations, especially Turkey, Haiti, the Philippines, Nigeria, and Guinea-Bissau, are now routinely approached by advanced nations to become sites for the dumping of toxic waste. A virtual armada of ships circles the globe in search of cheap storage facilities to dump waste that can cause cancer and birth defects. Some of the waste has even been found radioactive. International toxic dumping is currently a $10-billion-a-year business, and much corruption accompanies it.[61]

The advanced nations of the world generate about 400 million tons of toxic waste annually; 60% comes from the United States. The EPA requires U.S. companies to provide on-site disposal facilities for toxic waste that cost upwards of $30 million and take years to build. However, such waste can be dumped in third world nations for a fraction of this cost, even providing handsome financial rewards to the recipient nations. For example, Guinea-Bissau, which has a gross national product of $150 million, will make $150 to $600 million over a 5-year period in a deal to accept toxic waste from three European nations.[62]

Third world participation in the waste dumping of advanced nations has generated a host of scandals.

- In April 1988, five top government officials in Congo were indicted after they concluded a deal to import 1 million tons of chemical waste and pesticide residue, receiving $4 million in "commissions" from a firm specializing in hazardous waste disposal. The total contract was worth $84 million.
- After dumping toxic waste in Nigeria and Lebanon in 1988, Italy agreed to take back some 6,400 tons. Nigeria recalled its Italian ambassador and arrested 25 people when it discovered that some of the waste was radioactive. To complicate matters, Italian dock workers in 10 port cities have refused to handle the waste. Italy has pledged to ban further toxic exports to the developing world and plans to spend $7 billion a year to clean up its own toxic dumps at home. The Italian government has also sued 22 waste-producing firms to force them to turn over $75 million to pay for transporting and treating incoming waste.[63]
- In 1987, Weber Ltd., a West German waste transporter, found a Turkish cement plant willing to accept 1,500 tons of toxic-waste-laden sawdust for about $70 a ton. Instead of being burned, the sawdust waste sat in the open air for nearly 16 months, slowly leaking poison into the ground. A newspaper reported that the sawdust contained lethal PCBs, and a scandal ensued. Under pressure from the governments of Turkey and West Germany, Weber finally agreed to transport the waste back to West Germany. Normally, Weber charges its customers $450 to $510 a ton to dispose of waste in Germany. With third world costs of $110 per ton, the amount of profit involved is substantial.

- In late 1991, three South Carolina metal smelting firms contracted with waste disposal firms to send waste containing life-threatening levels of cadmium and lead to Bangladesh. Once in that country, the waste was used to make fertilizer and used by Bangladeshi farmers.

Ironically, the greatest problem with toxic dumping in third world nations is that much of the time it is perfectly legal. About all that concerned citizens in developing nations can do is publicize the dangers involved. What environmental disasters may befall such nations in the future is anyone's guess.

Third world dumping involves a series of related implications. For instance, some suggest that deliberate racist and genocidal policies are being practiced by certain corporations and government agencies. We suggest that corporate dumping may well have such effects on the non-White people of the world. The same may be said concerning support by corporations and governments for regimes that violate human rights.

## Human Rights, Multinationals, and U.S. Foreign Policy

Under Presidents Ford and Carter, the United States went on record as supporting the cause of human rights around the world. In a United Nations speech of March 17, 1977, President Carter pledged to "work with potential adversaries as well as . . . close friends to advance the cause of human rights."

The United States is also a party to the International Bill of Rights. Passed by the UN General Assembly in 1948, this document supports a variety of civil and economic rights and specifically pledges member nations not to subject anyone to "torture or to cruel, inhuman or degrading treatment, or punishment" or to "arbitrary arrest, detention, or exile."

Finally, the United States is also a signatory to the famous Helsinki Agreement of 1975, which contains a detailed human rights clause, specifically stating that participating nations will "respect human rights and fundamental freedoms, including freedom of thought, conscience, religion, or belief, all without distinctions as to race, sex, language, or religion." Thus, by pronouncement and by legal agreement, the United States has firmly committed itself to the cause of human rights.

Unfortunately, a mounting body of evidence indicates that U.S. policy makers have, on many occasions, either placed in power and/or aided in retaining power some of the world's most repressive dictatorships. The chief characteristic of such regimes is that they are right-wing, military dictatorships and hence friendly to the goals of multinational capitalism. With U.S. support (ranging from foreign aid to military protection), many third world regimes have done away with democratic practices and instituted brutally repressive measures, including arbitrary imprisonment, torture, death squads, and kidnapping.

In fact, a pattern has been established showing that U.S. economic and military aid (and aid from U.S.-dominated lending agencies) has been "positively related to investment climate (for U.S. multinationals) and inversely (negatively) related to the maintenance of the democratic order and human rights." This relationship is described in Table 5.1. Moreover, the decline in aid for South Korea and Chile is somewhat misleading. In South Korea, the decline was caused by the end of expenditures for the Vietnam War, in which South Korea participated. And the decline in aid for Chile was, in fact, due to a successful right-wing coup (supported by the CIA) in 1973; high levels of aid had been given before that date.

Between 1973 and 1978, the United States continued its aid to many of the regimes cited by Chomsky and Herman, as well as to others cited by organizations such as Amnesty International, the UN Commission on Human Rights, and the International Commission on Human Rights for persistent "torture, assassination, and arbitrary arrest."

Moreover, the Foreign Assistance Act of 1974 provides that the president "shall substantially reduce or terminate security assistance to any government which engages in gross violations of human rights." Under this act, it became illegal (as of July 1, 1975) to provide aid to any law enforcement organization (e.g., police prisons) of any foreign government. However, under the International Narcotics Control Act, both training and weapons have been given to police departments in many foreign countries, including those listed in Table 5.1.

In the cases of Guatemala (1953), Iran (1953), the Dominican Republic (1965), and South Vietnam (1963), U.S. troops and/or the CIA played an active role in actually installing such regimes, through either aid or armed forces or both. Aside from bringing advantages to multinationals, these regimes have done little to improve the lot of the people over whom they rule. This is especially the case in third world nations in Asia, Africa, and Latin America.

- In 1996, Nigerian troops executed nine environmentalists, including a former Nobel Prize winner. The activists were involved in protests against Shell Oil's parent company, which had destroyed large tracts of farmland in its quest for Nigerian oil. Shell refines and imports into the United States almost 50% of Nigeria's entire oil production. Evidence uncovered by the *Village Voice* in 1995 indicates that Shell Oil had been paying the Nigerian military to take action against environmental protesters and that Shell had offered bribes to witnesses in trials of murdered protesters.[64]
- In 1996, released manuals from the CIA-run School of the Americas (SOA) indicate that the training advocated such tactics as murder, extortion, physical abuse, and bounty for enemy dead. Other tactics advocated included the use of blackmail, false arrest, imprisonment of parents, and execution of all other members of the "enemy's" local cell.

**TABLE 5.1  Relationship Between U.S. Aid, Investment Climate, and Human Rights in 10 Countries**

| Country | Strategic Political Dates (1) | Positive (+) or Negative (−) Effects on Democracy (2) | (−) Means an Increased Use of Torture or Death Squads (3) | (−) Means an Increase in Number of Political Prisoners (4) | Improvement in Investment Climate: Tax Laws Eased (+) (5a) | Improvement in Investment Climate: Labor Repressed (+) (5b) | Economic Aid (% Change) (6) | Military Aid (% Change) (7) | (6) + (7) (% Change) (8) | U.S. and Multinational Credits (% Change) (9) | Total Aid (8) + (9) (% Change) (10) |
|---|---|---|---|---|---|---|---|---|---|---|---|
| Brazil | 1964 | − | − | − | + | + | +14 | −40 | −7 | +180 | 112 |
| Chile | 1973 | − | − | − | + | + | +588 | −8 | +259 | +1,079 | +770 |
| Dominican Republic | 1965 | − | − | NA | + | + | +57 | +10 | +52 | +305 | +133 |
| Guatemala | 1954 | − | − | NA | + | + | NA | NA | NA | NA | +5,300 |
| Indonesia | 1965 | − | − | − | + | NA | −81 | −79 | −81 | +653 | +62 |
| Iran | 1953 | − | − | − | + | + | NA | NA | NA | NA | +900 |
| Philippines | 1972 | − | − | − | + | + | +204 | +67 | +143 | +171 | +161 |
| South Korea | 1972 | − | − | NA | + | + | −52 | −56 | −55 | +183 | −9 |
| Thailand | 1973 | + | + | NA | − | − | −63 | −64 | −64 | +218 | +5 |
| Uruguay | 1973 | − | − | + | + | − | 11 | +9 | −2 | +32 | +21 |

*Source:* Chomsky, N., and Herman, E. S. U.S. vs. human rights, in the third world. *Monthly Review* 29 (July/August 1977), 30–31. Reprinted by permission.

Such tactics are illegal for U.S. intelligence agents, in part because they violate the human rights treaties to which the United States is a signatory. The SOA has trained members of death squads throughout Latin America. The squads are responsible for the deaths of thousands of innocent civilians in Latin America since 1954.

Examples of human rights abuses in Latin America and elsewhere by regimes supported by U.S. military aid and having death squads or police units trained by the CIA are legion.

- In the 1980s and 1990s, Colombia had the highest recorded homicide rate in the world, averaging about 35,000 murders per year (10 times higher than the United States). Many people assume that the high homicide rate is due to drug cartels, but only 2% of such killings are drug related. Over 70% of Colombia's homicides are due to the activities of the Colombian army, police, and paramilitary killer squad organizations, originally trained by the CIA. Among the frequent targets of government murderers are farming co-op members, who have protested for higher wages, and protesters fearing that Colombia's state-owned oil company will soon be privatized. Government groups received $1.6 billion in military aid from the United States between 1986 and 1996, with about $1 billion more scheduled for release in 2001.[65]
- In Turkey, an automobile accident in 1997 killed Abdullah Calti, a convicted drug trafficker and murderer, and his girlfriend, Conca Us, a Mafia hitwoman and former beauty queen. Evidence found at the crash scene indicated that Turkish officials had given special diplomatic credentials and various weapons permits to Calti. A subsequent investigation demonstrated the following:

> Calti had ties to the Turkish Secret Police and he belonged to a neofacist terrorist group called the Grey Wolves. The Wolves were responsible for bombing attacks that killed thousands of Turkish civilians in the 1960s and 1970s and were responsible for the 1981 shooting of Pope John II (which the CIA tried to blame on the Russians).[66]

> Calti also possessed close ties to the Turkish crime syndicate, which smuggles arms and heroin across Eastern Europe to various nations in the Middle East. The same smuggling mechanism was also used by the CIA in the 1980s to get weapons to the Nicaraguan Contras. The Grey Wolves also received funds and training from U.S. advisers and were affiliated with the CIA in the 1970s. In 1980, the violence committed by the Wolves led to a CIA-backed military coup in Turkey. Following the collapse of the USSR in 1991, extremist Grey Wolf members infiltrated many of the former Soviet provinces (now independent nations) and became active in the politics of a number of Central Asian nations. Meanwhile, the Turkish government continues to use the Wolves to repress Turkish minorities, especially the Kurds.

# Iran

In 1953, the CIA was responsible for placing the Shah's family in power when it assisted in overthrowing leftist Prime Minister Mohammad Mossadegh in a violent coup. From 1953 until the 1979 Khomeini revolution, Congress, the U.S. military, the CIA, and private corporate interests all supported the Shah's army and secret police with various types of aid. Under the U.S. Office of Public Safety program, between 1961 and 1973, Iran received $1.7 billion. This money was used to purchase police hardware (e.g., guns, teargas grenades, computers, and patrol cars) and to train 179 Iranian police officials at the International Police Academy in Washington, D.C. (and other special U.S. police schools). From 1946 to 1976, Iran received $1.6 billion under a variety of U.S. military assistance programs: outright grants of arms, equipment, and services; credit for purchasing U.S. arms; training Iranian military personnel; and subsidies awarded under an act designed to aid threatened pro-U.S. regimes. Between 1950 and 1976, 11,025 Iranian military officers received training under these programs.

Iran also purchased arms from private concerns. For example, the Bell Helicopter Company helped Iran develop a Sky Cavalry Brigade, operating from helicopters, which was modeled after similar U.S. units that fought in Vietnam.[67] Finally, between 1971 and 1978, the United States sold Iran $15 billion in military supplies.[68] Moreover, at the moment of the revolution, some 40,000 military advisers,[69] along with an unknown number of CIA agents, were stationed in Iran. In short, the United States had a long history of assistance to the Shah's regime.

While the Shah was in power, almost 1,500 people were arrested every month. In one day alone (June 5, 1963), the SAVAK (Iran's secret police) and the Shah's army killed 6,000 Iranian citizens. Amnesty International's report for 1975 indicated that Iranian authorities had arrested and imprisoned between 25,000 and 100,000 political prisoners.[70] The Iranian press was strictly controlled by the police under the Shah's direct orders. Minorities were not allowed to learn their native languages, and poverty was widespread. Iran was a nation in which political stability was maintained by repression—a nation on the brink of massive political turmoil.

Since 1973, Iran has been one of a number of nations cited for constant abuses of human rights by organizations such as Amnesty International, the International Commission of Jurists, and the UN Commission on Human Rights.[71] Thus, while U.S. officials and the press knew full well what was taking place in Iran, the government continued to support the Shah with various types of military aid, and the press remained nearly silent on the Shah's abuses.

By mid-1980, the United States had paid a tragic price for its rather blind support of the Shah's regime: in 1979, an anti-American revolution led by Muslim holy man Ayatollah Ruholla Khomeini, exiled from Iran by the government in 1963, overthrew the Shah's rule. U.S. support for the Shah may also have been partially responsible for the catastrophic increases in oil prices since 1973 (see Chapter 2). A number of sources, including Jack Anderson and CBS's *60 Minutes,* reported that the Shah:

> Was installed in power in the 1950s when the Rockefellers helped arrange the CIA coup that overthrew Mossadegh.

> Demonstrated his gratitude to the Rockefellers by making heavy deposits of his personal funds in the Rockefeller-owned Chase Manhattan Bank.

> Raised Iranian oil prices in 1973–1974 by 470%, with the approval of then secretary of state Henry Kissinger, a Rockefeller associate. (This cost the oil-consuming nations of the West an estimated $95 billion in inflated oil prices.)[72] The price hike was requested by the Shah in part to purchase American-made arms.

> Was admitted into the United States for medical care in 1979 as a result of pressure by Chase Manhattan president David Rockefeller and Henry Kissinger.[73] As a result, in November 1979, militants overran the U.S. embassy in Tehran, capturing 61 U.S. employees. An aborted effort to rescue the hostages in early May 1980 resulted in the deaths of eight U.S. servicemen.

Speculation still persists whether a secret deal was made by the Reagan campaign regarding the release of the hostages in exchange for weapons (see Chapter 9).

The Khomeini regime spread anti-American fever throughout the Middle East. In October 1983, a truck driven by members of a Khomeini-supported regime smashed into a Beirut, Lebanon, building housing U.S. marines, killing 241 servicemen.[74] Such terrorism and instability have seriously weakened perception of the strength and consistency of U.S. foreign policy.

U.S. support for the Shah was quite profitable for Chase Manhattan, which continued to be the repository for the Shah's sizable fortune, and Exxon Oil, which is controlled through Rockefeller trust funds and private holdings.[75] Yet these events have never been investigated by Congress. The consequences suffered in return for U.S. support for the Shah are also indicative of other consequences of supporting regimes that violate human rights.

## Latin America

In Latin America, another trouble spot, U.S. support for authoritarian dictatorships contributes to suffering and political instability throughout the region.

- From 1976 to 1983, some 15,000 to 20,000 residents of Argentina simply disappeared. Many were tortured to death and then buried in secret locations in unmarked graves by Argentina's military dictatorship. In 1982, the U.S.-backed government declared amnesty for those responsible for the disappearances of these 20,000 suspected subversives, which primarily benefited those guilty of torture and murder. However, in December 1983, Argentina elected a democratic government under Raul Alfonsin, and judicial action began against many of the military officers responsible for the crimes.[76]

- In El Salvador, a poor Central American nation, 2% of all families own 60% of the nation's most fertile land. And between 1961 and 1975, the number of families owning no land at all grew from 30,000 to 167,000. Between 1979 and 1983, some 40,000 civilians were killed largely by government-supported, right-wing death squads, and 20% of the Salvadoran population (800,000 people) became refugees. U.S. aid to El Salvador between 1979 and 1984 was $100 million, six times that provided in the previous 29 years, despite the fact that the government's death squads brutally raped, tortured, and murdered four U.S. nuns in 1980. Amnesty International declared that the Salvadoran death squads were a gross violation of human rights. Nonetheless, aid continued, as the Reagan administration continued to argue that the situation was constantly improving. Meanwhile, investments in El Salvador by U.S.-based MNCs, such as Chevron, Texaco, and Kimberly-Clark, totaled $100 million in the 1980s.[77]

- In 1994, a declassified cable sent by special envoy General Vernon Walters confirmed U.S. knowledge of Salvadoran leader Roberto d'Aubuisson's plan to murder U.S. ambassador Thomas Pickering in 1984. Other cables demonstrated that the United States suspected d'Aubuisson of death squad activity as early as 1978 but feared alienating him. The CIA was aware of the death squad's plan to murder Archbishop Oscar Romero, which it did. D'Aubuisson also had a close relationship with North Carolina's senator Jesse Helms throughout the 1980s. D'Aubuisson's death squads murdered several thousand leftists and suspected leftists in the 1970s and 1980s at the behest of wealthy landowners. D'Aubuisson died of throat cancer in 1992.[78]

- In March 1993, the UN commission on the truth on crimes committed against civilians in El Salvador's 12-year civil war released its official report. Among its conclusions was that the majority of the political murders in that nation's civil war occurred at the very least with the reluctant agreement and financial support of the Reagan and Bush administrations. More than 80,000 people, 1 in 70 Salvadorans and mostly unarmed civilians, were murdered in the war. The CIA in its own report described one leader, Roberto d'Aubuisson, as a drug trafficker, arms smuggler, and plotter in the assassination of Archbishop Oscar Romero.[79]

- In another poor Central American nation, Guatemala, the United States sponsored a CIA-directed coup in 1954 when it was learned that Guatemala's president, Jacobo Guzman, planned to redistribute 387,000 of the 500,000 acres of Guatemalan land owned by a U.S.-based company, United Fruit. Secretary of State John Foster Dulles, whose law firm had represented United Fruit in the 1930s, and CIA director Allen Dulles

(J. F. Dulles's brother and former president of United Fruit) launched a massive public relations campaign, accusing Guzman's government of being communist. The CIA coup that overthrew the Guatemalan president replaced him with a U.S.-trained army officer, Castillo Armas. Under Armas, political parties and trade unions were abolished, and U.S. aid totaling $6 million was used to thwart guerrilla resistance in the 1960s in which 10,000 people were killed and 100,000 people were left refugees. Even the U.S. Department of State criticized the operation.

Since 1954, 80,000 Guatemalan civilians, mostly peasants, have been murdered, many women and children. Eyewitness accounts report children being hacked to death with machetes and their heads smashed against walls, whereas infants have been thrown into the air and bayoneted. In 1982 alone, 80,000 peasants fled Guatemala, and Amnesty International estimates another 10,000 were killed. Yet the Reagan administration insisted that criticism of Guatemala was a "bum rap."[80]

Since July 1982, the Guatemalan government has been involved in the attempted genocide of ethnic groups living on its northern border, violating a 1948 UN convention against genocide (to which Guatemala was a signatory). In August 1983, General Montt was overthrown in a barracks coup and replaced by another military leader, General Victories. At the time of the coup, unemployment was 40% and business was angered over Montt's policies restricting oil investment.

Following the coup, the Reagan administration quickly approved an aid package totaling $10.25 million in military aid and $66.5 million in development aid.

- In Guatemala in 1982–1983, 1 million Indians were "internally displaced" in a counterinsurgency campaign by the government. Between 1978 and 1984, 75,000 Guatemalans were killed and another 200,000 fled across the Mexican border. By 1988, another 60,000 to 70,000 Indians were forcibly relocated by the government. Moreover, 10,000 homeless children now roam the capital city.[81]
- Between 1929 and 1979, the U.S.-backed Samosa family ruled Nicaragua with a dictatorial hand. Ousted by a popular revolution in 1979, Samosa's former supporters were armed and trained by the CIA in Central America and Miami. Although the revolutionary Sandinista government reduced illiteracy in Nicaragua from 50% to 12%, redistributed land, and achieved self-sufficiency in food production, its regime was forced to turn to the Soviet Union for aid when the Reagan administration cut off $30 million in funds approved under the Carter presidency. The United States has engaged in a covert war against Nicaragua, training counterrevolutionaries in more than a dozen Latin American nations, giving $3.1 million in military aid to the Honduran military, and arming 4,000 to 10,000 men in Nicaragua itself. The United

States also illegally mined harbors in Nicaragua and refused to accept judgment against this action by the World Court. The CIA also used the Salvadoran air force to fly sorties over Nicaragua.[82]

- Another case concerns the activities of General Roberto Viola. Invited to the White House in 1981 by newly elected President Reagan, the meeting marked the beginning of U.S. recruitment of right-wing regimes in its attempted overthrow of Nicaragua's Sandinista government. Aid to Viola's regime had been suspended during the Carter administration, when it was learned that the military junta engaged in human rights abuses against its own people. Viola was eventually sentenced to 17 years in prison for murder, kidnapping, and torture and for commanding death squads that killed 9,000 Nicaraguans. Nevertheless, the Reagan administration gave substantial covert military aid to the Nicaragua junta and entered into covert actions against the Sandinistas with Viola's regime.[83]

## Chile

Perhaps the most repressive noncommunist nation in the world was General Pinochet's Chile. By 1975, 2 years after Pinochet's CIA-assisted bloody coup, 1 in every 125 Chileans had been detained for more than a day. By 1988, 1 in every 55 Chileans had become a political exile. People were routinely held up to 20 days without government acknowledgment of their arrest. A wide range of torture methods was reported, including the use of electrodes on the genitals and knees, mock executions, sleep deprivation, constant loud music, sexual abuse, and submersion in water. Live rats were sometimes shoved into victims' mouths. One captive described his experience:

> I shouted and screamed from the intensity of the pain, and the method used: It was as if pincers were being applied to my testicles. . . . Scabs formed on my mouth. I couldn't speak. . . . My penis, testicles, and glands were torn open and all bloody. Later they told me they had run over my younger son, who is six, and that he was dead. . . . They told me they were going to torture my daughter also, that they would open her up and leave her menstruating for the rest of her life.[84]

Commonly, police and military troops searched entire poor neighborhoods in the early morning and pulled all adult males from the houses. The men were then transported to sports complexes, where their identifications were checked against computerized lists. This done, they were either released or taken into custody for several days.[85]

In short, this regime that the United States helped to install tortured hundreds of thousands of its own people. The economy was in a shambles, with unemployment in poor areas around 60% and those employed at the minimum wage unable to afford less than half their essential food costs. Social programs for the poor were either drastically cut or completely eliminated. And the work of artists, poets, novelists, and writers was suppressed.

In the meantime, the Pinochets lived in a 15,000-square-foot house, built at a cost of between $10 and $13 million, with 80 guards and an infrared security system. In late 1988, Pinochet lost a plebiscite (vote of public confidence) on his regime,[86] and a new president was elected. Pinochet fled in 1999 to England, which has refused to extradite him for trial. He returned to Chile in 2002 and was indicted for tax evasion in 2005 and for murder and kidnapping in 2006. He died of heart failure in late 2006.

## Assessing U.S. Support

Amnesty International has declared that more than one-third of the world's governments use some form of torture. The choice faced by the United States is one between supporting a butchering regime that faces opposition from a revolutionary movement or supporting a resistance willing to accept aid from wherever it can get it. The result is often a completely unstable situation.[87]

The assessment of U.S. support for regimes that violate human rights may be made by viewing (1) the conditions of people who live under them and (2) the effect of such support on U.S. foreign policy. It must be stressed that the inhabitants of the third world often live under conditions that violate elementary human rights. Thus, throughout Asia, Africa, and Latin America:

- An estimated 1.5 billion people are without effective medical care. There is an average of 4,000 people per doctor; in some areas, the ratio goes above 50,000 per doctor.
- Half the school-age children are not yet in schools.
- Twenty thousand persons per day die from starvation, 12,000 of them in Africa alone. Another 1.5 billion suffer from malnutrition.
- Unemployment is now 30% in most countries.
- Per capita income ranges from less than $250 per year (e.g., Ethiopia, India, Kenya, and Pakistan) to less than $1,600 per year (e.g., Turkey, Mexico, and Chile).
- More than 700 million adults are unable to read and write.[88]

To the extent that U.S. support for such regimes is based on arms rather than development, U.S. policy becomes a factor in exacerbating these wretched conditions. By 1993, yearly U.S. weapons sales to foreign nations had reached $33 billion. In 1983, the United States was the primary supplier to at least 20 of the world's nations engaged in war at the time.[89] Moreover, in 1982–1983, the United States signed another $24 billion in arms export agreements.[90] By 1984, the United States was the supplier of half the arms bought by third world nations.

Although it is true that not all third world peoples live under repressive dictatorships, the majority of third world governments are repressive. Such sales of weapons help to maintain repressive regimes and fuel wars in the third world. They do not foster peaceful economic development.

In the India–Pakistan War of 1965, for example, "the Sherman tanks of the Indian Army battled the Patton tanks of the Pakistani Army."[91] These weapons were sold to the two nations with the promise that they would be used defensively to resist communist aggression, yet they helped to support a war between the two noncommunist nations. Such incidents have also taken place between Israel and its Arab neighbors. Certainly, U.S. arms sales to nations in conflict are not the sole cause of such wars. But the presence of arms may contribute to the heightening of tensions. In any case, it is unfortunate that a world that spends billions of dollars a year on arms cannot (or will not) spend funds for projects so desperately needed in the third world.

U.S. support for dictatorships in underdeveloped countries helps to create a favorable business climate for multinational firms. However, the economic activity of multinationals is often a hindrance to the development of these countries. Consider, for example, the effects of repatriation (return of profits made overseas to the corporation's home base): "From 1950 to 1970 . . . U.S. firms added $1.7 billion to their holdings in four . . . countries—Chile, Peru, Bolivia, and Venezuela—primarily to increase production of such export commodities as copper, tin, and oil. But in the same period, these multi-nationals repatriated $44.2 billion to the United States, leaving a net loss to those countries of $9.5 billion."[92]

This net loss often translates into massive indebtedness, with such debts usually owed to multinational banks, governments, and other lending institutions made up largely of members from advanced industrial countries. The results have been very favorable for multinational banks but devastating to third world nations. From 1965 to 1972, overseas assets of U.S. banks grew from $9 billion to $90 billion. By 1976, U.S. banks held $181 billion in overseas assets, a 100% increase over 4 years.[93]

A great share of such assets was actually loans to third world governments. By the late 1970s, this indebtedness reached about $200 billion, a 300% increase.[94] By 2002, third world governments owed $2.4 trillion, an increase of nearly 1,200% over just 10 years.[95] This means that certain MNCs have an immense stake in preserving certain third world governments so that they may collect on their loans. Such stakes have sometimes required multinationals to favor foreign policy measures that are bitterly opposed by the U.S. public. The Panama Canal treaties are a case in point. Thirty-nine percent of the national budget of Panama is spent just to pay the interest on that country's national debt of $1.8 billion, 77% of which is owed to multinational banks. Ronald Steel claims that it was for this and other reasons favorable to business interests that MNCs lobbied hard for the passage of the canal treaties, which assured Panama of an income from the canal, plus various foreign aid payments, which in turn assured Panama's creditors that repayment would continue.[96] The passage of the treaties also meant continued military assistance to the repressive regime of

General Omar Torrijos. This, despite polls showing a majority of Americans opposed the treaties!

Not only does support for repressive regimes inhibit economic development and foster unpopular foreign policy measures, such support often has a detrimental effect on U.S. foreign policy, as well. That is, repressive regimes and U.S. support of them are often very unpopular with third world peoples. As seen in Iran, such support has touched off revolutions in nations that are anti-American and often anticapitalist, as well. U.S. support for regimes that violate human rights sometimes has the effect of driving poor nations into the hands of the communists. This has been the case with Cuba and certain African nations and may yet be the case with Nicaragua, the Philippines, and dozens of others. Thus, the policy designed to prevent communist influence in developing nations often has precisely the opposite effect.

## Conclusion

In this chapter, we have examined those U.S. defense and foreign policy areas in which deviance abounds: questionable defense contracting practices, bribery, the sale of hazardous goods by multinational firms, and U.S. support for repressive third world regimes. A closer look at these types of deviance indicates that they are interrelated. That is, many of the corporations involved in defense contracting with the federal government have also been found guilty of bribery overseas (e.g., Lockheed and Northrop). And many of these same firms are enriched by U.S. arms sales to repressive regimes. Likewise, the needs of the U.S. economic system for cheap labor, raw materials, and investment outlets have contributed immensely to the worldwide deployment of U.S. military forces and U.S. support for dictatorships that are ostensibly anticommunist.

These policies prove profitable for major corporations in the short term but may be devastating to the nation and much of the world in the long term. Waste, inefficiency, and cost overruns within the Department of Defense threaten to create domestic inflation and a weakened U.S. military capability. And bribery, the sale of hazardous products, and support for repressive regimes often foster resentment toward the United States, further weakening its strength at home and abroad. Such practices also hinder the economic development of the world's poorest and most desperate citizens. In short, nothing less than the future well-being of the United States and much of the world is now at stake, in part because of such deviance.

### CRITICAL THINKING EXERCISE 5.1
**The Pentagon Follies**

Use the Infotrack II database, Internet libraries, or a database chosen by your instructor to locate examples of fraud, waste, and abuse in Pentagon weapons contracting since the publication of the current edition of this book. List the number and types of problems in a table. Do you think that such deviance has become more or less serious in recent years? Write a brief (one- to two-page) paper to explain your answer.

## ENDNOTES

1. See Simon, D. (2004). *Tony Soprano's America: The criminal side of the American dream* (pp. 68–69). Boulder, CO: Westview; Orth, M. (March 2002). Afghanistan's deadly habit. *Vanity Fair*, 150ff.

2. Lyman, M. D., & Potter, G. W. (2004). *Organized crime* (3rd ed., pp. 389–394). Upper Saddle River, NJ: Prentice-Hall; MSNBC, September 15, 2001; CNN, 2001.

3. *Is Bush family protecting Bin Laden Family??* http://www.automotiveforums.com/vbulletin/index.php (February 9, 2004); Phillips, P., & Project Censored. *Censored 2005: The Top 25 Censored Stories* (pp. 63–64). New York: Seven Stories Press, 2006.

4. http://usa.mediamonitors.net/content/view/fill/2692/.

5. Ibid.

6. http://musingsoniraq.blogspot.com/2010/03/new-examples-of-corruption-in-iraq.html (25 March, 2010).

7. *New York Times*, October 29, 2004.

8. http://oversight.house.gov/investigations.asp?Issue=Iraq+Reconstruction, February 7, 2007

9. Http://www.csmonitor.com/2005/1019/dailyUpdate.html, October 19, 2005; Baldor, L. C. (February 19, 2005). *Defense Vows Crackdown on Fraud in Iraq.* Associated Press; http://news.yahoo.com/s/ap/20070320/ap_on_go_ca_st_pe/us_iraq_fraud, March 20, 2007; Tirman, J. (2006). *100 ways America is screwing up the world* (p. 22). New York: Harper Perennial.

10. Sprengelmeyer, M. E. (January 10, 2004). Despite report, Cheney says war was justified. *Seattle Post Intelligencer*, A-1. The full report can be found at http://www.ceip.org. See also *Politics*, January 9, 2004. Heard on The Thom Hartmann Show (October 2010).

11. Hersh, S. M. (May 10, 2004). Torture at Abu Ghraib. *New Yorker*.

12. *Florida Times Union*, May 16, 2004, A-1.

13. http://abcnews.go.com/Politics/us-troops-charged-corruption-iraq-afghanistan/story?id=10952163(20June,2010). http://www.onpointradio.org/2010/09/corruption-afghanistan.

14. http://english.aljazeera.net/news/europe/2009/11/20091117104858836370.html

15. Strobel, W. P., & Taylor, M. (November 5, 2010). $69.3 million Afghan-contracting fine may be a record. *McClatchy Newspapers*.

16. The following is based on Scahill, J. The Secret US war in Pakistan. 2 Scahill, J. (January 20, 2010). Blackwater wants to surge its Armed Force in Afghanistan. *Antiwar.com*, http://original.antiwar.com/scahill/2010/01/19/blackwater-wants-to-surge; and http://www.cnn.com/2010/WORLD/asiapcf/12/02/afghanistan.wikileaks/index.html

17. Edwards, D., & Kane, M. (August 7, 2009). Ex-employees claim Blackwater pimped out young Iraqi Girls. *Raw Story*.

18. http://www.projectcensored.org/top-stories/articles/5-blackwater-xe-the-secret-us-war-in-pakistan/.

19. http://news.dawn.com/wps/wcm/connect/dawn-content-library/dawn/the-newspaper/national/12-corruption-in-pakistan-can-invite-another-coup-icg-report-820--bi-01.

20. http://www.washingtonpost.com/wp-dyn/content/article/2010/09/05/AR2010090502816.html.

21. See Moyers, B. (1988). *The secret government*. Berkeley: Seven Locks.

22. See Bacevich, A. J. (2010). *Washington rules: America's path to permanent war* (pp. 20–21). New York: Henry Holt & Co.

23. Former President Jimmy Carter recently expressed his view that Americans believe they have the right to militarily intervene anywhere in the world they choose and impose

American values on any culture because God has willed it. This ideology is an extension of the doctrine of Manifest Destiny. See Real Time with Bill Mayer. *HBO*, 31 October 2010.

24. Huffington, A. (2010). *Third world nation* (Chapters 1–3). New York: Crown.

25. Bacevich, A. J. (2009). *The limits of power*. New York: Henry Holt: 24ff, and Huffington, A. (2010). *Third world nation* (Chapter 2).

26. Lens, S. (May 1978).Thirty years of escalation. *Nation, 27*, 624.

27. Riddell, T. (1988). The political economy of military spending. In R. Cherry et al. (eds.). *The imperiled economy* (vol. 2, p. 229). New York: Union for Radical Political Economics.

28. Lens (p. 624).

29. Klare, M. T. (1972). *War without end: American planning for the next Vietnams* (p. 25). New York: Knopf.

30. Sivard, R. L. (April 8, 1977). Arms or alms. *National Catholic Reporter, 24*, 8.

31. Zepezauer & Naiman (p. 15).

32. Eisenhower, D. D. (1972). Farewell address. In C. W. Pursell Jr. (ed.). *The military-industrial complex* (p. 206–207). New York: Harper & Row.

33. Senator Proxmire, W. (1970). *Report from Wasteland: America's military-industrial complex* (p. 162). New York: Praeger.

34. Center for Defense Information. (February 1996). *The Defense Monitor, 3*.

35. Reprinted from Sanseri, A. (1977). The military-industrial complex in Iowa. In B. F. Cooling (ed.). *War, business, and American society: Historical perspectives on the military-industrial complex* (pp. 158–159). Port Washington, NY: Kennikat Press; and *World almanac and book of facts, 1994* (p. 705). Mahwah, NJ: Funk & Wagnalls, 1993.

36. Fallows, J. (1981). *National defense* (p. 65). New York: Random House.

37. *World almanac and book of facts, 1994* (p. 704).

38. Data in this section come from Riddell (p. 229).

39. Stubbing, R., & Mendel, R. (June 1989). How to save $50 billion a year. *Atlantic Monthly*, 55.

40. Zepezauer & Naiman (p. 15).

41. Stubbing & Mendel (p. 55).

42. Weiner, T. (1990). *Blank check: The Pentagon's black budget* (p. 187–188). New York: Simon & Schuster.

43. Zepezauer, M., & Naiman, A. (1996). Military waste & fraud: $172 billion/year excerpted from the book *Take the rich off welfare*. New York: Odonian Press. Online http://www.thirdworldtraveler.com/CorporateWelfare/Military_Fraud.html (February 11, 2005).

44. Mokhiber, R., & Weissman, R. (December 2004). The ten worst corporations of 2004. *Multinational Monitor, 25*; and Kay, J. (December 17, 2003). Bush administration embroiled in boeing scandal. http://www.wsws.org.

45. Mokhiber, R., & Weissman, R. (October 5, 2004). The ten worst corporations of 2004, and Watch, H. Where profiteering isn't a dirty word. *Guerilla News Network.Org*.

46. O'Conner, J. (1973). *The fiscal crisis of the state* (pp. 350–351). New York: St. Martin's Press.

47. *South China Morning Post*, February 27, 2000.

48. *London Daily Telegraph*, February 27, 2000.

49. *Reuters*, January 2000.

50. Tobacco giant 'condoned smuggling into Mainland'. *South China Morning Post*, February 2, 2000.

51. *South Korean Times*, December 31, 1999.

52. See Simon, D. R., with Henderson J. (1997). *Private troubles and public issues: Social problems in the postmodern era* (pp. 304–307). Ft. Worth, TX: Harcourt Brace.

53. See Thurow, L. (1996). *The future of capitalism*. New York: Penguin, for an elaboration of these and other global economic themes.

54. Verhoogen, E. (April 1996). The U.S.-Haiti connection: Rich companies, poor workers. *Multinational Monitor*, 5.

55. Dowie, M. (November 9, 1979). The corporate crime of the century. *Mother Jones 10*, 24–25. © *Mother Jones Magazine*. Used with permission.

56. Tirman, J. (2006). *100 ways America is screwing up the world* (pp. 14–16). New York: Harper Perennial.

57. Satchell, M. (June 10, 1991). A vicious circle of poison. *U.S. News & World Report*, 32.

58. Ehrenreich, B., et al. (November 9, 1979). The charge: Genocide; U.S. government. *Mother Jones, 10*, 28.

59. Castleman, B. (Winter 1978/1979). Industries export hazards. *Multinational Monitor, 1*, 14.

60. Weir, D., et al. (November 1979). Boomerang crime. *Mother Jones, 10*, 43.

61. The global poison trade. *Newsweek*, November 7, 1988, 66–68.

62. Schurman, F. (October 1988). Opinion. *National College Newspaper*, 9; and *Multinational Monitor*, June 1988, 4.

63. Brooks, J. (July 1988). Waste dumpers turning to West Africa. *New York Times, 17*, 1.

64. Phillips, P., & Project Censored. (1997). *The 25 most censored news stories of 1996* (pp. 31–32). New York: Seven Locks.

65. Conklin, M. (February 1997). Terror stalks a Columbian town. *Progressive*, 23.

66. See Lee, M. (April 28, 1997). The cop, the gangster and the beauty queen. *In These Times*, 18–20.

67. For several interesting assessments, consult the following articles: Falk, R. (February 10, 1979). Iran's home-grown revolution. *Nation*, 135–137; Cockburn, A., & Ridgeway, J. (February 19, 1979). The worst domino. *Village Voice, 1*, 11–12; Laqueur, W. (September 23, 1978). Trouble for the Shah. *New Republic*, 18–21; Kondracke, M. (November 18, 1978). Who lost Iran? *New Republic*, 9–12; and Halliday, F. (December 26–28, 1978). Shah's dreams of economic growth and income nightmares. *In These Times*, 9.

68. Klare (pp. 20, 33, 36, 41, 45).

69. Kondracke (p. 12).

70. Baraheni, R. (October 28, 1976). Terror in Iran. *New York Review of Books*, 21.

71. Amnesty International. (1975). *Report on torture* (pp. 227–229). New York: Farrar, Straus, and Giroux.

72. Anderson, I. (December 5, 1979). Kissinger cleared Iran's oil gouge. *Washington Post*, 13–17.

73. Anderson, J. (December 26, 1979). Rockefeller–Shah–Kissinger connection. *Washington Post*, D-12; and *60 Minutes*, May 4, 1980.

74. Octoberfuss. *New Republic*, May 13, 1991, 7–8.

75. Anderson, J. (December 10, 1979). Kissinger cast in a questionable light. *Washington Post*, C-27.

76. White, R. A. (1984). *The morass* (pp. 29–30). New York: Harper & Row.

77. Caldicott, H. (1984). *Missile envy* (p. 160). New York: Morrow; and Kwitney, J. (1984). *Endless enemies* (pp. 10–11). New York: Cogdon/Weed.

78. *San Francisco Chronicle*, January 4, 1994.

79. See Hagan, F., & Simon, D. (). Elite deviance in the Bush era. *The Justice Professional*, 1997.

80. Caldicott (p. 98); and White, R. A. (1984). *The morass* (p. 97). New York: Harper & Row.

81. Lernoux, P. (November 28, 29, 30, 1988). Guatemala's new military order. *Nation*, 556–558; and Neir, A. (March 17, 1988). Repression in Central America since the Arias Plan. *New York Review of Books*, 22ff.

82. Caldicott (p. 100).

83. Weiner (pp. 203–204).

84. Timerman, J., & Cox, R. (November 2, 1987). Reflections: Under the dictatorship. *New Yorker*, 74.

85. Neier, A., & Brown, C. (June 25, 1987). Pinochet's way. *New York Review of Books*, 17–20; and Padilla, A, & Gomez-Diaz, L. (November 1986). A state of fear. *Psychology Today*, 60.

86. Timerman & Cox (p. 130ff); Neier & Brown (p. 20).

87. See Barber, J. D. (December 1985). Rationalizing torture: The dance of intellectual apologists. *Washington Monthly, 17*, 17.

88. Sivard (p. 9); Scheer, R. (1974). *America after Nixon*. New York: McGraw Hill.

89. Evans. (April 7, 1997). A year in corporate crime. *The Nation, 16*.

90. Sherrill (p. 128); and *Defense Monitor,* June 6, 1984, 6–7.

91. Freeman, H. (February 1977). On consuming the surplus. *Progressive, 41*, 20–21.

92. *Daily World in U.N. Action Pact for World Development* (New York: United National Information Division, n.d.), 1.

93. Lens, S. (May 1978). The sinking dollar and the gathering storm. *Progressive, 5*, 23.

94. Ibid.

95. Tossaint, E. (2005). Your money or your life (Updated Ed.). Books. Google.com?.

96. Steel, R. (March 23, 1978). Beneath the Panama canal. *New York Review of Books,* 12.

# CHAPTER

# 6

# Political Corruption: Continuity and Change

In the summer of 1787, the Philadelphia convention that produced America's Constitution met behind locked doors. From colonial times to the 1820s, voting rights were restricted to White, adult males who met a property qualification. Frequently, established seacoast areas had maintained their political power in the state legislatures at the expense of the growing western frontier. Some historians believe that secrecy at the convention existed so that the founding fathers could speak their minds openly, make compromises freely, prohibit partisan press coverage, and avoid all chances of a public clamor over difficult issues that might break up the convention.

Yet an examination of the attitudes of convention attendees reveals some disturbing realities:

- The vast majority of common people were viewed as "parochial spend-thrifts who never paid their debts and who advocated inflated paper money."[1] Small farmers of the day were plagued by heavy and chronic indebtedness and serious tax burdens. Many people were jailed for nonpayment of debts and/or taxes. In the winter of 1787, a rebellion against repressive debts and taxes was led by Daniel Shays and left 11 dead and many more wounded. This weighed heavily on the minds of the wealthy elites who met at the Constitutional Convention and feared dangerous factions of the masses of people. Some of the remedies for these situations included "the full faith and credit clause," which allowed creditors from one state to pursue debtors fleeing to other states. Second, the Constitution created a standing military to put down future Shays-like rebellions and protect other interests as well.
- The members of the Philadelphia convention who drafted the Constitution were, with a few exceptions, immediately, directly, and personally interested in, and derived economic advantages from, the establishment of the new federal system.
- The leaders who supported the Constitution in the state ratifying conventions represented the same economic groups as the members of

the Philadelphia convention, and in several instances they were also directly and personally interested in the outcome of their efforts.[2]

As Charles A. Beard[3] has noted:

- Thirty-seven of the 55 delegates were holders of Revolutionary War Bonds, and the taxing powers under the Constitution obligated the new government to pay off all debt incurred from the Revolutionary War. On the contrary, Treasury Department records of the 1790s listed the names of several prominent Federalist leaders and also those of many other delegates to the Constitutional Convention. Several of these leaders held varying amounts of old Continental notes. These had rapidly depreciated from the outset because the Continental Congress had not secured them with gold or silver. During the 1780s, there existed a large national debt, and few if any steps were taken to pay it off or to redeem the Continental notes. They consequently decreased in value to only about 20 cents on the dollar. This produced a rash of speculation, wherein many people bought up the paper money for a fraction of its original worth, hoping that the federal government might someday pay off the bills at a higher rate. The notes were eventually honored at 100%, and the financing of this debt consumed almost 80% of the federal treasury's receipts in the 1790s.
- Eleven of the 55 delegates were engaged in either shipping or trade and benefited from the Interstate Commerce Clause, which eliminated state control over commerce, creating a free trade area among the states.
- Twenty-four of the attendees of the Convention were bankers and investors and benefited from congressional powers to coin money and regulate its value, establish post offices and postal roads, grant copyright and patent powers, and punish pirates and felons on the high seas and those guilty of counterfeiting.
- Fourteen of the 55 delegates had speculated in land west of the Appalachian Mountains. Some of these lands contained hostile Native American tribes and a few British forts. The Constitution also gave the federal government the power to raise a military, declare war, and levy taxes. This allowed the new federal government to put down mass riots such as Shays' Rebellion and to rouse Indian and British troops from the newly emerging frontier west of the Appalachian Mountains. The land speculators that held claims in these new lands were anxious to make a return on their investment. The new federal troops were utilized to rid these lands of Native Americans and a few remaining British troops.[4]
- Fifteen of the 55 delegates were slave owners, who greatly feared slave revolts and benefited from the establishment of a federal army and navy. The import of slaves was not to be outlawed until 1808, and the Constitution (until passage of the Thirteenth Amendment) required the forced return of slaves who escaped to free states.[5] The slave trade was

never abolished by the Constitution, and for census purposes, slaves were counted as three-fifths of a human being. This gave slave-owning states increased representation in the House of Representatives.

The Constitution was essentially a document based upon the concept that the fundamental private rights of property are outside governmental jurisdiction and beyond the influence of popular majorities.[6] The entire process, from the calling of the Philadelphia convention to the ratifying of the Constitution, was unrepresentative and undemocratic; there was no popular vote on calling the convention; the masses of small property holders were not represented at Philadelphia; and only a small minority in each state voted for delegates to the ratifying conventions.[7]

1. A small band of highly organized men with particular economic and political interests shaped and directed the drive toward holding a Constitutional Convention.
2. When the convention was held at Philadelphia in 1787, it was under strict instructions from the Continental Congress only to prepare a list of amendments to the Articles of Confederation; the convention was not authorized to draw up a whole new Constitution, but only to advise the Continental Congress about what it should do to meet the needs of the Union. Therefore, the delegates had exceeded their instructions and were acting illegally.
3. The delegates at Philadelphia wrote a document that was in their direct economic and political interests; the new government would be in their hands, and its fiscal policy helped directly to enrich the personal fortunes of the original Philadelphia delegates.
4. The delegates at Philadelphia met in secrecy and not in an open forum that was subject to public scrutiny. Moreover, they never wanted publication of their debates or even the minutes of the convention. All the records were given to George Washington to take home with him at the end of the meeting in the belief that the great patriot of the Revolution would never be challenged for them. Conspiracy historians point out that by getting Washington into their camp, the pro-Constitution forces went a long way in fending off critical opposition.
5. The kind of government established was in fact not a democracy, although a fledgling democracy had been developing under the Articles of Confederation. The founding fathers wished to curb and restrain majority will and found the notion of popular sovereignty acceptable only when so indirect as to make a mockery of the concept.
6. The ratification procedure was patently illegal. According to the Articles of Confederation, which was the fundamental law of the land at the time of the Constitutional Convention, any change in the powers of the central government had to have the unanimous approval of all 13 states as represented in the Continental Congress. The founding

fathers changed this because they knew they could not get ratification under this procedure, so they said that the new Constitution would take effect for all the states when nine of them had registered their approval. The Continental Congress was completely sidestepped, it being asked to send the proposed Constitution along to the states immediately and without any debate or discussion.

7. The ratification procedure was also clearly undemocratic. The most democratic procedure would have been to have each state hold a popular referendum on the Constitution, with the people merely asked to indicate acceptance or rejection. Instead, the people were not directly consulted in any of the states. State constitutional conventions were held that decided the question of whether to approve the Constitution or not. In most instances, the people were asked to elect the delegates to these conventions, but this was not universal. Under these schemes, it has been estimated that only about 15% to 25% of the people even voted in the elections held to send delegates to the state conventions.

8. Finally, with regard to ratification, it has been pointed out by several historians that in key states like New York and Virginia those opposing the Constitution were in a clear majority at the beginning of the state conventions, but in the end were outvoted. What happened? Some say bribery and other illegal or at least immoral tactics were used to push the Constitution through.[8]

On the very eve of the Philadelphia convention in 1787, a short-lived revolt occurred in Massachusetts, where western farmers were up in arms about the high level of taxes that they were required to pay. This was quelled when an army was raised against them by the Bay State and the old tax policy was reinstituted. But, even so, the merchants of Boston and state and national political leaders had been given quite a scare. They knew that if the farmers had been more determined, they might well have been able to seize the state capitol. The weak national government had no army or authority to put down a rebellion successfully. Thus when the founding fathers gathered in Philadelphia, they were mostly concerned about the state of the union and the general economic conditions of the day.[9]

Political corruption has been an integral part of U.S. politics from its beginnings.[10] Political corruption is defined as "any illegal or unethical use of governmental authority for personal or political gain."[11] Corruption occurs, then, to accomplish one of two broad goals, material gain or power. Material gain can involve personal enrichment or illicit contributions to election campaigns. Abuses of power involve illegal acts of electioneering, violations of civil and human rights, and, more recently, sexual harassment by the powerful (usually men) of the less powerful (usually women).

This chapter is divided into two sections, one discussing each goal. In each case, the discussion will illustrate political corruption at one or more of the various levels of government: community, state, and national. We should note at the outset, however, that the examples used are just a small sample of the political crimes, known and unknown, that have occurred throughout U.S. history.[12]

## Money and Politics

Money and politics have always been closely intertwined. As political campaigns are costly, candidates must either be relatively affluent or accept money from the wealthy or special interests. We have discussed some aspects of the money–politics relationship already, but our concern in this section is with another facet: graft.

Political graft is the illegal act of taking advantage of one's political position to gain money or property. Graft can take several forms. First is the outright bribe, through which an individual, group, or corporation offers money to a public official for a favor. Or the government official may demand money in return for a favor, which is political extortion. Second is a subtle form of bribery: the public figure accepts exorbitant lecture fees from organizations or accepts retainers at his or her law office.

A third type occurs when a public figure is offered the opportunity to buy securities at a low price; then, when the price goes up, the briber purchases the securities back, at a great profit to the person bribed. Finally, a fourth variant is the kickback: contractors, engineering and architectural firms, and others pay back a percentage of a contract to the official responsible for granting the lucrative government contract.

The government, city, state, and national, is involved in a number of activities, including law enforcement, the granting of contracts, the use of public funds, the hiring and firing of employees, tax assessment, and land use. Quite certainly, all these activities are prone to corruption.

Under the current campaign finance laws, there is plenty of legal graft to fund all the trips and restaurant wining and dining that legislators desire, with enough left over to finance a winning presidential reelection campaign. Although federal campaign finance laws severely restrict the amount that can be given directly to a candidate, virtually nothing restricts individuals from going out and collecting massive amounts of other people's money for delivery to a single candidate. In the 2004 Bush reelection campaign, people who raised at least $100,000 were rewarded with the title "Pioneer." A special "Ranger" label was created for those super-fund-raisers who brought in more than $200,000. More than one-sixth of the 940 bundlers for Bush's campaigns were professional lobbyists, lawyers, and political operatives—people who possess the necessary connections to raise $100,000 or more from wealthy individuals and corporations.

These donations can be paid by legal campaign contributions as long as they are labeled "campaign expenses." Every day Congress members receive checks from interests eager to gain influence. In 2006, some Congress members crossed the line between such "legal bribery" and the illegal bribery by promising legislative favors for cash. Those who broke the law either sold this access to others or used it for themselves. Many of Bush's Pioneers and Rangers ended up violating the law. Nine of Bush's fund-raisers are under investigation, under indictment, or convicted of state or federal crimes.

> In the current election cycle (2010), "the Tea Party wouldn't exist without a gusher of cash from oil billionaire David H. Koch and the vast media empire of Rupert Murdoch. Many of the small donations to Tea Party candidates have been cultivated by either Fox News Channel, a property of Murdoch's News Corporation, or the Americans for Prosperity Foundation, chaired by Koch. The movement's major organizations are all run, not by first-time, mad-as-hell activists, but by former GOP officials or operatives.
>
> Taken together, Americans for Prosperity, Freedom Works (another far-right political group seeded by the Koch brothers) and (Rupert) Murdoch's News Corp, owner of Fox News and the *Wall Street Journal*, form the corporate headquarters of a conglomerate one might call Tea Party, Inc. This is the syndicate that funds the organizing, crafts the messages, and channels the rage of conservative Americans at their falling fortunes into an oppositional force to President Obama and to any government solution to the current economic calamity. Groups such as Tea Party Express, Tea Party Nation, and the FreedomWorks-affiliated Tea Party Patriots; the bevy of political consultants for hire; and various allied elected officials can be understood as Tea Party, Inc.'s loosely affiliated subsidiaries"[16]

## Purchasing Goods and Services

The federal government spends billions of dollars on an array of goods and services from U.S. businesses, including military hardware, space systems, research projects, musical instruments, desks, clothing, and brooms. Suppliers and repair contractors have been guilty of graft by billing the government for undelivered materials and work never performed. Also, store managers have accepted money and other gifts from firms that sell to the government; in return, the companies were allowed to charge in excess for their merchandise. What is more, Government Services Administration (GSA) officials have deliberately purchased inferior goods at premium prices for their personal gain, with both the companies and the GSA officials sharing in the bounty.

Bidding for contracts is a process that is very susceptible to bribery, especially when the bidding is not competitive. Approximately 90% of all contracts for new weapons systems are exempt from competitive bidding so that the Department of Defense may select the superior system rather than just the most economical one. Unfortunately, this process is especially open to graft.

A common exception to competitive bidding is the purchase of professional services by engineers, architects, auditors, and others. Although the rationale for this exception is logical, that is, the need for a specialist may mean that there is no competition, the negotiation process is vulnerable to graft. The most celebrated case involving this type of corruption caused Spiro Agnew to resign as vice president of the United States. Let us briefly look at this interesting and common type of graft.

During the 1960s, suburban Baltimore County was growing rapidly. This growth required the creation of new streets, sewers, and bridges, as well as numerous rezoning decisions. Great sums of money were made by those fortunate to receive favorable zoning or contracts from the county. A government investigation revealed that those favorably treated (including contractors, architectural firms, and engineering firms) often kicked back 5% to those responsible for the decision. This practice of kickbacks was not new. In fact, it was a time-honored Maryland custom.

Included among those regularly receiving kickbacks was Spiro Agnew. The payoffs began in 1962 when Agnew became a Baltimore County executive and continued when he became governor in 1967; even as late as 1971, when Agnew was vice president, he received a payment in the basement of the White House. Agnew received these payments for all the design jobs in the county, and later, as governor, he received a percentage of the highway contracts and other engineering work. While serving as vice president, the payments continued, amounting to $80,000 during those few years.

During the dark days of the Watergate investigation, the inquiry into Agnew's possible criminal activities became public. The evidence against him was irrefutable, and he was forced to plea-bargain to reduce the penalty. Agnew resigned, pleaded no contest to one charge of income tax evasion, and was given a sentence of 3 years of unsupervised probation and a fine of $10,000.

## Public Funds

The use of public money is a ready source of corruption by those in political power. In fact, the first corruption scandal in American history involved a sort of "insider trading" arrangement whereby public funds were used to enrich those close to the office of the U.S. Treasury secretary. Forty of the 55 delegates to the Constitutional Convention of 1787 held debt certificates issued by the federal and state governments during and after the Revolutionary War (1776–1783) with Great Britain. These certificates were worth $5,000 or more when issued, but their value had steadily declined as the new nation became embroiled in financial chaos under the Articles of Confederation.

The delegates had some important decisions to make about land, especially about where to locate the new national capitol after the Constitution's adoption. Benjamin Franklin, who had loaned the national government $3,000 at 6% interest, noted that such loan certificates had fallen drastically in value and hoped and believed that their value would "mend when our new Constitution was adopted."[17]

The nation's first Treasury secretary, Alexander Hamilton, had to decide what to do about the $80 million owed by national and state governments. He decided that the government would honor what had become worthless paper. Word of this policy was leaked to Hamilton's friends and in-laws, all of whom began buying up certificates at a record pace. The policy was officially announced on January 14, 1790, at which time the certificates were almost totally owned by speculators. Hamilton agreed to pay in full people owning the certificates at the time of redemption, not necessarily the original owners.

Hamilton's assistant, William Duer, ignored all charges of conflict of interest and engaged in numerous shady schemes. Besides benefiting from insider information about the debt certificates (he bought as many as he could with borrowed money), Duer demanded kickbacks on government contracts. An outraged public finally forced Hamilton to request Duer's resignation. But Hamilton's relatives and associates were guilty of some of the same conflicts of interest, and their punishment was merely to have their fortunes greatly increased.

## Public Property

Another potential area for corruption is the misuse of public property. Government officials have discretionary powers over public lands. They decide, for example, which ranchers will have grazing rights, which lumber companies will have rights to timberlands, and what policies will control the extraction of minerals and petroleum from lands owned by the government. Fortunes can be made or lost, depending on favorable access to these lands. Of course, such a situation is susceptible to bribery and extortion.

Early in U.S. history, there were several instances of the improper use of political influence in the disposition of public lands. One example involved a large area of virgin land west of South Carolina known as the Yazoo Territory (much of which is now Alabama and Mississippi), which was claimed by the federal government, Georgia, and numerous Indian tribes. In 1794, the Georgia legislature sold its land (30 million acres) to four companies for 1.5 cents per acre. "The haste of the legislature in concluding such an unprofitable sale was apparently the result of the attentions paid them by the companies which had peddled shares at very low prices to nearly all the legislators."[18]

This congressional largesse to help business for mutual gain was typical after the Civil War. "Congressmen gave huge grants, subsidies, and loans to railroad promoters, and bought their stocks at preferred prices or accepted gifts outright. . . . In 1876 they repealed all restrictions on the sale of public federal land in the South, ordering it sold to private interests as soon as possible—and got huge shares of it as the silent partners of the timber speculators who bought it."[19]

The most infamous case involving the fraudulent use of public lands was the Teapot Dome scandal. During the administration of Warren Harding (which, along with that of Ulysses S. Grant, is considered among the most corrupt in U.S. history), a scandal broke concerning the leasing of oil lands. In 1921, Secretary of the Interior Albert Fall persuaded President Harding and the navy secretary to transfer naval oil reserves from the navy to his jurisdiction in the Department of the Interior. When this was accomplished, Fall then transferred the oil reserves at Teapot Dome, Wyoming, and Elk Hills, California, to two private oil producers, Henry Sinclair and E. L. Doheny, for their use. The leases were signed secretly and without competitive bidding. In return, Fall collected $100,000 from Doheny for Elk Hills and $300,000 from Sinclair for Teapot Dome. When the scandal broke, the government canceled the leases. Fall was sent to prison for a year (the first cabinet officer in U.S. history to be put in prison), but no penalties were given to the two guilty oil companies or their officers.

The taxation function of government is one that has enormous potential for graft. Tax assessors have great latitude because many of their decisions are subjective. They are obvious targets for bribes to reduce assessments. In the 1920s, Chicago had a particularly corrupt tax system. Individual members of the board of review could raise, lower, or eliminate assessments made by the tax assessors. Workers in Chicago's political machine "were rewarded by ridiculously low assessments, a precinct captain's house being assessed at one-fifteenth the value of a similar house next door."[20] The situation in Cook County (where Chicago is located) was remarkably similar some 50 years later. In 1972, the county assessor was investigated by the state for assessing certain properties on a system subject to manipulation and preference. Upon learning of the pending investigation, the assessor, P. H. Cullerton, reassessed nine high-rise properties in Chicago, adding $34 million to the city's tax base.[21]

Officials at the federal level are also susceptible to bribes involving taxation. Internal Revenue Service (IRS) personnel investigating income tax evasion can be bribed to look the other way. So, too, can customs officials. An additional example of an abusive practice involving taxes is illustrated by the 1875 Whiskey Ring scandal, which broke during the Grant administration. More than 350 distillers and government officials were indicted for defrauding the government of tax revenues. This was accomplished when distillers falsified reports on the amount produced and bribed government inspectors to verify the fraudulent reports.[22]

## Regulation of Commercial Activities

Government officials are required by law to inspect foods (such as grain and meat) to ensure that they are not contaminated and to grade them according to quality. Again, we know of numerous instances when agents have received bribes to allow questionable items to pass inspection. Abuses also abound in government efforts to control certain business activities, such as gambling and the sale of alcohol. Because these activities are generally restricted by law, the granting of licenses is a lucrative plum for which people are willing to pay extra. They are also willing to pay for favorable legislation.

## Zoning and Land Use

The areas of zoning, planning, and building codes are highly subject to graft because the decisions can provide or eliminate great financial advantage. Decisions in these areas can establish which individuals or organizations will have a monopoly. Overnight, such decisions can make cheap land valuable or priceless land ordinary. And the decisions can force all construction to be done by certified employees, and so on. Again, we can see that the government's discretionary powers, while necessary, can be abused by government officials and businesspeople. The problem, of course, is that the decisions are not always made in the public interest.

The examples of graft in zoning decisions are plentiful, but we will present only two illustrative cases.[25] The first example occurred in a small borough in southern New Jersey called Lindenwold. From 1950 to 1970, it had undergone rapid population growth, tripling in size. In this setting, a group of speculators was able to make a 2,400% gross profit on a tract of 69 acres because of favorable zoning decisions greased by bribes. They purchased the land at public sale for $40,000. At that time, the land was relatively cheap because of strict zoning and a clause that demanded that the land be developed within a specified time or revert to the city.[26]

## The Legislative Process

What effect does receiving campaign contributions and other favors have on a legislator? Will his or her actions be biased? Clearly, it is difficult to affirm that a legislator acted because of money, as Amick has argued.

> When people are exercising legislative roles, they have to be given wide latitude. The law can and does forbid them to sell their votes, but it cannot force them to cast those votes in an objective way, or an intelligent way, or a well-informed way. And there is no test that can be designed that will automatically disclose whether a given vote is corrupt; the necessary freedom given to legislators to make honest decisions also makes it easier for them to get away with making dishonest ones.[27]

The relationship between giving money to and receiving favorable decisions from legislators is not always a subtle one, however. A few examples make this point, beginning with the Credit Mobilier scandal.[28] In the late 1860s, some of the major stockholders of the Union Pacific Railroad concocted a scheme whereby they would get their company, the railroad, to contract with their construction company, Credit Mobilier. This cozy arrangement allowed the conspirators to charge Union Pacific exorbitant costs. In effect, then, the money that Union Pacific raised through the sale of stocks went to the construction company, which made enormous profits. Concerned over a possible congressional investigation, one member of the conspiracy, who was also a U.S. representative from Massachusetts, Oakes Ames, gave away or sold Credit Mobilier stocks at very low cost to selected members of Congress. In 1872, the bribes were exposed, which led to the expulsion of Ames and another congressman, James Brooks. Also implicated were the outgoing vice president of the United States and a future president, James A. Garfield.

The largest congressional scandal in recent years was the FBI sting operation known as ABSCAM. This operation set up a fictional Arab sheik, Kambir Abdul Rahman, who offered financial inducements to legislators for their favors. Meetings between the sheik and legislators were secretly video-taped. Seven legislators (six representatives and one senator) were indicted and convicted of accepting cash or stock as bribes for their favorable influence. Most noteworthy, only one legislator, Senator Larry Presler of South Dakota, was offered the rich inducement but refused the bribe.[32]

The Housing and Urban Development (HUD) scandal is somewhat typical of the influence-peddling scandals that have taken place in recent years.

- During the Clinton administration, former San Antonio mayor Henry Cisneros resigned as head of HUD after he was accused of lying by the FBI. It seems he made improper payments to his longtime mistress, who taped their conversations and sold them to a supermarket tabloid.
- During G. W. Bush's presidency HUD secretary Alfonso Jackson revoked a contract from a man who said he didn't like President Bush, proving how political the awarding of HUD contracts has always been.
- In New York, the attorney general indicted 30 HUD tenants because they stole money from HUD by lying about their incomes.
- In Chicago, a former HUD Section 8 manager was indicted for investing funds in nonexistent "ghost residents."[33]

For reasons considered in Chapter 8, padding one's own pocket remains the most widespread form of elite deviance. One of the long-cherished functions of members of Congress is to secure government facilities and contracts for their districts. The study of which districts are the recipients of government largesse is a reliable guide to who is in power in Washington.

- $3.1 billion to convert a ferry boat into a crab restaurant in Baltimore.
- $3 million for Steamtrain, USA in Scranton, PA, to recreate an old rail yard.
- In a 2009 Spending Bill, 200,000 for tattoo removal, $40 million in funds for three presidential libraries, $150,000 to study the Hatfield-McCoy Feud, and $19 million to exam emissions from cow farts.[35]

Although the Fourteenth Amendment to the Constitution gave African Americans the right to vote following the Civil War, the white majority in southern states used a variety of tactics to keep blacks from voting. Most effective was the strategy of intimidation. African Americans who tried to assert their right to vote were often subject to beatings, destruction of property, or even lynching. A more subtle approach, however, was quite effective in eliminating the black vote in the southern states. Through legal means, laws were passed to achieve illegal discrimination. One tactic was the white primary, which excluded blacks from participating in the party primary. The Constitution prohibited the states from denying the vote on the basis of race. A political party, however, since it was a private association, could discriminate. The Democratic Party throughout most of the South chose the option of limiting the primary to whites. African Americans could legally vote in the general election, but only for candidates already selected by whites. And since the Democratic Party in the South was supreme, the candidate selected in the primary would be the victor in the general election. This practice was nullified by the Supreme Court in 1944.

Other legal obstacles for African Americans in the South were the literacy test and the poll tax, which were eventually ruled illegal by the Supreme Court, but only after many decades of denying Blacks the right to vote. Both obstacles were designed as two southern suffrage requirements to admit Whites to the electorate and exclude Blacks, without mentioning race. The literacy test and its related requirements were blatantly racist.[34] The object of the test was to allow all adult White males to vote while excluding all Blacks. The problem with this test was that many Whites would be excluded because they were also illiterate. In response, legislators in various southern states contributed alternatives to the literacy requirements that would allow the illiterate Whites to vote. One loophole was the "grandfather clause," which, using Louisiana law as the example, exempted persons from the literacy test who were registered voters in any state on January 1, 1867, or prior thereto, the sons and grandsons of such persons, and male persons of foreign birth naturalized before January 1, 1898."[35] Another alternative designed to allow illiterate Whites to vote was the understanding clause, which allowed a person who could not read any section of the Constitution to qualify as an elector if he could understand and give a reasonable interpretation of what was read to him. This procedure gave registrars great latitude to decide who could vote. Thus, they had the ability to discriminate, which they did uniformly. A similar law in some states authorized registration of illiterates if they were of good character and could "understand the duties and obligations of citizenship under a republican form of government."

Unfortunately, efforts by Whites to limit the power of African Americans are not just a historical anomaly. A number of racist strategies are still employed. Howard Ball, head of the political science department at Mississippi State University, has noted a number of "voting wrongs" still used by the White power structure in Mississippi to keep Whites in power, even though Blacks hold a numerical majority.

1. Holding at-large elections in multimember legislative districts gives Whites the advantage even when outnumbered because more than twice as many Whites as Blacks are registered voters.
2. Counties have been gerrymandered to dilute African American voting strength. As a result, Blacks, who represent 35% of Mississippi's population, hold only 7% of the county supervisor positions.
3. Once African Americans have been successful in winning elections, elective offices have been changed to appointive ones.
4. White subdivisions have been annexed to produce municipalities, thus diluting the Black vote.
5. Polling places have been switched literally the night before an election.[36]

## Election Fraud

Certainly, more than one election has been won through illegal activities. Violence and intimidation have been used by the supporters of certain candidates to control the vote. Various forms of harassment were used especially prior to 1850, when voting was done orally. This practice allowed bystanders to know how votes were cast and thus intimidate or punish persons who voted contrary to their wishes. In the 20th century, violence was aimed at southern African Americans to keep them from registering, thus ensuring White supremacy.

Most election frauds involving illegal voting, false registration, and bribery have occurred in areas of one-party dominance, especially in cities controlled by a political machine. This has kept the machine in power at the local level and has delivered votes in state and federal elections to one party, thus increasing the scope of the machine's power.

> In the heyday of machine politics, the use of repeaters and impersonators—to "vote early and often"—was widespread, from the North Side in Kansas City to the South Side in Chicago, from the Strip in Pittsburgh to South of the Slot in San Francisco. No less important, and generally used in conjunction with these, was the practice of wholesale manipulation of registration lists. The names of aliens (sometimes as the result of illegal naturalization), minors, and nonresidents were added to the registration list, along with fictitious names and the names of reliable nonvoters. In combination, such illegal techniques could yield large numbers of fraudulent votes. In the 1869 election in New York, for example, between 25,000 and 30,000 votes were attributed to repeating, false registration, and illegal naturalization.[37]

These tactics have been used throughout history to influence elections in the United States. For example, Harry Truman would not have been elected senator from Missouri without the help of 50,000 fraudulent votes from the Pendergast machine in Kansas City.[38] So, too, have more recent Democratic victories been predicated on the massive help from Mayor Richard Daley's delivery of the votes in Cook County, Illinois.

Votes have also been purchased and continue to be today, especially in poor areas, through bribes of money and liquor. The *Los Angeles Times* alleged, for example, that $5,000 was channeled through four African American ministers for street money to recruit votes during the Carter campaign in the 1976 California primary.[39]

Another form of election fraud is to bypass manipulation of the voters in favor of forgery and false accounting by election officials. Corrupt election officials can (1) complete ballots when the voter has failed to vote for a particular office, (2) declare ballots for the opposition invalid by deliberately defacing them or marking two preferences for a single office, (3) destroy ballots for the opposition, (4) add premarked ballots to the total, and (5) simply miscount.

One of the most famous instances of election fraud involved the election of Lyndon Johnson to the Senate.[40] In 1948, Johnson ran for the Democratic nomination (which meant certain election in Democratic Texas) against Governor Coke Stevenson. Stevenson won the primary by 71,000 votes but lacked a majority in the crowded field. A runoff was then held for the two top vote-getters, Stevenson and Johnson. Stevenson again won, or so everyone thought. Days after the polls had closed, a questionable correction of the vote from Duval County gave Johnson 202 more votes than the original count, enough to give him the Democratic nomination by 87 votes. The new vote was orchestrated by George B. Parr, the Democratic county boss. It was alleged that the new votes came from the graveyard and Mexico; some Chicanos testified that Parr had voted their names without their knowledge. When the defeated candidate charged fraud, the Senate voted to investigate. Senate investigators found, however, that the ballots had mysteriously been destroyed. The investigation ended and Johnson became a senator, taking a big step in his political career, which later included terms as the powerful majority leader of the Senate and finally as president of the United States.

## Unfair Campaign Conduct

In March 2010, the Texas Board of Education decided "that the author of the Declaration of Independence, main author of the Constitution and third president of the States; the person whose radical ideas about democracy are credited with touching off revolutionary fervor through Europe and the Americas; . . . has been removed from Texas world history schoolbooks."[41] Why? Because Jefferson was not a Christian, but, like many of America's founders, was a deist (believed God made the universe then walked away from it, never to intervene in its daily affairs again.)

During the 2010 health care bill debate, an anonymous caller to Democratic Congresswoman Louise Slaughter's office threatened "snipers" would kill the children of lawmakers who voted affirmative. Michigan Democrat Bart Stupak, a prolife congressman, who voted for the health care bill over the objections of antiabortion activists, was called a "bastard," a "baby-murdering scumbag" and warned he would die "either by the hand of man or by the hand of God." Ten members of congress asked for increased security. Bricks were thrown through the local offices of some members of congress.[47] Some Democratic members of congress were spat on, called "fags," and "niggers" by Tea Party protesters. The President was termed a "Bolshevik," "a Nazi," "the anti-Christ" for simply wanting to reform abuses in the health insurance industry. This hateful rhetoric occurred in the only advanced democracy that still lacks universal health care coverage. It is now considered patriotic in some rightwing circles to demonstrate love of country by hating one's government. Many charges of unfair campaign conduct marked both of George W. Bush's elections.

## Scandal-Plagued America: The Bush Years as Metaphor

The presidential election of 2000 was one of the closest in American history.[48] Vice President Al Gore topped then Texas governor George W. Bush by some 500,000 votes, yet lost the contest. The final outcome rested on results from Florida, which Bush won by a very close vote on election night. A number of postelection investigations by the U.S. Commission on Civil Rights, investigative journalists, and others revealed a host of unethical and illegal behaviors in Florida:

- More of the punch-card ballots were disputed or nullified in pro-Gore precincts (4%) than in pro-Bush areas (1.4%). This was because more pro-Bush precincts possessed modern optical scanning technology.
- Some 32,000 voters, largely African Americans, were denied their right to vote because, even though they had registered, their names were never added to voter lists.
- Telephone lines to the central registrar's office were continually busy on election day. In response, Florida governor Jeb Bush (George W. Bush's brother) ordered laptop computers be made available. A *New York Times* analysis demonstrated that the computers were disproportionately sent to counties that voted for Bush.
- In a number of Democratic precincts, voting ceased early, leaving lines of potential voters abandoned.
- Numerous ballots were not counted or were mislaid; some seven ballot boxes were found in mysterious locations, and two bags of votes were found uncounted in a poll worker's car trunk. One Black church that had served as a polling location in many elections was unable to get election workers to collect its ballots at day's end.
- State troopers under the command of Governor Bush set up search checkpoints in largely African American precincts near Tallahassee. The searches of voters' vehicles delayed voters from getting to polling places for 2 hours.

- Many Black voters without police records were denied their right to vote due to being mislabeled as "convicted felons."
- Despite Florida law requiring voters to show only one form of identification, Orange County Puerto Rican voters were required to present two forms of photo ID.
- In a Dade County recount, Bush militants, brought in from different states, physically attacked a Canvassing Board member. This created an environment of intimidation that forced the board to stop the recount and accept the original Bush winning total.

Despite a media blackout, indications continued to emerge that something deeply troubling had taken place in 2004:

- Nearly half of the 6 million American voters living abroad never received their ballots or received them too late to vote—after the Pentagon mysteriously shut down a state-of-the-art Web site used to file overseas registrations.[49]
- The consulting firm Sproul and Associates, hired by the Republican National Committee to register voters, was discovered shredding Democratic registrations.
- In New Mexico, which was decided by 5,988 votes, machines inexplicably failed to properly register a presidential vote on more than 20,000 ballots.
- Nationally, the U.S. Election Assistance Commission charged that possibly 1 million ballots were spoiled by faulty voting equipment.
- Exit polls in 30 states were not just off the mark—they deviated to an extent that cannot be accounted for by their margin of error. In all but four states, the discrepancy favored President George W. Bush.
- Tens of thousands of eligible voters were purged from the rolls in Ohio, the critical battleground state that clinched Bush's victory in the Electoral College.
- Registration cards generated by Democratic voter drives were not processed and in precincts where voting machines were allowed illegally derailed a recount that could have given Kerry the presidency. A Miami County precinct whose polling place was an evangelical church recorded an impossibly high turnout of 98%, whereas a polling place in inner-city Cleveland recorded an equally impossible turnout of only 7%. In Warren County, GOP election officials even invented a nonexistent terrorist threat to prevent the media from monitoring the vote count.
- In Ohio alone, at least 357,000 voters, the overwhelming majority of them Democratic, were prevented from casting ballots or did not have their votes counted.
- Astoundingly, one in every four Ohio citizens who registered to vote in 2004 showed up at the polls only to discover that they were not listed

on the rolls, thanks to GOP efforts to stem the unprecedented flood of Democrats eager to cast ballots. Evidence of fraud indicates that close to 80,000 votes for Kerry ended up being counted for Bush.

## Continuing Corruption

The U.S. Congress has also suffered its share of scandals, and these have badly damaged its credibility.

- In 1993, the former House postmaster Robert Rota and three House Post Office employees pled guilty to stealing cash and stamps. Rota claimed that he gave two House members, Dan Rostenkowski (D-IL) and Joe Kolter (D-PA), $30,000 in Post Office funds. Rostenkowski, powerful head of the House Ways and Means Committee, was under indictment but has since been pardoned.[50]

The leading issue of the 2006 election concerning voters was corruption, and there was much to be concerned about. Members of Congress were involved in numerous scandals:

- Representative Randy "Duke" Cunningham accepted numerous bribes from a defense contractor, including the following:[42]
    - $200,000 toward the purchase of his Arlington, Virginia, condominium
    - $140,000 to a third party for the *Duke-Stir* yacht, which was moved to his boat slip for his use
    - $16,867.13 to a marine services company for repairs to his own yacht, the *Kelly C.*
    - $12,000 paid to an antique store for three nightstands, a leaded glass cabinet, a washstand, a buffet, and four armoires
    - $6,632 paid to a furniture store for a leather sofa and a sleigh-style bed
    - $7,200 paid to an antique store for a circa 1850 Louis Phillippe period commode and a circa 1830 Restoration period commode
    - $13,500 toward the purchase of a Rolls-Royce
    - $17,889.96 for repairs to the Rolls-Royce
    - $11,393.56 paid to a moving company to ship his belongings from his Arlington condominium to his San Diego–area home
    - $2,081.30 paid to a Washington, DC, hotel for his daughter's graduation party
    - $9,200 paid to a manufacturer for two Laser Shot shooting simulators
    - $10,000 paid to various hotels, resorts, and restaurants for his meals and entertainment expenses
    - Hundreds of thousands of dollars in cash to him and a company he controlled.[51]

- Former House majority leader Tom DeLay (R-TX) was indicted in 2006 for alleged campaign funding illegalities, and in 2010 was convicted of money laundering by a Texas jury.
- Former Republican Senate majority leader Bill Frist (R-TN) was subpoenaed in an insider-trading investigation.[52]
- House Administration Committee chairman Robert W. Ney (R-OH) declined to seek reelection after becoming involved in a lobbying scandal.
- Ralph Reed, the former Christian Coalition leader, was defeated during his 2006 campaign for lieutenant governor of Georgia after failing to shake off suggestions that he received Indian gambling money to mount a lobbying effort against rival casinos.[53]
- In May 2006, FBI agents entered the office of William Jefferson, a Democratic congressman, and seized from the freezer $90,000 in neatly wrapped cold cash. Republicans greeted this event with the thought, "Aha, the Democrats are crooks too. They will not be able to as readily use the corruption charge against Republicans." Judging from the responses of Democratic and Republican leaders, these Republicans are wrong. Now, more than ever, corruption charges against Republicans will resonate strongly. The FBI is probing allegations that Jefferson took hundreds of thousands of dollars in bribes to promote business ventures in Nigeria, Cameroon, and Ghana. The FBI states it has videotaped evidence of Jefferson taking $100,000 in bribe money.[43]
- Perverted e-mails were exchanged between 52-year-old Congressman Mark Foley (R-FL) and some 16- and 17-year-old children. Foley asked the 16-year-old boy to measure his penis and asked another child to describe how he masturbates. The congressman ended up resigning his House seat just before the 2006 election.

A series of scandals tainted an unusually high number of incumbents during 2005 and 2006, but no individual represented the corrupting influence of money on politics more than convicted lobbyist Jack Abramoff.[44] Nine Republican officeholders, whom the Center for Responsible Politics identified as having received political contributions from Abramoff, lost House, Senate, or gubernatorial elections in 2006. Other incumbents tied to Abramoff barely held on to their usually safe seats. Several more Republicans had to resign before election day because of the lobbying scandal or other disgraces, and their party lost those seats to Democrats.

Sheila Krumholz, acting executive director of the Committee for Responsive Politics, said, "Once again, politicians in Washington have demonstrated they're out of touch with their constituents on a key issue. They underestimated voters' concerns about ethics in government. Members of Congress in both parties said all year that they were serious about combating corruption. But by Election Day, they had very little to show they meant it—and many examples that showed they didn't take voters' concerns seriously."[54] In fact, more than one source has termed the 2006 Congress the most corrupt ever.

The Bush White House itself faced a nearly unprecedented number of scandals. The Abramoff scandal also resulted in two additional, unanticipated scandals. First, David H. Safavian, Carl Rove's former business partner, who served as the top White House procurement official, resigned and was arrested on charges that he lied about and impeded an investigation into his dealings with Abramoff. Second, Timothy E. Flanigan, Bush's nominee for deputy attorney general, the number two job at the Justice Department, withdrew his nomination after questions were raised about his interactions with the lobbyist.

The Center for American Progress has released a one-page document detailing "Intimigate." The document shows that the White House has developed a pattern of firing, intimidating, and defaming anyone who has had the courage to tell the truth about Iraq. In fact, the Iraq policy makers whose influence has grown in the White House are largely those who parsed and distorted intelligence and misled the American people.[45]

One of the most senior officials in the White House, Vice President Cheney's chief of staff Lewis Libby, was convicted of lying to the FBI. Libby's sentence was recently (2007) commuted by President Bush.[46] Libby lied about leaking the name of CIA agent Valerie Plame, which may have been part of an administration effort to destroy the credibility of Plame's husband, Ambassador Joseph Wilson, who wrote an article critical of the claim that Iraq had obtained nuclear fuel rods from an African country.[47] The army's top civilian official resigned in March 2007 due to a scandal over care and conditions for wounded Iraq War veterans at Walter Reed Army Medical Center in Washington, DC, and in other veterans' hospitals. Army secretary Francis Harvey resigned one day after firing the general in charge of Walter Reed. Harvey's resignation was requested by defense secretary Robert Gates.[48]

These incidents and numerous others documented throughout this book are symbolic of the major scandals that have made elite wrongdoing of major concern in America. The public believes that money has a pervasive influence in political campaigns, wherein candidates often spend millions of dollars to secure $100,000-a-year positions. The crisis of confidence continues to this day. Moreover, large corporations have proved every bit as deviant as political organizations.

- Interpol on December 3, 2010 issued an arrest warrant for former vice president Cheney from Nigeria. The indictment is for Halliburton's illegal bribery of Nigerian officials while he was the CEO. Sadly, it was not for war crimes.[55]
- Finally, 40-year House veteran Charlie Rangle was censured on December 2, 2010 on 15 ethics violations. Rangle claims that the decision to censure him was extremely political, and that he never benefited personally from any of the violations.[56]

# Conclusion

This chapter has focused on the dark side of politics. Hopefully, politics is not completely corrupt, as one may be tempted to conclude from our discussion.

We have looked at two types of political deviance: the use of political clout for material gain and the unfair means used to gain, maintain, or increase political power. In both cases, the deviance can be achieved by corrupt individuals or by a corrupt system. But even when accomplished by individuals, the important sociological point is that the deviance is only possible because the elite occupy positions of power. Because of the duties and powers inherent in their political positions, they are susceptible to the appeals of the moneyed interests who want to use them or they are persuaded by the appeal of greater power.

Although political corruption is found in all types of societies and in all types of political and economic systems, the amount of political corruption found in the United States is astounding. Benson, after carefully studying the phenomenon, offers this conclusion:

> Today it is probably fair to say that America has as much corruption, both absolutely and proportionately, as any other modern constitutional democracy. There are no international indices of corruption, but the available data indicate that corruption here is at least as severe and extensive as in other modern democracies. American idealism does not appear to be reflected in our political ethos.[52]

Why is the United States plagued by this high rate of political corruption? The answer is complex and requires an understanding of the historical factors, character, values, and political–economic systems that characterize the United States. The rip-off mentality that pervades the economic system is found throughout the social structure, as this chapter has amply demonstrated. The goal of individual or corporate success supersedes group concerns; therefore, any means are used to achieve the goal. The following chapter should provide further insight into this complex societal problem.

## CRITICAL THINKING EXERCISE 6.1
### Subsidies Without Reason

Senator William Proxmire used to present an annual "Golden Fleece" award for the most ridiculous expenditures by the federal government. One of his awards included things like funding research to discover why monkeys fall in love. As you can tell from our discussion of subsidies, the federal government continues to spend money on wasteful projects. Do a search of databases like Infotrac, Proquest, or the Reader's Guide for the past 3 years. Make a list of what newspapers and magazines consider the most questionable expenditures. On what basis are most of these grants and subsidies questioned? Who are the recipients of most such programs?

# ENDNOTES

1. Parenti, M. (2002). *Democracy for the Few* (7th ed., p. 44). New York: Bedford/St. Martin's.
2. See Thomas Dye and Harmon Zeigler *The Irony of Democracy*, Millennial ed. (Upper Saddle River, NJ: Prentice-Hall), 50ff.
3. Beard, C. A. (1913). *An economic interpretation of the constitution.* New York: Macmillan.
4. See Dye, T. R. (2001). *Politics in America* (4th ed., p. 67). Upper Saddle River, NJ: Prentice-Hall.
5. Ibid.
6. Parenti, M. (2002) *Democracy for the few* (7th ed., 44ff).
7. Brown, R. E. (1956). *Charles beard and the constitution.* Princeton, NJ: Princeton University Press, passim, but especially first and last chapters.
8. Morgan, E. (1956). *The birth of the republic, 1763–1789* (p. 128). Chicago. For George Washington's attitude on the convention and first years of his presidency, see Cunliffe, M. (1958). *George Washington: Man and monument* (pp. 120–132). New York.
9. The best review of these issues by legal scholars is contained in Latham, E. (1952). *The Declaration of independence and the constitution.* Boston, especially the selection by Robert Schuyler.
10. The organization and many of the examples used in this chapter are from two sources: Amick, G. (1976). *The American way of graft.* Princeton, NJ: Center for Analysis of Public Issues; and reprinted by permission of the publisher, from Benson, G. C. S. (1978). *Political corruption in America.* Lexington, MA: Lexington Books, D. C. Heath.
11. Benson (p. xi).
12. In addition to Amick and Benson, the following source provides an excellent review of the magnitude of political crime in the United States: Friedrich, C. J. (1972). *The pathology of politics.* New York: Harper & Row.
13. Kenny, C. (July 31, 2006). Capital crimes. *In These Times*, http://www.inthesetimes.com/article/continued/2732/capital_crimes/.
14. Benson (p. 49).
15. Amick (pp. 40–41).
16. http://www.alternet.org/news/148598/tea_party_inc.%3A_the_big_money_and_powerful_elites_behind_the_right_wing%27s_latest_uprising/. The Agnew case is taken primarily from Amick (pp. 42–50); and Lukas, J. A. (1976). *Nightmare: The underside of the Nixon years* (Chapter 12). New York: Viking.
17. This section is based on the discussion in Nathan Miller's (1992) *Stealing from America* (88 ff). New York: Paragon House.
18. Browning, F., & Gerassi, J. (1980). *The American way of crime* (p. 214). New York: Putnam's.
19. Ibid.
20. Benson (p. 12).
21. Amick (pp. 98–99).
22. Benson (pp. 81–82).
23. Amick (pp. 146–149).
24. Ibid (pp. 109–114).
25. Ibid (pp. 76–94).
26. Turetsky, D. (April 1988). New York City: Where money talks and ethics walks. *In These Times*, 5.

27. Amick, G. (1976). *The American Way of Graft*. Princeton, NJ: Center for Analysis of Public Issues.

28. Ibid (pp. 146–149).

29. Benson (p. 13).

30. Green, M. (1984). *Who runs congress?* (4th ed., pp. 255–258). New York: Dell.

31. Ibid (pp. 235–239).

32. Ibid (pp. 258–262).

33. See Gross. *National suicide* (pp. 173–175).

34. The following is taken from Key, Jr., V. O. (1949). *Southern politics* (Chapter 26). New York: Vintage.

35. Gross, M. (2009). *National suicide* (pp. 136–140). New York: Berkely Books.

36. Ball, H. (January 26, 1982). Mississippi's voting wrongs. *Washington Post*, A-19.

37. Benson (p. 171); reprinted by permission of the publisher.

38. Lasky, V. (1977). *It didn't start with Watergate* (p. 122). New York: Dial Press.

39. Benson (p. 172). (Originally appeared in *Los Angeles Times*, August 8, 1976, 1, 24).

40. Lasky (pp. 199–223).

41. See Parenti, M. (2002). *Democracy for the few* (7th ed., pp. 209–210). Boston: Bedford/St. Martin's; *New York Times*, 30 November, 2000, A-1; *Voting irregularities in Florida during the 2000 presidential election*. Washington, DC: U.S. Commission on Civil Rights, June 2001.

42. This discussion is based on the following sources: Center for Media and Democracy. (September 14, 2006). http://www.sourcewatch.org/index.php?title=U.S._election_irregularities_in_2004; Piven, F. F. (2004). *The war at home* (pp. 119–120). New York: New Press; Kennedy, Jr., R. F. (June 1, 2006). Was the 2004 election stolen? *Rolling Stone*.

43. Hoffman, M. (1992). *The world almanac and book of facts 1993*. (p. 53). New York: Pharos Books.

44. Ferrighetti, R. (1994). *The world almanac and book of facts 1994* (pp. 60, 75). Mahwah, NJ: Funk & Wagnalls.

45. Associated Press. http://news.yahoo.com/s/ap/2005.

46. http://www.washingtonpost.com/wpdyn/content/article/2005/10/13/AR2005101301955.html.

47. Ibid.

48. Congressional corruption. http://www.watchblog.com/democrats/archives/003676.html (May 12, 2006).

49. http://americablog.blogspot.com/2006/10/white-house-downplays-foley-scandal-as.html.

50. http://www.opensecrets.org/pressreleases/2006/PostElection.11.8.asp.

51. http://www.blackcommentator.com/164/164_cover_corrupt_congress.html.

52. http://www.commondreams.org/news2003/0930-12.htm.

53. http://www.nytimes.com/2007/03/07/opinion/07weds1.html.

54. http://www.capitolhillblue.com/artman/publish/article_7564.shtml.

55. http://www.sportfishermen.com/board/f17/cheney-indicted-nigeria-no-less-1169169.html.

56. ——. House votes to censure Rangle. *Reuters*. http://www.reuters.com/article/idUSTRE6B200S20101203.

# 7

# Political Deviance

In early 1998, the Clinton White House was reeling from news of a sleazy 3-year sexual relationship involving a 24-year-old former White House intern, Monica Lewinsky, and the 50-year-old president. Charges of Clinton's infidelities surfaced in the 1992 campaign when a former Arkansas state employee, Jennifer Flowers, sold her story of her affair with then-governor Clinton.

Clinton lied about the affair in a 1992 *60 Minutes* interview. Flowers had tapes, authenticated by audio experts, of her 12-year affair with Clinton. Flowers sold the tapes to a supermarket tabloid, the *Star*, for $175,000 after audio experts reviewed them. Clinton was soon thereafter elected president, and Ms. Flowers posed naked in the December 1992 issue of *Penthouse*. Betsey Wright, Clinton's chief of staff when he was governor of Arkansas, expressed relief that yet another "bimbo eruption" (sexual affair with a tattletale) had been survived.[1]

After Clinton was elected president, another Arkansas woman, Paula Jones, sued him for sexual harassment. Shortly after Clinton gave a deposition in the Jones suit, the first by a sitting president, news of his alleged relationship with Lewinsky exploded in the press on January 21, 1998.

Charges of late night phone sex, a gift of a dress, and late night trysts in the White House Theatre were countered with charges of a plot to get the president by right-wing Republicans and GOP independent prosecutor Kenneth Starr.

Mysterious tape recordings of conversations between Lewinsky and Linda R. Tripp, a Pentagon employee whose telephone call to independent prosecutor Starr on January 12, began an investigation into the Clinton–Lewinsky scandal (also known as "Zippergate").

There was evidence of a late December 1997 meeting between Clinton and Lewinsky after she had been subpoenaed in the Paula Jones sexual harassment case against the president, and intensive efforts by presidential confidant Vernon E. Jordan Jr. to help find the lowly White House intern a job at the time she prepared her affidavit were undertaken.[2] Allegedly, Lewinsky had been instructed by the president to lie under oath concerning their affair, which, if true, amounts to a felony, suborning perjury, a possible impeachable offense. Likewise, allegations of the president lying under oath while being deposed in the Paula Jones case were said to amount to the crime of perjury (a possibly impeachable offense).

The allegations stunned press and public alike, for this was the post-Watergate generation, familiar with scandals involving abuses of power, not sexual deviance in high places. Had more news media members or their public remembered the history of scandals on the federal level, the news may not have been so traumatic. Since Americans live in a culture with a long history of sexual repression and other sexual contradictions, scandals about their president's peculiar sexuality still evoke strong emotions.

Due in large measure to America's numerous contradictions about sexual matters, the nation has a very long history of sexual scandal in places high and low. So far as we know, it all began in 1702 (before the nation's independence) when Lord Cornbury, the colonial governor of New York, addressed the state assembly wearing a dress and elaborate headgear and waving a fan, supposedly to better represent his queen. From there, sexual scandals became a somewhat institutionalized feature of the trappings of political power in America.

- In 1730, Benjamin Franklin brought home an illegitimate child (by his mistress) for his common-law wife to raise. Franklin had numerous affairs throughout his life, most of which he wrote about in depth.
- George Washington, while single, wrote a love letter to his neighbor's wife, and Thomas Jefferson, while single, had children by one of his slaves, Sally Hemings. Jefferson had affairs with Betsey Walker, wife of his next-door neighbor, and Maria Conway, spouse of an English miniaturist.
- Married Treasury secretary Alexander Hamilton published accounts of his sexual liaison with Maria Reynolds, for which he paid her husband. Eventually, the Reynoldses blackmailed Hamilton over the affair.[3]
- In 1880, President James Garfield became the first known married president to have an extramarital affair, and in 1884, President Grover Cleveland openly confessed to fathering an illegitimate child.
- During the 1920 presidential campaign, the Republican National Committee sent Senator Warren Harding's mistress, Carrie Philips, on an all-expense-paid trip to China. She was one of Harding's two mistresses. The other, Nan Britton, had an illegitimate child with Harding.

In short, sexual scandal is a very common phenomenon in American life, perhaps even more the norm than bribery incidents. It is also the case that sex, mixed with other morally questionable behaviors, has been the source of many recent federal scandals.

- As president, Franklin Roosevelt carried on an affair with Lucy Mercer Rutherford when his wife, Eleanor, was out of town. Mrs. Roosevelt carried on a lesbian relationship with Loreana Hickok, who actually lived in the White House in a room directly across from the First Lady's.[4]

- Kay Summersby wrote a book about her extramarital affair with President Eisenhower when he was supreme commander of the Allied forces during World War II.

- From 1961 until his assassination in 1963, John F. Kennedy seduced a wide variety of women in the White House, including actress Judith Exner, a girlfriend of Chicago Mafia don Sam Giancana. Kennedy was introduced to Exner by his close friend entertainer Frank Sinatra, whose Mafia ties were already decades old. J.F.K. broke off the affair after Federal Bureau of Investigation (FBI) director J. Edgar Hoover wrote a secret memo to Attorney General Robert Kennedy expressing alarm over the president's involvement with a woman with Mafia ties. Another woman with whom J.F.K. was involved was thought to be an East German spy. Kennedy may have swum nude with his brothers and various women in the White House swimming pool, while the Secret Service guarded the pool entrance.[5]

- J.F.K. was involved with literally hundreds of women. Two blonde secretaries, nicknamed Fiddle and Faddle, regularly brushed Kennedy's hair for him, as well as cavorted nude with the president in the White House pool. J.F.K. and artist Mary Pinchot Meyer made love and smoked pot together in the White House. Actresses Jayne Mansfield and Angie Dickinson and stripper Blaze Starr were some of his lovers, as was Marilyn Monroe, who had affairs with both President John Kennedy and Attorney General Robert Kennedy. The Kennedys' sexual and other scandals were kept out of the public realm by an admiring press and their father's active discouragement of press leaks until 1969. Then Senator Ted Kennedy drove his 1967 Oldsmobile off a Chappaquiddick bridge, killing his companion, Mary Jo Kopechne, and dashing the senator's hopes as a presidential candidate. Supermarket tabloids and numerous additional press organs have detailed the personal lives of the senator and other Kennedy offspring ever since.

- Likewise, Lyndon Johnson made a habit of seducing members of his secretarial staff while president. Johnson once crawled into bed in the middle of the night with an aide (who was visiting his ranch) while uttering, "Move over, this is your president."[6] Johnson also had a special bell system installed in the White House so the Secret Service could warn him of his approaching wife as he was seducing various secretaries.[7]

- Johnson's chief of staff resigned after being arrested for homosexual encounters at a Washington YMCA men's room.

- In 1974, House Way and Means Committee chair Wilbur Mills (D-AK) was arrested for drunk driving at the Washington tidal basin. In the car with Mills was his mistress, striptease artist ("the Argentina Firecracker") Fanne Fox, who tried to flee by plunging herself into the water.[8]

- Richard Nixon, the only president to resign from office, had an off-again on-again relationship with Marianna Liu, an attractive cocktail lounge hostess at the Hong Kong Hilton's Den lounge. The affair lasted from 1958 to 1969, when Nixon's wife, Pat, insisted it cease. Nixon personally aided Liu in securing American citizenship.
- In 1976, Ohio Democratic representative Wayne Hayes resigned after revelations that his mistress-"secretary," Elizabeth Ray, was being paid $17,000 a year to use her sexual prowess to entice businessmen and political associates to close deals with Hayes.
- Another 1981 case involved several members of Congress and former lobbyist and attractive blonde Paula Parkinson. Parkinson allegedly took three members of Congress, including future vice president Dan Quayle, and six other males on a Florida golfing vacation. Rumors ran wild that Parkinson had videotapes of a number of her powerful guests in embarrassing positions. Parkinson was bewildered by all the press coverage and claimed that she had had affairs with eight members of Congress including a number of members of the ultraconservative Moral Majority. In the end, none of the politicians involved admitted much of anything about the incident, especially since the FBI was investigating it. Parkinson finally resigned her lobbying post, proudly proclaiming, "My morals might be low, but at least I have principles."[9] Following the scandal, Parkinson did the customary thing, posing nude for a men's magazine.
- The House censured Representative Gary Stokes (D-MA) in 1983 for having had sex with a 17-year-old male congressional page.
- In 1988, Representative Jim Bates (D-CA) was accused of sexually harassing his female aides and using his congressional staff to do campaign work.
- In 1988, married Colorado Democratic senator Gary Hart withdrew from the presidential race following the *Miami Herald*'s story that Hart had spent the night with a young model, Donna Rice, on board a yacht.
- In 1989, Representative Don Lukens (R-OH) was convicted of contributing to the delinquency of a minor by having sex with a 16-year-old girl. After spending 30 days in jail for the offense, Lukens was subsequently accused of fondling a Capitol building elevator operator and soliciting sex from her.
- In the early 1990s, Senator Robert Packwood (R-OR) resigned from office after it was revealed that he had sexually harassed numerous female staff members and campaign workers.
- Newt Gingrich, former Republican Speaker of the House of Representatives (1995–1999), admitted in March 2007 that allegations that he was having a sexual affair while serving as Speaker were true.
- Bob Livingston resigned as Speaker of the House of Representatives in December 1998 after it was revealed during the height of the impeachment debate surrounding the Lewinsky scandal that *Hustler* magazine

was preparing to publish an article detailing sexual indiscretions by Republican politicians, including the married Livingston.

- Gary Condit, a California Democratic congressman, was revealed to be having an affair with his intern, Chandra Levy, which, it was alleged, may have led to her murder in 2001.
- Strom Thurmond, the late U.S. Senator, had an African American daughter out of wedlock. He fathered the child with Carrie Butler, then a 16-year-old maid in his parents' household. Six months after Thurmond's death in 2003, a 78-year-old African American woman named Essie Mae Washington-Williams revealed that the former senator was her father, a fact that Thurmond's family confirmed.
- James McGreevey, former governor of New Jersey, admitted an extramarital homosexual affair with aide Golan Cipel in 2004, making him the first openly gay state governor in American history.
- Larry Craig, a Republican U.S. Senator from Idaho, resigned in September 2007 after being arrested in June 2007 in a men's public restroom at the Minneapolis–St. Paul International Airport and pleading guilty in August 2007 to a disorderly conduct charge related to the arrest. Police had been investigating reports of gay sexual activity in the restroom when an undercover, plainclothes police officer arrested Senator Craig. Senator Craig later admitted to reporters that he had "made a poor decision." Despite his claims that he was not gay and that he was entrapped in a toilet stall, he resigned after being pressured by fellow Republicans.
- Republican U.S. Senator David Vitter (R-LA) was found on a list of clients of an infamous escort service run by Deborah Jeane Palfrey, know as the "D.C. Madam," in 2007. He admitted that his telephone number was included in the D.C. Madam's phone list.
- Randall L. Tobias (R) Appointed by George W. Bush as Deputy Secretary of State, the "AIDS Czar" who stated that U.S. funds should be denied to countries that permitted prostitution resigned April 27, 2007 after confirming he had been a customer of Deborah Jeane Palfrey.
- Glen Murphy Jr. (R), 33-year-old president of the Young Republican National Federation, was investigation for oral sexual assault of a sleeping 22-year-old man (2007).
- Tim Mahoney (D-FL) was elected to fill the seat left when disgraced Congressman Mark Foley (R-FL) resigned due to inappropriate emails sent to male congressional pages. He ran on a campaign promise to make "a world that is safer, more moral." In October he admitted he placed his mistress on his staff and then fired her saying "You work at my pleasure." He then admitted to multiple concurrent affair (2009).
- In July 2011, Rep. David Wu (D-Ore.) resigned after it was discovered he had sex with the teen aged daughter of a childhood friend and supporter. In an even more notable scandal , Rep. Anthony Weiner (D-NY) resigned after involvement in a sex scandal where no actual

intercourse took place, only nude and semi-nude pictures and text messages that Weiner posted to various women on the internet (one of whom was only 17).

So what can be learned about corruption from this minihistorical review of the deviant sexual behavior of America's political officials? One way to draw useful conclusions is by using it to dispel a number of myths that were being reported in conjunction with the recent Clinton sex scandal.

**Myth:** The recent Clinton sex scandal is an aberration. Most American scandals are about abuses of power, not sex. When sex becomes an issue, usually the Democrats are involved. When money is an issue, it's usually a Republican doing.

**Fact:** Both political parties have a long history of sexual scandals among their members. The key factor operating here is not sex or money but the relationship between sexual scandals and all other abuses of power. Anyone in a position of authority who takes up with any underling is, almost by definition, abusing a basic form of power—the power to hire and fire. Reviews of the record reveal that most politicians accused of sexual misconduct also misbehave in other areas.

This brings us to a related notion; namely:

**Myth:** What presidents (or other politicians) do in their private lives is unrelated to the performances of their jobs.

**Fact:** In this post-Watergate, post-Chappaquiddick era, tattling on celebrities, including politicians, has become a cultural obsession. As a result, politicians clearly put their careers at risk and endanger their chances for future success by engaging in reckless sexual behavior or by committing perjury or obstruction of justice in order to cover it up. Sex with women affiliated with organized crime, or other unsavory interests (especially enemy spies) today would place any powerful politician in a vulnerable position, one that may result in blackmail, endangering the nation's security, and/or removal from office.

**Myth:** Sexual scandals are only about sex.

**Fact:** The line between sex, status, power, and money in this most materialistic of cultures grows blurrier by the day. Lewinsky was offered $2 million by *Penthouse* for her photos and story. Many other women involved in political and sexual scandals with the wealthy and powerful have posed naked in men's magazines, written books, or starred in movies or nightclub acts due to the incidents that made them famous. This includes Elizabeth Ray and prostitutes visited by televangelist Jimmy Swagart and actor Hugh Grant, among many others. The sex scandal industry is a cottage industry in contemporary democratic societies. Women with a modicum of intelligence are well aware of the possibilities offered by sexual encounters with the rich and famous, and the Clinton sex scandal was no different.

Given America's cultural contradictions concerning sex, its constant craving for knowledge of the "backstage" behavior of the powerful, rich, and famous, and the media's werewolf-like yearnings to make profitable commodities out of everything and anything, the sex scandal business can only continue to grow. Were the public to tire of such matters, were illicit sex to become unprofitable, and those who related only the sleazy hearsay that initiates reportage of sexual scandal were publicly condemned, the results might be quite different.

Trashy and tragic as it may sometimes become, sexual news is an economic mainstay of mass-media journalism, entertainment, and advertising. Given satellite TV news, tabloid journalism, and so many men and women on the make, the sexual scandalization of politics is probably in the infancy of a new era. As media critic John Carman relates, when it comes to sleazy and hearsay reporting of sexual deviance, the seemingly ashamed media behave like the pet dog that has been scolded by its master for chasing cars. "Seemingly contrite and stricken, the dog trudges to a corner of the yard and plops down miserably to contemplate his bad behavior. The next car drives by and the dog bolts after it. It's difficult to change the nature of things. . . . Traditionally the greatest journalistic virtue was to get the story right. The next greatest virtue was to get it first. In the new climate. . . factualness and speed appear to have changed places."[10]

Given these realities, it would be very unsurprising if news broadcasts of videotape of politicians engaging in all manner of illicit sex did not become something of a custom in the near future. There is also a need to assess the causes of these scandals. It is tempting to attribute these episodes to the personalities of those involved. However, there are important elements of the Washington environment that contribute to all manner of corruption.

# The Corrupting Environment of Politics

A major contributor to political corruption in the United States concerns all manner of privileges and perks that politicians of all stripes and at all levels of government have conveyed upon themselves. Together these costly freebees contribute to an atmosphere of elitism and arrogance—an environment conducive to the idea that holders of political power can do no wrong. According to Martin Gross[11]:

- Congress's 535 members employ a supporting staff of more than 25,000 at a cost of well over $1 billion.
- There are numerous tax deductions, exemptions, and free tax preparation by the Internal Revenue Service (IRS).
- The National Gallery of Art lends original paintings to members of Congress for use in decorating their offices.

- A special gift office wraps packages free of charge to representatives, senators, and their senior staff. There are special stationery stores inside the Capitol that heavily discount all items sold. This congressional subsidy costs America's taxpayers $1 million annually.
- There are free photos with constituents taken, cropped, and sent out at no cost. The same service also frames posters and snapshots for free.
- If airline tickets are paid for by the government (a not infrequent occurrence), Congress members and their staffs are allowed credit for airline frequent flier miles. When using their privately owned vehicles, above-average mileage reimbursement is allowed.
- After leaving Congress, members may use their office desks and chairs free—at home! Members of Congress and their staffs are also provided with free, unlimited long-distance phone service—even when calling from their own homes.
- The Library of Congress charges no fines on overdue books and other items for Congress members and their staffs. Each year, thousands of books go unreturned. Members of both houses hire children of friends and constituents to fill various patronage jobs—such as congressional page—at taxpayers' expense. Likewise, the White House has numerous such posts. Likewise, a number of congresspersons have been caught by Capitol police engaging in oral sex in their vehicles with various pages.[12]
- Leaders of the House and Senate, of course, must be transported from one place to another, and they are provided (at taxpayer largesse) free limousines and chauffeurs. There are radio and television studios inside the nation's Capitol, used for free by elected officials there for making tapes that are subsequently sent out to media outlets in their districts. Challengers in elections must, of course, pay to have such messages made.
- People in Congress have free medical, life, and other insurance, as well as an unparalleled pension plan. Some 40 million American citizens, mostly members of the "working poor," are without medical insurance during part of any given year largely because Congress refuses to pass national health care legislation.
- In 1996, the average retired Congress member received $100,000 from the government. Each member of Congress receives a postal budget of some $108,000—known as the franking privilege—paid for by the taxpayers. Most of the mail (printed for free) sent goes for reelection purposes. The cost of this self-serving subsidy is more than $65 million a year in the House of Representatives alone. This great campaign aid is, of course, denied to those challenging Congress members in elections.
- Finally, there are congressional "junkets." These are merely free air and other forms of travel on government-owned and government-operated airplanes. One junket alone involved four congresspersons, their senior staffs, and 25 of their spouses going on a "fact-finding" tour of China and Japan at a cost of $550,000. Part of the tour included an entire day spent at a reserve for Chinese panda bears.

Lest you think this ridiculous example unusual, other trips have included:

- More than 100 Congress members, staff members, spouses, and guests went to a Paris air show at a cost of more than $200,000.
- Some 19 members of the House toured Saudi Arabia and Israel and billed America's taxpayers $322,402 for the privilege.
- House committee members "investigated" Eastern Europe with their mates for $99,000.
- A foreign policy investigation of Singapore by one senator, six of his friends, and their spouses cost $359,000.

The point is not simply that these game show–like prizes are unfair on their face. The key issue here is that such nonsensical expenditures create an atmosphere in which illegal and unethical behaviors are certain to flourish.

This claim is borne out by a similar examination of the White House environment. If the congressional atmosphere can be described as one of special privileges, the White House environment can only be termed one of royalty.

- A White House operator dials phone numbers for important personnel. The minute the president takes off his suit, a servant carries it off to be cleaned. There are helicopters available to transport the president and guests to a fleet of state-of-the-art jetliners waiting at Andrews Air Force Base. The White House also has a fleet of 29 limousines and drivers, as well as Secret Service agents, to transport the president wherever he wants. There are five calligraphers at an annual cost of $260,000.
- No one really knows how much all the White House perks cost. The White House has 132 rooms that are run and maintained like a world-class luxury hotel. Priceless paintings decorate the walls. The land it sits on is assessed at $314,974,600, and the building itself at more than $25 million. There are also numerous executive office buildings for use by the executive branch. The president receives a $200,000 yearly salary, which is nothing considering the $9.7 million to run the White House executive residence, $24.9 million for the Office of Administration, $38.9 million for the White House Office, and an additional $93.8 million for remaining costs. In total, the executive office of the president is budgeted at over $300 million per year. The president's airplane alone costs $391 million because it is specially equipped. Another $356 million is spent by the Secret Service to protect the president and vice president. In 1992, the Office of Personnel Management tried to estimate all remaining costs and came up with a figure of $978.5 million annually, but this does not include the other support costs that are part of the budget of other agencies besides the Secret Service.[13]

Ronald Kessler has assessed the consequences of all this largesse:

"The dizzying combination of power and perquisites is corrupting. The percentage of White House aides who have had to consult psychiatrists is far out of proportion to the general population. . . . The White House is an environment that magnifies character flaws, a catalyst that has led to such scandals as Watergate and the Iran-Contra affair."[14]

Theories such as differential association, differential reinforcement, and rational choice, as well as other learning and control crime theories, emphasize operant conditioning principles in crime causation. Our discussion of the immediate environment of secrecy, power, and great privilege indicates that some of the more important aspects of reinforcement may not take place in face-to-face situations. The perks of power and wealth may in and of themselves act as important reinforcers that encourage corruption in many ways, some obvious, others more subtle. These reinforcers, coupled with other mechanisms such as groupthink and neutralizations concerning who "the real criminals" are (see Chapter 8), add some interesting dimensions to our notions of white-collar crime causation.

Criminologists interested in political crimes have traditionally concentrated on acts by individuals and organizations against the government, that is, attempts to change the political system through violating the law. Although these political acts are important to understand, this exclusive focus neglects those crimes perpetrated by the government against the people. The purpose of this chapter is to attempt to right this imbalance by focusing on the deviance of the political elite (see also Chapter 6).[15] Political deviance is an omnibus concept, including a number of practices. Under this rubric are the numerous forms of political corruption noted in Chapter 6, as well as the consequences of the government's bias in favor of business that negatively affects the powerless.

The remainder of this chapter catalogs additional political acts that are deviant. Specifically, we examine deviance in the domestic and foreign spheres. On the domestic level, we consider (1) the secrecy and deception used by government officials to manipulate public opinion; (2) the abuse of power by government officials and agencies; (3) political prisoners; and (4) official violence, as manifested in police brutality and the use of citizens as unwilling guinea pigs. On the international level, we will focus on two illegal warlike acts: clandestine intervention and war crimes.

# Domestic Political Deviance

## Secrecy, Lying, and Deception

The hallmark of any democracy is the consent of the governed based on a reliable flow of information from the government. Unfortunately, a number of mechanisms serve to thwart this principle in U.S. society.[16] One common technique used to withhold information is the presidential exercise of *executive privilege*. The doctrine of executive privilege is the constitutionally questionable belief that the president and his staff cannot be made to testify and that presidential documents cannot be examined without the president's permission. The argument given for this immunity is that such information might compromise national security. However, the more realistic effect is that executive privilege allows the executive branch to withhold information from the courts and Congress, not to mention the general public.

Executive privilege has been used several times in U.S. history:[17]

- President Truman refused to turn over to the House Un-American Activities Committee a Federal Bureau of Investigation report on a government scientist.
- In 1963, General Maxwell Taylor declined to appear before the House Subcommittee on Defense Appropriations to discuss the Bay of Pigs invasion.
- In 1972, the Securities and Exchange Commission refused to give certain information to the House Interstate and Foreign Commerce Subcommittee concerning its investigation of ITT.
- In 1973, President Nixon refused to surrender the White House tape recordings to Special Prosecutor Archibald Cox.

Another method used to stonewall is to designate information as memorandums. The following is an example of a secret memo from Assistant Secretary of Defense Daniel McNaughton to Secretary Robert McNamara:

> 70 percent [of the reasons for fighting in Vietnam are] to avoid a humiliating U.S. defeat (to our reputation as a guarantor), 20 percent, to keep South Vietnam (and the adjacent territory) from Chinese hands, 10 percent to benefit the people of South Vietnam [with] a better, freer way of life.[18]

> What would have happened had these goals been made public?

> Would Congress have authorized a major war and more than 50,000 U.S. combat deaths for these goals? Would the American people have supported a war for these goals? And if not, was an American President justified in going to war for them anyway? More importantly, was an American President justified in concealing these goals and our own acts of provocation while he was, in fact, making a unilateral decision to go to war?[19]

Most likely, the people would not have supported the war if they had known about the government's goals. Realizing this, President Nixon (who broadened the war from Johnson's policies) attempted to suppress publication of the Pentagon Papers, which would have revealed the true U.S. intentions and behaviors. In addition, the weight of the government's force was brought to the prosecution of those who had leaked the Pentagon Papers (Daniel Ellsberg and Anthony Russo). The government even went so far as to offer the judge in that case the directorship of FBI while the case was being heard.[20]

Officials can also deceive the public by the "you did not ask me the right question, so I did not give you the right answer" game.[21] As an example, when Richard Helms was director of the Central Intelligence Agency (CIA), he was asked before Congress if his agency had been involved in Watergate. His reply was no. Much later, when it became known that the CIA had lent equipment to the Watergate burglars and concealed the laundering of checks used in the cover-up, Helms was reminded of his previous answer. He explained that he had not been asked the right question, for he had assumed that the original question meant involvement in the actual break-in at Democratic headquarters.

Although all the above tactics work to deceive the public, none is more onerous than outright lying by government officials, which has occurred many times in U.S. history.[22]

- In 1954, Secretary of State John Foster Dulles said that Americans were not involved in the coup in Guatemala that deposed the regime of leftist President José Guzman, even though the operation was financed, organized, and run by the CIA.
- In 1960, a U.S. spy plane, flown by a CIA pilot, was shot down over the Soviet Union. Although the United States had been using U-2 planes to spy on the Soviets for the preceding 4 years, officials denied the incident, saying that the United States had not violated Soviet air space.
- In 1961, the CIA, under President Kennedy, organized an invasion of Cuba at the Bay of Pigs. Yet, when the Cubans charged in the United Nations that the United States was behind the operation, ambassador Adlai Stevenson responded that no U.S. personnel or government planes were involved.
- In 1963, the United States supported but officially denied its involvement in the coup against South Vietnam President Ngo Dinh Diem.
- In 1964, President Johnson used an incident in which U.S. ships were allegedly shot at in the Tonkin Gulf to give him a free hand to escalate the war in Vietnam. Congress was deliberately misled by the official representation of the facts.[23]
- President Johnson praised U.S. Asian allies for sending supposed volunteers to fight in Vietnam when in fact our government had paid Thailand and the Philippines $200 million each to make this gesture.
- President Nixon and his advisers told the U.S. public that the neutrality of Cambodia had not been violated when the United States had already conducted 3,600 bombing missions in that country over a 5-year period. To carry out this deception, the U.S. government falsified the death certificates of Americans who died in Cambodia.
- U.S. military and government officials in the Vietnam War deliberately underestimated enemy troop strength to provide the illusion of military progress.[24]

- In February 1976, George Bush, then director of the CIA, said, "Effective immediately the CIA will not enter into any paid or contractual relationship with any full-time or part-time news correspondent accredited by any U.S. news service, newspaper, periodical, radio, or television network or station." At the time of this announcement, the CIA employed about 50 members of U.S. media organizations and kept 25 journalists on the payroll, despite official pronouncements to the contrary.[25]

In 1994, the CIA was haunted by a series of miniscandals involving fraud and corruption by its own agents.[26]

- An agent stationed in Venezuela knowingly allowed several shipments of cocaine into the United States. At the time, the agent was romantically involved with a Drug Enforcement Agency (DEA) official.
- In the mid-1980s, an FBI investigation revealed that CIA contract officers were illegally shipping arms back into the United States. The agents were dismissed but never prosecuted.
- The CIA spent more than $13 million to spirit its agents out of Ghana after one of its secretaries revealed the agents' identities to her lover.
- The CIA has lost all of its Iranian agents twice. The first time occurred in 1979 when the U.S. embassy was taken over by Iranian revolutionaries. This episode probably cost Jimmy Carter his bid for reelection. The second loss occurred in the late 1980s and is still going on. Since 1988, Iranian authorities have hunted down at least 30 Iranians who spied for the CIA. The CIA knew of this threat to its own agents, but the officer in charge of operations in Iran ignored numerous warnings of the impending danger. Most of these spies were tortured and executed for lack of proper protection.
- One agent working in Moscow was personally trained by the director of operations there. However, the agent had a criminal record involving assault with a deadly weapon and drug abuse problems. When these were revealed, he defected to Russia, with numerous CIA secrets.
- Finally, consider the case of agent Aldrich Ames, who sold intelligence secrets to the Russians for years and was paid some $2 million for doing so. Ames and his wife spent large sums of money overtly, buying a $540,000 house and a $40,000 Jaguar. Nevertheless, their treasonous activities went undetected by the CIA for years.

In addition to these examples, we must remember cover-ups of CIA involvement in the takeover of the Allende government in Chile, the attempted whitewashing of the sheep deaths in Utah because of an unintended release of chemicals used in biological warfare, the denial by Attorney General John Mitchell that ITT had offered $400,000 to underwrite the 1972 Republican National Convention, and so on. Cover-ups, lies, and secrecy by the government certainly run counter to the long-standing philosophical commitment of the United States to an open system in which the public is included in the decision-making process. Thomas Emerson, a Yale law professor, alleges that secrecy in a democratic society is a source of illegitimate power, for several reasons.

1. When the people are assumed to be the master and the government, the servant, it makes no sense that the master should be denied the information upon which to direct the activities of the servants.
2. Each branch of government has its constitutional role to play, and for one branch to withhold information from another undermines the whole principle of checks and balances.
3. Secrecy denies the individual due process, which demands that the citizen be furnished all the information upon which his or her destiny rests.[27]

Of course, at times, the public must be kept in the dark. The question, though, is, when is secrecy legitimate? The burden of proof lies with those imposing the secrecy. The key is whether the intentional tampering with the free flow of public information is more beneficial to the public interest than disclosure.[28]

The determination of whether the public is better served by secrecy or disclosure is difficult to assess because one can argue that the public interest is *always* paramount, regardless of the situation. For example, most Americans believed the actions of Daniel Ellsberg were wrong when he disclosed the secrets of the Pentagon Papers. Thus, the secret leaker was deemed guilty, whereas the secret keepers were innocent because the public interest required secrecy in these militarily sensitive matters. Others, in contrast, perceived Ellsberg as a hero, one with courage enough to reveal the errors of the establishment. In this view, the secret keepers were guilty and the secret leaker was honored because public policy in Vietnam was against the public's interest.

David Wise has bluntly summarized the secrecy problem:

With its control over information supported by an official system of secrecy and classification, the government has almost unlimited power to misinform the public. It does so for various reasons. The government lies to manipulate public opinion, to generate public support for its policies, and to silence its critics. Ultimately, it lies to stay in power.[29]

The CIA has also had a long history of involvement with drug traffickers. On August 18, 1996, the *San Jose Mercury News* published a front-page story claiming that

for the better part of a decade, a San Francisco Bay Area drug ring sold tons of cocaine to the Crips and Bloods street gangs of Los Angeles and funneled millions in drug profits to a Latin American guerrilla army run by the U.S. Central Intelligence Agency.

This drug network opened the first pipeline between Colombia's cocaine cartels and the black neighborhoods of Los Angeles. . . . The cocaine that flooded in helped spark a crack explosion in urban America . . . and provided the cash and connections needed for L.A.'s gangs to buy automatic weapons.[30]

The army's financiers, who met with CIA agents both before and during the time they were selling the drugs in Los Angeles, delivered cut-rate cocaine to the gangs through a young south–central crack dealer named Ricky Donnell Ross. Unaware of his suppliers' military and political connections, "Freeway Rick," a dope dealer of mythic proportions in the Los Angeles drug world, turned the cocaine powder into crack and wholesaled it to gangs across the country. The cash Ross paid for the cocaine, court records show, was then used to buy weapons and equipment for a guerrilla army named the Fuerza Democratica Nicaraguense (Nicaraguan Democratic Force), or FDN, the largest of several anticommunist groups commonly called the *Contras.*

The fact that the CIA aided drug traffickers in the 1980s was confirmed by a number of sources, including the *Nation*, which argued the fact that the "government turned a blind eye to Contra drug trafficking has long resided in Washington files."[31]

Likewise, an investigative report by Peter Kornbluh confirmed that

[U]sing the Freedom of Information Act, the National Security Archive obtained the declassification of thousands of pages of secret White House documents, regarding the Contra war . . . Those records revealed a sad and shocking truth: U.S. officials—White House, National Security Council and CIA—not only knew about and condoned drug smuggling during the Contra operations, but in some cases collaborated with, protected, and even paid known dope traffickers who were deemed important players in the Reagan administration's obsessed covert effort to overthrow the Sandinista government in Nicaragua.

"This is a scandal," Kornbluh claimed, "and it is a scandal that demands a full accounting."[32] According to Project Censored, Congress, in 2000, refused to hold any public hearings on the question of CIA-Contra-cocaine links, acting more secretively than the CIA itself.[33]

The Contra–CIA drug trafficking link is a symptom of several much more widespread conditions. First, the CIA has been a major force in international drug trafficking for decades:

- In France in 1950 the CIA recruited Corsican gangsters, the Ferri-Pisani family, to break a strike by dockworkers. The workers had refused to ship arms to Vietnam (where France was then at war). Corsican gangsters assaulted picket lines of communist union members and harassed union officials. In return for stopping the strike, the Ferri-Pisani family was allowed to use Marseilles as a shipping center for heroin.
- For more than 30 years the U.S. government supported opium production in Southeast Asia's Golden Triangle by providing arms, military support, and protection to corrupt officials—all in the name of anticommunism,

of course. This relationship began in the 1950s, after the Chinese Communists defeated Chiang Kai-shek's Nationalist Chinese army (the Kuomintang) in 1949. The CIA helped the Kuomintang regroup and settle in Burma's Shan states, bordering on China. The Shan area is a rich source of opium poppies. The CIA even helped smuggle the heroin out of Laos on its own airline, Air America. The CIA was aided in this project by American Mafia members whose lucrative Cuban market had dried up after Fidel Castro ousted the corrupt dictator Fulgencio Batista. (The story of Air America was made into a movie starring Mel Gibson in the 1980s.)

- In the 1970s the Kuomintang's Cholon (Chinese Mafia) began producing injectable heroin and importing it into Vietnam. It has been estimated that 100,000 American soldiers in Vietnam had become addicted to heroin by 1974.
- The CIA also aided its Southeast Asian drug producers by establishing money-laundering facilities for them in Australia. The Nugen Hand Bank was established by a number of former CIA agents and U.S. military officers. William Colby, former director of the CIA, was hired as the bank's lawyer. The bank was involved in numerous illegal activities, including a scheme to defraud U.S. oil workers in Saudi Arabia of their wages.
- Other incidents link U.S. government agencies to drug trafficking by the Nicaraguan Contras in the 1980s. The Medellín cocaine cartel paid the Contras $10 million to allow its agents safe passage through Contra-held territory, with the full knowledge of the CIA. The Enterprise operation established by Lieutenant Colonel Oliver North and Admiral John Poindexter provided airplanes to the Medellín cartel in 1984–1985. The cartel paid the Enterprise for use of planes, landing strips, and labor to load drug shipments. The proceeds were allegedly used to buy arms for the Contras.
- In 1985, the CIA supplied arms to the Afghans under General Hekmatyar. The CIA aided the Mujahedin (holy war fighters) after the Soviet army invaded Afghanistan to prop up the communist regime it had installed there. Hekmatyar and his army promptly went into the heroin business, and by 1988 they had 100 to 200 heroin refineries just across the border in Pakistan. By the late 1990s, heroin from these Southwest Asian nations accounted for about 75% of the European heroin supplies.[34]

Scandals involving the CIA and drug traffickers are symptomatic of an age in which elite deviance in both government and business has become an institutionalized feature of global capitalism.

## Abuse of Power by Government Agencies

Watergate revealed that the highest U.S. leaders had conspired, among other things, to win an election by using such illegal means as dirty tricks, burglary of opponents, and soliciting of campaign funds by threats and bribes. But these White House transgressions, which we examined earlier in some detail, are only one expression of illicit government intervention. In this section, we focus on the deviant actions of government agencies in several key areas.

Many government abuses have occurred under the guise of internal security. Domestic surveillance is one example. Government agencies have a long history of surveilling citizens.[35] The pace quickened in the 1930s and increased further with the communist threat in the 1950s. Surveillance reached its peak during the height of antiwar and civil rights protests during the late 1960s and early 1970s. The FBI's concern with internal security, for example, dates back to 1936, when President Roosevelt asked FBI director J. Edgar Hoover to investigate domestic communist and fascist organizations in the United States.[36] In 1939, as World War II began in Europe, President Roosevelt issued a proclamation that the FBI would be in charge of investigating subversive activities, espionage, and sabotage and that all law enforcement offices should give the FBI any relevant information on suspected activities. These directives began a pattern followed by the FBI under the administrations of Presidents Truman, Eisenhower, Kennedy, Johnson, Nixon, Ford, Carter, Reagan, and Bush.

The scope of these abuses by the FBI, the CIA, the National Security Agency (NSA), and 18 other federal agencies engaged in surreptitious surveillance is incredible.[37] Indeed, many questionable acts against U.S. citizens have been performed in the name of national security.

- From 1967 to 1973, the NSA monitored the overseas telephone calls and cables of approximately 1,650 U.S. citizens and organizations, as well as almost 6,000 foreign nationals and groups.[38]
- Between 1953 and 1973, the CIA opened and photographed nearly 250,000 first-class letters in the United States.
- As director of the CIA, William Colby acknowledged to Congress that his organization had opened the mail of private citizens and accumulated secret files on more than 10,000 Americans.[39]
- Over the years, the FBI has conducted about 1,500 break-ins of foreign embassies and missions, mob hangouts, and the headquarters of such organizations as the Ku Klux Klan and the American Communist Party.[40]
- During the last 5 years of the Reagan administration, the FBI spied on numerous U.S. citizens and groups that opposed the administration's Central American policies. The groups under surveillance included the Committee in Solidarity with the People of El Salvador, the Southern Christian Leadership Conference (SCLC), the Maryknoll Sisters, and the United Automobile Workers.[41]

These are but a few examples of government abuses against its citizens. To make the point clearer, we will describe in greater detail two nefarious (but representative) government campaigns: (1) the FBI's vendetta against Martin Luther King Jr. and (2) the FBI's campaign to nullify the effectiveness of the Socialist Workers Party (SWP).

The FBI campaigned to destroy civil rights groups. The most infamous example was the attempt to negate the power of Martin Luther King Jr. King had been openly critical of the bureau's ineffectual enforcement of civil rights laws. This apparently led the director, J. Edgar Hoover, to label King "the most notorious liar in the U.S." and to launch a vendetta against him.[42] From 1957, when King became prominent in the Montgomery bus boycott, the FBI monitored his activities under its vague authority to investigate subversives. The more powerful King became, the more the FBI pursued him.

King was indexed in the files as a communist; as a result, he was to be imprisoned in the event of a national emergency. This charge against King was based on the allegation that two of his associates in the SCLC were communists.

Because Hoover had convinced Attorney General Robert Kennedy of the possible link between King and the communists, Kennedy authorized wiretaps of King's phones, which continued for the next 2 years. Kennedy did not know, however, that the FBI planned to use the wiretaps to discredit King.

The FBI's efforts to neutralize or even destroy King were intensified with King's increasing popularity, as exemplified by his "I Have a Dream" speech before 250,000 in Washington, DC, in August 1963. King was thus characterized in an FBI memo: "He stands head and shoulders over all other Negro leaders put together when it comes to influencing great masses of Negroes. We must mark him now . . . as the most dangerous Negro of the future of this Nation from the standpoint of Communism, the Negro and national security."[43]

The efforts then escalated to include physical and photographic surveillance and the placement of illegal bugs in King's living quarters. Tapes of conversations in a Washington hotel were used by the FBI to imply that King engaged in extramarital sexual activities. The FBI used these tapes, which may or may not have been altered, to dishonor King. At the very time King was receiving great honors including the Nobel Peace Prize, *Time* magazine's "Man of the Year" award, and numerous honorary degrees, the FBI countered with briefings, distribution of the tapes to news people and columnists, and congressional testimony about King's supposed communist activities and questionable private behavior. The FBI even briefed officials of the National Council of Churches and other church bodies about King's alleged deviance. The smear campaign against King reached its zenith when the FBI mailed the tapes to the SCLC offices in Atlanta with a covering letter suggesting that he commit suicide or face humiliation when the tapes were made public on the eve of the Nobel award ceremonies in Sweden.

Summing up the sordid affair, Halperin and his associates editorialized as follows:

> The FBI had turned its arsenal of surveillance and disruption techniques on Martin Luther King and the civil rights movement. It was concerned not with

Soviet agents nor with criminal activity, but with the political and personal activities of a man and a movement committed to nonviolence and democracy. King was not the first such target, nor the last. In the end we are all victims, as our political life is distorted and constricted by the FBI, a law enforcement agency now policing politics.[44]

This comment is critical of the FBI and justifiably so. Clearly, the FBI's tactics were illegal, whether King was a communist or not. And that is a moot point because King was not a communist. In testimony before a Senate committee, the FBI's assistant deputy director, James Adams, was asked by Senator Frank Church if the FBI ever found that King was a communist. Replied Adams, "No, we did not."[45]

Another example of an FBI vendetta against a nonexistent threat involved the SWP, a small, peaceful, and legal political group. This party became the target of FBI abuses because it supported Castro's Cuba and worked for racial integration in the South. For these transgressions, the FBI kept the SWP under surveillance for 34 years. FBI documents have revealed that, in one 6½-year period in the early 1960s, the agency burglarized the offices of the party in 94 raids, often with the complicity of the New York City Police Department. Over this period, FBI agents photographed 8,700 pages of party files and compiled dossiers totaling 8 million pages.[46] The FBI tried to destroy the party by sending anonymous letters to members' employers, by working to keep the party's candidates off the ballot, and by otherwise sabotaging political campaigns. Informants were also used to collect information about the political views of the organization.

Several points need to be made about these FBI activities. Obviously, they were a thorough waste of time and money. As one observer put it, "If they had devoted tens of thousands of man-hours to pursuing true criminals, say those involved in organized crime, they might have served the public interest as they were meant to."[47] Most important, the FBI's tactics not only were illegal but were directed at an organization that was working legally *within the system.*

> One legal organization, the Socialist Workers Party (SWP), ran candidates for office at various levels of government. The SWP was targeted by the FBI in an official secret memo. The FBI illegally burglarized the SWP's headquarters some 1,500 times in the1960s.[48]

Some justice was finally served when the SWP sued the FBI for violation of civil rights. This, too, was accomplished by working legally within the system.

Finally, it is important to recognize that the government's violation of the rights of its citizens was not just an aberration of the Nixon years. For instance, illegal wiretaps were commonplace during the Roosevelt and Truman years. Although bugging declined during the Eisenhower administration, it rose sharply during the Kennedy and Nixon presidencies. And under President Reagan, illegal wiretaps reached an all-time high.[49] This increase can be attributed in part to the Electronic Communication Privacy Act of 1986, which deleted from the federal wiretap law the need for authorization of government surveillance.

## Political Prisoners

In 1978, when he was ambassador to the United Nations, Andrew Young commented publicly that the United States was guilty, as were other nations, of having political prisoners. Young's accusation was widely denounced by politicians and editorial writers, many of whom saw such wild statements as reason enough for the ambassador's ouster. Andrew Young, however, was correct. Exactly what is meant by *political prisoner?* The key is that a political prisoner is prosecuted by the criminal justice system because of his or her political activities.[50] McConnell describes this concept:

> Socrates, Charles I and Patty Hearst, despite their widely varied times, circumstances and beliefs, shared the common characteristic that at a certain time in their lives they were placed on trial because of behavior found reprehensible by the political elite of their day, for activities thought highly prejudicial to the welfare of the state, and tried in legal proceedings from which a large political element and an inflamed public opinion could not be severed. And they were tried, moreover, by bodies seeking to foster official values or notions of public policy which the victims repudiated.[51]

Three factors are central to our distinction of political prisoners. First, political repression begins with the assumption that the law serves the interests of those with the power to make and enforce it. The law, therefore, is a tool by which the powerful retain their advantages. They do this by legally punishing those who threaten the status quo.

Second, although political criminals and other criminals may both pose a threat, the former are considered a direct threat to established political power.[52]

> If the members of a ruling elite believe a particular individual or group to be imminently hostile to the prevailing pattern of value distribution, and if they activate the criminal process against him (or them) for that reason, what results is a political trial. Additionally, if members of the ruling elite feel someone seriously intends to alter the way in which the government distributes those values, and if the elite activates the criminal process against them for that reason that, too, constitutes a political trial.[53]

Third, political criminals do not perceive themselves as animals but as people who have violated the law out of a set of convictions to create a better society. Thus, they see the system and its agents as the criminals and the enemy.

Of course, according to our view of political prisoners, acts such as assassination, treason, mutiny, and conspiracy to overthrow the government are examples of dissent by perpetrators who will be punished by the legal system. Throughout U.S. history, groups that were oppressed resorted to various illegitimate means to secure the rights and privileges that they believed were justly theirs. The revolutionary colonists used acts of civil disobedience and finally 8 years of war to accomplish their goals. Native Americans have fought the intrusions of White settlers and systematic suppression by the U.S. government. And other groups, such as farmers, slaveholders, WASP (White Anglo-Saxon Protestant) supremacists, ethnic and racial minorities, and laborers, have at times broken the law in efforts to change what they considered an unfair system. Although these are extremely important, we will concentrate here on the efforts by dissenters during the Vietnam War to change the government's course, as well as the governmental efforts to silence these critics.

The Vietnam War was never formally declared by Congress.[54] It escalated from presidential decisions and commitments that were camouflaged from the public. In effect, the United States had taken a side in an Asian civil war without the consent of the people. Even if this consent had been given, it would have been achieved through the manipulation of events and information by our leaders, as we know now. Because of the uniqueness of our involvement in this war, many young men refused to serve. Some became fugitives from the law by hiding in the United States or by fleeing to other countries. Others accepted imprisonment. Some 20,000 Americans of all ages refused to pay all or part of their taxes because the money would be used to support a war that they considered illegal, immoral, and unjust. As a result, they risked harassment by the Internal Revenue Service and possible imprisonment.

At one demonstration before the Oakland induction center in 1965, one David Miller set fire to his draft card, saying, "I believe the napalming of villages to be an immoral act. I hope this will be a significant political act, so here goes."[55] He was arrested and later sentenced to 2½ years in prison. This started a rash of similar protests that the establishment considered a threat to its power. At one rally, the Reverend Sloane Coffin, Dr. Benjamin Spock, and two others announced that they would henceforth counsel young men to refuse to serve in the armed forces as long as the Vietnam War continued. They were arrested for conspiracy, convicted, and sentenced to 2 years' imprisonment for treason.

One of the most infamous political trials of this era involved the Chicago Eight.[56] In 1968, a year of ghetto riots and the assassinations of Martin Luther King Jr. and Robert Kennedy, Congress passed the Rap Brown Amendment (Brown was chairperson of the Student Nonviolent Coordinating Committee [SNCC] at the time), which nearly outlawed interstate travel by political activists. In the summer of that year, the Democratic National Convention was held in Chicago. Because Hubert

Humphrey, a hawk on Vietnam, was the leading nominee, thousands of youths flooded Chicago, bent on protesting the war and venting their anger against what they perceived as an unresponsive political leadership. They protested and the police reacted violently, adding to the volatility of the situation.

Months later, when Richard Nixon took office and John Mitchell became attorney general, the federal government issued indictments against individuals believed to be the leaders of the Chicago riots: David Dellinger, Rennie Davis, Tom Hayden, Abbie Hoffman, Jerry Rubin, Lee Weiner, John Froines, and Bobby Seale, soon to be known collectively as the Chicago Eight. These persons were charged with conspiracy to cross state lines with intent to cause a riot (violating the Rap Brown law). Together, they represented various kinds of dissent, such as radical pacifism, the New Left, political hippies, academic dissent, and Black militancy. The case was heard in the U.S. district court in Chicago, Judge Julius Hoffman presiding.

Many knowledgeable observers, including former attorney general Ramsey Clark, felt that the trial was a political gesture by the new Nixon administration to demonstrate a no-nonsense policy against dissent. The conspiracy charge made little sense because the actions of the defendants and their constituencies were uncoordinated. Moreover, Bobby Seale, an alleged coconspirator, knew only one of the other defendants.

The Chicago Eight trial was a symbolic showcase for the defendants as well. Because of their disrespect for the system, the defendants refused to accept the traditional role.[57] Instead of allowing the system to keep them quiet while the long judicial process wound down, the defendants acted so that their actions would be headline news. Thus, they continually challenged the judiciary's legitimacy. Sternberg has characterized their rationale as follows:

> The argument that the court is illegitimate rests on the defendants' analysis and condemnation of the existing situation in the United States. They see themselves as political prisoners trapped by a power structure of laws created by societal groups hostile to their interests. The court is both an agent for these groups and institutions most significantly, monopoly, capitalism, racism, colonialism, the military-industrial complex, and incipient fascism, and also an oppressive power group in its own right. Although defendants may vary somewhat in the rank or order of their targets, all are in agreement that the criminal court's allegiances are squarely with the oppressor groups and directly hostile to the powerless classes in American society.[58]

As a result of their disrespectful behavior toward the court, Judge Hoffman found the defendants and their lawyers guilty of 159 contempt citations and sentenced them to jail for terms ranging from 68 days to 4 years and 13 days. In addition, each defendant was found guilty of inciting a riot, receiving a sentence of 5 years in prison and a $5,000 fine. However, all were acquitted of conspiracy. Before the sentences were passed, each defendant was allowed to make a final statement. The speech by Tom Hayden captured the essence of the problem from the perspective of the accused:

> Our intention in coming to Chicago was not to initiate a riot . . . it was to see to it that certain things, that is, the right of every human being, the right to assemble, the right to protest, can be carried out even where the Government chooses to suspend those rights. It was because we chose to exercise those rights in Chicago . . . that we are here today . . . We would hardly be notorious characters if they had left us alone in the streets of Chicago last year. . . . It would have been testimony to our failure as organizers. But instead we became the architects, the master minds, and the geniuses of a conspiracy to overthrow the government. We were invented. We were chosen by the government to serve as scapegoats for all that they wanted to prevent happening in the 1970's.[59]

Daniel Berrigan, himself a political prisoner, has discussed his concern for the direction of the government and the need for dissent.

> Indeed it cannot be thought that men and women like ourselves will continue, as though we were automated heroes, to rush for redress from the King of the Blind. The King will have to listen to other voices, over which neither he nor we will indefinitely have control: voices of public violence and chaos. For you cannot set up a court in the Kingdom of the Blind, to condemn those who see; a court presided over by those who would pluck out the eyes of men and call it rehabilitation.[60]

More recently, the sanctuary movement has raised the issue of political prisoners, highlighting the conflict between law and morality. This movement is composed of liberal religious groups that provide shelter, transportation, and other aid to illegal immigrants who have fled to the United States to escape tyranny in their native countries of El Salvador and Guatemala. The U.S. government prosecutes persons who aid these refugees because they disobey the law by harboring an illegal immigrant. These individuals argue that they are simply showing humanitarian concern for the suffering. Moreover, they argue, if they were providing shelter to those fleeing communist countries (e.g., Cuba or Nicaragua), the government would treat them as heroes. But because they give sanctuary to those fleeing governments that are friendly to the United States (but nonetheless repressive), they are treated as criminals. Hence, these individuals are political prisoners.

## Official Violence

We do not usually think of government actions as violent. Most often, violence is viewed as injury to persons or property. We make this distinction because the powerful, through the lawmaking process and control of communication, actually define what behavior is violent. In this section, we examine instances of what we have called *official violence*, including overt acts by the government and subtle ways that the system operates to do harm.

Consider, for example, the violence perpetrated against minorities throughout U.S. history according to official government policy. The government supported slavery. The government took land forcibly from the Native Americans and for a time had an official policy to exterminate them. During World War II, Japanese Americans were relocated in detention camps, causing them great losses of property and wealth. The law itself has helped to cause violence against minority groups. Amnesty International, in its study of the death penalty in the United States, concludes:

> There is strong evidence of racial discrimination in the application of the death penalty up to 1967, especially in the southern states. About two thirds of offenders executed there from 1930 to 1967 were black, although they constituted a minority of the population. In some individual states, an even higher proportion of those executed were black. The greatest disparities were in rape cases, in which the death penalty was imposed almost exclusively on blacks, usually in cases involving white victims—405 (or 89 percent) of the 455 prisoners executed for rape after 1930 were black.[61]

This is a historic problem. Former attorney general Ramsey Clark commented on this disparity in sentencing some 20 years ago: "There can be no rationalization or justification of such clear discrimination. It is outrageous public murder, illuminating our darkest racism."[62] The system also injures when reforms that would adequately house, clothe, feed, and provide medical attention are not instituted. Carmichael and Hamilton describe how this phenomenon does violence to minority members.

> When white terrorists bomb a black church and kill five black children, that is an act of individual racism, widely deplored by most segments of the society. But when in that same city, Birmingham, Alabama, five hundred black babies die each year because of the lack of proper food, shelter and medical facilities, and thousands more are destroyed and maimed physically, emotionally, and intellectually because of conditions of poverty and discrimination in the black community, that is a function of institutional racism.[63]

Of the many forms of official violence, we consider two in some detail: police brutality and the use of citizens as unknowing guinea pigs.

*Police Brutality.*    What is or is not classified as police brutality depends on one's placement in the hierarchy of power. An act is perceived as violent if it challenges existing arrangements. Thus, what a victimized group may perceive as police brutality is viewed by those in power as the legitimate enforcement of law and order.[64] Police are legally permitted to carry weapons and use them against citizens. This unique power results occasionally in citizens being killed by their law enforcement officers. Five times as many citizens as police are killed in these shoot-outs.[65] Also, the killings appear to be selective by the social characteristics of the victims. For example, research has shown that very few women are killed by police (0.8%), whereas a disproportionately large proportion of non-White males are killed (49.6% of all males killed).[66] Put another way, statistically, the number of shooting deaths of African Americans and Hispanic Americans by police is 10 to 13 times higher per 100,000 population than that of White Americans.[67] These data support the charge of police brutality that is so often heard from minority communities.

The use of deadly force by police varies greatly from community to community. For instance, data show that each year more than 2 persons per 100,000 die at the hands of the police in New Orleans, a rate nearly 27 times as high as that in Sacramento, California.[68]

Four of the most publicized instances of police brutality are (1) the Chicago police's treatment of civil rights demonstrators at the 1968 Democratic convention; (2) the Ohio National Guard's firing of 61 shots that killed four college students and wounded nine at Kent State University in 1970; (3) the killing of 43 inmates at Attica Prison in 1971; and (4) the 1991 beating of a Black motorist, Rodney King, by Los Angeles area law enforcement officers.

Let us examine the Attica incident. The Attica case is noteworthy because the revolt was a result in part of a raised consciousness among the prisoners that they were in jail for political reasons.[69] They tended to think of themselves as political prisoners and as victims rather than as criminals for two reasons:

1. As members of largely African American or Hispanic ghettos, they were acutely aware of the inequities of society.
2. They were especially aware of the ways the criminal justice system singled them out unfairly.

Many factors caused the inmates' rage, but one was particularly symbolic: the corrections staff did not include one African American or Puerto Rican American. The primary concern of the all-White staff from rural western New York State was that the inmates "knew their place." This typical attitude clashed with the inmates' view that they were victims rather than criminals, which resulted in a rising level of tension as inmates increasingly refused to adhere to the demands of the corrections officers.

Under these conditions, a spontaneous riot occurred after an incident, with 1,281 inmates eventually controlling four cellblocks and 40 hostages. Negotiations took place over a 4-day period, with the prisoners demanding 28 prison reforms and amnesty for the uprising. Governor Nelson Rockefeller was convinced that the revolt was led by revolutionaries, and he refused to negotiate. As he told the commission investigating the Attica incident:

> One of the most recent and widely used techniques of modern-day revolutionaries has been the taking of political hostages and using the threat to kill them as blackmail to achieve unconditional demands and to gain wide public attention to further their revolutionary ends. . . . [T]olerated, they pose a serious threat to the ability of free government to preserve order and to protect the

security of the individual citizens. Therefore, I firmly believe that a duly elected official sworn to defend the Constitution and the laws of the state and nation would be betraying his trust to the people he serves if he were to sanction or condone such criminal acts by negotiating under such circumstances.[70]

Thus came the decision to retake the prison by force. The time had come to reassert the sovereignty and power of the state over the rebels. A full-scale assault was launched, and in 15 minutes the state police had retaken the prison at a cost of 39 dead and 80 wounded, the bloodiest 1-day encounter between Americans since the Civil War, with the exception of the American Indian massacres of the late 19th century.

Although the charge of police brutality is often made, it is seldom punished. Few of the officers involved in fatal cases of brutality have ever been indicted for murder. Some have been suspended from the force, whereas others have been tried for lesser crimes (such as justifiable homicide or manslaughter) and then been acquitted or given light sentences.[71]

*The Use of Citizens as Guinea Pigs.* Nazi Germany is often cited as a horrible example of a government's disregard for human life. Among the Nazis' crimes was medical experimentation on human subjects. For example, Josef Mengele, the infamous Nazi doctor known as the "Angel of Death," conducted a variety of inhumane experiments using the Auschwitz inmates as subjects. Included in Mengele's so-called medical experiments were sewing together 3-year-old twins, back to back, and injecting dye into infants' eyeballs.

The United States has also used unwilling and unknowing subjects in potentially dangerous medical experiments. One case that clearly rivals Nazi Germany for its contempt for the human subjects was conducted by the U.S. Public Health Service. Beginning in 1932, doctors under the auspices of the Public Health Service began observing 400 African American male syphilis patients in Macon County, Alabama. The patients did not know they had syphilis; rather, they were told that they had "bad blood." The purpose of the study was to assess the consequences of not treating the disease. So during the 40 years of the experiment the men were not treated; their pain was not even alleviated. When the men's wives contracted syphilis, again, they were not treated. And when their children were born with congenital syphilis, they, too, were not treated. Likewise, in 2010, it was learned that from 1946 to 1948, U.S. Public Health Service doctors deliberately infected nearly 700 Guatemalans—prison inmates, mental patients and soldiers—with syphilis in order to test the reliability of penicillin. Prostitutes already infected were hired to sleep with prisoners. If the prostitutes' efforts in infecting the men failed, some prisoners were administered syphilis directly through wounds on their penises, faces, arms, or some sometimes via injection into the spine. The U.S. officially apologized on October 1, 2010. The President of Guatamala, called the tests crimes against humanity.[72]

Also consider this example: From 1946 to 1963, between 250,000 and 300,000 soldiers and civilians were exposed to radiation during 192 nuclear bomb tests. Among the tests conducted by the army was one that assessed the resultant psychological effects on soldiers who observed an atomic blast four times the size of the bomb dropped on Hiroshima from a distance of 2 miles. The army wanted to determine whether soldiers could perform battlefield assignments after being exposed to such an explosion. These exposed soldiers suffered severe, long-term negative effects from this experiment, yet the government has been unwilling to accept blame for the higher than usual incidence of leukemia and cancer. Instead, the government has tried to suppress scientific research findings linking low-level radiation exposure to medical problems. In addition, many of the medical records of the men exposed have mysteriously disappeared.[73] In August 1986, the Veterans Administration deliberately shredded thousands of case records of military personnel who had been exposed to nuclear radiation since the 1940s.[74]

Federal agencies also conducted radiation experiments on human subjects from the mid-1940s until the 1970s. The House Energy and Commerce Subcommittee on Energy Conservation and Power reviewed Department of Energy documents and concluded that U.S. citizens were tested as nuclear calibration devices to measure the biological effects of radioactive material. Some of the participants did so knowingly, but others were unaware of the purpose of the test. A number of experiments were cited in the report.[75]

- From 1963 to 1971, X-rays were applied to the testes of 131 inmates at Oregon and Washington state prisons.
- Between 1953 and 1957, 12 terminal brain tumor patients at Massachusetts General Hospital, most of them comatose or semicomatose, were injected with uranium.
- Radioactive iodine was deliberately released into groundwater seven times from 1963 to 1965 at the Atomic Energy Commission's National Reactor Testing Station in Idaho. Experiments that followed include having seven people drink milk from cows that had grazed on contaminated land and placing people in pastures during radiation release.
- In the early 1960s, 20 elderly adults were fed radium or thorium at the Massachusetts Institute of Technology.

In the late 1970s, declassification of government documents revealed that U.S. people had been subjects in 239 open-air bacteriological tests conducted by the army between 1949 and 1969. The objectives of these tests were to investigate the offensive possibilities of biological warfare, understand the magnitude of defensing against biological warfare, and gain data on the behavior of biological agents as they are borne downwind. During one of these tests, San Francisco was blanketed with poisonous bacteria known as *Serratia*, which cause a type of pneumonia that can be fatal. One hospital treated 12 persons for *Serratia* pneumonia, and one victim died.[76]

Finally, in 1994, the Department of Energy revealed that more than 50 separate experiments were done on unknowing subjects between the 1940s and the 1980s. These experiments involved exposure to radiation:

- Ninety-five previously secret nuclear bomb tests took place at a Nevada test site.
- Pregnant women scheduled for therapeutic abortions were injected with radioactive iodine 131 to test the effects of radiation on aborted fetuses.
- In 1946, six laboratory employees were given plutonium-contaminated water to drink to test plutonium absorption.
- As late as the 1980s, subjects were exposed to radioactive isotopes at government weapons laboratories. The extent of consent obtained has not been made public.
- To date the federal government has spent $3.7 million just to learn more about the extent of radiation testing on unknowing human subjects since 1945 and will probably spend a total of $24 million just to document searches on its own experiments.[77]

Another example of the exposure of Americans to potentially dangerous chemicals without their knowledge or consent was the behavioral-control experiments conducted by the government after World War II.[78] For 35 years, various government agencies used tens of thousands of individuals to test several mind-control techniques: hypnosis, electronic brain stimulation, aversive and other behavior-modification therapies, and drugs. Many of the subjects in these experiments were volunteers, but many others were not. Throughout U.S. history, one government agency in particular, the CIA, has proved its disregard for the rights of citizens in its quest for national security.

- Documents revealed in the 1950s under the Freedom of Information Act show that, during the height of the cold war, the CIA developed knock-out substances and incapacitating agents. The pool of subjects used to develop these compounds consisted of terminal cancer patients, who had no idea that they were being used as guinea pigs.[79]
- In 1953, a CIA scientist slipped LSD into the after-dinner drinks of scientists from the Army Chemical Corps. The drug had an especially adverse effect on one of these persons. He experienced psychotic confusion and 2 days later leaped to his death from a hotel window. The CIA withheld these facts from the victim's family for 22 years.[80]
- The CIA hired prostitutes in San Francisco to give their customers drugs. The behavior of the victims was then observed through two-way mirrors and heard through hidden microphones.
- The CIA administered LSD to borderline underworld "prostitutes, drug addicts, and other small timers who would be powerless to seek any sort of revenge if they ever found out what the CIA had done to them."[81]

Agents working on the project would randomly choose a victim at a bar or off the street and, with no prior consent or medical prescreening, would take the individual back to a safe house and administer the drug. For many of the unsuspecting victims, the result was days or even weeks of hospitalization and mental stress.[82]

- In 1996, it was learned that U.S. troops serving in the Persian Gulf in 1991 were exposed to ammunition composed of depleted uranium (DU). In one case, the 144th Army National Guard Service and Supply Company performed battlefield cleanup for 3 weeks, without protective clothing or knowledge of what they were handling. At least 40,000 DU rounds were fired by U.S. troops in Kuwait. DU is linked to many illnesses, including cancer, birth defects, and so-called Gulf War syndrome. For 6 years the Pentagon denied that U.S. troop exposure to DU and other dangerous chemicals in the Gulf was in any way related to Gulf War syndrome.[83] However, a 1997 investigation found that the CIA knew in the mid-1980s that Iraqi bunkers (attacked in the 1991 Gulf War by U.S. soldiers) contained stored chemical weapons. The CIA failed to warn military commanders clearly enough to avert possible exposure of U.S. troops. In June 1996, the Pentagon disclosed that several hundred soldiers, possibly even thousands, may have been exposed to sarin and other toxic agents because Iraqi weapons were blown up in a bunker at Khamisiyah. The Pentagon had denied for 5 years that any U.S. soldiers had been exposed. The Pentagon claimed that information about the Khamisiyah bunker had been lost.[84]

These examples demonstrate the arrogance of the CIA, a government agency that is willing to victimize some of its citizens to achieve an edge in its battle against U.S. enemies. Some would argue that this behavior, so contrary to life in a free society, is more characteristic of the enemy.

# International Crimes

Crimes by the government are not limited to those directed at its citizens. War is an obvious example of one government's willful attempt to harm citizens of another country. Other government acts short of war, including trade embargoes, arms sales, colonial arrangements, and the like, are also harmful to others. In this section, we discuss two other types of crimes perpetrated by the U.S. government against other nations: intervention in domestic affairs and war crimes.

## U.S. Intervention in the Domestic Affairs of Other Nations

How would the United States respond if foreigners assassinated the president? What if foreign agents tried to influence the outcome of an election? Or, what if a foreign power supported one side in a domestic dispute with money and weapons? Obviously, Americans would not tolerate these attempts by outsiders to affect U.S. domestic affairs. Such acts would be interpreted as imperialistic acts of war. The irony, of course, is that we have perpetrated and continue to perpetrate such acts on other countries as part of U.S. foreign policy.

The number of clandestine acts of intervention by the U.S. government is legion. Evidence from Senate investigating committees has shown, for example, that, over a 20-year period, one government agency, the CIA, was involved in more than 900 foreign interventions, including paramilitary operations, surreptitious manipulation of foreign governments, and assassinations.[85] We limit our discussion here to several well-known cases of CIA involvement in foreign assassinations. In 1975, the Senate Select Committee on Intelligence reported on the activities of the CIA over a 13-year period. The publication of this report occurred over the objections of President Gerald Ford and CIA director William Colby. The reason for their fears was obvious: the government was embarrassed for citizens to find out that the CIA was actively involved in assassination plots and coups against foreign governments.[86]

- Between 1960 and 1965, the CIA initiated at least eight plots to assassinate Fidel Castro, prime minister of Cuba. The unsuccessful attempts included applying instantly lethal botulinium toxin to a box of Castro's cigars, hiring the Mafia to poison him, and presenting him a gift of a wet suit (for skin diving) treated with a fungus.
- In 1975, the Senate Select Committee on Intelligence found strong evidence that CIA officials had planned the assassination of Congolese (Zaire) leader Patrice Lumumba and that President Eisenhower had ordered his death.
- The United States was implicated in the assassination of Dominican dictator Rafael Trujillo, South Vietnam's President Ngo Dinh Diem, and General Rene Schneider of Chile.
- In 1985, CIA director William Casey arranged for the assassination of Sheikh Mohammed Hussein Fadlallah, a Lebanese Shiite Muslim leader, in coordination with Saudi Arabian intelligence. During the assassination attempt in Beirut, 80 innocent people were killed when a car bomb exploded.[87]

The CIA's actions are contrary to U.S. principles in fundamental ways. Aside from supporting regimes notorious for their violation of human rights (see Chapter 5), the United States, which based its independence on the people's right to self-determination, is now actively involved in manipulating foreign governments to achieve its own will. The infusion of money in foreign elections, the use of propaganda, assassination attempts, and the like are all contrary to the guiding principle of the Monroe Doctrine, that is, self-determination of peoples, which we invoke readily when other nations intrude in the affairs of state in any Western Hemisphere nation.

## War Crimes

War crimes can be interpreted in three ways. According to the first view, crimes in war are illogical, war is hell, anything goes. The only crime, from this position, is to lose. A second view is that war crimes are acts for which the victors punish the losers. The winners denounce the atrocities committed by the enemy while justifying their own conduct. Thus, the Germans and Japanese were tried for war crimes at the conclusion of World War II, but the United States was not, even though it had used atomic bombs to destroy two cities and kill most of their inhabitants. For even if one assumes that the bombing of Hiroshima was necessary to bring an early end to the war (a debatable assumption), the bombing of Nagasaki 2 days later was clearly an unnecessary waste of life. A third view of war crimes is one that applies a standard of morality to war, applicable to winners and losers alike. The chief U.S. prosecutor at Nuremberg, Robert Jackson, summarizes this inter-pretation: "If certain acts in violation of treaties are crimes, they are crimes whether the United States does them or whether Germany does them, and we are not prepared to lay down a rule of criminal conduct against others which we would be unwilling to have invoked against us."[88]

We will use this last view in our examination of war crimes. And, in doing so, we will see that throughout history, nations, including the United States (examples include the oppression of Native Americans and the 1900 counterinsurgency campaign in the Philippines),[89] have been guilty of war crimes. Since the government, the media, and the schools traditionally remind us of the heinous acts of our enemies throughout history, we will focus on the war crimes perpetrated by the United States, limiting the discussion to the Vietnam experience. The principle we will apply is the definition of war crimes established by the Nuremberg tribunal (Principle VI, b):

> Violations of the laws or customs of war which include, but are not limited to, murder, ill-treatment or deportation to slave-labor or for any other purpose of civilian population of or in occupied territory, murder or ill-treatment of pris-oners of war or persons on the seas, killing of hostages, plunder of public or pri-vate property, wanton destruction of cities, towns, or villages, or devastation not justified by military necessity.[90]

The Vietnam War provides many examples of U.S. actions in clear vio-lation of this principle.

***Indiscriminate Shelling and Bombing of Civilians.***   The enemy in the Vietnam War, the National Liberation Front, was difficult to fight because it was everywhere. It was often impossible to distinguish allies from ene-mies. Thus, in strategic terms, the entire geographic area of Vietnam was the enemy. As Roebuck and Weeber have observed, "In order to 'save' Vietnam from Communism, it was therefore necessary to destroy the entire country."[91]

As a result, civilian villages were bombed in the enemy region of North Vietnam and in South Vietnam, as well. The amount of firepower used was unparalleled in history.

Perhaps the most significant (and certainly the most infamous) bomb used by the United States was napalm, a jellylike, inflammable mixture packed into canisters and dropped from aircraft. This mixture of benzene, gasoline, and polystyrene is a highly incendiary fluid that clings. It is an anti-personnel weapon that causes deep and persistent burning.

The most infamous incident of the war was the March 1968 massacre at Song My (also known as My Lai). Under orders from their superiors, U.S. soldiers slaughtered more than 500 civilians.[92] In Operation Cedar Falls, 30,000 U.S. troops were assigned the task of destroying all villages in a 40-square-mile area. In this and other operations, groups of soldiers known as "Zippo squads" burned village after village.

*Ecocide.*    The use of anticrop chemicals. The air force sprayed defoliants on 100,000 acres in 1964 and 1,500,000 acres in 1969. Herbicides were used to destroy foliage that hid the enemy, as well as the crops that fed the Vietcong soldiers and their civilian supporters, including the infamous toxic chemical Agent Orange. The results of this campaign were devastating in a number of ways.

The U.S. government has privatized many of the functions previously performed by the military. Firms have been retained to employ trained civilians to fill positions as inmate guards, police, and at many U.S. military bases, including those in Iraq, Afghanistan, and Cuba. These employees are governed by military law. Many of the recruits are former police officers, soldiers, and mercenaries who fought for repressive regimes in South Africa, Chile, and Yugoslavia. Some of these employees have been involved in prisoner abuse in the Abu Ghraib scandal, including assault and possible rape, as discussed in Chapter 5.

In 2000, Congress passed the Military Extraterritorial Jurisdiction Act (MEJA), which allows for the prosecution of civilian employees contracted with the Department of Defense and is limited to felonies committed overseas. Some employees responsible for prisoners' deaths, but hired by the CIA, are not subject to the MEJA law. Amnesty International is seeking accountability for private contractors at Abu Ghraib. It can be reached at http://takeaction.amnestyusa.org/action/index.asp?step=2&item=10897.[93]

- The U.S. Supreme Court ruled in 2006 that the military tribunals set up by the Bush administration to try detainees at Guantánamo Bay are unlawful under U.S. and international law.[94]

A 2007 report, "Ghost Prisoner: Two Years in Secret CIA Detention," contains a detailed description of a secret CIA prison from a Palestinian former detainee who was released from custody in 2006. President Bush claimed that the last 14 CIA prisoners were sent to Guantánamo, and none remain in CIA custody. But many other prisoners have been "disappeared" by the CIA. Their fates remain unknown, and Human Rights Watch worries that many of them have been transferred to secret CIA prisons where they may face torture. The 2007 report explains that these prisoners' treatment by the CIA constitutes enforced disappearance, a practice that is absolutely prohibited under international law.[95]

British and U.S. troops continue to use DU in Iraq. DU is very hard and is made into shells and armor-piercing bullets. It is also radioactive and contains a small amount of the isotope U-235; in 2001 a World Health Organization study linked it to cancer. Its remains are inhaled as dust or consumed in toxic food or water near sites where shells have landed. It enters the body and circulatory system, potentially threatening bone marrow, the lymph system, and the kidneys.[96]

Furthermore, one study estimates that as many as 500,000 innocent Iraqi civilians have been killed as a result of U.S. war and occupation. Estimates are that 80% of violent deaths were caused by the U.S. military and that most of the civilians killed were women and children. Iraqis are 58 times more likely to die a violent death than before the U.S. war. "The violence is deliberately encouraged by 'legal immunity' from prosecution enjoyed by 'trigger happy' U.S. soldiers and mercenaries trained to dehumanize Iraqi[s]. . . . In addition, tens of thousands of mercenaries, armed militias and death squads—armed and financed by U.S. forces—are terrorizing and murdering Iraqi civilians at an alarming rate. Tens of thousands of innocent Iraqis have been murdered in cold blood, including thousands of prominent Iraqi politicians, intellectuals, scientists and academics."[97]

## Conclusion

In this chapter, we have cataloged many overt and horrifying forms of political deviance. We also observed the ultimate irony: the United States, a country that takes pride in calling itself a free and open society, has sponsored repressive government organizations that, in the name of national security, operate to make society anything but free and open. Thus, it seems that to protect the national interest means to punish dissent and manipulate foreign governments. Somehow, the FBI, the CIA, and other such agencies have come to believe that it is necessary to break the law in order to protect the system. In so doing, their actions reap the very results that they wish to abolish. Supreme Court Justice Louis Brandeis has summarized this, saying, "For to break some laws in order to enforce other laws is not to fight anarchy and terrorism but to create them."[98] Harris concurs:

> In a government of laws, existence of the government will be imperiled if it fails to observe the law scrupulously. . . . Our government is the potent, the omnipresent teacher. For good or for ill, it teaches the whole people by

its example. Crime is contagious. If the government becomes a lawbreaker, it breeds contempt for the law; it invites every man to become a law unto himself; it invites anarchy. To declare that in the administration of the criminal law the end justifies the means, to declare that the government may commit crimes in order to secure the conviction of a private criminal would bring terrible retribution.[99]

## CRITICAL THINKING EXERCISE 7.1
### The CIA's Higher Immorality

This chapter is largely about the abuses committed by the CIA since its inception in 1947.[100] Among the abuses documented here are the following:

1. *Immorality of covert actions and a lack of oversight of covert operations.* CIA officials have failed to tell their own boss, the director of central intelligence (DCI), the truth. The DCI found that plans for covert action were rarely scrutinized formally and their approval was given informally. CIA misdeeds have been supported by Congress, which has neglected oversight responsibilities.
2. *Reckless excesses.* The CIA's past attempt to humiliate Castro "by trying to get his beard to fall off—is something that only someone whose level of maturity had not advanced beyond kindergarten could have dreamed up." The CIA "is also secretive—sometimes foolishly so. . . . Even newspaper clippings have been stamped 'secret.' "[101]
3. *Deviance by CIA agents.* One common form of fraud is when CIA personnel claim that they have paid a local agent and actually have kept the money for themselves.
4. *Corrupt personnel.* New recruits are sought for their character and loyalty, yet recruits are asked to spend their lives in false identities.
5. *Perversion of democratic principles.* The CIA has sabotaged the democratic processes of other countries, sometimes by overthrowing legally and democratically elected leaders, sometimes by outright assassination, including (at times) hiring organized crime figures to engage in such work.
6. *Illegal domestic spying.* The CIA has opened the mail of U.S. citizens going to or coming from communist nations.
7. *Experimenting with LSD without subjects' consent.* Such experiments resulted in at least one suicide.
8. *Illegal investigative methods.* Wiretapping the telephones of newsmen to learn about their sources and conducting illegal break-ins and installing wiretaps while investigating CIA employees have been carried out.
9. *Laundering of money.* The CIA has laundered its money at the Nugan Hand Bank, the Bank of Credit and Commerce International (BCCI), and various S&Ls, sometimes in cooperation with organized crime (see Chapter 2).

Are these deviant practices something that is merely an outgrowth of cold war necessities, or are they built into the structure of the CIA and its organizational culture? To answer this question, go to Infotrack II or another online data-based site and read stories about the CIA's scandals since the cold war's end (1989).[102] Does the CIA continue to suffer scandals like those mentioned above? If so, do the scandals in question fit into any of the above categories? Are there any deviant acts committed by the CIA since 1990 that do not fall into these categories? What do you think is causing the CIA's deviance in the post–cold war era?

## ENDNOTES

1.  The following discussion is based on Simon, D. R., & Hagan, F. (1999). *White collar deviance* (pp. 50ff). Boston: Allyn & Bacon. See also Kessler, R. (1996). *Inside the White House* (p. 164). New York: Bantam.

2.  Balz, D. (February 1, 1998). The story so far in week two: A survival strategy emerges. *Washington Post*, A-1.

3.  Ross, S. (1988). *Fall from grace* (pp. 3–43). New York: Ballantine. http://en.wikipedia.org/wiki/Political_scandals_of_the_United_States (27 Oct., 2010).

4.  Kessler. *Inside the White House* (p. 2).

5.  Hersh, S. (1997). *The dark side of Camelot*. New York: Random House.

6.  Ross. *Fall from grace* (pp. 40ff).

7.  Kessler (p. 1).

8.  Ross (pp. 191–214), and *Sex Scandal* http://en.wikipedia.org/wiki/sex-scandal (September 6, 2007) are the sources for the following discussion.

9.  Ross (p. 261).

10.  Carman, J. (February 4, 1998). Media can't help chasing the story. *San Francisco Chronicle*, A-1, A-11.

11.  Gross, M. (1996). *The political racket: Deceit, self-interest and corruption in American politics* (pp. 190–193). New York: Ballantine.

12.  Kessler (Chapter 1).

13.  Gross. *The political racket* (p. 14); Kessler (pp. 7–8).

14.  Kessler, R. (1996). *Inside the White House.* (p. 164). New York: Bantam.

15.  For other sources emphasizing government deviance, consult the following: Roebuck, J., & Weeber, S. C. (1978). *Political crime in the United States: Analyzing crime by and against government.* New York: Praeger; Wolfe, A. (1978). *The seamy side of democracy: Repression in America* (2nd ed.). New York: Longman; Wise, D. (1978). *The American police state: The government against the people.* New York: Vintage; Reasons, C. E. (1974). *The criminologist: Crime and the criminal.* Pacific Palisades, CA: Goodyear; Etzioni, A. (1984). *Capital corruption.* New York: Harcourt, Brace, Jovanovich; Coleman, J. W. (1993). *The criminal elite* (3rd ed.). New York: St. Martin's Press; and Parenti, M. (1989). *The sword and the dollar: Imperialism, revolution, and the arms race.* New York: St. Martin's Press.

16.  The discussion here is limited to the federal government, especially the executive branch. However, attempts to deceive the public are found at all levels of government. For examples of cover-ups, secrecy, and the like at other levels, see Hersh, S. M. (1972). *Cover-up.* New York: Random House; Manning, P. K. (1974). The police: Mandate, strategies, and appearances. In Richard Quinney (ed.). *Criminal justice in America: A critical understanding* (pp. 170–200). Boston: Little, Brown; Royko, M. (1971). *Boss: Richard J. Daley of Chicago.* New York: E. P. Dutton; and Henderson, J., & Simon, D. R. (1994). *Crimes of the criminal justice system.* Cincinnati, OH: Anderson.

17.  Dorsen, N., & Shattuck, J. H. F. (1974). Executive privilege: The president won't tell. In N. Dorsen & S. Gillers (Eds.). *None of your business: Government secrecy in America* (pp. 27–60). New York: Viking.

18.  Cited in McCloskey, Jr., P. N. (1972). *Truth and untruth: Political deceit in America* (p. 54). New York: Simon & Schuster.

19.  McCloskey, P.N., Jr. (1972). Truth and Untruth: *Political Deceit in America.* (p. 54) New York: Simon & Schuster.

20.  Parenti, M. (1980). *Democracy for the few* (3rd ed., p. 157). New York: St. Martin's Press.

21.  Lewis, A. (1974). Introduction. In N. Dorsen & S. Gillers (Eds.). *None of your business: Government secrecy in America* (pp. 3–24). New York: Viking.

22.  The examples in this section are taken from Wise, D. (1973). *The politics of lying: Government deception, secrecy, and power.* New York: Random House Vintage Books.

23.  See also "The 'Phantom Battle' That Led to War. *U.S. News & World Report,* July 23, 1984, 56–67.

24.  Schneir, W., & Schneir, M. (May 12, 1984). How the military cooked the books. *Nation,* 570–576.

25.  Corn, D. (August 27, 1988). The same old dirty tricks. *Nation,* 158.

26.  The following examples are taken from Walcott, J., & Duffy, B. (July 4, 1994). The CIA's darkest secrets. *U.S. News & World Report,* 34–47. That a conservative magazine such as this one blew the whistle on the CIA is a good indication that the agency has finally fallen into the disrepute its critics have warned of for the last 50 years.

27.  Emerson, T. L. (March 30, 1974). The danger of state secrecy. *Nation,* 395–399. See also Miller, A. S. (December 1973). Watergate and beyond: The issue of secrecy. *Progressive,* 37, 15–19.

28.  Galnoor, I. (May/June 1979). The politics of public information. *Society,* 16, 20–30.

29.  Wise, D. (1978). The American Police State: *The Government against the People.* New York: Vintage

30.  Webb, G. (August 18, 1996). America's 'Crack' Plague Has Roots in Nicaragua War. *San Jose Mercury News,* A-1.

31.  See *Nation,* October 21, 1996, 4.

32.  Kornbluh, P. (November 18, 1996). Special to the *Baltimore Sun.*

33.  Phillips, P., & Project Censored (2001). *Censored 2000: The year's top 25 censored stories* (p. 108). New York: Seven Stories.

34.  See Simon, D. R. (with Joel Henderson). (1997). *Private troubles and public issues: Social problems in the postmodern era* (pp. 15–16). Houston, TX: Harcourt Brace.

35.  For a history of the government's monitoring of its citizens, see Wolfe, A. (December 1971). Political repression and the liberal democratic state. *Monthly Review,*23, 18–38; Davis, D. B. (1972). Internal security in historical perspective: From the revolution to World War II. In R. H. Blum (ed.). *Surveillance and espionage in a free society* (pp. 3–19). New York: Praeger; "It's official: Government snooping has been going on for 50 years," Intelligence Activities and the Rights of Americans: *Book 11,* Report 94–755, 1,120. In Ermann, M. D., & Lundman, R. J. (Eds.) April 26, 1976. *Corporate and governmental deviance* (pp. 151–173). New York: Oxford University Press, 1978.

36.  This brief history of the FBI is taken from Harris, R. (August 8, 1977). Crime in the FBI. *New Yorker,* 30–42.

37.  Young, T. R. (September 1981). *Political surveillance, inequality and the democratic state* (p. 1). Red Feather, CO: Red Feather Institute.

38.  Project minaret. *Newsweek,* November 10, 1975, 31–32.

39.  U.S. Senate, Select Committee to Study Governmental Operations with Respect to Intelligence Activities, Intelligence Activities, *Book 11,* 156. See also "Who's chipping away at your privacy?" *U.S. News & World Report,* March 31, 1975, 18.

40.  "The FBI's 'black-bag boys.' " *Newsweek,* July 28, 1975, 18, 21.

41.  See "G-Men at it again." *Progressive,* 52, March 1988, 9; "Events the FBI watched." *First Principles,*13, February/March 1988, 3; and Shenon, P. (January 28, 1988). FBI papers show wide surveillance of Reagan critics. *New York Times,* A-1, A-8.

42.  The following account is taken from several sources: Halperin, M. H., et al. (1976). *The lawless state: The crimes of the U.S. intelligence agencies* (pp. 61–89). New York: Penguin; The truth about Hoover, *Time*, December 22, 1975, 14–21; and Tales of the FBI and The crusade to topple King, *Time*, December 1, 1975, 11–12.

43.  U.S. Senate, Final Report of the Select Committee to Study Governmental Operations with Respect to Intelligence Activities. (1976). Dr. Martin Luther King, Jr., case study. In *Intelligence activities and the rights of Americans: Book 111* (pp. 107–98). Washington, DC: Government Printing Office (cited in Halperin et al., 78).

44.  Morton H. Halperin et al., The Lawless State: The Crimes of the U.S. Intelligence Agencies (New York: Penguin, 1976), 61–89

45.  Quoted in The crusade to topple King. (p. 11).

46.  The evidence presented on the FBI's campaign against the SWP is taken from Harris; Associated Press release, March 29, 1976; and Monitoring repression. *Progressive, 41*, January 1977, 7.

47.  Harris (p. 40).

48.  Harris, R. (August 8, 1977). *Crime in the FBI.* (pp. 30–42). New Yorker.

49.  Ostrow, R. J. (December 18, 1983). Electronic surveillance hits new highs in war on crime. *Los Angeles Times*, 1–4.

50.  Goodell, C. (1973). *Political prisoners in America* (pp. 3–13). New York: Random House.

51.  McConnell, W. H. (1978). Political trials East and West. In C. E. Reasons & R. M. Rich (Eds.). *The sociology of law: A conflict perspective* (p. 333). Toronto: Butterworth.

52.  We will consider political crimes only in the narrow sense of crimes against the establishment. We are sympathetic, however, with the view expressed by Alexander Liazos: "Only now are we beginning to realize that most prisoners are political prisoners—that their criminal actions (whether against individuals, such as robbing, or conscious political acts against the state) result largely from current social and political conditions, and not the work of 'disturbed' and 'psychotic' personalities" (p. 108).
In this view, then, all prisoners are political in the sense that they became criminals as a result of struggling against the inequities of society. See Liazos, A. (Summer 1972). The poverty of the sociology of deviance: Nuts, sluts, and perverts. *Social Problems, 20*.

53.  Becker, T. (ed.). (1971). *Political trials* (pp. xi–xii). Indianapolis, IN: Bobbs-Merrill.

54.  Much of this account is based on Goodell (pp. 126–159).

55.  Quoted in ibid (p. 130).

56.  The following account is based primarily on Danelski, D. J. (1971). The Chicago conspiracy trial. In T. Becker (ed.). *Political trials* (pp. 134–35). Indianapolis, IN: Bobbs-Merrill. We have used this case as representative of many others from the same time period. For other illustrations of the existence of political trials and political prisoners, see the following trial accounts: for the vendetta against the Panthers, B., & Hayden, T. (1970). *Trial*. New York: Holt, Rinehart and Winston; the trials of the Berrigans, Berrigan, D. (1970). *The trial of the Catonsville nine*. Boston: Beacon Press; and the trial of the Wilmington 10, Anderson, J. (December 11, 1978). U.S. is cited for human rights violations. *Rocky Mountain News, 61*. For general statements on political criminals, see Frutig, J. (August 27, 1976). Political trials: What impact on America? *Christian Science Monitor*, 16–17; Goodell; and Becker.

57.  See Sternberg, D. (1974). The new radical-criminal trials: A step toward a class-for-itself in the American proletariat?" cited in Quinney (pp. 274–294).

58.  Ibid.

59.  Danelski, D.J. (1971). The Chicago conspiracy trial. In T. Becker (ed.). *Political Trials* (pp. 134–35). Indianapolis, IN: Bobbs-Merrill.

60.  Berrigan, D. (1970). The Trial of the Catonsville Nine. Boston: Beacon Press.

61.  Amnesty International. (1987). *United States of America: The death penalty* (pp. 10–11). London: Amnesty International Publications.

62.  Clark, R. (1970). *Crime in America: Observations on its nature, causes, prevention and control* (p. 335). New York: Simon & Schuster.

63.  Carmichael, S., & Hamilton, C. V. (1967). *Black power: The politics of liberation in America* (p. 4). New York: Random House.

64. See Skolnick, J. (1969). *The politics of protest* (pp. 3–8). New York: Ballantine Books.

65. Kobler, A. L. (Winter 1975). Police homicide in a democracy. *Journal of Social Issues, 31,* 163–184.

66. U.S. Public Health Service data, quoted in ibid (p. 164).

67. Takagi, P. T. (August 27, 1979). Abuse of authority is a very explosive situation. *U.S. News & World Report,* 29.

68. Reported in Wiessler, D. A. (January 10, 1983). When police officers use deadly force. *U.S. News & World Report,* 59.

69. The following is taken from the New York State Special Commission on Attica. (1972). *Attica: The official report.* New York: Bantam, excerpted in Douglas, J. D., & Johnson, J. M. (Eds.). (1977). *Official deviance* (pp. 186–194). Philadelphia: Lippincott.

70. The following is taken from the New York State Special Commission on Attica, Attica: The Official Report (New York: Bantam, 1972), excerpted in Official Deviance, ed. Jack D. Douglas and John M. Johnson (Philadelphia: Lippincott, 1977), 186–94.

71. Parenti, M. (1983). *Democracy for the few* (4th ed., p. 154). New York: St. Martin's Press.

72. Jones, J. H. (1981). *Bad blood.* New York: Free Press and http://www.talkleft.com/story/2010/10/1/23130/2580

73. Rosenberg, H. L. (June 1976). The guinea pigs at camp desert rock. *Progressive, 40,* 37–43.

74. Project censored. *Editor and Publisher, 120,* June 13, 1987, 20.

75. Reported in Lawrence, J. (October 25, 1986). Americans served as guinea pigs for radiation testing. *Fort Collins Coloradoan,* A-10.

76. Cousins, N. (November 10, 1979). How the U.S. used its citizens as guinea pigs. *Saturday Review,* 10. See also United Press International release, December 4, 1979.

77. See *San Francisco Chronicle,* June 28, 1994, A-4; and *New York Times,* June 28, 1994, A-6.

78. See Bowart, W. H. (1978). *Operation mind control: Our government's war against its own people.* New York: Dell; and Marks, J. (February 3, 1979). Sex, drugs, and the CIA. *Saturday Review,* 12–16.

79. Lee, M. A. (June 5, 1982). CIA: Carcinogen. *Nation,* 675.

80. Bowart (pp. 87–91).

81. Marks (pp. 12–16).

82. Halperin, M.H., et al. (1976). The Lawless State: *The Crimes of the U.S. Intelligence Agencies.* (pp. 61–89). New York: Penguin.

83. Messler, B. (May 26, 1997). Pentagon poison: The great radioactive cover-up. *In These Times,* 17; and Phillips, P., & Project Censored. (1997). *Project censored, 1997* (pp. 47–51). New York: Seven Stories.

84. Pine, A. (April 10, 1997). CIA knew of chemical weapons in Iraq bunker military. *Los Angeles Times,* A-1.

85. Roebuck, & Weeber (p. 82).

86. The following list is taken from "CIA murder plots weighing the damage to U.S." *U.S. News & World Report,* December 1, 1975, 13–15; and "The CIA's hit list." *Newsweek,* December 1, 1975, 28–32.

87. Johnson, H. (September 26, 1987). Casey circumvented the CIA in '85 assassination attempt. *Washington Post,* A-1. For other examples, see Corn, D. (August 27, 1988). The same old dirty tricks. *Nation,* 158.

88. Quoted in Knoll, E., & McFadden, J. N. (Eds.). (1970). *War crimes and the American conscience* (p. 1). New York: Holt, Rinehart and Winston.

89. For information regarding U.S. treatment of Native Americans, see Johansen, B., & Maestas, R. (1979). *Wasi'chu: The continuing Indian wars.* New York: Monthly Review Press; and Brown, D. (1972). *Bury my heart at wounded knee: An Indian history of the American west.* New York: Bantam. For information regarding U.S. involvement in the Philippines, see Miller, S. C. (September 1970). Our My Lai of 1900: Americans in the Philippine insurrection. *Trans-action, 7,* 19–28; and Taylor, T. (1971). *Nuremberg and Vietnam: An American tragedy* (pp. 173–174). New York: Bantam.

90. Cited in Knoll, & McFadden (p. 193). See also Mallison, W. T. (1972). Political crimes in the international law of war: Concepts and consequences. In F. Adler & G. O. W. Mueller (Eds.). *Crime and the international scene: An inter-American focus*. (pp. 96–107). San Juan, Puerto Rico: North-South Center Press.

91. Roebuck & Weeber (p. 70).

92. See Taylor (pp. 122–153); and Falk, R. A. (January 1970). Song My: War crimes and individual responsibility. *Trans-action*, 33–40.

93. Chatterjee, P. (March 7, 2005). Intelligence, Inc. *Project Censored*, http://www.projectcensored.org/censored_2006/www.corpwatch.org and May 11, 2004.

94. Dworkin, A. (June 30, 2006). Supreme court overturns Guantanamo military tribunals. *Crimes of War Project*, http://www.crimesofwar.org/onnews/news-commissions3.html.

95. ———. (February 27, 2007). U.S. Secret CIA prisoners still missing. *Human Rights Watch*, http://hrw.org/english/docs/2007/02/26/usint15408.htm

96. *BBC News*, http://news.bbc.co.uk/2/hi/middle_east/6105726.stm (November 1, 2006).

97. Hassan, G. (June 18, 2006). False Jubilation in Iraq. *Global Reach*, http://www.globalresearch.ca/index.php?context=viewArticle&code=HAS20060618&articleId=2667

98. Harris (p. 35).

99. Harris, R. (August 8, 1977). Crime in the FBI. (pp. 30-42). New Yorker.

100. Weiner, Tim (2007) *Legacy of Ashes* (New York: Doubleday).

101. Kessler, R. (1992). *Inside the CIA*. New York: Simon & Schuster.

102. See, for example, Baker, R. W. (September 10, 1991). CIA: Out of control. *Village Voice*, for one analysis of the CIA's recent abuses.

# 8 Understanding Elite Deviance

## Why Elite Deviance?

Those reading the previous chapters of this book, as well as the next chapter and epilogue, usually realize the seriousness of the problems related to elite deviance and white-collar crime. The myths attached to these types of wrongdoing are in and of themselves great harms to our nation and the global society as a whole. Busting through the myths is a first step in understanding the true nature of America's crime and deviance problems.

**Myth:** Common criminals ("street criminals") kill and injure more people than white-collar crooks.

**Fact:** The FBI estimates that the losses from "street crime" are around $16.6 billion per year, whereas the losses from economic crime may be as high as $3 trillion.[1]

**Myth:** Ordinary criminals kill and injure more people than elite criminals.

**Fact:** The FBI estimates that there are 11,000 gun-related murders each year in the United States. Conservative estimates are that 55,000 workers die each year from injuries or illnesses caused by dangerous working conditions. Another 30,000 die from unsafe products, and environmental toxins kill another 20,000 citizens.

**Myth:** The public is apathetic about elite crime and defines the crime problem as involving only ordinary crime.

**Fact:** Every study and public opinion poll done on the subject reveals that the public regards elite crime as serious, lightly punished, and very costly to American society. Likewise, as will be explained, ordinary crime and crimes by elites do not exist in vacuums. Numerous interrelationships between the two contribute to the formation of the overall crime problems that America faces.[2] Finally, deviance by elites creates measurable distrust in both the economic and the political system that manifests itself in a variety of ways, as we shall now examine.

Aside from the exposure of myths, the facts above are also important for another reason. The problem that runs through these examples has many names: "social breakdown,"[3] "social disintegration," the rise of "the morally loose individual,"[4] instrumental and expressive "wilding," and the "ethical crisis of Western civilization."[5] Whatever one chooses to call it, the problem of moral decline is a major cause of elite deviance as well as many other types of deviant behavior.

## Elite Deviance and the Sociological Imagination: A Paradigm for Analysis[6]

We began our discussion of elite deviance with a look at the power structure of American society. The power elite model was developed by C. Wright Mills in the 1950s.[7] As our examination reveals, a great deal of evidence exists to support this notion of interrelated corporate, media, political, and military elites. Further, in Chapter 2, we explored the existence of the so-called higher immorality, that set of deviant practices that Mills claimed goes on in elite circles. Again, our examination demonstrated case after case of the higher immorality that has taken place since Mills wrote in the 1950s. We have also noted how the nature of the higher immorality has changed, with scandal now an institutionalized phenomenon within the executive office of the president, Congress, and the national security state's intelligence apparatus. What remains is to account for the theoretical causes of elite deviance.

Again, we turn to one of Mills's conceptions, the sociological imagination.[8] The sociological imagination is a paradigm, a model for looking at social reality, in this case social problems such as elite deviance. Paradigmatic models can be used to develop a number of scientific theories. "What is important," Mills notes, "is the fact that neither the correctness nor the inaccuracy of any of the specific theories necessarily confirms or upsets the usefulness or the adequacy of the models. The models can be used for the construction of many theories."[9]

Thus, in this chapter we will first lay out the paradigm for constructing a theory of elite deviance and then proceed to make various theoretical statements derived from the model.

The paradigm raises questions regarding three levels of social analysis. These include the following:

1. *The macro level of analysis.* Here we explain how the institutional structures and the cultural values of a given society contribute to elite deviance.
2. *The immediate milieus.* Here we must explain how the immediate environment of everyday life, especially the structure and characteristics of the bureaucratic organizations in which people work, contribute to the planning and commission of acts of elite deviance.
3. *The individual level.* Here we must explain how individual personality characteristics of elites and those in their employ figure in the planning and commission of acts of elite deviance. Specifically, how do issues of character structure and alienation contribute to the commission of elite deviance?

We begin with an analysis of macro-level concerns, specifically values and institutional structures.

## Elite Deviance and American Values: The American Dream

Messner and Rosenfeld[10] argue that the causes of crime lie within the same values and behaviors that are usually viewed as part of the American version of success. The American Dream is defined as a "broad cultural ethos that entails a commitment to the goal of material success, to be pursued by everyone in society, under conditions of open individual competition." The power of the American Dream comes from the widely shared values that it includes

1. *An achievement orientation:* This includes pressure to "make something" of oneself, to set goals and achieve them. Achieving material success is one way personal worth is measured in America.[11] Although this is a shaky basis for self-esteem, it is nevertheless true that Americans view their personal worth much like a stock, one that rises or falls with the realization of moneymaking.
2. *Individualism:* This refers to the notion that Americans possess not only autonomy but also basic individual rights. Americans make individualistic decisions regarding marriage and career choices, religion, political outlook, and probably thousands of other issues. The result is that individualism and achievement combine to produce anomie because fellow Americans often become rivals and competitors for rewards and status. Intense personal competition increases pressure to succeed. Often this means that rules about the means by which success is obtained are disregarded when they threaten to interfere with personal goals.
3. *Universalism:* This includes the idea that the American Dream is open to all. Universalism means that the chances of success and failure are possibilities that are open to everyone. Fear of failure is intense in America and increases pressure to abandon conformity to rules governing proper conduct in favor of expedience.
4. *The "fetishism" of money:* Money has attained an almost sacred quality in American life. It is the way Americans keep score in the game of success, and, as noted, there are no rules that tell us when enough is enough. What is stressed in the American Dream is ends over means. As Elliott Currie[12] notes in his discussion of a market society, the pursuit of private gain has become the organizing principle for all of social life. Charles Derber[13] argues that, during the Reagan–Bush era, increasing inequality, along with an ethic of "greed is good," combined to give the American character an element of narcissism. Narcissism is a personality disorder, a mental illness, characterized by distorted

self-love and, most important, selfishness coupled with a lack of guilt. The Reagan–Bush ideology of self-reliance stimulated large numbers of upper-world crooks to engage in a quest for power, status, and attention in a "money culture." The result was an unrestrained quest for personal gain.

Sociologist Robert Merton pointed out more than a half century ago that the great contradiction of American culture concerned its stress on winning and success but a lack of opportunity to achieve such success. A portion of this contradiction is due to what sociologist Emile Durkheim[14] described as *anomie*, a social situation in which norms are unclear. Success in America has no official limits; the private accumulation of wealth is without "a final stopping point."[15] No matter what their income level, most Americans want about 50% more money (which, of course, becomes 50% more once it is achieved).

Achieving success via force and fraud has always been considered smart, so smart that for a number of decades our culture has lionized gangsters. Beginning with Al Capone, we have come to admire Mafia dons who do not hesitate to take shortcuts to success. Thus, *People Magazine*'s 1989 cover story on Gambino family godfather John Gotti pictured the don as so tough that he could punch his way through a cement block. A multimillionaire, with plenty of charisma, *People* noted, Gotti is also a loyal family man, who has never cheated on his wife. The fact that he personally has murdered a number of rivals is talked of as largely an occupational requirement.

Merton[16] also noted that crime "is a very common phenomenon" among all social classes in the United States. A study of 1,700 middle-class New Yorkers in 1947 indicated that 99% of them admitted to committing crimes violating one of New York's 49 criminal offenses, for which they could have been imprisoned for at least a year. Moreover, 64% of the men and 29% of the women reported committing felonies. A 1991 survey by Patterson and Kim also showed a high percentage of Americans engaging in criminal behavior (summarized in Chapter 1). Thus, one of the myths about crime is that America is divided into two populations, one law-abiding and the other criminal.

Social critic James Adams,[17] who coined the term the *American Dream*, once remarked that many people coming to America's shores were relatively law-abiding before they arrived here. People "were made lawless by America, rather than America being made lawless by them." It has been American elites who have served as role models (examples) to ordinary people. Thus, elite deviance provides an excuse for nonelites to engage in crime without feeling guilty. Elite deviance also sends the message that it is stupid not to commit crime if one has the opportunity. Many a drug dealer and street gang member have remarked that they are just doing what the Rockefellers, Carnegies, and other robber barons did in the 19th century—establishing monopolies.

Aside from the values associated with the American Dream, elite deviance is also related to the social structure of American society.

## Social Structure: The Dominance of Elite Institutions

The *structure* of American society is that of a mass society. A *mass society* is characterized by a capitalistic economy dominated by huge multinational corporations. Corporate elites (owners and managers) frequently take temporary positions in government and its military establishment. In the United States, the economic institution has always taken precedence over other institutions in American life. This has immense implications for the nature of America's social problems.

America is the only nation in the history of the world whose founding creed involved the inalienable right to pursue happiness. The American concept of happiness has always involved the unlimited accumulation of profit and property, and the goal of making money has been widely accepted as the definition of happiness and success, a central feature of what is called the American Dream.

So important has the goal of accumulating wealth, of achieving the American Dream, become that profit in America has frequently taken place without the restraints placed on capitalist economies in other nations. In the United States, attempts to regulate the excesses of business have been criticized as government interference, or "socialism."

Second, other institutions in American life have had to accommodate the needs of business. Thus, most people go to college not because they are fascinated by learning but because it leads to a middle-class occupation afterward. America has always been the most anti-intellectual nation in the Western world—precisely because its primary definition of success involved making money. Thus, colleges and universities offer evening and weekend programs, many of them in business, because people's jobs take precedence over the needs of educational and other institutions. The requirements of work also take precedence over the needs of family life. The United States remains the only advanced industrial democracy without paid family leave, without national health care, without an extended family vacation policy precisely because the needs of business are given precedence over everything else in the American institutional order. Moreover, despite all the political rhetoric about the importance of the American family, it is nearly impossible to support a family in this country if parents are unemployed.

Government, too, has historically been subservient to the needs of business. Now that the government is a central part of the economy, the primary responsibility of modern government is not to provide for the needs of its citizens but to ensure economic growth. Much of American foreign and defense policies are about protecting the holdings of multinational corporations, not ensuring that human rights and democracy are encouraged in other nations. As discussed in Chapter 5, the United States has a long history of supporting oppressive regimes that are friendly to American business interests. Moreover, American government at all levels grants generous subsidies, tax breaks, loans, and loan guarantees as well as government contracts to American businesses in the hope of stimulating economic growth. This is one reason that the American federal government has spent more than $4 trillion on defense since 1947, much of it on expensive weapons systems. For all these reasons it is now more appropriate to speak of a political economy in which political and economic activities have become interrelated in a myriad of ways.

Likewise, elite deviance often requires the explicit coordination of a number of bureaucratic institutions in order to be planned and executed yet remain undetected and unpunished. Thus, in the I. G. Farben case the Nazi government participated in selling slave labor to a chemical firm for the purpose of building synthetic chemical plants. Similarly, throughout this book, we have cited numerous additional examples, illustrating how elite deviance involved interorganizational cooperation.

- For years, government and business groups have employed organized crime to perform illegal and unethical acts. In the early 1960s, the Central Intelligence Agency (CIA) hired Mafia members to assassinate Fidel Castro. Mafia-generated drug money is routinely laundered through banks in Miami, often with the bankers' full knowledge.[18]
- In Chapter 5, we described the cozy relationship between Pentagon employees and defense industry consultants. Promises of positions in the defense industry for retiring Pentagon employees sometimes resulted in providing insider information to defense contractors.
- In Chapter 2, we described further episodes of Mafia–CIA ties in money laundering through a variety of savings and loans. In Chapter 7, we noted the possible ties between CIA and Mafia personnel in the execution and cover-up of the assassination of President John F. Kennedy. In Chapter 9, we explore more fully the implications and history of this so-called secret government.[19]

These examples show that elite deviance often involves links between business, government, and, at times, other institutions, such as organized crime syndicates. And because of these interorganizational ties, elite deviance has a great chance of going undetected and unpunished (or at least lightly punished). As we have discussed, economic elites regularly participate in political processes involving candidate selection, monetary contributions to candidates and parties, and lobbying. This means that elites have great influence over the content and character of the law. As a result, many acts that might otherwise become crimes are prevented from becoming illegal in the first place. Thus, Hoffman–LaRoche, a drug company, successfully kept amphetamines out of federal control by paying a Washington law firm three times the amount of the annual budget of the Senate subcommittee seeking legislation for tighter controls. Moreover, when elite deviance is made illegal, it is often treated quite differently from nonelite deviance. For instance, a number of the environmental protection laws require corporations to monitor the pollution levels at their own factories. Other laws only address breaking regulations per se, and what happens as a result of the infraction is ignored. For example, in England, a company was found to be responsible for an accident that resulted in the deaths of five workers. The firm was prosecuted for not properly maintaining or inspecting the equipment; it was not charged with the deaths of the workers. Such laws focus on intention in order to substantiate guilt, which makes it virtually impossible to prove fault in the case of worker injury or fatality.[20] Under these circumstances, it is little wonder that many acts of elite deviance constitute violations of civil or administrative law rather than criminal law. Moreover, the penalties for such violations, barring a serious public outcry or a request by elites themselves for government regulation, tend to remain relatively lenient.

Other institutions in American life have been penetrated by the language, ethics, and requirements of American business. Terms such as *bottom line, leverage,* and *cash flow* have become part of everyday language. Many politicians believe the way to solve the problems of government is to run government like a business. Thus, in 1992 Ross Perot ran for president promising to bring the principles that had made him a billionaire businessman to bear on governmental problems. Moreover, many individuals from the private sector are appointed to cabinet-level positions in America.

The causal links between the macro-level variables of the American Dream and institutional dominance by the political economy are depicted in Figure 8.1. Two possible hypotheses related to the sociological imagination paradigm follow from this macro-level theory:

1. Rates of elite and nonelite deviance are not constant. They wax and wane in response to changes in the American value system and changing institutional conditions. Thus, both elite and nonelite deviance will be higher in those historical periods when there is more emphasis placed on the values associated with the American Dream than in periods when the culture emphasizes values such as community, teamwork, and spirituality.
2. Likewise, now that the government has become a central part of the economy, and that the ethics of business now dominate governmental institutions, both corporate crime and political scandals will occur at the same time and frequently be interrelated.

Rates of deviance are influenced not only by macro considerations but by organizational considerations as well.

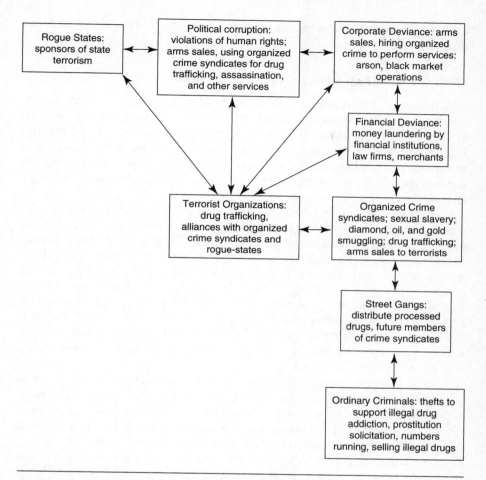

**FIGURE 8.1**   *Links Among Tangible Forms of Deviance*

## Characteristics of Bureaucratic Structures

We agree with Braithwaite and others that elite deviance is explained in part by examining the nature of the actors' roles within an organization, as well as the bureaucratic structures (characteristics) that shape such roles.[21] Bureaucracy, as a form of social organization, possesses certain structural characteristics that account for both its amoral ethical nature and its potential to generate acts of great harm.

Modern bureaucracies are characterized by several things, including these qualities: (1) centralization of authority, (2) creation of specialized vocabularies and ideologies, and (3) fragmentation and routinization of tasks. Each of these characteristics in turn often produces a number of social and psychological processes, all of which help create the environment for elite deviance.

## Centralization of Authority

Obedience to elite authority is of central importance to the study of organizations and the deviance they commit. Orders, decisions, and plans that are unethical or illegal are often carried out by underlings, in part because they feel they have no choice; they feel powerless to disobey, regardless of the intent of the order. Examples of such cases are numerous and include the massacre at My Lai, Watergate, and the General Electric price-fixing case of 1961.

Surprisingly, those who seem most powerless include both those "far removed from the centers of power and . . . those relatively close."[22] Thus, although such perceived powerlessness is usually characteristic of the lower–middle and lower classes, Kelman found a striking degree of such conformity among high-level military officers and bureaucratic functionaries, as well. Kanter and Kanter and Stein have discussed the existence of widespread feelings of powerlessness at both top and middle levels of organizations.[23] However, the empirical aspects of such powerlessness and its relationship to organizational and interorganizational deviance remain understudied. We do know that conformity among those in the higher circles of the power elite results for a variety of reasons.

One important structural condition that perpetuates elite deviance is the massive centralization of power in the hands of the elite themselves. Such centralization tends to guarantee the conformity of underling bureaucrats, either corporate or governmental, for two reasons. Because they possess such overwhelming power, elites can often secure nonelite cooperation by giving direct orders to engage in deviant acts. Refusal to conform to such directives may result in severe sanctions for potential dissidents, including being fired, court-martialed, blacklisted, demoted, or not promoted. Still other sanctions might include transfer to a less desirable assignment or geographic location or forced early retirement.[24]

Thus, the distinction often made between those deviant acts committed by workers for their personal enrichment and those committed on behalf of their employer is misleading. That is, given the centralization of power in organizations, acts committed on behalf of an organization often involve personal rewards for nonelites, as well as the threat of sanctions for noncompliance with elite directives. Moreover, people who occupy positions in bureaucratic organizations play roles for which they have been trained. As such, they are acutely aware that as people they are replaceable, interchangeable parts, mere occupants of bureaucratic positions.[25] This is certainly a dehumanizing realization for the individuals involved. Nonetheless, such conformity is the rule rather than the exception.

Quite clearly, much conformity is due to feelings of powerlessness. However, no organization operates by the threat of sanction alone. Elite authority, especially that of a national president or an upper corporate manager, is obeyed in large measure because it is recognized as legitimate. Such authority is seldom questioned. This legitimacy is part of another aspect of elite deviance, the higher immorality. As we discussed in Chapter 2, the higher immorality includes many forms of deviance that are not considered to be particularly wrong by the elites who engage in them (e.g., antitrust violations). A number of social psychological factors account for elite approval of such deviance.

## Specialized Vocabularies and Ideologies

From a social–psychological perspective, the higher immorality consists of a subculture that forms at the top of bureaucratic organizations. A small group of power holders tends to develop precepts and customs delicately balanced between conventional and criminal (deviant) behavior, as well as objectives that may be obtained through both deviant and nondeviant means. Part of this subculture of elite behavior consists of norms and sentiments that make deviance permissible. That is, deviant acts are filtered through a sanitizing, ideological prism, which gives them the appearance of not being criminal or deviant.[26]

Part of this sanitizing ideology involves the adoption of special vocabularies of motive. According to Mills, "It is an hypothesis worthy of test that typical vocabularies of motive for different situations are significant determinants of conduct."[27] A number of recent case studies of elite deviance report the construction of an elaborate vocabulary designed to provide both motive and neutralization of guilt.[28]

Likewise, the Nazi SS, in their extermination of the Jews, adopted such a vocabulary in dealing with "the Jewish problem." Special language rules were adopted: terms such as *special treatment* and *clearing up fundamental problems* were utilized as euphemisms for mass murder.[29] Moreover, such vocabularies are symptomatic of the alienation, stereotyping, and dehumanization involved in elite deviance (also see the following section).

A final aspect of the vocabulary of motives involves a series of mechanisms specifically designed to neutralize guilt. Although such mechanisms are found in almost all deviant subcultures, in the case of the elite, their adoption is more direct and absolute because the elite themselves have generated and established the ideology of deviance, as discussed earlier. When applied to elite deviance, the general ideology of deviance becomes interlaced with a number of guilt-reducing rationalizations.

1. *Denying responsibility:* The rationalization here is that what went wrong was not the organization's fault. Mechanical malfunctions in the workplace resulting in employee deaths are termed "accidents." Likewise,

consumers are blamed for their ignorance in "misusing" products that cause harm. Or, blame may be shifted to other officials or organizations, as when businesses blame a problem on a lack of government regulations.

2. *Denying victimization/dehumanization:* This guilt-reducing mechanism functions to convince interested parties that no real person was, or is being, victimized. Such denials usually take one of two forms. The first may be *object-directed dehumanization;* it involves the perception of others as statistics or commodities in a vast numbers game. People are no longer perceived as human beings but as a portion of a less than human collectivity (e.g., the enemy, the market, the competition, or the government).

Janis has described the presence of a second denial mechanism at work in elite circles. Termed *groupthink*, it refers to "a mode of thinking that people engage in where they are deeply involved in a cohesive in-group, where the members' striving for unanimity overrides their motivations to realistically appraise alternative courses of action."[30] Groupthink reduces individual capacity for moral judgment, enhancing the formation of stereotyped thought by in-group members. Thus, during the Vietnam era, members of the Johnson inner circle of policy makers created stereotypes portraying the poor of the world as wanting to take from the rich and espousing Asian disregard for human life. The Vietnamese were also the subject of racial stereotypes developed by U.S. troops, who used terms such as *mooks, gooks, slopes,* and *dinks* and described the people as barbaric and uncivilized, deserving of ruthless slaughter.

3. *Authorization/higher loyalties:* Another rationalization technique, termed *authorization*, stems directly from the legitimacy of elite power. Authorization is an ideological device involving the creation of some transcendent mission whereby elites stake claim to supposedly higher purposes that are clearly outside legal and ethical boundaries. In the case of government, such purposes usually relate to the national interest, executive privilege, fighting the communist menace or other foreign threat. In the case of corporate deviance, such notions usually involve meeting profit targets or protecting the interests of the stockholders. Such amoral justifications have been propagated for decades by conservative social critics. Milton Friedman, for example, has long argued that businesses possess virtually no social responsibility for their acts.

There is one and only one social responsibility of business—to use its resources and engage in activities designed to increase its profits so long as it stays within the rules of the game . . . [and] engages in open and free competition, without deception or fraud. . . . Few trends could so thoroughly undermine the very foundations of our free society as the acceptance by corporate officials of a social responsibility other than to make as much money for their stockholders as possible. This is a fundamentally subversive doctrine. If business people do have a social responsibility other than making maximum profits, how are they to know what it is?[31]

Such statements can easily be interpreted to mean that any profit-making behavior in which businesses engage is morally acceptable, as long as no laws are broken.

4. *Condemning condemners:* This mechanism is used to handle critics of deviant behavior. Namely, attention is diverted away from the real issue and focused on another topic or even the critics themselves. For instance, corporations often attack proposals involving further government regulation as being opposed to free enterprise. Governments, in turn, often view critics of civil rights abuses or war crimes as "communist sympathizers."

These neutralization techniques, along with an official ideology of deviance accepted by general society, ensure that elites may commit deviant acts without guilt or damage to their respectable self-images. Moreover, underlings will come to share these ideological visions and adopt the Adolf Eichmann excuse of elite authorization ("only following orders").

Finally, these ideological constructions allow elites to attribute real deviance and crime to the lower classes, thus mystifying themselves as to their own deviance and misdirecting perceptions of the distribution of societal harm in general. The dimensions of such harm are even greater when committed by organizations because of the nature of modern organizational life.

## Fragmentation and Routinization

Decisions to commit deviant acts—even murder—are carried out within established routines. Such routines involve more than filling out forms, reports, and schedules. Indeed, a number of scholars maintain that the large, complex nature of modern organizations encourages deviance, for two reasons: (1) specialized tasks involve the same routines, whether they are deviant or legitimate; and (2) elites both discourage being informed of scandals within organizations by lower functionaries and hide acts of elite deviance from functionaries and the public.[32]

Related to the specialization of tasks found in modern organizations is alienation, which denotes "a mode of experience in which the person experiences himself or herself [and other people] as alien."[33] Within bureaucratic organizations, alienation is manifested partially through distance. For example, workers engaged in producing dioxin never witnessed the effects of the chemical on the residents of Love Canal in Niagara Falls. Similarly, pilots serving in the Vietnam War convinced themselves that they were bombing geographic targets on maps, not killing civilians in their homes. In modern society, technology has produced a world of such extreme distances that victimization becomes impersonal.

## Image Construction and Inauthenticity

### Front Activities

The centralization of power and fragmentation of tasks in large organizations create still another important aspect of elite deviance: a world of image construction that masks acts of deviance behind a smokescreen of *"front" activities.*

A number of scholars have commented on the subject of front activities involved in elite deviance.[34] Yet the term is vague and has come to include everything from making deceptive or false statements about a deviant act (or series of acts) to creating pseudo-events and phony crises by news media, public relations firms, and governmental agencies.[35] Quite simply and directly, front activities may be described as management via image manipulation.

During the Watergate era, for example, a number of commentators observed that the White House staff felt that the basic problem was successfully managing public opinion.[36] And during the Carter era, White House staffers commonly complained that the confidence gap between the White House and the public was due to an image problem.

The use of front activities to camouflage deviance is a common and accepted practice of virtually all types of bureaucratic entities. Turk believes that lying within government agencies is "a routine tactic" and that its use is limited only by expediency.[37] Such lying is accompanied by many front activities: (1) providing only the information requested by investigating officials or citizens; (2) destroying or conveniently misfiling incriminating items before they have to be produced; (3) fragmenting information so it appears incomplete and out of sequence; and (4) depicting deviant acts as the work of "bad apples" or even past leaders. Another common ploy is to deny access to information on the basis of "need to know," "national security," or other justifications to hide embarrassing secrets.[38]

The discussion in this chapter has centered around the structural causes of elite deviance. A central portion of this discussion has emphasized that the causes and consequences of elite deviance are hidden from, even mystified by, both elites and nonelites, victimizers as well as victims. This mystification of elite deviance via an official ideology and a host of guilt-neutralizing techniques and front activities has serious implications for those who occupy positions in bureaucratic hierarchies. The alienation and dehumanization that characterize elite deviance produce a condition that has been described as *inauthentic*.[39] As an objective social condition, inauthenticity refers to maintaining overt positive appearances despite the presence of negative underlying realities.[40] Within powerful organizations, inauthenticity is indicated by the amount of resources spent on various front activities as the organization tries to convince workers, clients, and the general public of its positive attributes in the face of negative, often tightly held secrets.

Given these central variables regarding modern organizations, bureaucratic concerns may be hypothesized to cause elite deviance in a number of respects:

- *Hypothesis:* The more centralized authority is within an organization, and the more secrecy, the more elite deviance will be committed.
- *Hypothesis:* Organizations that engage in one type of elite deviance (e.g., price-fixing or environmental law violations) will also tend to engage in other types of elite deviance (e.g., sexual harassment or other civil rights violations).
- *Hypothesis:* Organizations that engage in high levels of inauthentic front activities (e.g., public relations and image-enhancing advertising) will also be engaging in high levels of other deviant activities.

Finally, it is likewise important to understand the types of personality traits that are likely to characterize individuals who engage in deviant acts within organizations.

## Elite Deviance and "Individual" Characteristics

Certain people who work in organizations also possess unique personality characteristics that lead them to engage in deviant acts of various kinds. Presthus has noted that one type of personality is particularly successful in making it to the top of bureaucratic organizations.[41] Such an individual exudes charisma via a superficial sense of warmth and charm. He or she is able to make decisions easily because matters are viewed in black-and-white terms. This requires the ability to categorize and thus dehumanize individuals as nonhuman entities for the purpose of making decisions concerning layoffs, firings, plant closings, and advertising campaigns.

Clinard's study of managers of large corporations found that those executives likely to engage in acts of organizational deviance were often recruited from outside the companies they administered.[42] These executives were interested in getting publicity in financial journals, showing quick increases in profits, and moving on to higher positions within 2 years.

Studies of work alienation demonstrate that people with such high extrinsic needs also tend to be workaholics, displaying what are called type A personality characteristics. Such traits involve "free floating hostility, competitiveness, a high need for socially approved success, unbridled ambitions, aggressiveness, impatience, and polyphasic thought and action" (trying to do two things at once).[43] These persons also frequently exhibit the lowest scores on mental health measures in such studies. Thus, victimizers in elite deviance often turn into victims, in a sense, dehumanizing both their victims and themselves.

Finally, there is evidence that, within organizational hierarchies, many of the same people who execute deviance on behalf of the organization also commit acts against it for their own personal gain. In a Canadian study, Reasons noted that supervisory personnel accounted for approximately two-thirds of the business dishonesty over the last decade.[44] Furthermore, within the organizations that commit deviant acts, those individuals who participated were likely to engage in acts of deviance for personal gain against their employers. This may be true because such employees resent being asked to engage in deviant acts and thus strike out against their employers in revenge. Or perhaps, having demonstrated their corrupt moral nature to their employees, such organizations invite acts of deviance against themselves by providing an untrustworthy role model. Again, we come to a similar conclusion regarding conformity within bureaucratic organizations.

One useful concept in explaining the deviant behavior of some individuals is *attachment disorder*, a condition that affects 30 million children in the United States.[45] These children are frequently the victims of incest, abuse, and neglect. They are unable to bond—to become attached—to other human beings. As children, they often strangle animals, start fires, try to drown their playmates, steal, lie, and inflict physical damage on other people's belongings.

The symptoms associated with attachment disorder involve severe forms of inauthenticity and dehumanization. Disordered children do not treat themselves or other people as human beings with needs for love and recognition. Consequently, the symptoms of disordered children reflect extreme forms of alienation:

- They are self-destructive. Disordered children often stab themselves with knives and exhibit no fear of dangerous heights or other risky situations (such as reckless driving or robbing convenience stores). In adulthood, these people become the salespeople who sell unsafe used cars, the bosses who steal their subordinates' ideas, the consumers who fail to pay their debts, or the serial killers (such as Ted Bundy and Charles Manson).
- They exhibit phoniness (personal inauthenticity). Attachment-disordered children have no idea how to relate to other people. Consequently, they tend to behave insincerely when expressing love or other emotions. They tend to be perceived as untrustworthy and come across as manipulators. One parent of an attachment-disordered child remarked that it was like living with a "robot."[46]

- Stealing, hoarding, and gorging of food and possessions are common among attachment-disordered children. Not knowing how to form attachments to other people, disordered children experience severe unmet emotional needs. As a substitute for needs involving love and human contact, disordered children often steal and hoard items such as food, even if they are not hungry.
- Conning behavior is also common. Acts of deception take place in both childhood and adulthood. As children, disordered persons often feign helplessness, act loving or cute, smart or beguiling—whatever suits their need at the time to obtain what they want. In adulthood, such behavior may manifest itself as fraud and con games.
- A final symptom of attachment disorder involves what is termed "crazy lying."[47] Such children lie even under the most extreme circumstances, especially when they are caught directly in the act of misbehaving. Crazy lying means that lies will be told even when such behavior is obvious.

## Organizational Conditions and the Production of Deviant Personalities

It is much too facile to argue that elite deviance is caused by deviant personalities, people who were predisposed to deviant acts before they arrived at the organization's doorstep. Reality, unfortunately, is a good deal more complicated and much more interesting than this. There are instances when organizations can and do influence workers to commit deviant acts. Such motivations are frequently associated with the presence of alienation within organizations.

Thus, Boston University professors Donald Kanter and Philip Mirvis[48] have substantiated that alienation is surprisingly widespread in America. In their analysis of a national sample of data, about half of their respondents agree with the statement that "most people are only out for themselves and that you are better off zapping them before they do it to you."[49] Among their most important findings are that many people in America now take a cynical approach to the work they do, and that this cynicism extends from the very top to the lowly bottom of the American occupational structure.

At the zenith of corporate America are "command cynics." These are senior managers who see themselves in a corporate jungle. They believe that their advancement has been an outcome of Darwinian logic, which holds that since they are on top, those beneath them must be "weak, naive, inept, or just plain dumb." Command cynics also hold that everyone has his or her price, and everyone can be had.

Beneath the command cynics are the "administrative sideliners," middle managers and upper-level government bureaucrats who view human nature as being cold and uncaring, and who have no genuine concern for people, except as means for their own ends. Next is a group of young game players, self-absorbed professionals who became visible symbols of the greed and narcissism of the 1980s. What these self-centered people have in common is willingness to do whatever it takes to move up the bureaucratic ladder. Kanter and Mirvis referred to them as "porcupine quills," people who take pleasure in putting others down as they climb to the top of corporate or government hierarchies.

In the middle levels of the bureaucratic layers of business and government sit "squeezed cynics," usually the sons and daughters of skilled factory workers and working-class clericals. This once upwardly mobile working-class group has been made cynical by the loss of manufacturing jobs and the decline of heavy industry. The jobs they once expected to give them security have been sent overseas, automated, or completely eliminated. They are now downwardly mobile Americans. They have lost faith in the American Dream, and their cynicism stems from a belief that their careers have reached a dead end. These sad people are hard-bitten cynics, who believe they cannot trust anyone at work or in business, and that "expecting anyone to help you makes you a damn fool."

White-collar workers often suffer from self-estrangement and other feelings of alienation associated with inauthenticity, previously discussed. One of the most interesting studies in this regard is Jan Halper's *Quiet Desperation*.[50] Dr. Halper is a humanistic psychologist and organizational consultant. She interviewed 4,126 Fortune 500 executives, middle managers, and other professionals; she also intensely interviewed and provided free therapy to a subsample of executives.

To advance in their firms, these men must go along, sacrificing for the sake of their careers and companies. What Dr. Halper discovered was that a large proportion of these successful men were self-estranged, cut off from their feelings, wishes, wants, and needs. Their socialization both within their families and at work has taught them to deny their feelings and to conform to the demands of job and family. Halper found that a large portion of these men, almost two-thirds, are tired of being dutiful, loyal employees, with no control over their jobs. Many suffer from reactions to denying their feelings for so long. Depression, feeling out of control, and other stress reactions are common. Some commit suicide.

Moreover, many of these men suffer the ill effects of not knowing who they are. They confuse the roles they play with who they are as people. Often they see themselves as a group of titles: "hero, breadwinner, lover, husband, father, warrior, empire builder, or mover-and-shaker."[51] Relinquishing a role or two, through dismissal, retirement, or divorce, often leads to an identity crisis in which they feel they are nothing without the identities they have lost.

The credo these men are taught is that they are responsible for others' needs over and above their own. Often they avoid thinking about their own needs in order not to feel anticipated guilt, feeling they have violated the male credo. Despite their considerable accomplishments in many cases, a large number of these professionals suffer from low self-esteem. Frustrated at work, not intimately related to their wives, many of these men lead rich fantasy lives, preferring to see themselves as what they want rather than who they really are. No matter how successful they are, many feel that they have not achieved success.

Most of these men also suffer from numerous contradictions. One of the most common among the executives is that they feel forced to demonstrate that they are both tough and nice guys at the same time. Halper found that 57% of managers do not delegate authority because they fear giving up control over decisions. As a result, many feel great stress over being constantly responsible for what takes place inside their firms. Related to this control over decision making is the fact that many corporate executives Halper interviewed find it difficult to trust their fellow employees. Moreover, this distrust between workers increased in the 1990s. This is because of the massive layoffs that have taken place in recent years in corporate America. No job seems safe anymore. Frequently, those not laid off feel the guilt, irritability, fatigue, and stress that come with being left on a job that requires more effort.

People have made a tacit bargain with the capitalist system, exchanging their work time for escapist consumption and leisure. Alienation at work is soon transformed into reification in the marketplace. It is often rendered in a reluctant, incomplete, and psychologically stressful manner. Moreover, such conformity is related to a number of types of more personal deviance, even among elites themselves. This is especially true when front activities fail and organizations are implicated in deviant acts. For instance, Eli Black, chairman of United Brands, committed suicide when it was revealed that his company was involved in a bribery scandal designed to hold down taxes on bananas. Similarly, Japanese executive Mitsushiro Shimada killed himself when his company was proved to be involved in the Grumman bribery scandal.[52] We can conclude then that if official ideologies of deviance were fully accepted, embarrassed organizational elites would probably not resort to such desperate acts.

Taken together, this body of evidence leads to the following hypotheses:

- *Hypothesis:* Those individuals likely to engage in acts of elite deviance will tend to exhibit weak attachments to friends, family, and coworkers. Elite deviants are thus likely to suffer from all of the symptoms that accompany attachment disorder, including the ability to freely lie and manipulate and the inability to delay any sort of gratification.
- *Hypothesis:* Organizations headed by people suffering from alienation and attachment disorder will likely be "polyoffenders." As we have seen with General Electric (Chapter 3), corporations that commit deviant acts in one area (e.g., defrauding the government in defense contracting) will likely commit deviant acts in other areas (e.g., ecological crime).

# Links Between Elite Deviance and Nonelite Deviance

Another critical aspect of elite deviance often overlooked when the subject is confined to so-called corporate criminality or political deviance involves the mutually dependent (symbiotic) relationship between certain types of elite and nonelite deviance. This point stems from an additional aspect of the sociological imagination that holds that society, as Mills put it, is "a network of rackets."[53] Such rackets arise because of institutional contradictions, permanent conflicts within social structures.[54] One of these contradictions concerns the relationship between elite and nonelite deviance. This symbiotic relationship exists on two levels: tangible (involving money, products, and/or services) and symbolic (involving the construction of ideological and social structural variables).[55]

## Tangible Links

The tangible links between elite and nonelite deviance are represented in Figure 8.1. As the figure shows, the great bridge between elite and nonelite deviance is organized crime. Profits from the activities of organized criminal syndicates are made from various types of street crime—including prostitution, illegal gambling, selling drugs—which include moneys obtained by burglars and robbers who need to support drug habits. Such proceeds, totaling some $150 billion in annual gross revenues, generate an estimated $50 billion in net profits, profits that must be reinvested in order to grow.[56] At times, such profits have been invested in partnership ventures with legitimate corporations, as when Pan Am and Mafia interests opened gambling resorts in the Caribbean following Castro's expulsion of the Mafia from Cuban casinos.

Likewise, business dealings between organized crime and legitimate corporations include the use of racketeers to suppress labor unions and the laundering of Mafia drug funds through banks and other legal enterprises. In addition, there are numerous financial links between organized criminal syndicates and the government, from campaign donations of Mafia moneys to outright bribery of politicians (not to mention the infamous activities of the CIA).

Finally, as mentioned above, numerous legitimate and illegitimate financial links exist between political and economic elites: political lobby groups, government contracts, bribery, and corporate efforts to influence governmental behavior overseas. This is not to say that all legitimate corporations working with legitimate politicians are also automatically linked to organized criminal syndicates. It is merely to say that such three-way links do exist. And obviously, many of the links between legitimate corporations and Mafia-owned businesses are of a customer–retailer nature. This includes phone calls made by bookies using AT&T lines, Mafia-owned automobile dealerships, syndicate influence in the legitimate gambling industry (e.g., Las Vegas and Atlantic City), and relationships between the Mafia-dominated

Teamsters Union, legitimate corporations, and politicians. (See Chapter 9 for further examples.)

## Symbolic Links

As discussed in Chapters 1 and 2, the most powerful U.S. elites have access to the nation's great socializing institutions, especially the mass media and the schools. Such access has been utilized in part to create an ideological view of deviance. This view holds that the U.S. crime problem is the fault of a supposedly dangerous lower class that is criminal in nature, deserving of its poverty and moral inferiority, and in need of increased social-control measures by the state. Such deviants are typically viewed as the products of certain individual pathologies (e.g., "evil, subculture of poverty"). The notion that justice is blind in its fairness—ignoring race, class, and power—is completely overlooked.

Because many people in the United States are convinced that the deviance of the powerless is a greater harm to society than that of elites, both moral indignation and financial resources are focused there. This further serves to convince elites of their own moral superiority, reaffirming that their acts do not constitute the real deviance of common criminals. Thus, the official (elite) ideology of deviance serves to convince elites of the rightness of their own conduct, even if unethical or illegal. It also serves to keep the attention of law from the deviance of elites, focusing instead on the apprehension, processing, and punishing of so-called street criminals.

Finally, the official ideology of deviance gives rise to a situation in which the deviance of the powerless reinforces the inequality between the powerless (nonelites) and powerful (elites). This occurs in part because the victims of nonelite street criminals are disproportionately members of the same powerless lower class. Such deviance tends to keep the lower class divided within itself, destroying any sense of community that might result in a united lower-class movement for social change.

For its part, the deviance of elites has both direct and indirect impacts on the deviance of nonelites. First, elites, under certain circumstances, may order relatively powerless people to commit deviant acts. We observed this in the Farben case, where the cruel Capos were ordered to oversee the slave-labor inmates of Nazi concentration camps. Second, as we have already noted, elite deviance often has a trickle-down effect, providing a standard of ethics and behavior by which nonelites can justify their own deviant acts. Finally, elite deviance often victimizes nonelites financially and in other ways. Such exploitation serves to reinforce the inequalities of power and wealth that are in large measure responsible for this symbiotic relationship between elite and nonelite deviance. To understand the causes of elite deviance, one must first understand the symbolic and symbiotic dimensions of the structure of wealth and power, in U.S. society and elsewhere.

## Elite Deviance and Victimization

A great deal of attention has been paid by sociologists in recent years to the effects of class, race, gender, and age on human behavior. Nowhere are these variables more relevant than in the study of the victims of elite deviance. Consider the following.

- In 1993, a Defense Department report stated that 83 women and seven men were assaulted during the 1991 Tailhook Association Convention at the Las Vegas Hilton. (The association's members are present and former navy fliers.) The 300-page report was based on more than 2,900 interviews. The report said that victims were "groped, pinched, fondled," and "bitten" by their assailants and that oral sex and sexual intercourse performed in front of others contributed to a "general atmosphere of debauchery."[57] Ultimately, navy secretary John Dalton asked for the removal of Admiral Frank Kelso, chief of naval operations, and three other admirals were censured. Then 28 other admirals and one marine general received letters of caution.[58] None of the officers involved ever went to prison.
- In November 1996, an army sexual misconduct scandal broke at the army's Aberdeen Proving Ground, Maryland, where company commander Captain Derrick Robertson was charged with rape, violation of the Ordnance Center and School Regulation that prohibits improper student/cadre relationships, conduct unbecoming an officer (fraternization), adultery, obstruction of justice, and related charges. Robertson was a company commander. Staff Sergeants Nathaniel Beach and Delmar Simpson, both drill sergeants, were arraigned on a variety of charges, including rape, forcible sodomy, adultery, and obstruction of justice. As part of the investigation, the army established a toll-free number for receiving calls from victims, parents, and anyone with information pertaining to the sexual misconduct investigation.[59]
- In April 1997, a former drill instructor was convicted of raping six trainees.[60] The Aberdeen Proving Ground incident was the most serious case arising from a sexual deviance scandal that spread to U.S. military bases worldwide. The same drill instructor had already been sentenced to 32 years in prison for having consensual sex with 11 trainees, a violation of army rules.
- Immediately following the former drill sergeant's conviction, General John Longhouser, the Aberdeen Proving Ground's base commander, announced his retirement, admitting he had had an adulterous affair in 1992, while separated from his wife. The general reportedly became the subject of a Pentagon inquiry after an anonymous tip was received over a telephone hot line, established because of the charges leveled at Aberdeen drill sergeants. Other sexual harassment complaints were leveled against Lieutenant Kelly Flinn, the air force's only female bomber pilot.

Flinn was given a general (less than honorable) discharge and forced to resign from the service. The incident touched off national debate over a sexual double standard wherein women charged with sexual misconduct are forced to resign under less than honorable conditions while males charged with similar behavior simply retire without penalty.

The debate intensified when air force general Joseph Ralston, vice chairman of the Joint Chiefs of Staff, admitted to an adulterous affair, but President Clinton refused to accept his resignation, noting that he wanted the general to become his new top military adviser. Likewise, retired Sergeant Major Brenda Hoster accused the army's highest-ranking enlisted man, Sergeant Major McKinney, of grabbing her and demanding sex during a business trip. Hoster made her charges public after learning that Sergeant McKinney had been appointed to a panel investigating sexual misconduct in the army.

As usual, the Tailhook scandal and the 1997 army sexual harassment scandals are symbolic of a much more widespread condition. In March 1994, four women serving in the military told a House committee that sexual harassment in the military is very common and that complaints about it often go unheeded. Although stronger harassment rules have been issued by all branches of the armed services, and sensitivity training initiated, the female personnel claim that complaints of sexual harassment are met with disdain, ostracism, and in some cases transfer to a dead-end job.[61]

Sexual harassment has long been part of the organizational culture of the military, but it is certainly not limited to the armed services. Harassment is most heavily centered in male-dominated occupations and organizations, and its toleration depends on the behavior of the elites in charge. If vigorously opposed, harassment can be overcome. The same is true of the denial of civil liberties to gays, more than 10,000 of whom have been forcibly discharged from the U.S. military in the last 32 years, and there exist many forms of institutional discrimination against homosexuals and lesbians in American life.[62]

Moreover, the Tailhook scandal points up one additional facet of organizational life, but this time the organization concerns the discipline of criminology itself. Recent publications have pointed out that women, as victims of "white-collar crime," have gone unstudied, as indeed all such victims have. As this book points out, many of the victims of international corporate dumping are women and children, but their victimization does not stop there:

- In 1991, 25 people were killed in a fire in a North Carolina chicken processing plant. More than 75% of the victims were female in a plant where doors were locked to prevent workers from stealing chickens.
- The Dalkon Shield intrauterine birth control device, which caused sterilization, infections, and death in some women, created a scandal that victimized women, as did Ovulen, an oral contraceptive, information about the dangerous side effects of which was withheld by its manufacturer,

Searle Company. Likewise, carpal tunnel syndrome (atrophy of thumb muscles) primarily affects assembly-line workers and typists, who are mainly female. The same is true for conditions related to the use of video display terminals in offices, which can cause a variety of neck, back, and shoulder problems, as well as eye strain and carpal tunnel syndrome. Likewise, in the textile industry, women make up from 62% to 89% of the workers in certain occupations that incur the risk of contracting "brown lung" disease from exposure to cotton dust.[63]

Finally, the elderly suffer very high rates of victimization from white-collar crimes, especially scams (confidence games) and frauds.

- More than 10,000 elderly residents of Arizona alone are victims of fraudulent auto repairs and other consumer frauds, situations that exist nationwide.[64]
- The elderly are among those prone to cons by televangelist hucksters. In 1990, Reverend Jim Bakker received a 45-year prison sentence (later commuted) for mail fraud and related offenses when he misappropriated moneys supposedly raised to support his PTL ("Praise the Lord") ministries. Bakker's $150-million-a-year "church" was well connected to the Reagan and Bush administrations, as well as to large corporations. One firm, Wedtech (later bankrupted in a scandal involving defense contracting fraud), paid thousands to silence Jessica Hahn, a secretary who was forced to engage in sex with Bakker and an associate. Many of the people who mailed money to Bakker were elderly, some of whom went without heat during the winter, and whose only incomes were their Social Security checks.
- Aside from numerous evangelical fraudsters, there are numerous additional types of white-collar crimes associated with various clergy. For example, a Catholic Priest, Randal Radic, who was sent to prison for embezzling his parish's donations, wanted to learn how widespread ripping off U.S. Catholic Churches is. According to a study by Villanova University, 85% of parishes in the United States suffer from embezzlement, 11% of which were over $500,000. One reason is that no auditing of Church monies takes place until a given priest leaves his parish. Other evidence reveals a worldwide sexual abuse scandal involving children among Catholic clergy, but the pope unwilling to testify about it on the grounds that he is the head of a country, and thus immune. Data from insurance firms confirm by a recent Associated Press report that the three major insurance companies for Protestant Churches in America say they typically receive 260 reports each year of minors being sexually abused by Protestant clergy, staff, or other church-related relationships. Likewise, over 100 Rabbis have been involved in sexual and political scandals over the past century, and numerous corruption scandals.[65]

Sutherland's Differential Association Theory focuses on how individuals learn how to become criminals, but does not concern itself with why they become criminals. They learn how to commit criminal acts; they learn motives, drives, rationalizations, and attitudes. It grows socially easier for the individuals to commit a crime. Their inspiration is the processes of cultural transmission and construction.

Differential association predicts that an individual will choose the criminal path when the balance of definitions for law-breaking exceeds those for law-abiding. This tendency will be reinforced if social association provides active people in the person's life. Therefore, the principles of Sutherland's Theory of Differential Association can be summarized into nine key points:

1. Criminal behavior is learned.
2. Criminal behavior is learned in interaction with other persons in a process of communication.
3. The principal part of the learning of criminal behavior occurs within intimate personal groups.
4. When criminal behavior is learned, the learning includes techniques of committing the crime, which are sometimes very complicated, sometimes simple and the specific direction of motives, drives, rationalizations, and attitudes.
5. The specific direction of motives and drives is learned from definitions of the legal codes as favorable or unfavorable.
6. A person becomes delinquent because of an excess of definitions favorable to violation of law over definitions unfavorable to violation of the law.
7. Differential associations may vary in frequency, duration, priority, and intensity.
8. The process of learning criminal behavior by association with criminal and anticriminal patterns involves all of the mechanisms that are involved in any other learning.
9. While criminal behavior is an expression of general needs and values, it is not explained by those needs and values, since non-criminal behavior is an expression of the same needs and values.[66]

    Yet, what seminary or rabbinical school have you ever heard about that teaches its prospective clergy that sexually molesting children is acceptable behavior? Which priest specifically learns that the parish's contributions from his "flock" are okay to "fleece?" And since when has the Vatican determined that covering up criminal deeds by its clergy is standard operating procedure? Given the widespread nature of these scandals, much like phony credit default swaps on Wall Street, they have become institutionalized behaviors in some religious institutions, as have the attempts to cover them up.

# Constructionist and Objectivist Positions on Elite Deviance

Throughout this book, we have presented a view of elite deviance that is admittedly controversial. Rather than take a safe position, involving only white-collar criminal acts, we have argued for a definition that encompasses both illegal and immoral acts. But, one may ask, whose morality is to be used as a basis in deciding what may be termed elite deviance?

In general, two answers may be offered to this question. First, there is the constructionist position, which views all deviance as acts occurring in a particular context: a given historical period, a specific culture, and even an isolated situation within a specific culture. Thus, a murder committed during peacetime may become a heroic act in war. But not all societies condone all wars or even war in general.

In this chapter, we have stressed the importance of reality as a social construction in our discussion of the official elite ideology of deviance.[67] This official ideology has several negative effects: (1) it blinds both elites and non-elites to the greater harms generated by elite deviance; (2) it focuses attention and resources on the less harmful deviance of the powerless; and (3) it serves as a basis for guilt-reducing rationalizations used by powerful individuals engaged in deviance. We have also examined the question of who possesses the power to construct such definitions or, conversely, to prevent competing definitions of deviance from being constructed. Finally, we have assessed the harmful consequences that follow from defining deviance in this way.

A central problem with the constructionist position is that it treats all moral positions as relative, denying the existence of any absolutes, including reality of human pain and suffering.[68] Erich Goode's argument in his otherwise excellent text, *Deviant Behavior*, is characteristic of the constructionist view on this point. Like most constructionists, he argues that human suffering is nothing but a social construct, thus implying that there is no human suffering until such misfortunes are officially defined as such. Moreover, just because new practices (such as various human rights violations) come into existence, and old ones (such as slavery) disappear does not mean that the pain of physical injury or death, or theft, or rape, or any other practice that causes suffering is less real. Goode also seems determined to limit the definition of elite deviance to violations of human rights, thus overlooking all our discussions of the higher immorality, the interrelated nature of deviance, and the like.

Ideologically, the constructionist position is safe because it easily excuses one from taking sides and advocating solutions, which leads to the implicit acceptance of the dominant ideology concerning social problems, including various forms of deviance. Thus, the constructionist position supports the stance that nothing matters, which for us is unacceptable.

An alternate position is that of the objectivists, which holds that there are moral absolutes regarding social problems.

There are social structures that induce material or psychic suffering for certain segments of the population; there are structures that ensure the maldistribution of resources within and across societies; . . . there are corporate and political organizations that waste valuable resources, that pollute the environment, that are imperialistic, and that increase the gap between the "haves" and "have nots" globally and societally.[69]

The objectivist (or normative) approach, unlike that of social constructionism, argues for the adoption of moral imperatives and human needs that are universal and ahistorical. To describe violation of these norms by elites as "wrongs," "deviance," or "social problems" is merely to state such universals using another label. Stated in the positive, such universals provide a coherent view of basic human needs that may serve as a foundation for policies designed to address the causes and consequences of the types of deviance we have described in this book. Among these basic needs are essential physical requirements (food, clothing, shelter, and medical care), as well as a host of nonmaterial needs, including the basic human rights discussed in Chapter 5. (Others are discussed in the epilogue.)

More important, however, is the realization that dangers are involved with adopting any set of basic "rights," "wrongs," and "shoulds," or causes and solutions. Objections can be offered to any position, as seen in the following examples.

1.  The only reason most of the examples that make up this book are here is because they constitute what Simon believes to be deviance. He's just being self-righteous.

This charge is profoundly untrue! The examples in this book constitute a case-by-case series of deviant acts that have offended the sensibilities of many leading social critics, muckrakers, and social scientists. The ethical foundation rests on the same moral principle on which the Judeo-Christian and many other non-Western ethical systems are founded: namely, the Golden Rule, which holds that one should treat others as he or she would like to be treated. What society would sanction the behavior related in this chapter's examples? Even I. G. Farben's use of slave labor would have been disapproved of by the mass of the German people had they known about it and been free to render a judgment.

2.  How dare you speak of the salaries of corporate executives, war crimes, antitrust violations, and pollution as if they all constitute equal wrongs! All you do is open up a Pandora's box! Now virtually anything elites do can be considered deviant by someone writing on the subject. As a result, the issue of criminal elite deviance is lost in the process.

Such an argument ignores the fact that we have introduced a standard by which to measure deviance: harm, including physical loss (death and injury), financial loss, and the destruction of public trust. Our argument is not that all deviant acts cause the same kind and degree of harm. Instead, we find that such acts—whether technically criminal or not—are harmful in some way. For instance, the three-martini lunch and other special privileges given elite executives cause harm by furthering massive federal deficits, as wealthy individuals and corporations legally evade paying taxes. In addition, citizens lose faith in taxation, thus destroying public trust. Those $3,000-per-day executive salaries and perks further contribute to many social inequalities, which are in turn related to many social ills, including crime at all societal levels. So yes, not all the wrongs we discuss are of equal dimension. Nonetheless, they remain wrongs and are symbolic and symptomatic of still greater problems.

3. Calling some practices "deviant" when they are not considered to be so by those who commit them is irrational. Practices such as corporate dumping, even if dangerous, are still legal and justified by those individuals involved. They have their reasons. Your approach completely rules out any understanding of the people involved.

Yes, and juvenile delinquents, Nazis, I. G. Farben executives, rapists, and all other criminals have their reasons, too. Deviant individuals erect ideologies and rationalizations to reduce the guilt they feel. Further, they feel that what they do is quite rational, according to their own value systems.

Still, just because corporate dumping in foreign countries is profitable and legal does not make the harm it causes any less serious than the harm to those who lose their lives to pesticide poisoning or suffer birth defects due to faulty contraceptives. And the fact that the victims of dumping are not Americans should not matter; they are still human beings. Calling such behavior "rational" misses the point. The harm is intrinsically real and empirically measurable, as this book documents.

Moreover, the rational pursuit of profit may not be as rational as we sometimes think. Practices such as corporate bribery actually have very negative consequences for many of the companies and officials involved. Therefore, in the long run, they may be viewed as irrational.

It is impossible to account for every individual rationale when trying to define elite deviance. So, instead, should we limit our definition to include only criminal acts? Doing so would be unfortunate. Many great harms would go neglected—harms that, if properly understood, would aid in our knowledge of how and why elite deviance works.

## Conclusion

The discussion in this chapter has analyzed how rationalizations for elite deviance are constructed and maintained through the use of front activities, and how they fail due to the emergence of scandal and opposing beliefs. Based on this analysis, we conclude that elite deviance is understandable from the deviant's perspective. In addition, we feel that elite deviance is empirically testable. To establish such empiricism, the following hypotheses must be verified:

1. *Hypothesis:* Public distrust and alienation are increased by elite acts that are considered to be immoral/unethical, as well as by those that are clearly illegal.
2. *Hypothesis:* Major corporations involved in scandals (such as pollution or dangerous working conditions) are likely to suffer from distrust among their employees, the result of which will be deviance: stealing from the workplace, absenteeism, and perhaps drug and alcohol abuse.
3. *Hypothesis:* Employees asked to participate directly in acts of organizational deviance may comply with such directives. But in some cases, especially when scandal occurs, intense psychological strain will result in acts of personal deviance (e.g., drug addiction, mental illness, suicide) and resentment against the organization (causing white-collar crime).

Each of these hypotheses may be tested via interviews, as a number of studies attest.[70] Thus, we see little incompatibility between our so-called ideological stance and the canons of empirical science. The fact that elite deviance is empirically testable is one of the major strengths of our view of deviance.

The discussion in this chapter has illustrated the complexity of the subject, elite deviance. It is quite clearly a product of our complex society, as a number of forces work together to provide the motive, the opportunity, and the structure necessary for deviance to occur (Figure 8.2).

Perhaps the most basic cause of elite deviance is the structure and internal workings of the contemporary political economy. Assigning structural causes requires one to examine solutions that are structural, as well. Not to include solutions in a text such as this does little more than contribute to the feelings of powerlessness and alienation that already plague U.S. society, not to mention much of social science. Not to propose such changes would be, we feel, intellectually dishonest. Unfortunately, we find that a double standard operates in this area. On the one hand, when so-called objective social scientists offer reformist solutions to the problems plaguing society, their work is labeled as "policy study," "social policy," "foreign policy," or some other pseudoscientific label. Most important, it is believed to be unbiased, scientific, and value free. On the other hand, when anyone proposes change that involves the basic distribution of wealth, power, and private property, the work is labeled as "utopian," "unscientific," "social criticism," or even "subversive."

In response to this arbitrary approach to social problems, we suggest that the time for labels is past. To avoid making proposals leaves students with a sense of hopelessness and fatalism that merely serves to perpetuate

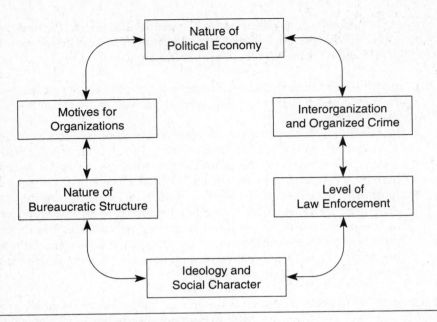

**FIGURE 8.2**  *Interrelated Causes of Elite Deviance*

such problems. To label our approach as being more ideologically biased than reformist is to deny the pluralistic nature of the U.S. political and intellectual landscape. However, to criticize our beliefs as being utopian does us great honor, for we, with Kenneth Keniston, hold that positive utopian visions are essential as a source of hope in an increasingly cynical, alienated, and negative world.[71]

## CRITICAL THINKING EXERCISE 8.1
### Elite Deviance and the Sociological Imagination

Write a short paper (three to five pages, double-spaced) stating your opinion in response to the following questions. *Be sure to make a copy of your paper. What is important now is your impressions of the issues raised here.*

1. *Social problem.* Select a magazine or newspaper article about a topic currently in the news—a murder in a high school, say, or an indictment of a politician on corruption charges, a kidnapping, a terrorist bombing incident, or a shoot-out between rival drug gangs. Does the article's topic indicate a more widespread problem in America? What types of harm result from this socially patterned problem? Consider the following dimensions of the sociological imagination.

**A.** *Contradiction.* What are the institutional contradictions surrounding the problem? For example, do some institutions in American society approve of drug use, either legal or illegal, whereas other institutions condemn it? What contradictions are inherent in American institutions that may cause the problem you selected?

**B.** *Historical epoch.* What events in the recent past have raised concern about this problem?

**C.** *Immediate milieu.* To what extent is this problem a part of your immediate environment? For example, do you know other students who abuse alcohol or illegal drugs? Has someone ever attempted to sell you illegal drugs? Have you experienced any direct contact with the problem you chose to analyze?

**D.** *Personal troubles.* Have you or members of your family experienced problems with the issue you chose? Are any of your friends experiencing problems with it? If so, what sorts of trauma have you experienced because of this social problem? Is the problem resolvable within your immediate environment, or do you believe that some larger effort is necessary—perhaps a private effort in your local community, or governmental legislation, or public service education by the mass media? If so, what kinds of efforts do you believe are necessary to rid your everyday life of this problem?

# ENDNOTES

1. See Kappeler, V., & Potter, G. (2006). *The mythology of crime and criminal justice* (4th ed., pp. 149–155). Long Grove, IL: Waveland, for an excellent discussion of these issues.

2. Ibid (pp. 268–270, 368–371), for a discussion of these issues.

3. See the Winter (1991) issue of *Dissent*.

4. See Nisbet, R. (1988). *The present age.* New York: HarperCollins.

5. Lipson, L. (1993). *The ethical crisis of civilization.* Newbury Park, CA: Sage.

6. The following is based in part on Simon, D. R. (1995). *Social problems and the sociological imagination.* New York: McGraw-Hill.

7. See Mills, C. W. (1956). *The power elite.* New York: Oxford University Press.

8. See Mills, C. W. (1959). *The sociological imagination.* New York: Oxford University Press, for an extended discussion of this point.

9. See Mills, C. W. (1960). *Images of man: The classic tradition in sociological thinking* (p. 3). New York: Braziller.

10. Messner, S., & Rosenfeld, R. (1994). *Crime and the American Dream* (p. 6). Belmont, CA: Wadsworth.

11. See, on this point, Horney, K. (1938). *The neurotic personality of our time.* New York: W. W. Norton; Fromm, E. (1966). *Escape from freedom.* New York: Avon; and Riesman, D. (1950). *The lonely crowd.* New Haven, CT: Yale University Press.

12. Currie, E. (Winter 1991). The market society. *Dissent*, 255–258, elaborated in a speech "The market society" at the 1994 meeting of the Academy of Criminal Justice Sciences, Chicago, Illinois.

13. Derber, C. (1992). *Money, murder, and the American Dream: Wilding from Wall Street to Main Street.* New York: Faber & Faber.

14. See Durkheim, E. (1966). *Suicide* (classic). New York: Free Press.

15. Merton, R. (1994). Social structure and anomie. In S. Traub & C. Little (Eds.). *Theories of deviance* (4th ed., pp. 114–148). Itaska, IL: Peacock Publishers.

16. Ibid (p. 116).

17. Adams, J. R. (1926). *America as a business civilization* (p. 44). New York: Holmes and Meier.

18. See, for example, Lernoux, P. (February 18, 1984). The Miami connection. *Nation*, 186–198; and Lernoux, P. (1984). *In banks we trust*. New York: Anchor/Doubleday Press.

19. Moyers, B. (1988). *The secret government: The constitution in crisis*. Berkeley: Seven Locks.

20. Box, S. (1983). *Crime, power, and mystification* (pp. 58–60). London: Tavistock.

21. Braithwaite, J. (1984). *Corporate crime in the pharmaceutical industry* (p. 26). London: Routledge and Kegan Paul.

22. Kelman, H. (Winter 1976). The social-psychological context of Watergate. *Psychiatry, 39*, 308; and Kelman, H. (Fall 1973). Violence without moral restraint: Reflections on the dehumanization of victims and victimizers. *Journal of Social Issues, 29*, 25–61.

23. Kanter, R. M. (1977). *Men and women of the corporation* (pp. 189–205). New York: Basic Books; and Kanter, R. M., & Stein, B. A. (Eds.). (1979). *Life in organizations* (pp. 80–96). New York: Basic Books.

24. On this point, see Glass, J. (Autumn 1976). Organizations in action. *Journal of Contemporary Business*, 91–111.

25. Ermann, M. D., & Lundman, R. J. (Eds.). (1982). *Corporate and governmental deviance: Problems of organizational behavior in contemporary society* (2nd ed., Chapter 1). New York: Oxford University Press; and MacCoby, M. (1976). *The gamesman* (p. 230). New York: Simon & Schuster.

26. Based on Box (pp. 54–57).

27. Mills, C. W. (1963). A diagnosis of our moral uneasiness. In I. L. Horowitz (ed.). *Power, politics, and people.* (p. 445). New York: Oxford University Press.

28. Sykes, G., & Matza, D. (May 1957). Techniques of neutralization: A theory of delinquency. *American Sociological Review, 22*, 664–670.

29. Arendt, H. (1964). *Eichmann in Jerusalem: A report on the banality of evil*. New York: Viking.

30. Janis, I. (1972). *Victims of groupthink* (p. 9). Boston: Houghton Mifflin. For more on dehumanization, see Bernard, V., et al., Dehumanization, in Sanford & Comstock (pp. 102–124); and Duster, T. Conditions for guilt free massacre, also in Sanford & Comstock (pp. 25–36).

31. Friedman, M. (1972). *Capitalism and freedom* (p. 133). Chicago: University of Chicago Press. For an interesting elaboration, see McKie, J. W. (ed.). (1974). *Social responsibility and the business relationship* Washington, DC: Brookings.

32. See Silver, M., & Geller, D. (Fall 1978). On the irrelevance of evil: The organization and individual action. *Journal of Social Issues, 34*, 125–136; Vaughn, D. (1980). Crime between organizations: Implications for victimology. In G. Geis and E. Stotland (Eds.). *White-collar crime: Theory and research* (p. 87) . Beverly Hills: Sage; Kramer, R. C. (1982). Corporate crime: An organizational perspective. In P. Wickman, & T. Dailey (Eds.). *White-collar and economic crime* (pp. 75–94). Lexington, MA: D. C. Heath; and Smigel, E. (February 1956). Public attitudes toward stealing in relationship to the size of the victim organization. *American Sociological Review, 21*, 320–347.

33. Fromm, E. (1955). *The sane society* (p. 111). New York: Holt, Rinehart and Winston.

34. Barnet, R. (1972). *The roots of war*. Baltimore: Penguin; Mills, C. W. (1956). *The power elite*. New York: Oxford University Press.354-356.

35. Boorstin, D. (1961). *The image: A guide to pseudo-events in America*. New York: Harper & Row.

36. For an analysis of conservative, liberal, and socialist reactions to Watergate, see Simon, D. R. (August 1978). Watergate as a social problem, paper presented at the meeting of the Society for the Study of Social Problems.

37. Turk, A. (February 1981). Organizational deviance and political policing. *Criminology, 19*, 231–250.

38. Bernstein, B. (Spring 1976). The road to Watergate and beyond: The growth and abuse of executive authority since 1940. *Law and Contemporary Problems, 40,* 57–86.

39. Seeman, M. (Fall 1966). Status and identity: The problem of inauthenticity. *Pacific Sociological Review, 9,* 67–73; Baxter, B. (1982). *Alienation and inauthenticity.* London: Routledge and Kegan Paul; Etzioni, A. (December 1968). Basic human needs, alienation, and inauthenticity. *American Sociological Review, 33,* 870–884; and Etzioni, A. (Spring 1969). Man and society: The inauthentic condition. *Human Relations, 22,* 325–332.

40. Plasek, W. (February 1974). Marxist and sociological concepts of alienation: Implications for social problems theory. *Social Problems, 21,* 316–328; and Schweitzer, D. (1982). Contemporary alienation theory and research. In T. Bottomore et al. (ed.). *Sociology: The state of the art* (p. 68). Beverly Hills: Sage.

41. Presthus, R. (1978). *The organizational society* (rev. ed.). New York: St. Martin's Press.

42. Clinard, M. B. (1983). *Corporate ethics and crime: The role of middle management* (pp. 136–138). Beverly Hills: Sage.

43. Kanungo, R. N. (1982). *Work alienation: An integrated approach* (p. 157). New York: Praeger.

44. Reasons, C. (1982). Crime and the abuse of power: Offenses beyond the reach of the law. In P. Wickman & T. Dailey (Eds.). *White-collar and economic crime* (pp. 59–72). Lexington, MA: D. C. Heath.

45. Keough, R. (1993). *Attachment disorder.* New York: Dell.

46. Ibid (p. 56).

47. Ibid (p. 55).

48. Kanter, D., & Mirvis, P. (1989). *The cynical Americans.* San Francisco: Jossey-Bass.

49. Ibid (p. 34).

50. Halper, J. (1988). *Quiet desperation: The truth about successful men.* New York: Warner Books.

51. Ibid (p. 66).

52. Fisse, B., & Braithwaite, J. (1983). *The impact of publicity on corporate crime* (p. 240). Albany, NY: SUNY Press.

53. Mills. *Images of man* (p. 17).

54. See Simon. *Social problems and the sociological imagination* (Chapter 2), for a detailed analysis.

55. See Thio, A. (1988). *Deviant behavior* (2nd ed., pp. 88–96). Boston: Houghton Mifflin; and Box, Chapter 1.

56. This argument is based primarily on Box, Chapter 2. For a related perspective, consult the following: Smith, D. C. In Wickman & Dailey (Eds.).(1980) White collar crime, organized crime, and the business establishment: Resolving a crisis in criminological theory (pp. 23–38); Smith, D. C. (January 1980). Paragons, pariahs, and pirates: A spectrum based theory of enterprise. *Crime and Delinquency, 26,* 358–386; and Terreberry, S. (March 1968). The evolution of organizational environments. *Administrative Science Quarterly,12,* 590–613. For estimates, see Cook, J. (September 29, 1980). The invisible enterprise. *Forbes,* 60–71.

57. *World almanac and book of facts.* Mahwah, NJ: Funk & Wagnalls, 1994, 52.

58. *New York Times,* October 1993, A-1, A-8.

59. Army News Service, November 8, 1996.

60. Associated Press, April 29, 1997.

61. *New York Times,* March 10, 1994, A-1, A-11.

62 See D'Emilio, J. (June 7, 1993). All that you can be. *Nation,* 806–808; and Blumfield, W., & Raymond, D. (1993). *Looking at gay and lesbian life* (pp. 252–254). Boston: Beacon Press, for a discussion of institutional homophobia.

63. See, for example, Gerber, J., & Weeks, S. (1992). Women as victims of corporate crime: A call for research on a neglected topic. *Deviant Behavior, 13,* 325–347.

64. See *60 Minutes,* July 10, 1994, first segment.

65. Radic, R. (2008). *Gone to hell: True crimes of America's clergy* (p. 25). Toronto, Canada: ECW Press; http://www.foxnews.com/story/0,2933,286153,00.html; Simon, D. R. (May, 2010). *Crime and religion.* Lecture presented to the First Coast Free Thought Society, Jacksonville, FL.

66.  http://en.wikipedia.org/wiki/Differential_association (18 October 2010).

67.  See Goode, E. (1997). *Deviant behavior* (5th ed., pp. 354–356). Upper Saddle River, NJ: Prentice-Hall, for a constructionist critique of the position discussed here.

68.  See Simon, D. (1997). *Private troubles and public issues* (Chapter 1). Fort Worth, TX: Harcourt Brace.

69.  The following discussion is based, in part, on Eitzen, D. S. (August 23–26, 1984). *Teaching social problems: Implications of the objectivist-subjectivist debate* (p. 7). Paper presented at the 1984 meeting of the Society for the Study of Social Problems, San Antonio, Texas.

70.  Clinard (pp. 136–138); and Fisse & Braithwaite (p. 240).

71.  See Keniston, K. (1965). *The uncommitted* (Chapter 2). New York: Dell.

# CHAPTER

# 9

# The Scandalization of America

## The Higher Immorality in an Era of Greed

Between 1860 and 1920, the United States suffered only two major crises involving corruption on the federal level. This amounts to about one scandal every 50 years. However, beginning in 1963 with the investigation into the assassination of President Kennedy, the American federal government has experienced repeated scandals. The scandals themselves are serious social problems, causing all manner of social harm.

- When President Kennedy was assassinated in Dallas, Texas, on November 22, 1963, a cover-up of the investigation into the crime was personally ordered by President Johnson, Assistant Attorney General Katzenbach, and Federal Bureau of Investigation (FBI) Director Hoover. They allegedly felt that communist elements from either Cuba or the Soviet Union (or both) might be involved and feared a war would result. These officials agreed that the public must be convinced that Lee Harvey Oswald acted alone in killing the president. This was President Johnson's motive in setting up the Warren Commission in December 1963. Moreover, the Warren Commission did indeed find that Oswald had acted alone in killing the president, and that Dallas nightclub owner Jack Ruby had acted alone in killing Oswald (who at the time was surrounded by nearly 200 armed law enforcement officers) in the Dallas Police Station.

    Subsequent investigations into the crime by the House Special Committee on Assassinations (HSCA), 1975–1978, found numerous inconsistencies in the case. The HSCA found that President Kennedy "was probably assassinated as a result of a conspiracy."[1] Likely suspects included members of organized crime.[2] The HSCA concluded that Mafia bosses Marcello of New Orleans and Trafficante of Florida had the "means, motive, and opportunity" to assassinate the president, and/or that anti-Castro activists may have been involved.

    Within the last few decades, a disturbing body of writing has emerged, raising questions about conspiracies in the killings of major political and civil rights leaders of the 1960s. These questions continue to tear at the soul of many Americans who look fondly upon the Kennedy era as a time of high public confidence and optimistic notions of progress and human concern. As noted in Chapter 1, conspiracy theory is extreme in its tone and incorrect in its substance. However, this does not mean that conspiracies do not happen. The issue becomes a matter of evidence either for or against conspiracy. Today, the evidence for conspiracy cannot be ignored:

- Several studies have examined the notion that President John F. Kennedy was assassinated by the Marcello crime family of New Orleans. Carlos Marcello supposedly ordered the murder in an attempt to stop then attorney general Robert Kennedy's efforts to deport Marcello to Costa Rica. There is also evidence that former Teamsters Union president Jimmy Hoffa, later imprisoned by Robert Kennedy, and Mafia family boss Santos Trafficante, solicited by the Central Intelligence Agency (CIA) in 1961 to assassinate Premier Castro of Cuba, were in on the conspiracy. In 1977, the HSCA found that these mobsters had "the motive, means, and opportunity to murder the president."[3] The committee's chief counsel, Robert Blakey, concluded: "The mob did it. . . . It's an historical fact."[4]

- Marcello also allegedly ordered associate David Ferrie to Dallas immediately after the assassination. Ferrie supposedly gave orders to Marcello family associate Jack Ruby to kill the president's accused assassin, Lee Harvey Oswald. Ruby did in fact murder Oswald on national television 2 days after President Kennedy was killed. Oswald also had long-standing ties to the Marcello family through his uncle, a bookie, for whom Oswald worked during the spring and summer of 1963, just preceding the assassination.[5] Telephone records document numerous phone calls between Ruby, top Marcello aides, Florida mobster Trafficante, and convicted Teamsters boss Hoffa just prior to Oswald's murder.

- FBI head J. Edgar Hoover knew about a conspiracy but covered it up to protect the bureau from criticism for its failure to investigate the case. Robert Kennedy was allegedly blackmailed into keeping quiet about Mafia involvement because Hoover had secret files on the Kennedy brothers showing their involvement in CIA plots to kill Castro, as well as President Kennedy's sexual dalliances with Marilyn Monroe and Mafia moll Judith Exner.[6]

- It has also been alleged that the Mafia was responsible for the 1968 murders of presidential candidate Robert Kennedy and civil rights leader Martin Luther King Jr. and the 1965 murder of Black activist Malcolm X. For example, it has now been established that 13 shots were fired at Robert Kennedy on June 5, 1968, five more than "lone" assassin Sirhan Sirhan's eight-shot revolver held, and the fatal bullets came from the rear, not from the front, where Sirhan stood in relation to Kennedy. Separate examination of all fired bullets demonstrated that two .22-caliber guns were involved. Moreover, Sirhan had ties to the Mafia. He worked on the

Carona horse-breeding farm, run by Frank Donnarumma, a convicted criminal and associate of the farm's part owner, Mafia member Mickey Cohen. Cohen was also an associate of Marcello and other mobsters implicated in President Kennedy's assassination. FBI director Hoover consistently argued against the very existence of a Mafia in the United States. Thus, he denied the possibility of conspiracy in any of these assassinations, most likely to protect the bureau.

Journalist Bill Moyers has commented on the assassination of President Kennedy and the work of the CIA and related agencies (the secret government):

> The accusations linger; the suspicion of a dark, unsolved conspiracy behind Kennedy's murder. You can dismiss them, . . . but since we know how our secret government had planned for Castro, the possibility remains: Once we decide that anything goes, anything can come home to haunt us.[7]

Some of the most thorough research done on President Kennedy's assassination has been the investigation by physicist David Lifton. Over more than 15 years, Lifton has painstakingly examined all forensic, autopsy, and photographic evidence available. He has drawn several conclusions.

**1.** Following the assassination, the president's body was brutally and surgically altered and the photos of it falsified so as not to show bullet entry holes in the back of his head, which was blown apart. Testimony by many doctors, nurses, and others who attended the president, as well as the original photos of his body, all document rear head wounds. The opening for the tracheotomy done on the president was also enlarged to cover up a wound to his throat. Kennedy's body also contained some unexplained abrasions and a "clip" device in his skull, which was designed to reattach the back of his head to the rest of his skull. This was done to hide the fact that the bullets that killed him came from more than one direction and were thus the work of more than one assassin. Lifton also found evidence that a bullet was surgically removed from the rear of Kennedy's head.[8]

**2.** The autopsy pictures and X-rays of Kennedy's body were never examined by the Warren Commission, which was established by President Johnson to investigate the assassination. Moreover, the Warren Commission was led to believe, by FBI director Hoover and Assistant Attorney General Katzenbach, that Oswald acted as the lone gunman, despite massive evidence to the contrary. Proof of Oswald's identity, gathered by the CIA, was also suppressed by various officials, including ex-CIA head Allen Dulles, himself a Warren Commission member[9] (see also Chapter 2).

In 1977, the HSCA found that the killings of President Kennedy and Martin Luther King Jr. were probably due to conspiracies, and that the FBI,

CIA, and other government agencies had deliberately withheld evidence from the Warren Commission.[10] Certainly, only legitimate government agencies had the level of access to Kennedy's body necessary for the surgical alterations that were made.[11]

Considerable circumstantial evidence implicates the CIA in President Kennedy's assassination. The CIA was upset that the Kennedy administration had refused to launch further covert operations against Cuba following the attempted assassination of Castro and the failed CIA-backed Bay of Pigs invasion. What is more, many of the government agents involved in Watergate were also in Dallas the day Kennedy was shot. Some of these agents played roles in the Iran-Contra scandal (see later section) and other CIA-related covert operations as well, including the secret war in Cambodia in the early 1970s.

Perhaps the most thought-provoking issues in considering why the CIA would have killed Kennedy surround the Vietnam War and covert operations. The Kennedy administration was actively planning withdrawal of all U.S. military personnel from Vietnam, which angered the CIA. Likewise, Kennedy's order for the CIA to cease paramilitary (covert) operations during peacetime also met with strong disapproval. Not surprisingly, U.S. involvement in the Vietnam War escalated dramatically within a month after President Kennedy's assassination. Clearly, in many ways, the course of U.S. history was violently altered. The country would never be the same.

The precise nature of the conspiracy as related to the actual assassination, and those persons or organizations that were involved, was never determined, and, consequently, numerous theories have been advanced. Between 1966 and 2010, more than 600 books and 2,000 articles were written about the Kennedy assassination. The dominant view in these writings is that government agencies killed their own president. They did this because the president was going to make peace with the Soviet Union and end the cold war. There is also speculation that Kennedy was going to disengage the United States from its involvement in Vietnam.

Since Oliver Stone's 1991 film, *JFK* (Warner Bros.), resulted in the passage of the 1992 JFK Assassination Records Review Board. The Board's creation resulted in the release of about 2 million classified documents, but there are still another 1 million files that will not be released until 2017. What researchers have discovered among the released files is that (1) despite Bobby Kennedy's orders, the CIA–Mafia plots to assassinate Fidel Castrol under CIA Director Helms; (2) Mafia figures James Hoffa, David Ferrie, Carlos Marcello, Santos Trafficante, San Giancana, and Johnny Rosselli worked with both the CIA and anti-Castro Cubans in efforts to kill the Cuban dictator; (3) Robert and John Kennedy also hatched their own plot to over throw Castro (the JFK–Alimeida coup), which was to take place on December 1, 1963 (This violated the agreement that JFK had made with Soviet premier Khrushchev never to attempt to reinvade Cuba.); and (4) the Mafia also participated in the assassinations of Robert Kennedy, Rev.Martin Luther King, Jr., and Malcolm X.[12]

The JFK assassination is important in that it marks not only the first major postwar scandal but the beginning of a drastic decline in public confidence in government agencies and politicians.

Following President Kennedy's death, the United States escalated its presence in Vietnam. As previously discussed, the Vietnam War was loaded with a number of scandalous incidents that divided American public opinion and, ultimately, contributed to public distrust in government. Vietnam was followed by the Watergate scandal, which caused public trust to decline even further.

# Watergate

The Watergate-related crimes committed by government officials represent acts of official secrecy and deception taken to the extreme. They demonstrate forcefully and fearfully just how far away from the democratic ideal the U.S. political system had moved at the time and how close it was to approaching totalitarianism. In the words of David Wise:

> Watergate revealed that under President Nixon a kind of totalitarianism had already come to America, creeping in, not like Carl Sandburg's fog, on little cat feet, but in button-down shirts, worn by handsome young advertising and public relations men carrying neat attaché cases crammed with $100 bills. Men willing to perjure themselves to stay on the team, to serve their leader. It came in the guise of "national security," a blanket term used to justify the most appalling criminal acts by men determined to preserve their own political power at any cost. It came in the form of the ladder against the bedroom window, miniature transmitters in the ceiling, wiretaps, burglaries, enemies lists, tax audits, and psychiatric profiles. It is not easy to write the word totalitarian when reporting about America, but if the word jars, or seems overstated, consider the dictionary definition: "Of or pertaining to a centralized government in which those in control grant neither recognition nor tolerance to parties of differing opinion."
>
> And that is very close to what happened, for, as we learned from the Watergate investigation, the enormous power of the government of the United States, including the police power and the secret intelligence apparatus, had been turned loose against the people of the United States, at least against those who held differing opinions, against the opposition political party, and the press.[13]

The Watergate investigation revealed a number of criminal and undemocratic actions by President Nixon and his closest advisers.[14]

- Burglars, financed by funds from the Committee to Re-elect the President, broke into and bugged the headquarters of the Democratic Party in the Watergate apartment complex. These individuals were paid hush money and promised executive clemency to protect the president and his advisers.

- Burglars also broke into the office of the psychiatrist of Daniel Ellsberg, the person who leaked the Pentagon Papers to the press. These papers, of course, were instrumental in showing the public how it had been systematically deceived by a series of presidents during the long Vietnam War. Although the trial was in session, the White House offered the judge in the Ellsberg case the possibility of his being named director of the FBI.
- President Nixon's personal attorney solicited money for an illegally formed campaign committee and offered an ambassadorship in return for a campaign contribution. Money gathered from contributions, some illegally, was systematically laundered to conceal the donors. Much of this money was kept in cash so when payoffs occurred, the money could not be traced.
- President Nixon ordered secret wiretapping of his own aides, several journalists, and even his brother. Additionally, he had secret microphones planted in his offices to record clandestinely every conversation.
- John Mitchell, attorney general of the United States, participated in preliminary discussions about bugging the Democratic headquarters. He even suggested that one means of gaining information about the Democrats was to establish a floating bordello at the Miami convention.
- The president's men participated in a campaign of dirty tricks to discredit various potential Democratic nominees for president, including the publication and distribution of letters—purporting to come from Senator Muskie—claiming that Senator Henry Jackson was a homosexual. The White House also requested tax audits of administration opponents.
- The White House used the CIA in an effort to halt the FBI investigation of Watergate. The director of the FBI even destroyed vital legal evidence at the suggestion of the president's aides.
- President Nixon offered aides H. R. Haldeman and John Erlichman as much as $300,000 from a secret slush fund for their legal fees after they were forced to resign.
- The president and his advisers, using the cloak of national security, strongly resisted attempts by the special prosecutor, the courts, and Congress to get the facts in the case. Various administration officials were found guilty of perjury and withholding information.
- When the president, under duress, did provide transcripts of the tapes or other materials, they had been edited.
- The president, on television and in press releases, lied to the U.S. public, over and over again.

This infamous list of discretions comprises a tangled web of activities that posed a significant threat to the democratic political system of the United States. All the efforts were directed at subverting the political process so that the administration in power would stay in power, regardless of the means. There was a systematic effort to discredit enemies of the administration, to weaken the two-party system, and to control the flow of information to citizens.

Although the Nixon administration was guilty of these heinous acts, we should not assume that Nixon was the first U.S. president to be involved in such chicanery. Watergate was no aberration. Rather, it was a startling illustration of government practices that have been significant throughout U.S. history.

Moreover, there is ample evidence of various linkages between the Watergate scandal and other major American scandals since 1963, including the Iran-Contra affair.[15]

## Iran-Contra

In 1987, news broke concerning what was to be the most damaging scandal of the Reagan administration, the so-called Iran-Contra affair. The root of the scandal involved the diversion of funds from profits on missiles sold to the Iranian government. The profits were diverted to the Nicaraguan Contras, a counterrevolutionary force virtually created by the CIA.[16] At first the entire episode was blamed on marine lieutenant colonel Oliver North, with virtually all high-ranking officials of the Reagan administration claiming they were "out of the loop" concerning any knowledge of the events. Subsequent investigations and trial testimony, however, pointed to a massive cover-up by White House aides and others.

North's 1989 trial revealed that at a 1984 national security group meeting composed of vice president Bush, the Joint Chiefs of Staff, several cabinet officers, and President Reagan, a discussion of Contra aid based on solicitation of "third" parties (foreign governments) took place. This was adopted as a strategy of getting around the Boland Amendment that forbad further military aid to the Contras. President Reagan personally solicited the largest contributions for Contra aid from foreign nations, and a number of Latin American governments were requested to cooperate by falsifying arms sales transactions so knowledge that the weapons were for the Contras could be hidden. Those nations agreeing to falsify such documents were promised increased U.S. foreign aid.

Both illegal arms sales and illegal solicitation of funds were orchestrated by a secret group, the Enterprise, set up apart from the CIA and other governmental agencies to ensure secrecy. The Enterprise was composed of retired military and intelligence personnel, arms dealers, and drug smugglers.[17]

Actually, the North trial was part of a cover-up that began when President Reagan appointed the Tower Commission to look into his handling of Irangate. In the end, the commission reported that President Reagan had been unaware of what was going on around him and that his management style was based on his being removed from decision making. The Tower

Commission also found that the Iranian arms sale was mismanaged by various members of the Reagan White House staff. Reagan had told the Tower Commission that he was unaware that North and the other Reagan appointees to the National Security Council (NSC), including Admiral John Poindexter and Colonel Robert McFarlane, had been aiding the Contras. But it was North who was first tried for creating an organization known as the Enterprise in order to execute the arms deal. Along with retired air force general Richard Secord and Iranian-born businessman Albert Hakim, North was charged with, among other things, making a profit from the sale of government property.

This was actually a trivial charge, considering that North could have stood trial for lying to Congress and perhaps even treason. Despite later remarks made about his lack of involvement, in 1987, President Reagan told the press that he had definitely been involved in the decision to support the Contras. In fact, North's trial revealed Reagan's direct involvement in Contragate. President Reagan was prevented from testifying at North's trial because classified information was withheld by the very government prosecuting North.

## Early Involvement With Iran

There is evidence that the Iran-Contra episode was rooted in two incidents that involved George Bush, who was then vice president. According to a recent documentary, vice presidential nominee Bush went to Paris before the 1980 election to meet with Iranian officials.[18] At the time, the Iranians were holding some 80 American hostages, who had been kidnapped from the U.S. embassy in Tehran by Iranian revolutionaries. The American hostages were a crucial issue in the 1980 U.S. presidential election, in which the Republican Ronald Reagan sought to unseat Democratic president Jimmy Carter. In 1980, Bush allegedly offered the Iranians arms to delay release of the American hostages until after the election in November. Had the hostages been released prior to the election, such an "October Surprise" surely would have increased Carter's chance of winning.

Tremendous controversy still surrounds this affair. In early May 1991, Gary Sick, former Ford appointee to the NSC, claimed that it was Reagan campaign manager and subsequent CIA director William Casey, not vice president Bush, who met in Washington, DC, in late February or early March 1980 with Jamshid Hashemi, an Iranian arms dealer.[19] Hashemi himself has admitted to meeting with Casey and two additional U.S. aides in Madrid in July 1980 and Paris in October 1980. He claims the outcome of the meetings was initial U.S. shipments of tires for Iranian fighting vehicles via Israel. Similar claims have also been made by former Iranian president Bani-Sadr.[20] Interestingly, a former CIA operative, Richard Brenneke, claimed in sworn testimony in 1988 that he met with Casey, Iranian Manucher Ghorbanifar, Israeli and French intermediaries, and Donald Gregg (then a CIA officer attached to the NSC).[21] Gregg went on to become vice president Bush's aide and is suspected of involvement in Operation Black Eagle, another scandal predating the Iran-Contra affair.

The possibility that George Bush attended the Paris meeting still exists,[22] but most observers now feel that Casey made the deal. Casey was also likely the man who arranged for the theft of President Carter's debate-briefing papers in October 1980.[23] There were calls for a congressional investigation into the October Surprise incident, but no such calls have yet arisen for a similar look into Operation Black Eagle.

## Diverting Funds to the Contras

Although this may have been the beginning of arms sales to Iran, the idea of diverting funds to the Contras did not take place until after the 1980 election, when President Reagan and CIA head William Casey actually created the Contras. The first illegal operation to aid them took place in 1983, once again involving George Bush. From 1983 to 1986, Bush was involved in Operation Black Eagle, the purpose of which was to find a way around the Boland aid prohibition. Black Eagle was run out of Bush's office by CIA agent Donald Gregg, a longtime friend from the days when Bush was head of the CIA. Gregg and other operatives negotiated an arrangement with Panamanian dictator Manuel Noriega, whereby Panamanian airfields and front companies would be made available to Black Eagle operatives in exchange for Panamanian use of Black Eagle cargo planes. In fact, the planes were used to smuggle cocaine and marijuana into the United States at the behest of Colombia's Medellin cartel. "Several of those involved in the operation were aware that Bush and Donald Gregg knew about Noriega's use of Black Eagle for drug running and that nothing was done to stop it."[24] It was also learned that General Noriega had dossiers and videotapes about vice president Bush's role in the Black Eagle project. Black Eagle itself was part of a plan to defy the first Boland Amendment, which Congress had passed in order to stop aid to the Nicaraguan Contras. Between October 1984 and October 1986, Congress acted further to prohibit aid to the Nicaraguan Contras by passing additional Boland Amendments. In response, the Reagan administration launched what ultimately became the Iran-Contra affair. Along with the Iran-Contra operation, involving Lieutenant Colonel North and Enterprise, there was also a further resupply effort whereby planeloads of Colombian cocaine were flown to Costa Rican farmlands owned by John Hull, CIA/NSC liaison to the Contras. Hull claimed in 1984–1985 to have received $10,000 a month from the NSC. The cocaine in question belonged to Pablo Escobar and Jorge Ochoa, two major Medellin cartel figures, whose business accounts for 80% of the cocaine smuggled into the United States each year. Once off-loaded at Hull's ranch, the drugs were shipped by sea and air to the United States. Hull was paid by the Medellin traffickers in return for the labor and facilities supplied for the operation. The proceeds Hull was paid allegedly went to buy arms for the Contras. In other cases, the Contras smuggled drugs directly, possibly purchasing them from the Medellin cartel. The drugs were again flown to Hull's Costa Rican ranch, where they were swapped for arms.[25]

## The Scandal: Contragate

The selling of arms to Iran and the diversion of funds from such sales to the Nicaraguan Contras were accomplished by setting up a private supply operation using a company owned by retired air force general Richard Secord. Secord's American National Management Corporation has been involved in other covert operations besides Contragate, including providing logistical support for the military elite's Delta Force commandos and short-term secret airlift operations.[26] In fact, it appears as though the Iran-Contra operation was conceived by Secord as part of a meeting on special operations held in March 1983 at the National Strategy Information Center at Georgetown University. The meeting was attended by a number of CIA officials, military officers (including North), Secord associate Ted Schackley (later involved in Contra shipments himself), and Carl Channel (used by North to raise private funds to buy weapons for the Contras and to raise money illegally for candidates supporting the administration's Contra policy). Secord's philosophy of the NSC's role is expressed in his master's thesis, written in the late 1970s at the Naval War College, in which he spoke of the need to circumvent Congress and the bureaucracy in setting up covert operations and argued that the NSC would be a likely place to attempt such circumvention.[27]

## The Nugan–Hand Bank Affair

Another scandal involving Secord and others associated with Contragate involves the Nugan–Hand Bank. This bank, set up in Australia by a host of former U.S. military officers and ex-CIA agents, hired as one of its attorneys former CIA director William Colby. Subsequently, bank personnel were involved in a scheme to defraud U.S. civilians working in Saudi Arabia of their wages, which were deposited with bank officials ostensibly for the purpose of investment. The bank has also been involved in laundering drug money and in a smuggling operation that included former CIA agent Thomas Clines, associate of another former CIA operative, and Edmund Wilson, who is now serving a prison sentence for selling arms to Libya's premier Muammar Kaddafi. In his Nugan–Hand dealings, Clines was involved in selling Philippine jeeps to Egypt and was convicted of submitting $8 million in false vouchers to the Department of Defense. Another Nugan–Hand arms sale involved Edmund Wilson directly, along with bank employee Bernie Houghton, a businessman with CIA and U.S. military connections in Australia since 1967.[28]

## The Iran-Contra Conspiracy: "Operation Polecat"

At the State Department, the Iran operation was described as "Operation Polecat" because they thought it stank so much. George Bush at first lied and claimed that he had been "out of the loop" and unaware of Iran-Contra activities. Even though, as vice president, Bush headed the Vice President's Task Force on Terrorism, which urged that it was futile to make deals with hostage takers, he later admitted that he was aware of the hostage deal but did not admit to knowledge of diversion of funds to the Contras. Ironically, by violating their own rules and dealing for hostages, the Reagan–Bush team proved their own point. Such secret operations released three hostages but encouraged the taking of more.

The entire cover-up—lying to Congress and hiding of evidence—had been intended to protect Ronald Reagan from possible impeachment. In June 1992, Special Prosecutor Walsh indicted former secretary of defense Caspar Weinberger in order to attempt to prove a conspiracy to cover up Reagan's involvement. The charges were that Weinberger had lied to Congress and obstructed justice, based upon entries in his diary.

Finally came the "Christmas Eve Massacre" (December 1992) in which lame-duck president George Bush issued pardons to most of those convicted or under investigation, claiming that they "did not profit or seek to profit from the conduct," that they were acting in what they believed to have been the national interest, and that the Iran-Contra investigation represented an unnecessary "criminalization of policy differences." Bush did not pardon Secord, Hakim, and Clines, who were convicted in Iran-Contra and whose motivations appeared to be more of a mercenary nature. The pardons left Lawrence Walsh little choice but to close down the probe.

The message sent by George Bush in issuing the pardons was that government officials are free to violate the law whenever they believe their behavior is for the good of the country, even if it is in violation of the Constitution.

## Connections and Conspiracies

A shocking set of additional Central American connections runs through the Contragate affair and involves such groups as the World Anti-Communist League (WACL), whose membership includes another of the Contragate arms dealers, former U.S. general John Singlaub, who was part of the North/Secord Enterprise venture. WACL's Latin American affiliate, known as CAL, possesses direct links to Bolivian officials involved in cocaine smuggling and now convicted ex-Nazi turned drug trafficker Klaus Barbie. Barbie is reputed to have supplied the CIA with a list of KGB agents operating in Latin America and organized a meeting, with CIA approval, of the Condor Group, made up of intelligence officials from right-wing regimes in Argentina, Chile, and Bolivia. Barbie was also a security consultant to Roberto Suarez, a major cocaine dealer and producer.[29] WACL members from Guatemala, Taiwan, and Argentina have been represented in Washington by former White House aide Michael Deaver, who lobbied for U.S. military aid. The Guatemalan and Argentine officials represented by Deaver have been tied to death squads in those nations. Also among CAL's members is Roberto D'Aubuisson, organizer

of El Salvador's death squads. Finally, it is known that the Argentine affiliate of the WACL was responsible for the deaths of Archbishop Oscar Romero
and 28 other liberation advocates in Latin America. Moreover, the former
Argentine interior minister has been tied directly to Paraguayan cocaine
trafficking. In turn, Paraguayan intelligence chief Pastor Coronel, coordinator
of local death squads, is a partner of Corsican drug smuggler Augusto Ricord,
who is linked to the Gambino Mafia family in New York.[30]

The Contras themselves were the study of an investigation by a human
rights organization mandated by Congress as a condition of military aid. The
investigating body cited 22 abuses of human rights by Contra troops between
December 1985 and June 1987, including the execution of eight Sandinista
prisoners, forced recruitment of Nicaraguan Mennonites, the killing of Baptist
relief workers and a Catholic social worker, the abduction of Sumo Indians,
the killing of three civilians, and the kidnapping of two civilian women.[31]

A Latin American drugs/arms connection also involves the Contras.
Colombian cocaine cartel launderer Ramon Milian-Rodriguez recently testified in front of a congressional committee on narcotics that he funneled
nearly $10 million to the Contras via CIA operative Felix Rodriguez in order
to gain favor with Drug Enforcement Agency (DEA) and CIA operatives.
Rodriguez (also known as Max Gomez) helped oversee the supplying of the
Contras in the Enterprise operation.[32]

Other reports of a Contra cocaine link are disturbing.

- A cable message from the U.S. ambassador to Costa Rica (Tams) to
  Lieutenant Colonel North dated March 27, 1986, noted that "Popp"
  Chamorro, a Contra leader on the Costa Rican border, was allegedly
  involved in drug trafficking. North aide Robert Owen also testified that
  a plane delivering rocket-launching equipment to the Contras, secured
  by the CIA, was involved in drug running. The company hired by the
  CIA had a long history of cocaine smuggling, according to Owen.[33]
- Perhaps most disturbing is the alleged episode concerning Tom Posey,
  head of the Alabama-based Civilian Military Assistance Group that aided
  in supplying weapons to the Contras. One Contra operative, Jesus Garcia,
  has testified that Posey hatched a plot to assassinate the U.S. ambassador
  to Costa Rica and blame it on the Sandinistas in an effort to draw the
  United States into a direct military confrontation in Latin America.[34]

## Contragate and the Changing Nature of American Power and Corruption

As power has become more and more concentrated at the federal level
and as the economy itself has become more militarized (see Chapter 5), the
nature of corruption has changed. What is not generally appreciated about

this prevalence of corruption is what it reveals about the structure of power in American society.

Contragate, the Wedtech scandal, former White House employee Michael Deaver, and the problems of Jackie Presser and the Mafia-linked Teamsters Union all seem totally unrelated at first glance. Yet a deeper look reveals a disturbing pattern of interaction among officials of the executive branch of the U.S. government, former CIA agents turned businessmen, organized crime figures and drug traffickers, and large corporations.[35]

Wedtech, now bankrupt, was linked to Attorney General Edwin Meese, who was accused of securing a large defense contract for Wedtech at a time when he owned stock in the company. By further coincidence, Lieutenant Colonel Oliver North belongs to the Officers of Christian Fellowship and the Full Gospel Businessmen's Association—groups that provided funds that helped launch the careers of right-wing preachers Jim Bakker and Pat Robertson.[36]

Other links show a disturbing pattern of relationships.[37]

- Wedtech paid Robert Wallach, attorney for and close friend of Attorney General Meese, $1 million in stocks and cash. In 1982, Meese's intervention on Wedtech's behalf obtained a $32 million army contract.
- Wallach used his ties to Meese to intervene in a scheme involving building a billion-dollar pipeline from Iraq to the Gulf of Aqaba and alleged payoffs to the Israeli Labor Party. Meese also solicited the aid of NSC adviser Robert McFarlane, who saw the project as a method of balancing the advantages to Iran in the Contragate arms-for-hostages deal, which he and Oliver North masterminded.
- International arms dealer Adnan Khashoggi, involved in financing the Irangate arms sale, is now under investigation by a New York grand jury for allegedly assisting Ferdinand and Imelda Marcos in transferring hundreds of millions of dollars' worth of Manhattan real estate and art objects to Khashoggi in order to keep the Philippine government from obtaining them. Khashoggi and the Marcoses were indicted for fraud but later acquitted.
- Francis D. Gomez of the Washington public relations firm International Business Communications, which was used by Lieutenant Colonel North to funnel funds raised by Carl Spitz to the Contras, was also serving, at $21,000 per month, as the Washington representative of Impulso Turistico y Financiero. Impulso was also used by General Manuel Noriega to perform certain tasks in the United States.
- Noriega, while in the employ of the CIA at $200,000 per year, aided North and Secord in support of the Contras in violation of the Boland Amendment. At the same time, Noriega also supplied arms to M-19, a Colombian left-wing terrorist organization aligned with the Medellin cocaine cartel. In turn, Noriega contributed to the organization of Lyndon LaRouche, found guilty in 1988 of credit card swindling. Noriega was tried for drug trafficking in Miami and convicted.

## Characteristics of Contemporary Scandal

All of the scandals listed above share a number of common characteristics:

**1.** They were all the result of secret actions of government agencies (especially the FBI, CIA, executive office of the president) that were either illegal or unethical and caused severe physical, financial, and/or moral harm to the nation. All have taken place since the passage of the National Security Act of 1947, which institutionalized the most secretive aspects of what President Eisenhower termed the military-industrial complex, and C. Wright Mills characterized as the power elite and higher immorality (as described in Chapters 1 and 2). The key here is that organizations with immense resources—not merely corrupt individuals—were involved in criminal acts and their cover-up.

**2.** All the episodes discussed were the subject of official government hearings or investigations, some of which were nationally televised. Despite official investigations, the original causes of most of these scandals remain unknown. Thus, motives for President Kennedy's assassination, the reason(s) for the Watergate break-in, and the possible involvement of vice president Bush, President Reagan, and CIA director Casey in planning the Iranian arms sales and diversion of funds to the Contras remain matters of heated debate. Indeed, one of the hallmarks of the official investigation of modern scandal is that the investigations tend to become part of the scandals themselves, leaving unanswered questions concerning the causes of and mysterious events surrounding scandals to linger.

Unanswered questions characterize scandals both large and small. Consider the Bush administration, which left office with a host of unanswered questions concerning its deviant activity. According to Hagan and Simon[38]:

- Brett Kimberlin, while serving time as a federal prisoner for drug offenses, was on two separate occasions placed in detention and *incommunicado* from the media in order to silence him. Kimberlin claimed that in the early seventies he frequently sold marijuana to Dan Quayle, then a law student and later to be vice president. During the 1988 presidential campaign, Kimberlin was invited twice by reporters to discuss these charges. In both instances, before he could speak, he was put into detention by order of J. Michael Quinlan, then director of the Federal Bureau of Prisons. This was unprecedented—never before had a bureau director isolated an individual inmate. A report issued by Senator Carl Levin (D-MI) and chairperson of the Subcommittee on Oversight of Government Management concluded that Kimberlin was silenced for political reasons. According to one source, the DEA had informed the Bush campaign that it had a file on Quayle alleging cocaine use. The truth or falsity of these allegations remains a mystery.

- The Inslaw case charges that the U.S. Department of Justice, beginning during the Reagan administration, stole proprietary software from the Hamiltons and tried to force their small company out of business in order to pirate its software and sell it for the benefit of Reagan cronies. Two court cases ruled in favor of the Hamiltons and against the Justice Department. The software that they had developed that was the subject of dispute was PROMIS (Prosecutor's Management Information System), which enabled the computerization of law enforcement and criminal justice system files. The Hamiltons' defense attorney, Elliot Richardson, discovered that Inslaw's lucrative contracts and software had been planned to be passed on to then attorney general Meese's friends. Further intrigue was added to the Inslaw case when, in 1990, a freelance writer Danny Casolaro mysteriously "committed suicide" while hot on the trail of what he described as an outlaw intelligence operation behind Inslaw. The Inslaw matter remains unresolved to this day.

**3.** Moreover, numerous unanswered questions concerning events within each scandal remain shrouded in mystery. What was Lee Harvey Oswald's true identity? Why did Jack Ruby, in front of more than seventy armed officers, shoot him? Was President Lyndon Johnson involved in President Kennedy's assassination? Did the Nixon White House hire Arthur Bremmer to assassinate George Wallace in 1972? Why was the FBI the first agency to meet Dorothy Hunt's (wife of Watergate burglar Howard Hunt) airplane following its bombing? Did the 1980 Reagan campaign arrange an "October surprise" of its own that eventually became the Iran-Contra scandal? These and many other questions await answers.

**4.** Recent political scandals, especially Iran-Contra and the savings and loan episode, interrelate, not only to each other but to other types of crime and deviance as well. As mentioned earlier, the secret government is a product of the National Security Act passed in 1947.

Almost immediately, intelligence agencies began classifying documents and budgets (see "The Pentagon's 'Black' Budget" case study in Chapter 5) and engaging in covert operations using a bewildering collection of personnel: ex-Nazis, Mafia gangsters, arms dealers, right-wing extremists, corrupt politicians and bureaucrats, and current and former CIA and military officials. By 1963, the secret government had become a force unto itself. Since then, it has been linked to every major scandal at the federal level in U.S. domestic and foreign affairs.

- Virtually every member of the Watergate break-in team (the "plumbers") was involved in the failed CIA Bay of Pigs invasion, the idea for which belonged to then vice president Richard Nixon. One Watergate team member, Frank Sturgis, was also part of the CIA–Mafia plot to assassinate Fidel Castro in the 1960s.[39]

Sturgis also knew and had dealings with Lee Oswald, the alleged lone assassin of President John F. Kennedy, as did former CIA agent E. Howard Hunt and many other CIA employees. Watergate burglar Bernard Barker was also involved with Jack Ruby, who killed Oswald several days after his arrest. Ruby was also tied to an anti-Castro group in New Orleans that had links to the New Orleans Marcello crime family, which was implicated in 1977 by the House Assassinations Committee in the killing of President Kennedy. Both Hunt and Sturgis participated in a plot to mislead investigators concerning Oswald's real identity.[40]

Sturgis was also linked to Mafia gambling operations in Cuba from 1959 to 1961. Indeed, there is evidence that the hush money paid by the Nixon administration to the Watergate team was obtained from the Mafia and paid in part to keep the burglars from revealing their participation in the CIA–Mafia attempt to kill Castro. Interestingly, 11 former members of the Warren Commission were hired by Watergate defendants, including President Nixon, as defense attorneys.[41]

- President Nixon, for his part, had long-standing ties to organized crime and the secret government. Nixon and close friend Bebe Rebozo invested in the Mafia-linked Keyes Realty Company, of which Watergate burglar Eugene Martinez was vice president. The loan for the investment came from Arthur Dresser, an associate of mob financier Meyer Lansky, and another suspected plotter in the Kennedy assassination, Teamsters boss Jimmy Hoffa. Rebozo was also a partner in the Mafia-financed Resorts International Paradise Casino, profits from which were skimmed by organized crime.[42]

- There are also some fascinating links between the Watergate and Iran-Contra scandals, most of which center around Reagan CIA director and former Nixon Securities and Exchange Commission (SEC) head William Casey. In 1970, Casey was a partner in an agribusiness called Multiponics; the firm filed for bankruptcy in 1971. Another partner in the business was Carl Biehl, associate of Mafia boss and suspected Kennedy assassin Carlos Marcello since the 1950s. Casey also represented a New Jersey waste disposal company, SCA, in 1977. SCA, according to New Jersey state police intelligence, had deep ties to organized crime. Two close Casey associates, Max Hugel and William McCann, men whom Casey sponsored for Reagan administration appointments, were also closely linked to organized crime.[43]

- As noted in Chapter 2, the Reagan administration also had numerous links with organized crime. Jacky Presser, the Teamsters Union head, was used as an informant for the FBI at the same time he was under investigation for defrauding the union's pension fund. Presser, long linked to the Cleveland Mafia, was later named as a special economic adviser by Reagan. Presser advised the Reagan team, including George Bush, to select two appointees with ties to organized crime: as labor secretary, Ray Donovan, who was later twice indicted for Mafia-linked union activity, and as a Labor Department official, Roy Brewer, who was former head of the Mafia-dominated stagehands union and a friend of Reagan's since his days as president of the Screen Actors Guild (1940s–1950s).

- Another close Reagan associate with Mafia ties was Senator Paul Laxalt (R-NV). Laxalt and his brother invested in a Carson City, Nevada, casino, Ormsby House, with partner Bernard Nemerov, who had a long association with the Mafia. Laxalt was also instrumental in the 1971 Nixon decision to commute the prison sentence of Jimmy Hoffa. Hoffa mysteriously disappeared, however, just before he was to testify concerning his knowledge of the assassination of President Kennedy. Laxalt was Reagan's campaign manager in 1976, 1980, and 1984 and was nearly nominated for vice president.[44]

Thus, there is an emerging body of evidence that much of what is mistakenly called the American "street crime" problem is actually part of a complicated network of relationships among criminals and organizations at all strata of society (see Chapter 8).

**5.** The episodes in this chapter also contain numerous examples of what William Chambliss has described as "state organized crime,"[45] which stems from the need of nations for legitimacy, which is rooted in the rule of law. Some laws, however, conflict with other needs of nations, especially the need to accumulate wealth. Chambliss explored the origins of state-organized crime in European nations' support for piracy in the New World between 1400 and 1800. In the modern era, state-organized crime involves institutionalized practices discussed in depth in this book, namely, state-sponsored drug and arms smuggling; assassinations of foreign leaders (with the cooperation of organized crime syndicates); illegal surveillance of U.S. citizens; illegal drug experimentation on unsuspecting subjects by the CIA; and the illegal harassment of dissidents by the FBI. Although Chambliss's concept of state-organized crime constitutes both a useful theory and a typology of deviance by governmental elites, it does not include the possibility of either assassination of domestic officials or what has been termed "state-supported corporate crime,"[46] wherein the state and private corporations cooperate in the commission of criminal acts (see Chapter 8). The many unanswered questions concerning the secret government's involvement in assassinations and scandals (e.g., the killings of President Kennedy, Martin Luther King Jr., Robert Kennedy, and Malcolm X; the 1972 attempt on the life of Democratic presidential candidate George Wallace; and the Bank of Credit and Commerce International [BCCI] scandal) lead us to conclude that the discipline of criminal justice has neglected this topic for far too long. Indeed, the CIA has trained more police forces around the world than virtually any other agency of U.S. government, yet it is almost never mentioned in criminal justice and law enforcement texts. Obtaining a working knowledge of the motives for, and depth of, state-organized and state-supported corporate crime is essential to understanding elite deviance—as well as how the overall political economy of the nation functions. For example, Chambliss claims that not all governmental agencies are likely to engage in state-organized crimes—usually just the more secretive ones. The CIA, FBI, DEA, and various intelligence agencies are in ideal positions to engage in such acts. Indeed, these agencies have repeatedly obstructed justice in the name of secrecy.

- The CIA and FBI covered up the crimes of former employee and Cuban exile Ricardo Morales, who, on CIA orders, bombed a Cuban airliner in Venezuela, killing 73 people.[47]

Although the activities of the secret government constitute a crucial topic, it is also a challenging one. It will require innovative research strategies as well as new theories about the nature of the American political economy and culture. Moreover, there are problems with validity in such research. Considering the secrecy of the organizations and the emotional nature of the issues involved, this is hardly surprising. But what may hang in the balance is the very freedom Americans have come to associate with democracy.

## The Study of Elite Deviance

What implications do these examples hold for elite deviance theory, methodology, and policy?

The power elite of which C. Wright Mills wrote so eloquently has taken on dimensions that might surprise him. Not only are corporations, politicians, and military officials interlinked with Mafia figures, international narcotics smugglers, and small-time street criminals, but the CIA seems to regularly employ a vast array of drug dealers, arms smugglers, and ex-military and ex-CIA officials in its covert operations. Contragate, it would appear, is the tip of an iceberg, the dimensions of which are currently unknown. We must await further revelation by whistle-blowers, investigative journalists, and perhaps even enemies of the United States who stand to gain from such an exposé. In any case, the American power elite is clearly more structurally and morally complex than Mills initially proposed.

"Most criminologists tend to separate white-collar crime and the explanations for it from the organizational context and the political economy of which it is a part."[48] Specific goals, such as profit and power, often create situations wherein values conflict and deviant and/or criminal activity becomes an acceptable means of achieving such goals.[49] Situations that have the potential of bringing considerable harm are perpetrated in the pursuit of organizational goals by persons who would be reluctant to commit such acts outside their organizational roles. Indeed, as Montagu and Matson note, the new face of evil in the world wears the mask of everyday normality precisely because evil is now committed without feelings of shame, guilt, or other moral recognition. Instead, elites commit acts of great harm, often without knowing they are doing anything wrong.[50]

Moreover, scholars have studied crime in general and white-collar crime in particular on a type-by-type and case-by-case basis. This approach stems from the individualistic bias built into the legal apparatus of Western society. Overlooked, however, are the links among different types of crime as well as among various scandals.

The Bush family represents one of the most powerful dynasties in the history of the U.S. power elite. Much of the history of U.S. corporate capitalism and politics consists of family dynasties of one kind or another, from the robber barons of the Du Ponts, Mellons, Morgans, Rockefellers, Carnegies, and Kennedys to the newcomers such as Halliburton, Bechtel, Harken, Carlyle, and the like. Like the elites of England, "they marry into each other's families, go to the same schools and universities, sit on each other's corporate boards and invest in each other's business dealings. Importantly (as we will see), they watch each other's backs."[51]

- **George Walker** was President George W. Bush's great-grandfather. Walker took over the Hamburg-America Line, which was a front for a Nazi espionage operation in the United States. In Germany, Bush hired future CIA director Allen Dulles to launder the profits from Nazi investments. In 1942, the government seized Union Banking Company assets under the Trading with the Enemy Act, and George Walker and Prescott Bush had to cease doing business with the Nazis.
- **Prescott Bush** was the president's grandfather. He made considerable profits off Nazi slave labor. Now President Bush is an heir to these Nazi dealings. Prescott Bush continued his dealings with former Nazis until 1952, when he became a U.S. senator. His Nazi-related activities were kept out of the press during his election campaign.
- **George Herbert Walker Bush** is President George W. Bush's father. When George H. W. Bush was director of the CIA, he paid drug dealers large amounts of cash. Manuel Noriega, the dictator of Panama, was paid $90,000 a year by the CIA to prevent drugs from being transported through his country. Noriega still allowed cocaine shipments from Colombia to go through Panama. As CIA director, Bush helped fund drug dealers in Latin America and Southeast Asia. Bush also had dealings with fugitive Nazi Klaus Barbie, "the Butcher of Lyon." Barbie, who escaped to Bolivia and started associating with

Colombian drug dealers, used drug profits to fund a coup that over-threw the Bolivian government. George H. W. Bush was deeply involved in the Iran-Contra scandal, secretly selling cocaine in the United States and weapons to Iran, and using the money to secretly fund the Contras and socialist governments in Latin America. As vice president, he illegally sold arms and biochemical weapons to Iraq's Saddam Hussein.[52]

- **Jonathan J. Bush** is the president's uncle, and a member of the president's $100,000 Club. He is an elite manager at Riggs Bank, which was fined $25 million for violating the money-laundering law.

- **Neil Bush**, the president's brother, was involved in the savings and loan scandal as a director of Silverado Bank. At Silverado he loaned $200 million to his partners in his own failing oil company.

- **Jeb Bush**, the president's brother and a former governor of Florida, was also involved in the savings and loan scandal. He and his partner borrowed $4.56 million from the now-defunct Broward Bank. Jeb Bush repaid only $500,000 and was allowed to keep the office building the loan funded. The deal cost taxpayers $4 million. As governor of Florida, Jeb Bush was involved in rigging the 2000 election (see Chapter 6 for details).

- **George W. Bush** is president of the United States. Before becoming president, he engaged in a number of business practices that led to an SEC investigation. One of Osama bin Laden's brothers and Bush were cofounders of Arbusto Energy. Later, Spectrum 7 Corp bought out Arbusto (now called Bush Exploration Company). In 1986, the company was almost bankrupt, but even with its $3 million debt it was bought by Harken. Harken gave George Bush $2 million for his stock. Harken Energy was founded in 1973 by two oilmen connected to a covert effort to destabilize Australia's Labor Party government. It was purchased in 1983 by a new investment group headed by New York attorney Alan G. Quasha. Quasha's father was an attorney in the Philippines and legal adviser to dictator Ferdinand Marcos, and to the notorious Nugen-Hand Bank in Australia, a CIA operation.

    Bush ignored his new business partners' backgrounds, received his $80,000 annual salary (which eventually was increased to $120,000), borrowing money from the company at very low interest rates and buying stock at 40% below market value. Bush sold his stock for $23 million but denied knowing the firm was in financial trouble. However, memos obtained from the firm discuss the company's failure before he sold his stock, and Bush was advised by the firm's attorneys not to sell his stock due to insider trading regulations. The firm's memos and SEC documents confirm that Bush reported Harken had lost $28.5 million and was in danger of losing another $11.8 million. Bush claims he sold his Harken stock to repay a loan that was used to buy an interest in the Texas Rangers baseball club. Bush filed his report for that sale of his Harken stock to the SEC 8 months late.[53]

Questions have also been raised about Bush's military record. Critics charge the following:

- Bush never showed up for the Alabama Air National Guard when directly ordered to do so by his commander in 1972. He was absent for 6 months while working in his father's unsuccessful senate campaign. Furthermore, none of Bush's commanders or the 700 members of his Alabama National Guard unit have any memory of his presence. No official records exist for Bush's service in Alabama.
- Bush was also suspended from flying planes on August 1, 1972, due to his failure to pass a physical.
- Former lieutenant governor Ben Barnes pulled strings to get George W. Bush into the Texas Air National Guard during the Vietnam War while ordinary citizens, mostly the poor and working class, were being drafted. Bush was admitted to the Guard ahead of a waiting list of hundreds of applicants. Unlike draftees, most Guard members were not sent to Vietnam.[54]
- As president, Bush has appointed six former Iran-Contra defendants to his staff and filled the White House and Defense Department staffs with members of the Project for a New American Century. Critics charge that the aims of the neoconservative think tank, funded by right-wing foundations, are militarization of U.S. foreign policy and global domination by the United States. Some critics believe that the U.S.-led invasion of Iraq (2003) was their idea. The invasion, as we have seen, has made billions for Cheney's Halliburton, Rumsfeld's Bechtel, and his own family's Carlyle group.[55]

# Conclusion

The discussion in this chapter has not been in the methodological tradition of social science. It has been devoid of the representative samples and empirical testing that characterize mainstream research. Clearly, the study of elite victimization and organizational behavior is in an embryonic state in terms of description and classification of events. Moreover, even when and if genuine testable propositions are put forth, traditional social science methodology will be of little use in much of the undertaking, for several reasons.

(1) Much of the information about this field of study is secretive. It does not lend itself to observation, survey, variation of experimental design, cost–benefit analysis, or other traditional methodology that has been used in social science research. (2) Much of the information available is often intentionally deceptive. That is, false records, fronts, and other devices are created to hide exactly what must be studied. There is also a legitimized value system, a profit motive, and a desire for self-preservation that support and encourage elite deviance. (3) The behavior to be examined involves both individuals

and organizations, thereby not allowing for a clear unit of analysis. Movement from individual to social structural conditions and from informal to formal groups is the rule rather than the exception, once again making traditional social science research methods implausible.

Do these methodological difficulties leave us unable as social scientists to accomplish systematic study? We contend that they do not, although it seems clear that such study will require new research standards and tools. Finally, contrary to the independent or separate traditional conceptualizations in this field, we argue that three behaviors in this area—namely, corporate (organizational) crime, corporate (organizational) deviance, and behaviors that are legitimate but socially harmful—are intricately related to the extent that to study them independently would provide an inaccurate picture. White-collar crime at the individual level is an important component in this field of inquiry, due to the individualistic nature of our criminal justice system. That is, behaviors at the organizational level can be understood structurally, and reducing them to individual incidents of criminal behavior distracts from the structural understanding. Thus, Contragate was about one presidential administration's attempt to circumvent laws that proscribed what it wanted to do. Yet individuals have been indicted and convicted, not the entire administration or even its leaders. Another crucial issue is the nature of the evidence gathered in support of whatever propositions may be put forth. Validity problems loom large in research of this nature because much of the information gathered comes from private memos, government cables, and testimony given by people who may all have personal axes to grind. Perhaps the only solid evidence comes in the form of criminal conviction, as documented by court transcripts and files of law enforcement agencies. And on occasion, confidential information is leaked to the media and reveals what would have otherwise remained suppressed or distorted. These incidents are rare, but the evidence they provide can be substantiated by interviews with remaining role players. Regardless of how information is obtained, validity problems will remain, calling into question whether the study of elite deviance falls within the purview of social science. This is a question that those who study and work in sociology, political science, and criminal justice must decide for themselves. Indeed, this promises to be an issue in the debate over the definition and scope of elite deviance. For our part, we do not see how those disciplines that call themselves the social sciences can avoid the study of behavior that is so prevalent and demonstrably harmful—not only to American society but to the entire world.

## CRITICAL THINKING EXERCISE 9.1
### Scandal: The Hidden Dimensions

This chapter began with a discussion of some of the characteristics of modern scandal on the federal level. One of the most interesting aspects of contemporary scandal concerns lingering questions that remain the subject of controversy and debate. For example, after more than 25 years, we still do not know why the Nixon administration decided to bug the Democratic National Committee headquarters in the Watergate apartment complex. This and many other unanswered questions are the subject of this exercise. Select one of the following scandals:

- The 2008 Financial Crisis or Mortgage Meltdown
- Watergate
- Iran-Contra
- Inslaw
- The savings-and-loan scandal
- Iraqgate

Look up articles about any one of the above scandals. Then write a paper answering the following questions:

1. What remains unknown concerning the causes of the scandal?
2. What other scandalous events are speculated about by writers as occurring during the scandal? For example, some people have speculated that the Nixon administration hired Arthur Bremmer to assassinate George Wallace during the 1972 election campaign.
3. What reforms are proposed to prevent such scandals from taking place in the future?

## ENDNOTES

1. Summers, A. (1980). *Conspiracy* (p. 14). New York: Paragon House.
2. U.S. Government Printing Office. (1979). *Report of the Select Committee on Assassinations of the U.S. House of Representatives* (p. 53, vol. IX). Washington, DC: U.S. Government Printing Office.
3. Ibid.
4. Moldea, D. (1986). *Dark victory: Ronald Reagan, MCA, and the mob* (pp. 234–235). New York: Viking.
5. See, for example, Davis, J. (1989). *Mafia kingfish: Carlos Marcello and the assassination of John F. Kennedy* (pp. 258–303). New York: Signet; Scheim, D. (1988). *The mafia killed President Kennedy* (pp. 288–294). London: W. H. Allen, also published in the United States as *Contract on America* (New York: Kensington, 1988); and Friedman, A., & Schwarz, T. (1989). *Power and greed: Inside the Teamsters empire of corruption* (pp. 184–187). New York: Watts.
6. See Beatty, J. (June 23, 1991). Jack be nimble: A question of character. *Los Angeles Times Book Review, 1,* 13; and Davis.
7. Moyers, B. (1988). *The secret government: The constitution in crisis* (p. 44). Cabin John, MD: Seven Locks Press.
8. Lifton, D. S. (1988). *Best evidence: Disguise and deception in the assassination of John F. Kennedy* (pp. 703–708). New York: Carroll and Graff. See also Waldron, L., with Hartmann, T. (2009). *Legacy of secrecy: The long shadow of the JFK assassination* (pp. 182; 185–186). Berkeley, CA: Counterpoint Press .
9. Scheim (pp. 208–211); and Davis (pp. 290–295).

10.  Scheim (p. 210).

11.  See Fletcher Prouty, L. (1973). *The secret team: The CIA and its allies in control of the United States and the World* (pp. 416–417). Englewood Cliffs, NJ: Prentice-Hall; and Groden, R., & Livingston, H. (1990). *High treason: The assassination of John F. Kennedy and the new evidence of conspiracy* (pp. 273–465). New York: Berkeley Books.

12.  This section on Watergate is based in part on Eitzen, D. S. (1980). *Social problems* (Chapter 2). Boston: Allyn & Bacon.

13.  Wise, D. (1966). *The politics of lying* (pp. x–xi). New York: Vintage. See also Waldron, L. (with Thom Hartmann). *Legacy of secrecy: The long shadow of the JFK assassination* (pp. xi–xix; 55–57; 66).

14.  See also Wise (pp. xi–xiv); The tangled web they wove. *Newsweek*, December 2, 1974, 32–37; Four key convictions in the Watergate affair. *U.S. News & World Report*, January 13, 1975, 15–17; Dobrovir, W. A., Gebhardt, J. D., Boffone, S. J., & Oakes, A. N. (1973). *The offenses of Richard Nixon*. New York: Quadrangle; White, T. H. (1975). *Breach of faith: The fall of Richard Nixon*. New York: Atheneum; and Dean, J. (1976). *Blind ambition*. New York: Simon & Schuster. For a sociological analysis of Watergate, see Douglas, J. D. (1977). Watergate: Harbinger of the American prince. In J. D. Douglas and John M. Johnson (Eds.). *Official deviance* (pp. 112–120). Philadelphia: Lippincott.

15.  See, for example, Colodny, L., & Gettlin, R. (1991). *Silent coup: The removal of a President*. New York: St. Martin's Press; Scott, P. D. (1976). From Dallas to Watergate: The longest coverup. In P. D. Scott et al. (Eds.). *Assassinations, Dallas and beyond: A guide to cover-ups and investigations* (pp. 357–376). New York: Random House; and Scheim (pp. 297–326).

16.  Moyers.

17.  The following account of North's trial is based on Draper, T. (August 17, 1989). Revelations of the North Trial. *New York Review of Books*, 27, 5:59. In June 1991, most of the charges against North were overturned on appeal. The charges on which he was convicted (e.g., making a profit from the sale of government property) failed to address the real harm of the Iran-Contra affair (e.g., usurping Congress's constitutional powers in foreign policy, lying to Congress, and perhaps even treason).

  For evidence on this point, see *Coverup* (Los Angeles: The Empowerment Project, 1988); Hoffman, A., & Silver, J. (September 1988). An election held hostage. *Playboy*, 9, 7ff.; Hitchens, C. (September 19, 1988). Minority report. *Nation*, 192–193; and *Los Angeles Times*, June 23, 1991, A-1.

18.  ABC News. *Nightline*. 1995.

19.  *Los Angeles Times*, June 23, 1991, A-1.

20.  Ibid.

21.  See Octoberfuss. *New Republic*, May 13, 1991, 7–8; ABC News. *Nightline*, June 19, 1991; Phillips, K. (May 12, 1991). Political scandals brew—Is this Bush's Watergate? *Los Angeles Times*, M-1, and Bush absence fuels hostage deal rumors. *San Diego Union*, May 11, 1991, A-1, A-6.

22.  Persico, J. (1990). *Casey: From the OSS to the CIA* (p. 193). New York: Viking.

23.  Ibid (pp. 196–198).

24.  Waas, M. (July 14 , 1987). Two roads to a cover-up. *Village Voice*, 29.

25.  See Geis, G. (March 1, 1988). From deuteronomy to deniability. *Justice Quarterly*, 1–32.

26.  Miller, M. (1976). *The founding finaglers* (p. 350). New York: McKay.

27.  Hosenball, M., & Isadorff, M. (April 4, 1988). One big scandal. *New Republic*, 12–15.

28.  Kwitney, J. (August/September 1987). Crimes of patriots. *Mother Jones*, 16, 15–23.

29.  See Scott, P. D. (Summer).(1987) Beyond Irangate. *Crime and Social Justice*, 6, 25–46.

30.  Ibid (pp. 40ff). See also Safire, W. (May 20, 1993). Iraq gate giveaway. *New York Times*, A-13. The following examples are based on the discussion in Hagan, F., & Simon, D. R. (1997). Elite deviance in the Bush era. *Justice Professional*.

31.  *San Diego Union*, July 29, 1987, A-11.

32.  Mills, J. (1987). *The underground empire* (pp. 138ff). New York: Dell.

33.  *Los Angeles Times*, June 29, 1987, A-4.

34. See *Nation,* June 13, 1987, 786.

35. See Moyers.

36. Ridgeway, J., & Jacobs, K. (March 17, 1987). Onward Christian soldiers. *Village Voice,* 32ff.

37. Hosenball & Isadorff (pp. 12–15) is the source of these examples.

38. Hagan & Simon.

39. Ridgeway & Jacobs (p. 32ff).

40. For discussion of possible CIA involvement in the Kennedy assassination, see Marrs, J. (1989). *Crossfire: The plot that killed Kennedy* (pp. 181–210). New York: Carroll and Graff; Scott, P. D. (1976). From Dallas to Watergate. In S. Blumenthal & H. Yazijian (Eds.). *Government by gunplay: Assassination conspiracy theories from Dallas to today* (pp. 113–129). New York: Signet; and Davis (400–417).

41. Scheim (pp. 296–297) and Moldea (pp. 294–296).

42. Scheim (pp. 316–317).

43. See Potter, G., et al. (1997). *Organized crime* (pp. 238ff). Upper Saddle River, NJ: Prentice Hall, for a detailed analysis of Nixon's ties to the Mafia.

44. Scheim (p. 39). A movie presentation of some of these events is found in Francis Coppola's *The Godfather Part III* (1990).

45. Chambliss, W. (1989). State-organized crime. *Criminology, 27,* 183–198.

46. Kramer, R. (August 1991). *State-supported corporate crime.* Presented at the 1991 meeting of the Society for the Study for Social Problems, Cincinnati, Ohio.

47. Chambliss (pp. 185ff).

48. Ermann, M. D., & Lundman, R. (Eds.). (1993). *Corporate and governmental deviance* (4th ed. (pp. 3ff). New York: Oxford University Press.

49. Chambliss (pp. 185ff).

50. Montagu, A., & Matson, F. (1983). *The dehumanization of man* (pp. 185ff). New York: McGraw-Hill.

51. The following discussion is based on Rosen, B. (January 29, 2000). *George W. Bush and his questionable business dealings.* http://www.nobodyaskedme.com/monologues/012900mono. htm. See also Phillips, K. (2004). *American dynasty: Aristocracy, fortune, and the politics of deceit in the house of Bush.* New York: Viking.

52. Project for a new American century. http://en.wikipedia.org/wiki/Project_for_the_ New_American_Century (March 30, 2007).

53. Bush crime family. *Old American Century,* http://www.oldamericancentury.org/ bushco/bush_crime_family.htm (2002–2006).

54. Skinner, N. (September 2007). Bush's top 10 lies, exaggerations and 'obsfucations' about his military service. http://archive.democrats.com/display.cfm?id=165.

55. Bush crime family. *Old American Century,* http://www.oldamericancentury.org/ bushco/bush_crime_family.htm (May 2006).

# EPILOGUE:
# ECONOMIC DEMOCRACY

## A Proposal to Transform Society

Deviance by American elites is no longer confined to the borders of the United States:

- With 5% of the world's population, the United States accounts for nearly 40% of the emissions responsible for global warming each year.
- Numerous covert wars by the CIA, assassination plots, alliances with drug traffickers, organized crime figures, former Nazis, the Vatican's "Rat Line," and support for regimes that repress human rights have been responsible for the deaths of hundreds of thousands of people since 1947.
- At times, the CIA has rigged elections in democratic nations, destabilized entire economies, and, in the case of Iraq, used lies and propaganda to advance an agenda shared by global empire builders and corporate war profiteers.
- At present (mid-2011), there is an historical crisis of confidence in American institutions The White House's ratings are at nearly all-time-low records at home. Only 10% of the public expresses confidence in Congress, or in their bosses at work to do right by them.[1]

At the elite level, such deviance is part of a higher immorality. C. Wright Mills[2] used the term *higher immorality* (see Chapter 2 of this book) to refer to an institutionalized set of values and practices among the nation's corporate and political elite. Mills believed that America's upper class loves money, has mediocre cultural tastes, and, most important, possesses a moral insensibility that allows for the commission of various criminal and deviant acts. The acts constituting the higher immorality were discussed in Chapter 2. The Enron scandal is but one in a long line of such behavior.

Since Mills wrote in 1956 about the higher immorality, the nation has experienced unprecedented forms of corruption. No longer are American scandals simply about politicians taking bribes from corporate elites seeking political favors. Organized criminal syndicates have become active players in scandalous situations. Today these practices run the gamut from material self-enrichment and corrupt acts of acquiring political power (as in

Watergate) to deception of public opinion to sexual perversion. What Mills perceived about American political power in the 1950s was the beginning of "the secret government."[3]

## The Real Secret Government

The Constitution grants Congress the power to declare war. Although war has not been officially declared since 1941, the United States has fought dozens of secret wars between 1954 and 2007, often without the knowledge of Congress or the American people. Abroad, the government has secretly backed corrupt military dictatorships and death squads. At home, the CIA has violated the civil rights of millions of Americans by collecting dossiers, opening mail, and enlisting the FBI to burglarize the headquarters of organizations who merely oppose U.S. government policies. The effects of the secret government have devastated the trust of the American people in their government and American prestige in many third world nations. In many ways, the new war on terrorism is an effort to restore trust in government.

Beginning with the overthrow of the duly elected government of Iran (1953), the CIA has repeatedly destabilized democracies unfriendly to U.S. multinational corporations. American military intervention has gone hand in hand with the militarization of the economy, and increasing secrecy in the making of defense and foreign policy. Within the United States, the effects of the secret government have been evident in scandal after unprecedented scandal. Beginning with the assassination of President Kennedy and the investigation thereof,[4] the United States has experienced a continual barrage of scandals at the federal level. The crimes associated with these incidents have been seriously harmful.

The secret government will stake out a new role for itself in the coming "new world order." Former CIA director, now secretary of defense, Robert Gates has already stated that the CIA needs to ensure corporate security as well as governmental security. The CIA is stressing the need for domestic counterterrorism, involvement in the drug war, and "crisis management" of low-intensity conflicts around the world. Such practices tend to have anti-democratic effects at home as well.

Moreover, the deviance within the elite differs markedly from that of other social classes because it involves so much more money, power, and resources than those to which people in other strata have access.

## America's Main Drift

Social character remains the great dependent variable, shaped by both the political economy and the dominant culture. The master trend in American social character revolves around identity confusion and uncertainty about the future of the nation and its values. Since 1945, the social character literature has come "full circle."[5] The social critics of the 1940s and 1950s complained that Americans were too conformist and insecure. The American people were described as "cheerful robots,"[6] "other-directed,"[7] and overly receptive to the opinions of other people. In short, the fear of the 1950s was that the population had lost its independence under the pressures of anti-communism and the conformity inherent in bureaucratic and suburban life.

There followed in the 1960s and 1970s a cultural revolution that encouraged "doing your own thing." An entire self-help movement sprang up that stressed consciousness expansion, sexual freedom, and experimentation. Many members of the middle classes, products of the civil rights, antiwar, and feminist movements of the 1960s, eagerly adopted lifestyles based on self-awareness and self-fulfillment. No sooner had these seemingly independent streaks emerged than did the literature of the day begin to criticize Americans for their narcissism (selfishness and self-concern) and neglect of the common good.

By the time the "yuppies" emerged in the 1980s, social critics had become alarmed over the new lifestyle "enclaves" based solely on material gratification, designer drugs, and greed. Robert Bellah and his colleagues[8] noted with alarm the inability of new members of the upper-middle class to form emotional bonds of any kind.

Thus in the literature, at least, one notes conflicting trends from one decade to the next. Perhaps the greatest change during the past 40 years has been a virtual end of the affluence the generation of the 1950s took as a birthright. One can point to a new and more problematic aspect of the American character, namely, uncertainty and confusion. Many Americans now possess conflicting values or no values at all regarding faith in their most basic institutions. They are fearful about the nation's future, but haven't a clue about what will solve the nation's problems. There is no longer a basic faith in any political ideology or political figure. Business executives are every bit as distrusted as politicians. The "main drift" of the American character is one of cynicism and alienation.[9]

Much of this alienation stems from the inauthenticity and dehumanization that are the hallmarks of postmodern culture (see Chapter 8). This means that Americans live in a world where it is increasingly difficult to separate fiction from fantasy, form from substance, and lasting values from fad. The result of these influences on social character is an unprecedented confusion about life's most basic questions. Such confusion serves to spread a diffuse anger toward American institutions. Thus, Americans will remain hostile to politics and big business for a long time to come. Such hostility is usually met with slick new forms of propaganda and advertising. These efforts serve to raise up candidates who, shortly after their election, demonstrate an ineffectual leadership and corrupt practices of various kinds (related to the higher immorality described above).

America's view of extreme individualism and intense competition for scarce rewards and values (money, recognition, and power) create a society in which relatively few people become great successes. Consequently, many people in America feel they have "failed," and their self-esteem suffers. Knowledge about America's reward system and the American sense of individualism is a useful form of self-help. Studying the attitudes and experiences of others, their biographies (as Mills would call them), can be a liberating experience in a society that encourages self-blame, appearances over realities, and materialism over caring, concern, and emotional intimacy. Studying these dynamics can give you an important lesson in what is really important and lasting in life, and it can aid you in developing a sense of self-worth. Self-esteem is a crucial aspect of one's well-being and one's ability to love and be loved in return. The American social character is experiencing unmet needs for love, recognition, and identity. These issues are social problems.

## The Local Community and Social Change

Although government has a role to play in positive social change, it has become clear since the 1960s that no government can be made to positively change society on its own. Today, there is a quiet revolution happening in the United States. Social change that will ultimately end poverty, hunger, and unemployment is taking place in thousands of voluntary organizations. In Milwaukee, Esperanza Unida runs businesses through which young people receive job training and jobs. In Ohio, Open Shelter operates a nonprofit auto repair shop that teaches young people how to repair vehicles, rehabilitates houses using carpenter trainees, trains welders, and places trainees into paying positions within the community.[10]

Habitat for Humanity, Jimmy Carter's favorite charity, builds houses for the poor with volunteer labor. Other groups feed and shelter the homeless, grow food in their own urban gardens, recycle bottles, cans, and newspapers, comfort victims of AIDS, operate neighborhood crime watch programs, and perform countless other necessary tasks. There is a growing body of opinion that argues such groups are much more creative than government bureaucracies, have much more community support, and provide services more efficiently in many cases. Their supporters argue that government funding for these nongovernmental organizations (NGOs) will not only promote positive solutions to problems but also allow these nonprofit groups to provide many jobs, which will be sorely needed as corporations and government at all levels continue painful downsizing and restructuring processes.

Meanwhile, numerous other reforms are needed to enhance the American condition. These include the following:

**1.** The democratic reorganization of large corporations. Multinational corporations are an important barrier to progressive change. They possess no local or national loyalties and are unconcerned with their role in causing inflation, unemployment, pollution, and the perpetuation of gross inequalities, inequalities that inherently corrupt democracy. One of the best ways to extend democracy and community responsibility to corporations is to have workers invest their pension funds in them until they own a majority of the company's stock. This would not only ensure worker ownership and control, but would take away the layers of secrecy, from which so much corporate scandal grows. Worker-owned companies are much less likely to experience strikes and the problems that accompany worker alienation, especially drug abuse, absenteeism, and sabotage.

Currently, the government is mostly reactive to corporate crime, rather than proactive, in that it takes steps to prevent its occurrence. Over the past three decades there have been many reforms proposed by liberal criminologists, but few, if any, have been adopted.

Finally, following the rash of corporate scandals of 2002–2003, which cost Americans an estimated $200 billion and 1 million jobs, Congress passed the Sarbanes–Oxley Law. This law requires that:

> the Securities and Exchange Commission (SEC) cause the stock exchanges and NASDAQ to prohibit the listing of any security of an issuer that is not in compliance with standards for audit committees set forth in the Act. The Act requires the SEC, by rule, to prohibit the listing of securities of any company not in compliance with standards established in the legislation, including the following.

1. The audit committee is given direct responsibility for appointment, compensation, and oversight of the work of any accounting firm employed by the issuer.
2. Each member of the audit committee must be independent, and in order to be independent may not accept any consulting, advisory, or other compensatory fees from the issuer and may not be an affiliate of the issuer.
3. Each audit committee must establish procedures for receiving complaints about accounting and auditing matters and must keep those complaints confidential.
4. The audit committee must have the authority to engage independent counsel and other advisers.
5. The issuer must provide funding, as determined by the audit committee, for the audit firm and the advisers employed by the audit committee.

The Sarbanes–Oxley Act is seen by some as a major improvement to corporate oversight, particularly since it gives control over the hiring, firing, and oversight of the outside auditors to the audit committee and because it gives the audit committee the right to hire its own independent counsel and other advisers. Others remain extremely skeptical that these reforms will work.[11]

**2. Reducing government's size.** For most Americans, the greatest problems represented by government concern deficit spending, high taxes, unfair welfare programs, and gridlock. The system now in place has degenerated into government by special (business) interests, with reelection campaigns of politicians financed by such groups. Overcoming these problems is a complex task, but it is not impossible.

The writers of the American Constitution never dreamed there would be a class of professional politicians who made being in office a life's work. The Constitution says nothing about political parties. Our current pathologies suggest the need for (1) campaign finance reform (federally financed congressional elections); (2) term limitations for senators and representatives; and (3) the abolition of "welfare" for able-bodied people of working age and its replacement with guaranteed full employment and paid job training. Perhaps the best way to reduce the debt and the deficit is to pare down all possible expenditures, including corporate subsidies, and increase government receipts without raising taxes on working people. Full employment is the best medicine for our economic woes.

**3.** Bringing about full employment. This may require issuing new tax write-offs to employee-owned corporations to expand factories and jobs here in the United States. It may also require making government the employer of last resort if not enough corporate sector jobs are available. There is no question that government is capable of playing such a role, as Roosevelt's New Deal demonstrated with the Works Progress Administration (WPA), Civilian Conservation Corps (CCCs), and similar programs. Moreover, attached to every job ought to be cradle-to-grave benefits: health and dental insurance, life insurance, family leave, and some system of day care for children of employees. Day care centers go back at least as far as World War II in America, and there is no reason such facilities could not experience a rebirth at job sites. Why not finance these benefits through a combination of government sponsorship, employer contribution, and employee payroll deduction? The vast majority of other industrial democracies already sponsor such programs as paid family leave and national health care. Are Americans any less valuable than citizens of other democracies?

The financing of such programs could also take place through increased taxes on the Americans who possess the greatest wealth and who earn the greatest income. It is now the case that the richest 2.5 million Americans earn more income than the poorest 100 million. Clearly this situation is incompatible with the growth of democracy in a nation where money buys access and influence. The framers of the Constitution assumed that America would be an upper-middle-class society, and Jefferson himself warned that if the United States became an urban, manufacturing nation, class conflict and the growth of a few rich and many poor would follow. "He believed that almost all Americans should continue farming to avert social ills, class distinctions, and social conflict."[12] Jefferson said all this decades before Karl Marx was born. As historian Charles A. Beard once noted, one does not have to be a Marxist to know that wealth and power go hand in hand. Americans have always believed in the unlimited accumulation of wealth. It is part of the American Dream, as well as part of our conception of individualism. The notion that a few ought to fairly sacrifice for the benefit of all has not become part of the American character. Would there be much harm to Americans' motivation if their wealth were limited to $100 million? Or $1 billion? For 98% of the population, such a limitation would be of no consequence. A national debate on such limits ought to begin soon.

4. A program of social reconstruction. Rarely has there been such unmet need in America. Hundreds of billions of dollars worth of streets, roads, and bridges are in disrepair. Millions of first-time home buyers cannot afford a home. In California, two-thirds of such home buyers cannot afford one. There is a need for better schools and smaller classes, more family doctors (and fewer specialists), more nurses, teachers, computers in education and in homes, police and fire personnel, libraries, and drug treatment facilities (to name just a few). What seems reasonable is a domestic Marshall Plan for America, one similar to the one that rehabilitated the economic stability of European nations after World War II, and to reconstruct Iraq in 2004.

The question is, of course, how to pay for these programs. Aside from the tax programs discussed above, there is a need to drastically reduce spending on defense weapons systems, and engage in economic conversion to meet these needs. Many corporations can convert their plants to engage in badly needed peacetime activity: manufacturing mass transit systems, prefabricated housing units, and development of future technology (such as interactive video, nonpolluting energy sources, and virtual reality systems).

Although economic democracy is a necessity in America, government also suffers from concentrated power within organizations. Secretive organizations can lead the nation into war without a congressional declaration. This is proof enough of democracy's erosion in America. Many proposals exist for extending democracy in America. Dr. Michael Lerner has advocated making extensive use of legislative initiatives (proposals for law or changes therein that come from citizens and appear on ballots after the proper number of petition signatures has been collected). People then vote the proposal(s) up or down in the next general election. Lerner also advocates more extensive use of the recall, where a majority of voters can vote a politician out of office. One of Lerner's more provocative notions concerns the use of television to extend democracy. Voters express their preferences through voting devices attached to their television sets. They would vote after an electronic town hall meeting that debated the issue(s) in question. Representatives would consider the results of the vote.[13] Lerner's ideas are not the last word concerning how to expand democracy in America. The need to do so, however, remains paramount.

5. Public health. America's most ridiculous war remains the so-called war on drugs. This is the fourth war on drugs we have fought in the last century, and each time the results have brought nothing but disaster and more contradictions. I often fantasize that each night in America a scenario is played out wherein an adult with a cigarette in one hand and a martini in

another gives his or her teenage child a lecture about the dangers of drugs. All the illegal drugs we are trying to save our children from kill some 10,000 people a year, whereas the ones we keep in our homes legally kill over 600,000. Does this seem rational to you? And there are very strong relationships between the abuse of tobacco and alcohol and the consumption of the illegal drugs we say we are so concerned with eliminating.

Clearly these contradictions must cease. A national law similar to the ones in California, Florida, and New York City banning tobacco use in all restaurants, bars, hotel lobbies, and office buildings would be a good beginning. So would a ban on all alcohol advertising. Evidence exists demonstrating that the more alcohol is advertised in a given culture, the higher the per capita consumption of alcohol in that culture. There is also ample evidence that alcohol is sold to underaged children in minority neighborhoods as a matter of course.

A number of Congress members stated they did not know we were losing the drug war until they saw the movie *Traffic!* If our policy makers are not informed as to the status of the drug war, why should the public take an interest? The Congress has shown almost no imagination and little interest in the public health approach to drug treatment, as has been successfully utilized in Holland, England, and other European nations. In the United States, we only hear about the failures, it seems. As a nation, we have never made up our minds whether drug addicts are criminals or patients in need of treatment. The drug-addicted criminals of this generation are the urban rioters of the future. It makes no sense to have this population coming out of prison more angry, resentful, and in need of treatment than when they entered. They are a ticking time bomb waiting to explode into America's next crime epidemic. Let us treat them now while there is still time. For treatment is much cheaper than prison, and much cheaper than rioting.

## Foreign Policy and Population Crisis

Because we live in an interdependent world, whatever happens elsewhere is a matter of concern everywhere. The United States has political and economic relations and commitments everywhere. Consequently, America's true interest and moral principles lie in promoting peace, democracy, and prosperity/full employment wherever possible. Militarily, the United States has evolved into the military-industrial complex that President Eisenhower warned us against in his farewell address in 1961. The combined values of Pentagon programs and property, now planned for 10 to 20 years at a time, are about $1,450 billion, an amount equal to nearly 60% of the gross stock of fixed private capital in U.S. manufacturing industries.[14] There are now between 25,000 and 30,000 corporations who are prime Pentagon contractors. The result is that 2.2 million people are now employed in firms managed by the Pentagon, and military budgets have been kept at cold war levels.

The resources spent on Pentagon capitalism have meant less innovation in other sectors of the economy. Much of the manufacturing sector of the American economy has now lost its competitive edge to other European nations, especially Germany, in machine tools. Millions of manufacturing jobs have been transferred outside the United States to third world nations, such as Mexico, nations in Asia, and so on. Between 1977 and 1996 the number of machine tool factories in the United States alone declined by 50%. At the same time, top paid American corporate executives now earn more than 1,000 times the wages of the average American worker, a figure more unequal than in any other modern capitalist democracy.

Seymour Melman has recently argued that America's concentration of wealth, its deindustrialization, and Pentagon capitalism are exactly the same sort of economic variables that have produced the economic crisis that is currently wreaking havoc in the former Soviet Union. Melman's claim is that we are well on our way to experiencing the same sort of calamity.[15]

The United States is, after all, only one nation in a world composed of nearly 150 nations. America can, nevertheless, do more than it is doing now. One valuable policy the United States could promote is to have as many third world nations as possible coalesce into common market trading partners. Such arrangements can serve indirectly to promote freedom of travel and other human rights. The arrangement has worked so well in Europe that much of that continent is on the verge of forming a united, economic superpower, complete with multiple citizenship privileges, a common currency, and many additional advantageous features.

Given the depth of the global population crisis and environmental crises, organized groups of people must engage in nonviolent action to oppose shortsighted corporate and governmental environmental policies.

## Why Change Must Come

The reforms we have considered are not merely utopian. If we look at the history of progressive social change in America, we will soon discover a central trend. All the progressive reform of the 19th and 20th centuries, such as the abolition of slavery, the right to vote for women, the 8-hour workday, the right to collective bargaining, the Civil Rights Acts, or the Voting Rights Act are the outcome of protracted struggle by collective social movements. Such movements were products of marches and demonstrations by groups of people who aided each other. Despite all the American folklore about the importance of individual heroes and the apathetic and alienated masses, it is collectivities that produce progressive social change.

Possessing a sociological imagination involves the realization that positive social change in America has come about not so much through acts of individual heroism as through the episodes of collective action. These movements involve groups of people who share a genuine concern for each other's well-being and human rights. This is what Americans call "teamwork." If you wish to extend democratic life in this society, you must be willing to work for worthy causes. This means creatively participating in democratic social movements and joining worthwhile groups. The need for people to work for social change has rarely been greater, and the number of groups looking for dedicated volunteers and paid employees is astounding. Pick a cause: helping the poor, improving the environment, extending human rights here and overseas, ending hunger and malnutrition, extending gun control, befriending parentless children, world peace. The list is almost limitless. Such lists appear in nearly every issue of the *Utne Reader*. Part of developing a sociological imagination can mean experience in such organizations.

Second, working for social change also means staying informed about the issues of the day. One of the assumptions made by many of the writers of the Constitution was that the American citizenry would consist of people who took an active interest in public issues, who would stay informed and engage in ongoing public debate. Our democracy has degenerated into a place where 10-second sound bites and meaningless political slogans have nearly replaced serious debate about complex issues.

Having duly noted the limitations involved in predicting master trends, one can still point with some confidence to a number of institutional conditions that will continue to cause numerous social problems. Increasing inequalities of wealth and political power will worsen the numerous macro- and micro-level problems that have been the subject of this book (unemployment, recession/depression, corporate crimes and political corruption, and related woes).

Partially as a result of these trends, the social character of our age suffers from a lack of, and yearning for, stable moral values that will serve as a guide to decision making in daily life. Given the constant social changes concerning economic conditions, cultural fads, technological breakthroughs in birth control devices, medicine, and invasive technology, stable values seem a long way off at best. Moreover, there is every reason to believe that the current mass disrespect for political and economic elites will continue, perhaps culminating in collective social movements that will result in the basic structural reforms necessary to resolve the great social problems of our age.

From a sociological imagination perspective, solutions to the problems of our age must take place on the individual, community, and societal levels. Along with a humane transformation in social character, masses of people must be encouraged to engage in collective action that will extend both economic and political democracy.

The existing global economy creates islands of power and privilege in a large sea of poverty. The fortunate hoard and squander resources on frivolous consumption, whereas others are denied a basic means of living. A former president of the World Bank recently informed me that a billion third world inhabitants exist on 1 dollar or less and another billion survive on 2 dollars a day. Furthermore, those who control the creation and allocation of money use this power to generate speculative profits. These profits increase the claims of the speculators to the wealth created through the labor and creative effort of others—while contributing nothing in return to the wealth creation process. In our present economy, unemployment, hoarding, and speculation are endemic, resulting in a grossly inefficient use of life's resources. In nature, unemployment and hoarding beyond one's own need are rare, and there is no equivalent to financial speculation.

Our most brilliant scientists, innovators, and teachers have been those driven not by the promise of financial rewards, but by an inner compulsion to learn, to know, and to share their knowledge. In our present global economy, corporate-controlled mass media create monocultures of the mind that portray greed and exclusion as the dominant human characteristics. Intellectual property rights are used to preclude the free sharing of information, technology, and culture essential to creative innovation in the community interest.

We live at a time when our very survival depends on rapid innovation toward the creation of living economies and societies. Such innovation depends on vigorous community-level experimentation supported by the creative energies of individuals everywhere. It is far more likely to come from diverse self-directed democratic communities that control their economic resources and freely share information and technology than from communities whose material and knowledge resources are controlled by distant corporate bureaucracies intent on appropriating wealth to enrich their shareholders.

## Coda

All this is to say that the world as it is has evolved into a place that is just too violent, too dangerous, and too contradictory. The fictional gangster Tony Soprano has become a symbol of a world that tries to have it both ways, one in which it is permissible to be a psychopath and a gangster, as long as one is undergoing psychotherapy.[16] Murder, narcotics trafficking, bribery, and sexual depravities are now grounds for celebrity worship, not contempt, in American culture. If fascism ever comes to America, it will be under the guise of these new celebrities. What Tony represents is the extreme but logical outcome of the narcissistic individualism of the postmodern era and all of its attendant social problems.

What is really needed, as this chapter has pleaded, are unconditional doses of love, healing, and caring in a world that is bleeding from wounds of violence, war, famine, ignorance, poverty, disease, ecological trauma, and a host of related ills. Both major political parties in America have learned to cater only to our fears. They compete to build more prisons and more missiles, spend more to save Social Security (lest it disappear). Meanwhile, the real problems that need addressing as discussed in this book go unaddressed and unresolved.

# ENDNOTES

1. For details see the discussions in Chapters 1 through 7. For discussions of the imperialistic nature of the Bush administration and its policy failures, see Tirman, J. (2006). *100 ways America is screwing up the world* (pp. 43–45). New York: Harper; Vidal, G. (2002). *Dreaming war*. New York: Thunders Mouth; Vidal. (2004). *Imperial America*. New York: Nations Books; Blum, W. (2004). *Freeing the world to death: Essays on the American empire* (pp. 85–188). Monroe, ME: Common Courage Press; Burbach, R., & Tarbell, J. (2004). *Imperial overstretch: George Bush and the Hubris of empire* (pp. 76–218). New York: Palgrave Macmillan.

2. Mills, C. W. (1956). *The power elite* (Chapter 13). New York: Oxford University Press.

3. Moyers, B. (1988). *The secret government*. Berkeley: Seven Locks Press.

4. See Simon, D. R. (2002). The scandalization of America: Political corruption in the postmodern era. In Gary Potter (ed.). *Controversies in white-collar crime* (pp. 137–147). Cincinnati: Anderson.

5. See Wilkinson, R. (ed.). (1992). *American social character*. New York: Harper Collins; and Wilkinson, R. (1988). *In search of the American character*. New York: Harper Collins.

6. Mills, C. W. (1956). *White collar*. New York: Oxford University Press.

7. Riesman, D., et al. (1950). *The lonely crowd*. New Haven, CT: Yale University Press.

8. Bellah, R., et al. (1986). *Habits of the heart*. Berkeley: University of California Press.

9. Patterson, J., & Kim, P. (1991). *The day America told the truth*. New York: Prentice-Hall.

10. Garr, R. (1995). *Reinvesting in America*. Reading, MA: Addison-Wesley.

11. *Report of the NYSE Corporate Accountability and Listing Standards Committee* (p. 1), June 6, 2002. For a skeptical view see Huffinton, A. (2003). *Pigs at the trough: How corporate greed and political corruption are undermining America*. New York: Three Rivers Press.

Corporate governance standards are also being addressed by the stock exchanges. Responding to a request from SEC chairman Harvey L. Pitt, the New York Stock Exchange appointed a Corporate Accountability and Listing Standards Committee to review the exchange's listing standards. The new standards for corporations on stock exchanges very much resemble those listed above for auditors, only they are for members of corporate boards.

12. Etzkowitz, H. (ed.). (1980). *Is America possible?* (p. 4). St. Paul, MN: West.

13. Lerner, M. (1973). *The new socialist revolution*. New York: Dell.

14. Melman, S. (2001). *After capitalism* (p. 25). New York: Random House.

15. Ibid.

16. See Simon, D. R. (2004). *Tony Soprano's America: The criminal side of the American dream*. New York: Westview.

# SOURCES

The following is a list of articles, books, and organizations relating to the issues raised in this epilogue.

# Publications

*BankCheck*. 1847 Berkeley Way, Berkeley, CA 94703. World Bank and IMF activities and opposition campaigns. Web site: http://www.irn.org.

*The Ecologist*. c/o M.I.T. Press, Journals, 55 Hayward St., Cambridge, MA 02142. Europe's leading journal on social and environmental issues; emphasizes the effects of globalization and grassroots resistance movements. E-mail: theecologist@gn.apc.org.

*Multinational Monitor*. P.O. Box 19405, Washington, DC 20036. Reports on corporate activity, emphasizing accountability, trade, worker health, indigenous rights, environment, and consumer issues. Web site: http://www.essential.org.

*Third World Resurgence.* Third World Network, 228 Macalister Road, 10400 Penang, Malaysia. Deep analysis of North-South economic, social, and environmental issues from perspectives of southern activists and governments.

# Books

Barlow, M., & Campbell, B. (1995). *Straight through the heart: How the liberals abandoned the just society.* New York: HarperCollins. Documents Canadian Liberal Party's dismantling of the world's most effective social welfare programs.

Barnet, R. J., & Cavanagh, J. (1994). *Global dreams: Imperial corporations and the new world order.* New York: Simon & Schuster. How 200 companies are weaving webs of production, consumption, finance, and culture, leading to social, environmental, and political disintegration.

Bello, W., with S. Cunningham and B. Rau. (1994). *Dark victory: The United States, structural adjustment, and global poverty.* London: Pluto Press. Reports on multilateral development banks and their effects on the poor.

Cobb, C., Halstead, T., & Rowe, J. (October 1995). If the GDP is up, why is America down? *Atlantic Monthly.* Blistering critique of gross national product (GNP) and other current economic measurements; suggests new measurements that account for social and environmental effects.

Daly, H. E. (November 1993). The perils of free trade. *Scientific American.* The inherent flaws of free trade; why it cannot possibly promote equity or ecological sustainability.

Daly, H. E., & Cobb, Jr., J. B. (1994). *For the common good: Redirecting the economy toward community, the environment, and a sustainable future.* Boston: Beacon Press. Critique of current economic theory and practice; promotes alternative economic values for sustainability, not growth.

Heredia, C. A., & Purcell, M. E. (1994). *The polarization of Mexican society: A grassroots view of world bank economic adjustment policies.* The Development GAP 1994. Study of the effect of World Bank policies on Mexico's small farmers and the urban poor.

Korten, D. C. (1995). *When corporations rule the world.* Washington, DC: Kumarian Press. How the rules of the global economy were created by and for transnational corporate gain while devastating the environment and social equity; also offers a relocalizing strategy.

Mander, J., & Goldsmith, E. (1999). *The case against the global economy.* San Francisco: Sierra Club Books. Forty-three authors present comprehensive analyses of globalization's effects, the corporations and theories that drive it, and some ideas for localizing alternatives.

Raghavan, C. (1990). *Recolonization: GATT, the Uruguay round, and the third world.* New York: Third World Network. Analysis of the latest round of global trade talks.

Rifkin, J. (1994). *The end of work.* New York: G. P. Putnam's. Scary study of how new technologies are destroying jobs in industry, agriculture, and the service sector globally.

Shiva, V. (1993). *Monocultures of the mind: Perspectives on biodiversity and biotechnology.* Third World Network. Analysis of effects of new technologies on third world cultures.

Wallach, L., Cooper, P., McGinn, C., et al. (January 1996). NAFTA's broken promises: The border betrayed. *Public Citizen.* Examines environment and health decline of the U.S.-Mexico border in NAFTA's first 2 years.

# Organizations

Council of Canadians. 904–251 Laurier Ave. W., Ottawa, Ontario K1P 5J6, Canada. Leading battler against NAFTA; works to safeguard Canada's social programs and the environment and advocates alternatives to free trade.

Development Group for Alternative Policies (D-GAP). 927 15th St. NW, 4th Floor, Washington, DC 20005. Brings southern grassroots voice into international economic policy making. Web site: http://www.igc.apc.org/dgap.

Earth Island Institute. 300 Broadway, Suite 28, San Francisco, CA 94133. Environmental group that has led resistance to GATT challenge of Marine Mammal Protection Act and other wildlife issues. Publishes excellent journal. Web site: http://www.earthisland.org/ei/.

Fifty Years Is Enough: US Network for Global Economic Justice. 1025 Vermont Ave. NW, Suite 300, Washington, DC 20005. International coalition challenging the World Bank–IMF economic model. E-mail: wb50years@igc.apc.org.

Friends of the Earth. 1025 Vermont Ave. NW, Suite 300, Washington, DC 20005. Leading environmental group that campaigns against globalization and current economic policies. Web site: http://www.foe.org.

Global Exchange. 2017 Mission St., Suite 303, San Francisco, CA 94110. Books and publications on globalization; builds links between international organizing efforts. E-mail: globalexch@igc.apc.org.

Institute for Agriculture and Trade Policy. 1313 5th St. SE, Suite 303, Minneapolis, MN 55414. Pioneer campaigner and publisher against NAFTA and GATT and for preservation of small and indigenous farms. Web site: http://www.iatp.org/iatp.

Institute for Food and Development Policy (Food First). 398 60th St., Oakland, CA 94618. Think tank and publisher supporting citizen action on issues of food, poverty, development, and globalization. E-mail: foodfirst@igc.apc.org. Web site: http://www.netspace.org/hungerweb/FoodFirst/index.htm.

Institute for Local Self-Reliance. 1313 5th St. SE, Suite 306, Minneapolis, MN 55414. Develops alternative economic and technological policies for local production, consumption, and political control. Web site: http://www.ilsr.org.

Institute for Policy Studies. Working Group on the World Economy, 1601 Connecticut Ave. NW, Washington, DC 20009. Progressive think tank that produces books, studies, articles, and films on globalization and strategies for citizen responses. E-mail: ipscomm@igc.apc.org.

International Forum on Globalization. P.O. Box 12218, San Francisco, CA 94112. New alliance of activists from 20 countries presenting public education events and publications against globalization. E-mail: ifg@igc.org.

International Labor Rights Fund. 110 Maryland Ave. NE, Suite 101, Washington, DC 20002. Pioneered international worker rights through legislative, consumer, corporate, labor, and social charter strategies. E-mail: laborrights@igc.apc.org.

International Society for Ecology and Culture. 850 Talbot Ave., Albany, CA 94706. Workshops and publications on counterdevelopment strategies, antiglobalization, and preservation of local cultures.

People-Centered Development Forum. International alliance seeking sustainable and equitable community-based economies. Web site:http://iisd1.iisd.ca/pcdf.

Program on Corporations, Law, and Democracy. P.O. Box 806, Cambridge, MA 02140 . Educational programs on corporate dominance; organizing strategies for challenging corporate charters. E-mail: poclad@aol.com.

Public Citizen/Global Trade Watch. 215 Pennsylvania Ave. SE, Washington, DC 20003 . Policy development; organizing and legal action on issues of trade and food safety, public health, the environment and democracy.

Rainforest Action Network. 450 Sansome St., Suite 700, San Francisco, CA 94111. Focuses on the threats that global trade rules pose to tropical and temperate forests and to native peoples. E-mail: rainforest@ran.org. Web site: http://www.ran.org/ran/.

Redefining Progress. One Kearny St., 4th Floor, San Francisco, CA 94108. Think tank challenging economic assumptions and measurements that ignore social and environmental costs. E-mail: info@rprogress.org.

Sierra Club. 85 2nd St., 2nd Floor, San Francisco, CA 94105. Mainstream environmental group opposing GATT and NAFTA. Web site: http://www.sierraclub.org.

Southwest Network for Environmental and Economic Justice. P.O. Box 7399, Albuquerque, NM 87194. Grassroots organization of people of color promoting regional strategies on environmental degradation and corporate behavior.

# AUTHOR INDEX

**337**

# SUBJECT INDEX